UP NORTH AGAIN

More of Ontario's Wilderness, from Ladybugs to the Pleiades

DOUG BENNET AND TIM TINER

Illustrations by Marta Lynne Scythes

Canadian Cataloguing in Publication Data

Bennet, Doug
    Up north again : more of Ontario's wilderness, from ladybugs to the Pleiades

Includes bibliographical references and index.
ISBN 0-7710-1115-6

1. Natural history – Ontario, Northern.   2. Natural history – Ontario, Northern – Miscellanea.
3. Natural history – Outdoor books.   4. Ontario, Northern – Miscellanea.
I. Tiner, Tim.   II. Title.

QH106.2.O5B452   1997   508.713'1   C96-932520-7

The publishers acknowledge the support of the Canada Council and the Ontario Arts Council for their publishing program.

Field checklists on pages 296–301 reprinted with permission of the Federation of Ontario Naturalists

Front cover photo by Robert McCaw

Typesetting by M&S, Toronto
Map of Central Ontario by Tim Tiner
Constellation maps and star charts by Doug Bennet
Printed and bound in Canada

McClelland & Stewart Inc.
The Canadian Publishers
481 University Avenue
Toronto, Ontario
M5G 2E9

1 2 3 4 5   01 00 99 98 97

Contents

Fish
(and Aquatic Companions)

Mammals

Reptiles

Plants

Trees and Shrubs

The Heavens

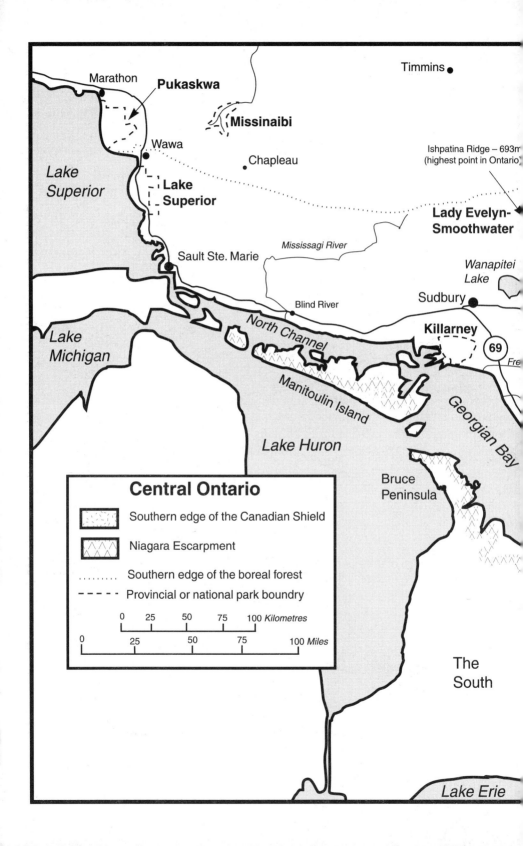

Timmins

Marathon **Pukaskwa**

Missinaibi

Wawa

Chapleau

Ishpatina Ridge – 693m
(highest point in Ontario)

Lake Superior

Lake Superior

Lady Evelyn-Smoothwater

Wanapitei Lake

Sault Ste. Marie

Mississagi River

Sudbury

Blind River

Killarney

Lake Michigan

North Channel

69

Fre

Manitoulin Island

Georgian Bay

Lake Huron

Bruce Peninsula

Central Ontario

Southern edge of the Canadian Shield

Niagara Escarpment

Southern edge of the boreal forest

Provincial or national park boundry

| 0 | 25 | 50 | 75 | 100 *Kilometres* |

| 0 | 25 | 50 | 75 | 100 *Miles* |

The South

Lake Erie

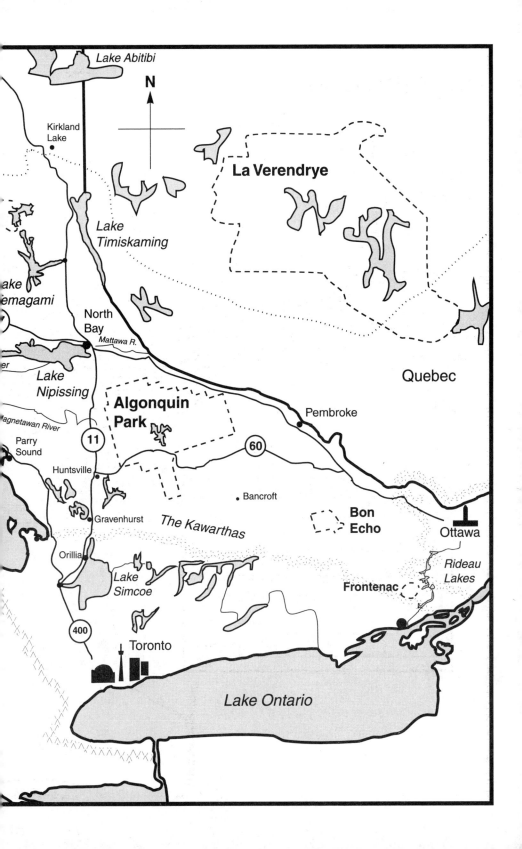

Introduction

THIS BOOK is very much a continuation of our first volume, *Up North*, published in 1993. Our original aim was to provide an eclectic guide to the plants, animals and other natural phenomena most commonly experienced outdoors in central Ontario. One of our most difficult tasks was selecting exactly what to profile in just 150 entries. Though we covered a good portion of the trees and mammals in the first book, there wasn't room to include many of the Canadian Shield's abundant birds, and space permitted only a small sampling of the region's superb assortment of wild plants and flowers.

Up North Again seeks to fill in the picture. Apart from birds and plants, considerably more aquatic creatures, including some of Ontario's legendary sport fish, are featured this time around. The Heavens section concentrates on the constellations of the autumn, winter and spring not covered by *Up North*. Most of the mammals, amphibians and snakes added here are as common as those in the first book, but less often seen or identified. A sprinkling of favourite creepy-crawlies is thrown in for good measure.

There are also completely new features in *Up North Again*. We have put together an almanac of the year's cycles of migrations, mating seasons, bloomings and other natural phenomena as they unfold in central Ontario, and we have also included field checklists, kindly provided by the Federation of Ontario Naturalists, to note sightings of birds, reptiles, amphibians and mammals. Included in the almanac and 121 entries on featured subjects is information on scores of other species. Their names appear in **bold** wherever mentioned at length in the main text. We strongly encourage using the index at the back of the book when searching for plants, animals or stars not appearing in the table of contents. The index also includes cross-references to *Up North*.

Like our first book, *Up North Again* deals primarily with Ontario's mixed forest, southern Shield region, to about Temagami and Wawa, also taking in the Kawarthas, Manitoulin Island and the Bruce Peninsula. This is the "up north" for most of the province's urban dwellers who, like ourselves, are drawn for revitalization to rocky hinterland lakes and forests. "Up north" is a state of mind as much as it is a geographic place. We've tried to reflect that spirit from the start, and thank the readers of *Up North* for encouraging us to think we achieved something of that sort, making this second book possible.

Tim Tiner
Doug Bennet

ANIMAL KINGDOM

AMPHIBIANS

W HILE BULLFROGS, toads, leopard frogs and spring peepers are probably the best-known amphibians in Ontario, others are abundant but less widely recognized. Green frogs are easily mistaken for small bullfrogs, but have milder voices and choose different surroundings. Wood frogs can similarly be passed over as diminutive forest toads without looking closely for their yellow-lined black masks. Though not usually seen, gray treefrogs and mink frogs add their own distinctive voices to familiar amphibian choruses.

Yellow-spotted salamanders are also seldom seen, and never heard. Yet they thrive in untold numbers in hidden places beneath the forest leaf litter. Several other Ontario salamander species are also visited in this section's yellow-spotted salamander entry. Like frogs, each salamander species has its own specialties, carefully adapted for its unique spot in the ecosystem.

GREEN FROG
Singing Down by the Pond

Average adult length: 6–9 cm
(2.4–3.6 in)

Maximum length: More than
11 cm (4 in)

Markings: Green to olive-brown
back, often with black spots or
blotches; bright green above
mouth; black hind-leg bands,
whitish undersides; distinct
ridge down both sides of the
back; mature males have
yellow throats and brown
eardrum circles twice the size
of the eyes

Alias: *La grenouille verte,*
Rana clamitans

Call: A deep, gulping "gunk,"
often described as sounding
like a low twang of a banjo;
4 different variations, each
sometimes repeated 2 or 3
times; males also growl softly
before or during fights

Preferred habitat: Slow, weedy
rivers, ponds, shallow marshes,
swamps and small, calm lakes
with lots of aquatic vegetation

ONLY TWO DISTINCT ridges down both sides of its back readily set the green frog apart from the bigger, more renowned bullfrog. The two species must have split from each other sometime in their recent evolutionary past. While the bulls came to rule the waves on larger marshy bays, their smaller look-alikes settled in along slow, quiet rivers and ponds. Green frogs may show up in bullfrog waters as well, on rare occasions even breeding with the big bulls. Mostly, however, they keep to themselves, hunting and calling along weedy shorelines.

Green frogs rouse from their muddy underwater winter beds after the surface ice has disappeared and late-April days consistently hover around 10°C (50°F). The groggy amphibians are quiet at first, concentrating on eating and building up their strength. Then in June, when rising water temperatures warm their blood and passions, males inaugurate their long breeding season with deep, twanging choruses. Their verbal declarations continue well into summer, gradually trailing off in August.

At the start of the mating season, males spend two or three weeks carving out territories by the water's edge and establishing dominance hierarchies. As the biggest, toughest characters call – especially at dusk and into the night – they display the yellow badge of experience on their throats. Boundary disputes are often settled by wrestling matches. With all the time spent calling, patrolling, threatening, chasing and fighting each other during the mating season, some males may lose up to a third of their weight. Subordinate frogs without their own territories are not harassed by property holders as long as they keep low in the water, like females, and call little attention to themselves.

Once things are fairly settled, towards the end of June and beginning of July, females inspect the breeding territories, looking for warm, shallow water and lots of veggy cover for their eggs. Once satisfied with a particular spot, a willing lass gives the lucky local male a nudge. He responds by grasping hold of her. As she releases her eggs, he gathers up 30 to 50 at a time with his hind legs, fertilizes them with his sperm and then pushes them away. While they are thus engaged, for up to half an hour, a subordinate male may take up the breeding host's calling perch in hopes of hooking up with the next inquiring female.

Sun-warmed fertilized eggs miraculously produce tiny tadpoles in just a few days. The algae-eating polliwogs lead a fishy existence until transforming into frogs the following summer. Almost immediately, they put their new legs to use, hopping onto land and, over the course of the summer, travelling up to 600 metres (650 yards) in search of new permanent bodies of water where they can settle. Along the way, they may sojourn in temporary ponds, puddles, creeks and streams. It's one of the few times green frogs move far from the water's edge, but it allows them to colonize smaller pools that the almost totally aquatic bullfrog never reaches.

In their new homes, the young frogs feed close to land during the day, then lie low to avoid being eaten by larger adults who swim into the shallows to hunt and sing under the cover of night. Perhaps not knowing any better, the young tend to go into hibernation later than older frogs.

Winter whereabouts: In mud between rocks and sunken logs at water's bottom

Food: Mostly flies, beetles, grasshoppers, spiders, snails, slugs and other insects; sometimes crayfish, little fish and smaller frogs; tadpoles eat algae, bacteria and decaying vegetation

Male breeding territory: 1–6 m (3.3–20 ft) along water's edge

Average clutch: 3,500–4,000 black-centred eggs, laid in a floating mat 15–30 cm (6–12 in) wide

Incubation period: 3–7 days

Tadpole: Green-brown with mottled tail, creamy, red-tinted belly; fat-bodied, 6–10 cm (2.4–4 in) long before transforming

Age at sexual maturity: Males 1–2 years, females 2 years

Maximum lifespan: More than 5 years

Predators: Snapping turtles, water snakes, raccoons, mink, foxes, herons, pike and bass; fish, dragonfly nymphs, giant water bugs and leeches eat tadpoles

Each frog's home range: 20–200 m^2 (25–250 sq yd)

Range: Southern Ontario to about Lake Timiskaming and Lake Superior hinterlands; also native to southeast Manitoba, Quebec and the Maritimes, and introduced in Newfoundland and British Columbia

Number of Ontario frog species: 9

Number of frog species worldwide: 2,770–3,500

Also see: Mink Frog. *Up North:* Bullfrog, Leopard Frog

MINK FROG
The Stinky Northerner

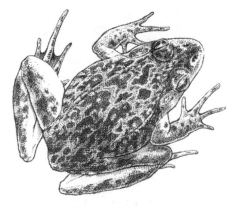

Average adult length: 5–7 cm (2–2.8 in)
Maximum length: 7.6 cm (3 in)
Markings: Dark-olive back and sides mottled with black spots, splotches and squiggles; bright-green snout; undersides creamy white on females, light yellow on males
Alias: *La grenouille du nord, Rana septentrionalis*
Call: A hollow knocking "tuk," usually several together
Preferred habitat: Still rivers and bays, swamps and bogs
Food: Dragonflies, damselflies, whirligig and diving beetles, water striders, aphids and minnows
Average clutch: 500–4,000 eggs
Incubation period: About 4 days
Tadpoles: Mottled olive green and black above; yellow bellies; transparent tails; up to 9 cm (3.6 in) long
Range: North central shore of Lake Ontario to southern James Bay; also eastern Manitoba, Quebec, New Brunswick and Nova Scotia

O N SLOW, WATER lily-clogged waters and boggy bays, the deep banjo twangs of lusty green frogs are accompanied by erratic bursts of percussion, sounding like the hollow knocking of wood. While the brawny green frogs are often seen near the tangled water's edge, the haphazard percussionists do their thing in obscurity amid the floating plants far from shore. There, male mink frogs stake out their breeding territories with their odd "knocking" calls. Like their bigger bullfrog and green frog cousins, mink frogs can, by living in permanent bodies of water, afford a fairly leisurely breeding season, and may be heard from June well into August, later than any other Ontario frog.

The mink frog comes by its name by foul means. When its skin is touched by predators or curious human hands, it gives off a stinky mink-musk smell, also likened to the odour of rotten onions. Few people have had the experience, since, besides keeping well offshore, the odoriferous amphibians are true northerners, found only sparingly south of Algonquin Park. Perhaps because they're geared for colder, northern waters, mink frogs remain in hibernation until May and develop slowly. Though they're smaller than green frogs, they spend two years as tadpoles before becoming three-centimetre-long (one-inch-long) froglets in June and July.

GRAY TREEFROG
Ontario's Arboreal Chameleon

THERE'S LITTLE WONDER why treefrogs are seldom spotted yet so abundant. They are the orang-utans of the frog world, living most of their lives high in the canopy of the tallest trees. In addition to being nocturnal and little, the long-toed, wide-mouthed amphibians are chameleons. In the space of about half an hour, by expanding or contracting three different layers of pigment cells beneath their transparent skin, they can change from bright green to brown to varying shades of grey, which-ever suits their surroundings. On cool days, and when breeding in the water, they often turn almost black to absorb as much heat from the sun as possible. Pressed into the service of science, treefrogs have even changed their colouring to approxi-mate checkered black-and-white backgrounds.

Like countless other amazing creatures in the wild, treefrogs alert other, more terrestrial, beings to their exis-tence only when caught up in the drama of reproduction. For several weeks around late May and June, males call out in the evening in loud, deep trills, inflating their throats like balloons. The sound might be mistaken for crickets, except it's far too early in the year for the chirp-ing insects to take their cue. Hopping down onto the ground and to nearby shrubby pools, swamps and swales, the singers perform on prominent overhanging alder and willow branches. They guard the territory around their perches closely, rumbling with any competitor that ignores their musical warnings to back off.

Trilling becomes faster as the air warms, reaching a frequency that finally draws females to the pond, usually a night or two after males arrive. The meeting of the sexes cranks up the music a couple of notches as the feminine frog makes her choice and invites a partner to cling to her

Average adult length: 3–5 cm (1.2–2 in)
Maximum length: 6 cm (2.4 in)
Markings: Variable grey, bright-green, brown or almost black back and sides, with irregular black-bordered darker blotches; bars across hind legs; yellowish-white belly; square white spot below each eye; yellow-orange beneath hind thighs; wide toe-disks; males have grey or black throats
Alias: Eastern gray treefrog, tree toad, greater gray treefrog, slow call gray treefrog, tetraploid gray treefrog, *la rainette versicolore*, *Hyla versicolor*
Scientific name meaning: *Hyla* is classical Greek for "wood," *versicolor* is "changing colour" in Latin
Call: Trills lasting 1–2 seconds

each, cricketlike but much deeper, repeated up to 700 times an hour

Preferred habitat: Forests most of year; shrubby wetlands, ponds and stream pools in June

Winter whereabouts: Beneath fallen leaves, rocks, logs and in old burrows of mice and other small animals

Food: Beetles, caterpillars, flies, moths, ants, spiders, leafhoppers

Breeding territory: At least 1.5 m (5 ft) across

Average clutch: Up to 2,000 grey and white eggs, in batches of 10–40

Incubation period: 2–5 days

Tadpoles: 2.5 cm (1 in) long and yellow after hatching, turning bright olive green, with white bellies and long, wide reddish tails; growing up to 5 cm (2 in) long

Reason for red tail: Possible warning to predators of protective tadpole skin toxins

Age at sexual maturity: 2 years

Lifespan: Usually less than 4 years, but up to 9 years in captivity

Swale: A wide, shrubby area in standing water, often with a creek or stream running through

Range: Southern Ontario to Lake Nipissing and Sault Ste. Marie; also Manitoba, southern Quebec and New Brunswick

Number of treefrog species native to Ontario: 3

Number of treefrog species worldwide: 630

before she drops to the water. The embrace may last up to several hours while she finds the spot for them to release eggs and sperm together. While they're gone, the singing perch may be occupied by a previously silent male waiting in the wings less than a metre (three feet) away, who tries to beckon a mate before the star returns.

Upon sticking the last batch of fertilized eggs to a submerged branch or stem, a mother treefrog departs the water for the rest of the year. The masculine singers hang around for the whole breeding period in hopes of another coupling with later-arriving females. Only about a quarter of all males, however, successfully mate each season, and very few get a second crack at it. When it's over, they return to the trees, occasionally breaking into song later in the summer on humid or warm, rainy evenings.

They may also use their sticky, bubbly toe-disks to walk up cottage walls and windows, hunting moths attracted by night lights

---

After hatching quickly in June and spending six to nine weeks of life as vegetarians, the tadpoles develop legs, lungs and an appetite for insect flesh. The newly transformed, cricket-sized froglets hunt near the water among shrubs and cattails in late August or September, waiting for a rainy night for their amphibious invasion of the trees beyond. They have smooth, brilliantly bright-green skin at first, which becomes rougher and bumpy, more like a toad, as they grow older and moult.

Blending perfectly with the grey bark, green leaves or lichens on which they rest, treefrogs can remain perfectly still for hours, then suddenly leap more than a metre into the air, catch a passing bug and land on another branch.

When they jump, bright yellow-and-orange markings on their inner legs suddenly flash into view, possibly serving to startle pursuing predators. On occasion, they may also use their sticky, bubbly toe-disks to walk up cottage walls and windows, hunting moths attracted by night lights. During the day, they generally sleep beneath leaves or bark or inside small tree cavities.

Around October, gray treefrogs come down to the earth and snuggle into the leaf litter, under rocks or in the abandoned burrows of small animals. Winter's deep layer of snow provides considerable insulation. Even so, during cold weather with little snow, up to 65 percent of their body fluids may actually freeze without causing the frosty frogs internal damage. High levels of glycerol and glucose usually keep them from freezing solid until they rouse from their slumbers again around mid-May.

Also see: Ribbon Snake, Wood Frog, Crickets, Willows. *Up North:* Spring Peeper, American Toad, Wetlands

WOOD FROG
The Skulking Forest Bandit

WOOD FROGS SHOULD be added to the pantheon of great Canadian wildlife symbols, alongside the beaver, loon and moose. The black-masked forest bandits inhabit the land from sea to sea to sea, hopping within sight of the Arctic Ocean in the Mackenzie River delta ("A river so Canadian it turns its back on America," said the poet F. R. Scott), farther north than any other amphibian on the continent.

Woodies are tough frogs, settling into dry forest litter in the autumn, pulling its cover over them and waiting for the snow to fall. They can slumber on a bed of frosted leaves as cold as −6°C (21°F) and withstand almost half their body fluids turning to ice crystals. In the late 1700s, Hudson's Bay Company explorer Samuel Hearne wrote of digging up wood frogs from the frozen moss that were as cold and hard as ice. To keep from completely freezing, wood frogs flood their bodies with glucose from carbohydrates stored in their livers. By thus elevating their blood-sugar levels to some 60 times the summertime norm, they create a natural antifreeze that prevents cell damage.

As soon as the snow is mostly gone and the litter layer thawed, in mid-April to early May, male wood frogs stir. The world's most posthumously famous idler, Henry David Thoreau, wrote of the early-rising frog in the spring of 1859: "He is wholly of the earth, sensitive as its skin in which he lives and of which he is a part. His life relaxes with the thawing ground." The newly roused bachelors make straight for the leaf-filled meltwater pools, ponds and wetlands where they first hatched. There, floating largely unseen in the water, they begin quacking like phantom ducks as the mercury rises towards 10°C (50°F). They may fall silent again if a cold front or late snowstorm

Average adult length: 3–5 cm (1.2–2 in)
Maximum length: 8.3 cm (3.3 in)
Markings: Distinct yellow-lined black "mask" running behind each eye; brown, tan, grey or reddish-brown back and sides; white undersides, sometimes darkly mottled; dark bars across legs
Vocal sacs: Gleaming white when inflated at the sides of males' heads
Alias: Robber frog, *la grenouille des bois*, *Rana sylvatica*
Scientific name meaning: *Sylvatica*, from Latin *sylva*, meaning "wood"
Call: Mating song sounds like high-pitched duck quacks; males also chirp when grabbed by other lusty fellows to tell them they've made a mistake
Preferred habitat: Damp portions

rolls in. The larger females join them a few days later, each drawing half a dozen or more males around her in a quacking frenzy. He who holds on the tightest remains fastened to the object of his desire anywhere from an hour to three days, until they finally spawn.

Parents have no time to lose if their young are to develop legs before natal swimming holes dry up. The mating prom may be over in as little as a few days at a given pond. With gatherings starting earlier on open marshes than in dark forest ravine pools, wood frog calls may be heard for two or three weeks before finally fading out, leaving a background chorus of spring peepers.

In a choice spot, where a submerged branch lies exposed to the sun, many wood frog mothers mass gooey globs of dark-centred eggs. The globs absorb and hold heat, protecting the eggs – especially those near the centre – from cold spells and re-forming ice. After a couple weeks, the tadpoles hatch and develop faster than the larvae of any other North American frog, with aquatic childhoods as brief as 40 days. By early summer, the few that have survived the cold, predators and competition for food take to land around their shrinking ponds as air-breathing, thumbnail-sized froglets. After growing up together with wriggling mosquito larvae, the newly carnivorous hoppers avidly pick off their insect pool-mates who are transforming around the same time.

Throughout the summer, wood frogs stalk insects in the forest. They are the most terrestrial of Ontario's frogs, often rustling in the leaves and ferns along trails, and are easily mistaken for tiny toads, save for their signature black masks. Though they assume the same earth-brown colour as the land-loving toad, wood frogs have smooth skin and, like other frogs, must remain moist, always dwelling in damp, shadowy haunts. If found and picked up, they also have the uncanny ability to purr like a cat.

of the forest floor; shrubby, temporary woodland ponds, swamps and marshes in early spring

Winter whereabouts: In the forest litter layer and under rocks, logs and stumps

Food: Beetles, spiders, mosquitoes and flies; tadpoles eat algae and bacteria

Portion of males that get to mate each year: About 20%

Portion of males that mate twice in a season: About 1%

Clutch: 400–2,500 black-centred eggs in a round clump, 2–10 cm (0.8–4 in) across, around a submerged stem or twig, turning green with algae after about a week

Incubation period: About 2–3 weeks

Tadpoles: Hatch 7–10 mm (0.4 in) long, grow to 3–5 cm (1.2–2 in), yellow-spotted olive backs with iridescent, pink-tinted bellies

Portion of eggs that yield tadpoles surviving to frogdom: About 4%

Maximum lifespan: At least 4 years

Predators: Raccoons, mink, garter, ringneck and ribbon snakes, herons, bitterns and other large birds; turtles, red-spotted newts, yellow-spotted salamanders, diving beetles, leeches and caddisfly larvae eat tadpoles

Range: Throughout Ontario; also in all other provinces and territories

Also see: Yellow-spotted Salamander. *Up North:* Spring Peeper, American Toad, Mosquitoes

YELLOW-SPOTTED SALAMANDER

Glistening Subsurface Beauty

Length: 15–18 cm (6–7 in)
Maximum length: 23 cm (9 in)
Markings: Black or dark-grey
back with bright-yellow spots;
light purplish-grey sides and
grey belly
Alias: Spotted salamander, mole
salamander, *la salamander
maculée*, *Ambystoma
maculatum*
Preferred habitat: Subsurface of
mixed and deciduous upland
forests; small woodland pools,
ponds and bogs in early
spring
Winter whereabouts: In underground passageways and
old mouse, vole or mole
burrows and tunnels below
frost line
Food: Worms, beetle larvae,
snails, slugs, crickets and other
small ground insects and
larvae; tadpoles eat mosquito
larvae, minute crustaceans,

THOSE WHO BELIEVE all that crawls beneath the ground is gruesome and ghastly have undoubtedly never beheld the glistening form of a yellow-spotted salamander. Unfortunately, very few people ever see the plump, puppy-faced amphibians, which spend most of their lives in narrow passages beneath damp fallen leaves and mossy rocks or inside very rotted logs and stumps. Yet the forest literally crawls with salamanders, the yellow-spotted variety alone collectively outweighing the biomass of all local birds put together.

Only the odd herpetologist, or an extremely lucky early-spring night hiker, ever gets to see how many yellow-spotted salamanders really live in the woods. On rainy April or early-May nights, when temperatures rise above 5°C (41°F), the moist beasts rise from their winter sleeping chambers in the ground and stream over the surface towards low ground flooded with melt-water. A single pool may draw scores of the lust-driven amphibians. In rare instances, armies of many hundreds congregate at very large ponds or small, boggy lakes. Yet even for the brief week or so that they're in the water, the salamanders remain out of sight during the day beneath vegetation at the bottom.

Some 60 to 80 percent of a breeding pond's occupants are males, who throng on the bottom in groups of up to 100, called "congresses." When members of the fairer, slightly fatter, sex begin arriving, anywhere from a few hours to several nights after the males, the congress erupts, churning the water with frothy excitement. Initially mobbed by many nuzzling suitors, a debutante gradually enters into a more meaningful courtship with one of them. After a little dancing and caressing, the favoured male leaves little packets of sperm at the pond bottom or on a submerged branch in hopes his partner will pick it up in her cloaca beneath the base of her tail. But if a competing male finds the spermatophore first, he buries it in the ooze and deposits one of his own.

Shortly after accepting this gift, a female lays her newly fertilized eggs in a mass around an underwater stick or stem. Water absorbed by the permeable egg casings may swell the globe of jelly to the size of a road-hockey ball. Algae also enters the eggs, turning them green after a week or two and producing embryo-sustaining oxygen, which is frequently depleted in small pools by decomposing leaves lining the bottom. The algae in turn feeds on carbon dioxide and other nutrients given off by the embryos as they develop. A neat arrangement.

Yellow-spotted salamanders are one of the most sensitive amphibians to acid rain and snow, which kills or deforms their embryos. Those in pools of snowmelt are totally at its mercy, and their numbers have declined in many locations. But other breeding populations in small, naturally acidic lakes seem to have a high acid-tolerance that leaves them largely unaffected.

Hatching long after their parents have left them, the salamander tadpoles develop lungs and legs and crawl out of their shrinking nursery ponds in late summer. The jet-black juveniles develop their adult spots a few weeks later, as they fan out through the forest in search of unoccupied ground shafts, such as unused mouse tunnels, natural crevices or channels left by decayed tree roots. Once

frog tadpoles and their own kind

Average home range: At least 100 m² (125 sq yd)

Average clutch: 50–100 transparent or milky, dark-centred eggs, laid in a single mass, 5–10 cm (2–4 in) wide, or in batches of 20–30 eggs

Incubation period: 3–8 weeks

Tadpoles: Light greenish-yellow back and sides, whitish bellies and feathery external gills; dorsal fins running from neck to tail; 1 cm (0.4 in) long upon hatching, up to 4 cm (1.5 in) before transforming

Age at sexual maturity: Males 1 year, females 2 years

Annual adult survival rate: About 90%

Maximum lifespan: 20 years in captivity

Predators: Snakes; red-spotted newts, caddisfly larvae and leeches eat eggs; herons and diving beetles eat tadpoles

Detachable tails: Salamander tails lost to predators can grow back, but take years, and are never as long and lack vertebrae

Range: Southern Ontario to the mid-boreal forest; also in Quebec and the Maritimes

Ontario's largest salamander: Mudpuppy, 25–30 cm (10–12 in) long, lives entirely at bottom of marshy rivers and muddy lakes

World's largest amphibian: Japanese giant salamander, 1.5 m (5 ft) long

Longest lived salamander: Giant salamander, 52 years

Gerrymander: Term meaning to rig something; coined when

early-19th-century Massachusetts governor Elbridge Gerry altered electoral boundaries to his advantage and created a voting district shaped like a huge salamander (he still lost the election)

Cloaca: All-purpose waste and sexual orifice common to most reptiles, amphibians, birds and fish

Number of salamander species native to Ontario: 12

Number of "mole" salamander species native to Ontario: 5

Number of salamander species worldwide: About 350

Also see: Wood Frog, Plankton, Five-lined Skink. *Up North:* Redback Salamander, Humus

ensconced, they stay put, sleeping by day, and by night ambushing any creepy-crawly they can tackle that happens by the entrance to their lair. They prowl only when warm, rainy nights bring an abundance of worms and other tasty things to the surface. While out and about, they mark their tiny territories with chemical scent, warning other salamanders to keep away.

After as many as seven years in sedentary seclusion, yellow spotted salamanders are drawn back to the pond where they hatched, from as far away as half a kilometre (0.3 miles). No one knows for sure how such low-to-the-ground animals navigate so well, especially after having been away so long. In subsequent springs, they continue to return to the pond at almost exactly the same spot each time. Though salamanders are deaf and virtually mute, some experts believe they may keep their bearings by photo-receptors in their eyes that somehow detect the Earth's magnetic field.

The **blue-spotted salamander** leads a life almost identical to that of its yellow-spotted cousin, but is smaller, averaging seven to 12 centimetres (three to five inches). The two are central Ontario's most common "mole" salamanders, so called because they live almost entirely below the ground, deeper than the ubiquitous redback salamander.

An even smaller species, the **northern two-lined salamander**, lives under streamside rocks or beneath logs on soggy forest ground. Just six to nine centimetres (2.4 to 3.5 inches) long and quite slender, it has a black-dotted, yellowish-brown back with black borders, grey sides and a yellow belly. The similar-sized **four-toed salamander** is reddish brown with an orange tail and lurks in the moss of bogs and swamps.

BIRDS

F OR MOST OF US, *every excursion to northern woods and lakes brings new birds into view. It may be gray jays materializing for the first time on a fresh, clear September canoe trip or the sound of a pileated woodpecker drumming thunderously in early spring. Each visit to the wilderness also brings new insights into the ways of birds such as ravens, song sparrows and grackles. This section looks at many of the common birds we couldn't get to in Up North. More warblers and woodpeckers, sparrows, finches and others are offered to broaden the picture of the region's rich assortment of avian life.*

BARN SWALLOW
Bird of Endless Summer

Length: 15–20 cm (6–8 in)
Wingspan: 30–34 cm (12–13.5 in)
Weight: 14–24 g (0.5–0.8 oz)
Maximum number of daily
  sorties flown to feed nestlings:
  More than 1,000
Markings: Blue-black back; red on
  throat and between the eyes;
  pale rusty-beige undersides;
  long forked tail; thin, pointy
  wings; very small beak; tails of
  males about 20% longer
Alias: House swallow, chimney
  swallow, *l'hirondelle des
  granges, Hirundo rustica*
Call: Soft, liquid chittering song;
  also chirping call notes
Food: Mosquitoes, midges, deer
  flies, horse flies, beetles, flying
  ants, caddisflies, mayflies,
  moths, small amounts of
  berries and seeds
Preferred habitat: Open areas
  near lakes, rivers and marshes
Home range: Usually within
  200 m (220 yd) of nest
Courtship: Males chase females in

S WIRLING OVER MORE lands than almost any other bird on Earth, the barn swallow has winged its way into the folklore of innumerable cultures. In stories from across Asia and Europe, the skybound bird brings fire to humans from supernatural realms, its back blackened, its breast singed red and its tail feathers burned into the classic forked swallow-tail shape. From ancient Rome to China, it was deemed good fortune to have barn swallows nest on a house and very bad luck to disturb them.

Originally, barn swallows specialized in nesting at waterside cliffs and caves and must have been much more sparsely scattered in Ontario than they are today. European settlement greatly increased the birds' housing stock of sheltered vertical surfaces and ledges largely beyond the reach of predators. While showing little taste for cities and towns, barn swallows have taken madly to barn beams, bridge rafters and cottage eaves everywhere. Today, 99 percent of their mud-vessel nests are on human-made structures, even turning up on moving boats, trains and the rotating dish of the radio-observatory in Algonquin Park.

Barn swallows are accomplished nest builders and aviators. After flying as far as 15,000 kilometres (9,300 miles) from southern Argentina in the spring, the birds pair off and begin their work. Over one to two weeks, they scoop up hundreds of dabs of mud in their beaks, forming pellets and sticking them together against a ledge or wall. The mud-brick structures may last as long as five years, needing only to be refurbished when the same couple returns to the site in following years. If there's room, they often have neighbours as close as a few metres away, with loose communities of 10 or so nests common. Swallows, though, have an adulterous streak, prompting husbands to guard their mates jealously in the small space around their quarters.

After their nestlings fledge around late June, a couple may start a second family. In a really good year, a few overachievers may even go for a third. Things are often made a little easier when one of the young from the first brood sticks around to help Mom and Dad warm and feed its younger siblings.

When not feeding or brooding their young, barn swallows are almost constantly in swirling flight as they chase down buzzing insects, usually six to eight metres (20 to 27 feet) above water. Long, narrow wings and sleek bodies allow them to stay aloft on far fewer calories than are required by most other birds. Even to drink or bathe, they prefer to swoop their beaks or bodies through the water rather than wade into it. Early American ornithologist Alexander Wilson estimated that barn swallows log almost 1,000 air kilometres (620 miles) a day, and that one reaching the ripe old age of 10 years will have flown more than 3.2 million kilometres (two million miles) in its lifetime. While perhaps an overestimation, it stands as a testament to the bird's aerial nature. Among native birds, only chimney swifts, which also nest mostly on buildings, spend more time in the air.

Just as summer gets more comfortable in late July as the mosquito hordes diminish, swallows, too, make themselves scarce in many areas. In a number of choice marshes and waterside groves, however, their numbers explode, as swallows of several different species congregate in huge pre-migration flocks. They usually leave on cold fronts in late August, heading for the Southern Hemisphere to become birds of endless summer. Unlike most small birds, they migrate by day, often veering low to feed as they fly.

the air; upon landing, they rub heads and necks, preen and lock beaks together

Nest: Deep cup of mud pellets and grass, lined with feathers, 10–18 cm (4–7 in) wide, built on a sheltered platform or plastered against a wall beneath eaves

Average clutch: 4–5 pumpkin-seed-sized eggs, white with reddish-brown spots

Incubation period: 13–17 days

Fledging age: 18–23 days

Age at sexual maturity: 1 year

Survival in first year: 20–30%

Annual adult survival: 30–60%

Lifespan: Most less than 4 years; maximum 15 years

Predators: Merlins

Portion of bird species with "helpers" assisting parents at nest: 3%

Average first arrival in central Ontario: Late Apr.

Average last departure from central Ontario: Late Aug.

Winter whereabouts: Panama and the Caribbean to Argentina

Range: Throughout most of Ontario, but very sparse in northern half; also in all other provinces and territories

World range: All continents except Antarctica, occasionally reaching Hawaii

Audubon Society genesis: Formed in response to mass slaughter during a craze in swallow-feather hats in the 1880s

Number of swallow species breeding in Ontario: 6

Number of swallow species worldwide: 75

Also see: Midges, Nighthawk. *Up North:* Tree Swallow

BLACK-AND-WHITE WARBLER

The Easygoing Treehugger

Length: 10–14 cm (4–5.5 in)
Wingspan: 20–23 cm (8–9 in)
Weight: Average 10 g (0.35 oz), up to 15 g (0.5 oz)
Markings: Irregularly striped black-and-white back and sides; white belly; males have black throat; females have white throat and breast and greyish cheeks
Alias: Black-and-white creeper, black-and-white nuthatch, creeping warbler, pied creeper, striped warbler, varied creeping warbler, *la paruline noire et blanche, Mniotilta varia*
Call: Simple, high, rapidly repeated notes sounding like the squeak of cleaning windows; often also likened to a squeaky wheel; written as "weesee, weesee, weesee, weesee, weesee"
Preferred habitat: Large stands of mixed and deciduous forests and cedar swamps
Food: Caterpillars, ants, beetles, moths, spiders, insect and spider eggs
Nest: Thick-sided cup of grass, twigs, rootlets, leaves and shreds of bark, lined with hair and plant down; 4.5–8 cm (1.8–3.2 in) wide; on ground at the foot of a tree, rock, log or stump, often covered by leaves or branches; less commonly on a low stump
Average clutch: 5 chickpea-sized eggs, white with brown specks
Incubation period: 10–12 days

I N THE VERTICAL world of tree-trunk buffets, brown creepers go up and nuthatches usually go down, but black-and-white warblers go any way they fancy. They work the larger limbs of trees as well. Handsomely attired in sharply contrasting stripes, they are one of the more easygoing warblers, wandering about on trees in plain view, often at eye level. There's nothing shy in their demeanour.

While most of Ontario's hungry hosts of warblers don't arrive until the leaves unfold, serving as platters for the birds' insect feast, black-and-whites get a jump on the crowds, usually landing around early May. They don't need to wait for leafout because they pick their meals from the bark-crevice sleeping chambers and egg stashes of overwintering bugs and spiders. They're also among the few warblers to nest on the ground. Females most often build their thick-walled nurseries between roots at the base of trees, usually hidden by a tuft of dead leaves or pine needles.

Regrettably, ground-nesting woodland birds are also the most vulnerable to forest fragmentation. Wherever logging and new roads create open fringes, nesting areas become more exposed to predators and to parasites such as brown-headed cowbirds. When threatened near their nests, female black-and-white warblers often feign a broken wing – killdeer-style – and try to lead would-be nest robbers away. During June nesting, fathers, who help tend the young, temporarily tone down their loquacious singing to avoid detection.

They are one of the more easygoing warblers, wandering about on trees in plain view

---

Males often continue their singing into August. Perhaps they're exuberant because they keep their attractive breeding colours, unlike other warblers that fade to drab greens and tans in late summer and early autumn. Also during that time, black-and-whites often join mixed flocks of foraging birds, making it worthwhile to take a second, closer look at what might appear to be a homogenous band of chickadees fluttering in the surrounding trees.

Fledging age: 8–12 days
Maximum lifespan: 11 years
Predators: Sharp-shinned hawks; nests raided by garter snakes, raccoons, jays, grackles
Nests parasitized by cowbirds: About 21%
Other birds sensitive to forest fragmentation: Ovenbird, wood thrush, red-eyed vireo
Other ground-nesting warblers: Ovenbird, mourning and Nashville warblers
Range: Most of Ontario except far north and extreme southwest; also in all other provinces and Northwest Territories
Average daily spring migration distance: 30 km (18.6 mi)
Average first arrival in central Ontario: Early May
Average last departure from central Ontario: Mid-Sept.
Winter whereabouts: Gulf of Mexico, Caribbean and northern South America
Number of wood warbler species nesting in Ontario: 36
Number of wood warbler species worldwide: 115
Also see: Brown Creeper, Red-breasted Nuthatch, Chestnut-sided Warbler, Grackle

BLACK DUCK
Falling for Mallard Magnetism

Top flying speed: More than
  40 km/h (25 mph)
Length: 53–63 cm (21–25 in)
Wingspan: 84–94 cm (33–37 in)
Weight: Females 1–1.2 kg
  (2.2–2.7 lb), males
  1.1–1.5 kg (2.5–3.3 lb)
Markings: Both sexes are mostly
  dark brown, with sandy face
  and neck, violet-blue wing
  patch, white inner-wing undersides and orange-red or olive
  feet; bills are yellowish on
  males, greenish and often
  mottled on females
Alias: Dusky duck, blackie, black
  mallard, brown duck, Labrador
  duck, blackjack, redleg, velvet
  duck, American black duck, *le
  canard noir, Anas rubripes*
Scientific name meaning: In
  Latin, *anas* is "duck," *ruber* is
  "red" and *pes* is "foot"
Call: Females quack like mallards, males make a low croak
Name for a group: A puddle of
  ducks

ONCE REPUTED to be the most common quacker in Ontario, the darkly mottled black duck today faces diminishing returns. Though still the fowl most likely to turn up in weedy Canadian Shield backwaters, the black duck is in retreat, a victim not of hunting or habitat loss so much as sex and assimilation.

The cause of black duck decline is an apparently irresistible green-headed waddler well known to most city dwellers: the ever-popular mallard. Native to both North America and Eurasia, mallards are the ancestors of most domestic ducks, and are genetically almost identical to black ducks. The two probably separated only during the past Ice Age, with black ducks becoming camouflaged for a wooded setting. After much of the continent's northeastern forests were cleared, however, western mallards moved into black duck country, where they have also been stocked by humans. Along the way, they've interbred extensively with black ducks, whose hens seem to prefer the brightly coloured, more dominant mallard drakes. Their hybrid descendants tend to look like mallards.

Hybrids are also fortified with black duck genes that make them fairly resistant to a blood parasite, causing avian malaria, spread by blackflies on the Shield. The parasite normally causes mallards to go duck-up. Accordingly, while mallards have increased eightfold below the Shield in southern Ontario in recent decades, blackies have declined by 90 percent. In central Ontario, black ducks are down by some 40 percent.

One reason blackies and mallards mate so readily with each other is that their courting customs are virtually the same. Either species will respond to the overtures of the other. These consist of a variety of posturings, including drakes cruising by females while shaking their heads and tails and holding their chests high. On their wintering grounds, small groups of males often circle around females, whistling catcalls, making nasal quacking small talk and flicking water at the duck that takes their fancy. For her part, a female may goad a drake she's entertaining to attack an interloping rival to test his mettle. Just before finally mating, pairs get in the mood by facing each other and rapidly raising and lowering their heads in tandem.

When not courting, mating or forming a nest, females spend most of their time in eating overdrive, concentrating on protein-rich invertebrates to nourish egg production. Black ducks are "dabblers," gleaning their food from the surface of the water or dipping their heads down to forage off shallow bottoms, and seeming to moon observers in the process. Once egg-laying begins, most males leave their mates and hang out with the boys instead, during which time they are flightless. Their single-parented offspring emerge from their shells in mid- to late May.

Mothers escort their downy ducklings out of the nest usually within a day of hatching, and continue tending them for up to a week or two before they begin flying. Unlike tame urban mallards, the young are taught in the ways that have earned blackies the reputation of being the most wary of ducks. Once they fledge, in midsummer, they will fly straight up out of the water at the slightest whiff of trouble. It's in the air that they must have earned their name, appearing very dark against the sky, save for the flashing white undersides of their wings. Both the challenge of their fast, elusive flight, and the fact that they are a large, tasty eating duck, have long made them a favourite with the autumn shotgun set.

Food: Aquatic vegetation, insects and their larvae, worms, tadpoles, snails, mussels, crayfish, seeds, berries, occasionally frogs and toads

Preferred habitat: Beaver ponds, boggy lakes, marshes

Nest: Depression in grassy vegetation, filled with leaves and stems, lined by down, amid brushy stands of sweet gale, sedge and wetland shrubs along shorelines and islands; sometimes on muskrat lodges or farther from shore

Average clutch: 8–10 creamy-white or greenish eggs, about the size of large chicken eggs

Incubation period: 26–29 days

Fledging age: 58–63 days

Lifespan: Up to 19 years

Predators: Raccoons, foxes and mink take hens or eggs; snapping turtles, pike and muskies prey on ducklings

Interspeciel breeding partners: Mallards, pintails and wigeons

Portion of North American birds that hybridize with other species: About 10%

First domestication of mallards: At least 1st century A.D.

Duckisms: Lame duck, sitting duck, dead duck, odd duck, just ducky, don't forget to duck

Population density: 10–28 pairs per 100 km^2 (39 sq mi)

Range: All of Ontario to the tree line; also in Quebec, the eastern and Prairie provinces

Average first arrival in central Ontario: Early Apr.

Average last departure from central Ontario: Late Nov.

Winter whereabouts: Southern Ontario to Texas and Florida

BLACKBURNIAN WARBLER
Firethroat of the Treetops

Length: 11–14 cm (4.4–5.5 in)
Wingspan: 19–22 cm
(7.5–8.7 in)
Weight: Average 10 g (0.35 oz)
Markings: Males have a bright-orange upper breast and throat and slightly paler orange head stripes, alternating with black, a streaked black-and-white back and sides and a white belly; females are similarly patterned, with yellow instead of orange, and backs streaked brownish grey; males are more like females in autumn
Average number of feathers on a songbird: 1,500–3,000
Alias: Fire throat, torch bird, hemlock warbler, orange-throated warbler, *la paruline à gorge orangée, Dendroica fusca*
Call: High, thin, accelerating and rising song, often in the rhythm of "tsit, tsit, tsit, teede, tseeee"
Preferred habitat: Mature evergreen woods, especially hemlocks
Food: Caterpillars, beetles, ants, crane flies and other insects; turns to berries when bugs lacking
Nest: Round tray of twigs, herb stalks, plant down, spiderwebs, lichens, rootlets, grass and hair high up in dense evergreen branches
Average clutch: 4 chickpea-sized, white or greenish-white eggs with brownish spots

A WARBLER *par excellence*, the blackburnian is one of those flighty little birds that appears as an explosion of colour through binoculars. The male's intensity of colour earned it the nickname "fire throat," and there's nothing quite like the stunning orange-on-black contrast of its face and throat as it dances through dense, dark-green conifer bows.

Blackburnians are also good examples of warbler specialization. Although almost two dozen warbler species are common in central Ontario, each focuses its insect-hunting on a slightly different zone or type of vegetation. Blackburnians both nest and forage primarily along the upper periphery of high evergreens, especially hemlocks. Males tend to hover from branch to branch at or near treetop level, straining the eyes and necks of observers seeking out the source of their high-pitched song. Females stay a little farther below, close to where they do all the nest-building, incubation and brooding of the young. From around late June to early July, it's not so much singing males but noisy, hungry nestlings that signal blackburnian treetop residency.

The same evergreen may also host **black-throated green warblers**, foraging around the tree's midsection, and yellow-rumped warblers, feeding mostly around the bottom. The black-throated green is perhaps best known for the words put to one of its songs, "Trees, trees, murmuring trees." **Cape May warblers**, as well, work the conifer peaks, often pushing off from their perches to catch insects flying by. They are usually rare, however, except in years of spruce budworm outbreaks, when populations of all conifer-dwelling warblers increase significantly. During those years of plenty, **bay-breasted warblers** also appear, probing deeply within the tree's densest inner sections.

Blackburnians are particularly intolerant of forest-cutting and other human activities, which have caused the decline of many tropical migrants

---

Despite their fiery image, blackburnians are hemmed in somewhat by more-aggressive warbler tree-mates. They're also particularly intolerant of forest-cutting and other human activities, which have caused the decline of many tropical migrants. Blackburnians were once common south of the Canadian Shield until a fungus blight introduced from China in the early 1900s killed virtually all the native chestnuts, the one deciduous tree they frequented.

Incubation period: 11–12 days

Average adult songbird lifespan: Less than 2 years

Namesake: An early ornithologist, believing himself to be the first to write on the warbler in 1788, gave it the scientific name *blackburniae* in honour of contemporary English botanist Anna Blackburne. Many years later, an obscure paper from 1776 surfaced that named the bird *fusca*, Latin for "dusky." By the international rules of scientific nomenclature, the blackburnian became *fusca*, but in popular usage Blackburne's name carried the day

Range: Most of Ontario south of James Bay, except far southwest; sparse south of the Shield; also in Quebec, the Maritimes and the Prairie provinces

Average first arrival in central Ontario: Mid-May

Average last departure from central Ontario: Mid-Sept.

Winter whereabouts: Mountain cloud forests from Costa Rica to Bolivia

Number of tropical migrant species nesting in Canada and the United States: About 360

Also see: Black-and-white Warbler, Common Yellowthroat. *Up North:* Yellow-rumped Warbler, Hemlock, White Spruce

BROWN CREEPER
Methodical Bark Bird

Length: 13–15 cm (5–6 in)
Wingspan: 18–20 cm (7–8 in)
Weight: 8–9 g (0.3 oz)
Markings: Mottled brown on top, white beneath; white stripe above the eye and a long, thin, slightly curved beak; rust-coloured tail
Alias: Tree creeper, common creeper, little brown creeper, American brown creeper, *le grimpereau brun, Certhia familiaris, Certhia americana*
Call: Song a brief, high, thin, lisping whistle of several jumbled, descending notes, a little like the squeak of chalk on a blackboard; also nearly inaudible, thin "seee" calls
Preferred habitat: Mature forests with wet sections, bogs, swamps
Food: Insect and spider eggs, insect larvae and pupae, adult spiders, beetles, moths,

S ITTING ALONE in the middle of a forest can be beautifully tranquil, providing the bug dope is holding up. It's during such quiet moments that one may see, from the corner of one's eye, a brown creeper lurking in the shadows. To come face to beak with the ominously named spectre is to discover one of the smallest and most fascinating woodland birds.

Brown creepers are always moving, spiralling up furrowed tree trunks in a never-ending quest for treats hidden in the bark's cracks and crevices. They are so small, silent and plain, blending in like bits of bark along their tree-trunk travelways, that they're easily missed among flashier, more eloquent birds. Stiff, stout tails help creepers hitch their way up vertical surfaces like woodpeckers. As they go, they probe beneath slender flakes of bark with their thin, curved beaks, hunting for insects, spiders and eggs that no other birds can reach. A minute or so after a creeper has started up one tree, it drops down to the base of another and begins again, scurrying mouselike up and around and around.

The inconspicuous bug gleaners often go about their business in close proximity to people; there are even reports of either nearsighted or over-absorbed birds creeping up human pantlegs in their methodical search of every tree in the forest. When suddenly alerted to danger, their first line of defence is to hunker down against the trunk and spread out their wings, becoming one with the bark.

In addition to providing sustenance and safety, tree bark also serves as the creeper's roost and nursery. Well-hidden, tiny crescent-shaped nests – built by both mates during one to four weeks in May – are usually wedged between a trunk and loose bark. Males feed their spouses while they're on the nest and help raise the young. True to their heritage, baby creepers can scoot up tree trunks within 10 days of hatching, and before they learn to fly. Once fledged, they continue to roost together for a time, huddled in a circle with their heads at the centre.

After families split up, the creeper has a reputation for being a loner, interested in nothing but plying the bark-gleaning trade. As the weather turns colder and the pickings become thinner, some join loose, mixed flocks of chickadees, nuthatches and downy woodpeckers foraging through the forest. Together, they form a bark-gleaning "guild," helping one another find concentrations of insects or eggs, each specializing in different parts of the tree or different types and sizes of prey.

> *True to their heritage, baby creepers can scoot up tree trunks within 10 days of hatching*

Sometimes, roosting brown creepers also nestle together for warmth in tree cavities during winter. Most, though, fly south. On their migratory night flights in September and October and again in April, they come down in mixed flocks during the day to refuel, and this is when they are probably most often seen.

aphids, ants and pseudoscorpions; some seeds and nuts

Courtship: Between spiralling flights around trees, males sing short, high-pitched snatches of creeper love verse

Nest: Crescent-shaped structure of twigs, moss, grass and shreds of bark, reinforced with spiderwebs; built in space between a dead tree trunk and a loose piece of bark, usually 1–4 m (3.3–13 feet) above ground; rarely in tree cavities

Average clutch: 5–6 raspberry-sized, lightly brown-dotted white eggs

Incubation period: 14–15 days

Fledging age: 13–14 days

Maximum lifespan: At least 6 years

Predators: Sharp-shinned hawks, northern shrikes; red squirrels and raccoons may raid nests

Range: All of Ontario except far northwest; also in all other provinces

Average first arrival in central Ontario: Mid-Apr.

Average last departure from central Ontario: Mid-Oct.

Winter whereabouts: Some stay on breeding grounds, others fly as far south as the Gulf of Mexico

Number of creeper species nesting in Ontario: 1

Number of creeper species worldwide: 6

Also see: Black-and-white Warbler, Ruby-crowned Kinglet, Red-breasted Nuthatch, Downy Woodpecker. *Up North:* Black-capped Chickadee

CHESTNUT-SIDED WARBLER
Songster of Young Forests

"PLEASED, PLEASED, pleased to meet-cha!" This oft-quoted phrase matches quite closely both the cadence and meaning of the chestnut-sided warbler's love song. Upon returning to Ontario, males set up shop in open, sunny stands of young trees and shrubs and in May and June sing their song from prominent perches up to 4,000 times a day. Their feminine counterparts, usually arriving on the breeding grounds about a week later than the males, flit through the territory of one greeting balladeer to the next until finally choosing the right fella. Once their bond is sealed, a groom changes his tune, concentrating on a territorial anthem that is a less distinctive series of rapid high notes, lacking the love song's rising crescendo. It translates as "Stay away from my wife and my home" or, in the Canadian vernacular, "Take off, eh!"

Though fast and lively as they pick off insects from shrubs and small trees, chestnut-sided warblers are not particularly shy, and they often offer fleeting views of their yellow caps and rich roan-brown flanks. They usually give themselves away with the bright-white undersides of their tails, which are usually cocked. The warblers were once quite rare, probably specializing in settling sites recovering from forest fires. Logging and wilderness reclamation of lands abandoned by farmers defeated by the rock of the Canadian Shield have, however, created ideal conditions for the birds to proliferate. Central Ontario today hosts more nesting chestnut-sided warblers than anywhere else on the continent.

Where their territories reach down towards damp riversides and swampy thickets, the birds often live beside the very closely related **yellow warbler**, whose range stretches from the Mackenzie River delta to Bolivia,

Length: 11–14 cm (4.4–5.5 in)
Wingspan: 19–21 cm (7–8 in)
Average weight: 10 g (0.35 oz)
Markings: Male has yellowish-green back and wings, streaked with black; 2 light-yellow wing bars, chestnut sides, white breast and belly; yellow cap on head, white cheeks, black eye stripe and moustache; back turns drab yellow-green in autumn; females similar to males, with less distinct chestnut sides and yellow-green cap; immatures more greenish above and no chestnut sides
Alias: *La paruline à flancs marron, Dendroica pensylvanica*
Call: Song a rapid phrase of high notes, rising at the end, usually described as "pleased, pleased, pleased to meet-cha"; also "chip" and "tsip" call notes

making it the most widespread of all warblers. Chestnuts perhaps split off from their yellow cousins when they took up their more specialized niche. With rust-streaked yellow breasts and greenish-yellow backs, yellow warblers look quite different but are similar in many ways, including their wooing song, commonly imitated by the phrase "Sweet, sweet, I'm so sweet." Males of both species sing from prominent perches while leaving the nest-building and egg-sitting duties to their spouses below.

The nests of both warblers, placed in the crotch of several ascending branches, are frequently found by **brown-headed cowbirds**, which lay their eggs in other birds' clutches. Usually, the freeloading egg is mistaken for one of their own by the nesters, who end up unwittingly raising a large, aggressive baby cowbird that elbows the real offspring away at feeding times, sometimes right out of the nest. Both warblers, however, occasionally recognize the foreign egg. If they've laid only one of their own eggs already, they react by building a new floor over the eggs, so that they're never incubated. They then lay a new clutch. Yellow warbler nests have been found with up to five false floors covering abandoned eggs. Of all species, only song sparrows are struck by cowbirds as often as yellow warblers.

Chestnuts also share their space with **redstarts** and mourning warblers. With bright-orange shoulder, wing and tail patches, contrasted against a mostly black body, redstarts are constantly on the move, fluttering back and forth from understorey perches to catch insects on the wing. Their short, thin snatches of song continue well into July. **Mourning warblers** are far less conspicuous, moving fluidly beneath the cover of bracken ferns and arching raspberry canes. Both sexes have olive backs, yellow bellies and grey heads. The males bear a large black breast patch, and this, and the bird's slow, low-pitched, solemn dirge, account for its grave name.

Preferred habitat: Pockets of young, shrubby deciduous trees amid mature hardwood forests and woodland margins

Food: Caterpillars and other insects, spiders, some seeds and berries

Nest: Loose cup of bark strips, stems, grass, lined with rootlets, hair and plant down; within 1 m (3.3 ft) of ground in upright fork of a shrub or sapling, such as beaked hazel and chokecherry, or in raspberry canes

Average clutch: 4 raspberry-sized, white or cream-coloured eggs with brown and purple spots

Incubation period: 12–13 days

Fledging age: 10–12 days

Common neighbours: Alder and least flycatchers, yellow warblers, common yellowthroats, redstarts and mourning warblers

Range: Southern Ontario to Moosonee; also found in Quebec, the Maritimes, Manitoba and Saskatchewan

Average first arrival in central Ontario: Mid-May

Average last departure from central Ontario: Mid-Sept.

Winter whereabouts: Nicaragua to Panama and the West Indies

Average altitude of migrating birds: 1.5–6 km (5,000–20,000 ft)

Highest recorded migrating bird: Whooper swan, at 8.7 km (29,000 ft)

Also see: Common Yellowthroat, Indigo Bunting

CHIPPING SPARROW
Bold Beaked Hair Stealer

Length: 13–14 cm (5–5.5 in)
Weight: Average 12.5 g (0.5 oz)
Wingspan: 20–23 cm (8–9 in)
Flying speed: 24–32 km/h (15–20 mph)
Markings: Both sexes have a brown back and dusky brown wings, grey breast and cheeks, a bright brick-red cap and a white streak between cap and thin black eye bar
Alias: Chippy, chip-bird, hair bird, hair sparrow, little house sparrow, *le bruant familier*, *Spizella passerina*
Call: Song a rapid-fire, even, staccato trill, lasting 2 or 3 seconds, usually given about 6 times a minute; call an oft-repeated "chip"
Preferred habitat: Open coniferous forests and open areas close to woods or thickets
Food: Grass and weed seeds, beetles, caterpillars, grasshoppers, ants, wasps, spiders
Nest: Tight, tidy cup, 6–11 cm (2.4–4.4 in) wide, of grass,

U NLIKE MANY of their skulking kin, chipping sparrows aren't shy, and are often seen singing from a prominent perch or searching robinlike over open, grassy ground during or after a rain. Their long, staccato song is vaguely reminiscent of a cricket. They also call out incessantly in the single "chip" notes for which they are named. Originally birds of sparsely treed sections of evergreen forests, chippies have taken to the clearings of human settlement in a big way, happy to sport their smart roan berets on telephone wires and lawns and trees around cottages.

In the wild, females upholster their nests with a thick fabric of collected moose and deer hair to insulate their featherless hatchlings. With the coming of European settlers, horsehair soon became all the rage among sparrows in cleared rural areas, who sometimes daringly pulled directly from a horse's mane or tail. They were commonly called hair birds for the practice. After automobiles and tractors replaced horses, chippies in settled areas turned to pet and squirrel fur. Deep-sleeping dogs apparently provide chipping sparrow bonanzas. Other sparrow species use a certain amount of hair for their nests as well.

As soon as they arrive in Ontario, usually in late April and early May, males quickly carve out territories and proclaim the boundaries from strategic singing posts. Successful landholders find later-arriving mates, who assemble nests in less than a week. Before and during nest-building, a couple also engages in the feverish mating phase of their relationship. In the words of naturalist Louise de Kiriline Lawrence, who closely studied a pair of Madawaska River chipping sparrows through one breeding season, "Only after a wild pursuit is he able to bring her to earth where their bodies unite amid a great flutter of wings and loud cheepings."

Deep-sleeping dogs apparently provide chipping sparrow bonanzas

Within a month, most females have laid and hatched their eggs and seen their young fly from the nest. For most of the summer, juvenile chippers make sparrow identification even more complicated than usual, having streaked breasts and caps and a generally browner appearance than their seniors. Adults themselves can be confused with **tree sparrows**, which are almost identical, save for a small, central black spot on their grey breast. But the two species seldom cross paths, most tree sparrows generally leaving southern Ontario for their northern nesting grounds just before chipping sparrows arrive. In October, tree sparrows return for the winter as the chippies are winging their way south again. **Swamp sparrows**, which are common in marshes across the province, also resemble chipping sparrows, but are a little larger, darker, and lack a white bar over their eyes. Their song is similar, too, but is stronger, slower and, it is said, sung with more sweetness and feeling.

root fibres and plant stems, lined with hair; most often 1–3 m (3.3–10 ft) up on a dense evergreen tree

Average clutch: 4 pumpkin-seed-sized, light-turquoise eggs with brown, black and purple markings

Incubation period: Usually 11–14 days

Fledging age: 9–12 days

Lifespan: Adults average 2–3 years, up to 10 years

Predators: Sharp-shinned hawks, martens, mink, raccoons; red squirrels, grackles, jays and crows raid nests

Percentage of chipping sparrows that are polygamous: Probably more than 20

Average first arrival in central Ontario: Late Apr.

Average last departure from central Ontario: Early Oct.

Winter whereabouts: Eastern U.S. seaboard from Rhode Island through to Nicaragua

Range: Throughout most of Ontario; also in all other provinces and territories

Louise de Kiriline Lawrence: Canadian naturalist, 1894–1992, came to central Ontario after serving with the Swedish Red Cross during the Russian Revolution; author of perhaps the most quoted bird statistic ever, after devoting one day to counting how many times the tireless red-eyed vireo sings – 22,197

Number of sparrow species nesting in Ontario: 19

Number of New World sparrow and related Old World bunting species worldwide: 284

Also see: Song Sparrow

COMMON YELLOWTHROAT
Black-masked Balladeer

Length: 11–14 cm (4.4–5.5 in)
Wingspan: 17–19 cm
    (6.7–7.5 in)
Weight: Average 11–12 g
    (0.4 oz)
Markings: Olive-brown back and
    sides; yellow throat and
    breast; whitish belly; males
    have a wide black mask
    trimmed with white above
Alias: Yellowthroat, black-
    masked ground warbler,
    northern yellowthroat, olive-
    coloured yellow-throated
    wren, Maryland yellowthroat,
    la paruline masquée,
    Geothlypis trichas
Other common yellow-breasted
    warblers in central Ontario:
    Yellow, Nashville, magnolia,
    Canada, pine, northern parula
    and Cape May warblers
Call: Loud, rapid, rolling song,
    usually written as "witchety,
    witchety, witchety, witchety,
    witch" or a 2-syllable "whichy,
    whichy, whichy"; also a sharp,
    raspy "chip" call, sounding
    like dice knocked together
Preferred habitat: Shrubby
    swamps, marshes, wet thick-
    ets, bogs, streamsides, forest
    fringes and open areas
Food: Caterpillars, grasshoppers,
    dragonflies, mayflies, beetles,
    grubs, aphids, moths, butter-
    flies, ants, flies, spiders and
    some seeds
Breeding territory: 0.1–0.5 ha
    (0.3–1.2 acres)
Nest: Loose, bulky cup, about
    3 cm (1.2 in) wide, made of
    grass, sedge, stems, bark and

"BLACK-MASKED WARBLER" would probably be a better name for the common
yellowthroat, its Zorro mask the male's most
distinctive feature by far. Many other warblers also have
yellow throats; one is even confusingly called the yellow-
throated warbler, a foreign, grey-backed bird nesting no
closer than southern Ohio.

The bird is quite deserving of the epithet "common,"
though, being perhaps the most abundant warbler in
North America. Ontario certainly has plenty, chanting
their well-known "witchety, witchety, witchety" song
loudly from fields and forest fringes from May to July. In
their mating-season exuberance, males are known to hurl
themselves high into evening skies to perform carolling
"ecstasy flights." Passionate orators may climb up to 30
metres (100 feet) in the air to impress the opposite sex.

When not performing, common yellowthroats seek
anonymity, skulking low in deep vegetation, flitting from
branch to stem, seldom offering a clear, lingering view of
themselves. Their leaf-to-leaf insect-collecting speed is
legendary. By one count, a yellowthroat picked off 69
aphids in a single minute. They are, however, eminently

pishable – a human "pissssh!" quickly bringing them to the open to investigate the noise.

Yellowthroats are one of the most frequent victims of cowbirds, which lay their eggs in other species' nests so that their young are raised by the unwitting nesters. Most or all of the warbler brood is sometimes starved or pushed out of the nest by the larger, aggressive cowbird nestlings.

Yellowthroat young hop out of the nest when only eight or nine days old. They take their first leaps into the air within a day or two after that, and once fledged stick around home longer than most warblers, keeping adults busy all summer. Music goes out of their lives in early August, when fathers begin their moult and stop singing. In September, when their new set of sturdy fall migration feathers is complete, the males begin flying south a week or two ahead of their wives and children. While family units probably dissolve in the southbound flocks of songbirds, which swell to contain thousands, mates will meet again on the same breeding territory the following spring, provided they both survive.

When not performing, common yellowthroats seek anonymity, skulking low in deep vegetation

---

Beginning to leave about a month earlier, the **magnolia warbler** also has a black mask and yellow throat. Its yellow breast, however, is richly streaked with black. Topping off its sharp colour-contrasts, the magnolia has a dark-grey back and wings, with white wing patches and a yellow rump. It is a warbler of new-growth areas of bushy spruce and fir saplings, as well as the mixed and coniferous forest edge. In areas of ideal habitat, there can be 100 magnolia nests per square kilometre (0.4 square miles).

leaves, lined with fine root fibres and hair; on ground or up to 1 m (3 ft) high in a dense clump of tall dead grass, sedge, cattails or rushes or in a shrub
Average clutch: 3–5 cherry-sized, white or creamy eggs speckled brown, grey and black
Incubation period: 12 days
Fledging age: 9–10 days
Maximum lifespan: At least 7 years
Predators: Sharp-shinned hawks and, when perching near water level, snapping turtles, large fish and bullfrogs; snakes, raccoons, skunks and red squirrels raid nests
Nests parasitized by cowbirds: About 19%
Maximum population density: More than 100 pairs per km^2 (0.4 sq mi)
Range: All of Ontario except far north; also in all other provinces and territories
Average first arrival in central Ontario: Mid-May
Average last departure from central Ontario: Early Oct.
Winter whereabouts: Central eastern U.S. seaboard to Panama and the West Indies
Also see: Black-and-white Warbler, Chestnut-sided Warbler. *Up North:* Bullfrog

DOWNY WOODPECKER
The Tiniest Tapper

Length: 15–16 cm (6–6.4 in)
Wingspan: 28–30.5 cm (11–12 in)
Weight: 22–33 g (0.8–1.2 oz)
Hairy woodpecker weight: 62 g (2 oz)
Markings: White back and undersides; black wings with white barring; black tail trimmed with white; striped black-and-white head; males with red patch at back of the head
Alias: Black-and-white driller, little sapsucker, Tommy woodpecker, Batchelder's woodpecker, *le pic mineur, Picoides pubescens*
Call: A high, rapid, falling "whinny"; also a "pik" call
Drum-roll duration: About 2 seconds
Food: Beetles, carpenter ants, moths, aphids, gall wasps, spiders and their young or eggs make up 75–85% of diet; the rest consists of

BEING THE SMALLEST of their kind in Ontario, sparrow-sized downy woodpeckers are charged with the lightweight work, searching for insects out on thin branchlets that wouldn't support their bigger brethren. Among downies, though, it's the males that tend to pick away in the delicate upper-branch network. Their mates, with whom they share their territories year round, concentrate on gleaning food from the bark of trunks and larger limbs. Perhaps this way they avoid marital squabbles over food, though ornithologists don't agree on the reasons for this behaviour. Both tap erratically at their work surface and listen for the reverberations of insect tunnels and the sound of the hidden creatures munching away. Once targeted, the creepy-crawlies are doomed. The downy, like other woodpeckers, has a lightning-quick barbed and sticky tongue – one of the most effective weapons in birddom.

Downies don't drum as much as most woodpeckers, but mates do occasionally telegraph each other with some rapid-fire beak-banging on dry, dead, resonant branches. In March and April, they start to drum up the old enthusiasm in their relationships and reaffirm their territories with the onset of the breeding season. Pairs often join in percussive duets, each from his or her own private post.

Soon they begin searching for a nest site. While the female usually has last say on the location, her guy does most of the heavy labour, pecking out a tree cavity. It takes him two to three weeks, around the first half of May.

Fathers also do most of the brooding after their young hatch, and together the parents feed their nestlings up to 20 times an hour. Noisy fledglings remain dependent on their parents for up to three weeks before drifting away from home, usually around June. Many join loose, cosmopolitan foraging flocks of chickadees, nuthatches, kinglets, brown creepers and white-throated sparrows. While some downy woodpeckers shift slightly farther south in autumn, most remain, carving out tree holes into which they snuggle on cold winter nights. Mates, however, sleep separately in their own chambers. They eat more seeds during winter, but still find meat in cold storage, often raiding goldenrod galls for the juicy, sleeping wasp grubs within. Sociable downies also like to check out the buffet offered by humans. Suet balls, meat bones and sunflower seeds are menu favourites at birdfeeders.

Occupying much the same habitat, **hairy woodpeckers** are big, gangly, shyer versions of the more common downies. Though virtually identical, they are about 50 percent larger, approximately the size of a robin. Hairies also wield a more prodigious bill. It's as long as their heads and excavates deeper for bugs. The hefty bill also adds decibels to their tapping and drumming, and hairies have a much louder and more piercing call than their smaller cousins. Hairies lack the telltale black spots on the white tail feathers of downies, but these spots are often difficult to see on downies. The two birds are easiest to identify when seen side by side, but lacking that opportunity, look for the hairy's hammer.

And are downies downy and hairies hairy? No more or less than the other, so the origin of their names remains a taxonomic curiosity. The Latin family name for woodpecker is *Picoides*, from *picus*, meaning "woodpecker." The downy is *Picoides pubescens*, referring to the fine peach-fuzz hairs of puberty. The hairy is *P. villosus*, meaning "hairy."

berries (mountain ash, dogwood, poison ivy, serviceberry) and hazel nuts, beechnuts, acorns, seeds and sap
Preferred habitat: Deciduous and mixed forests with older trees
Territory: 12–30 m (40–100 ft) around nest
Nest: Cavity 20–30 cm (8–12 in) deep, up to 15 cm (6 in) across, with 4-cm-wide (1.5-in-wide) entrance, usually on south or east side of tree; floor covered by wood chips, normally 3–15 m (10–50 ft) up in dead tree or dead limb
Average clutch: 4–5 white, pumpkin-seed-sized eggs
Incubation period: 12 days
Fledging age: 21–25 days
Maximum lifespan: 10 years
Average population density: 1–10 pairs per km^2 (0.4 sq mi)
Range: Southern Ontario to southern James Bay; also in all other provinces and territories
Number of woodpecker species nesting in Ontario: 9
Number of woodpecker species worldwide: About 200
Also see: Brown Creeper, Red-breasted Nuthatch, Beetles, Goldenrod. *Up North:* Black-capped Chickadee, Yellow-bellied Sapsucker

EVENING GROSBEAK
Robust, Gregarious Newcomer

Length: 18–21 cm (7–8.5 in)
Wingspan: Average 33–35 cm
(13–14 in)
Weight: 52–63 g (1.8–2.2 oz)
Markings: Male has yellow
breast, undersides and
eyebrow, with brown head
blending to yellow above
black and white wing; also
black tails and greenish or
off-white beaks; female is
grey above, with brownish
head and touches of yellow,
black wings and tail with
scattered white
Alias: Eastern evening grosbeak,
American hawfinch, *le gros-
bec errant, Hesperiphona
vespertina, Coccothraustes
vespertinus*
Call: Loud, sharp "chip-chur"
notes; a warbled whistling
song is seldom heard
Preferred habitat: Coniferous
and mixed forests

THE PROSPECT of a bone-chilling winter sends most Ontario avifauna winging south for the season. Other species without the need, desire or Club Med reservations will stick around, however, and batten down for a long, cold blow. And there are a few for whom the winter is a time of boundless wandering and sometimes even opportunity. Robust, gregarious evening grosbeaks are among the most familiar in this group of wintry rovers, flocking wherever bountiful conifer cones yield their nutritious seeds. They're also attracted to roadside salt, and they often mob birdfeeders. They knock one another off feeder perches and platforms as if they were brawling in a hockey game, each bumped bird eager to rejoin the melee, like a little feathered Boston Bruin in its black-and-yellow-and-white uniform.

Originally nesting in western boreal forests, wayfaring evening grosbeaks seem to have found Ontario so much to their liking that they began staying year round in the 1920s, annually drawing hordes of naturalists to Camp Billie Bear on Muskoka's Bella Lake, one of the first spots they inhabited in summer. Birdfeeders and shade-tree plantings of Manitoba maples, whose seeds are a grosbeak staple out west, are credited with helping to lure the birds east. Logging, forest fires and grosbeaks' love of cherries probably have more to do with it, however. Vast numbers of chokecherry and pin cherry, which thrive in open sunlight, popped up across the province wherever forests were felled. In late summer, flocks of evening grosbeaks can be heard noisily devouring the wild fruits, cracking open the pits to eat the stones while discarding the sweet flesh. Each 60-gram (two-ounce) bird exerts 11 kilograms (25 pounds) of pressure with its vicelike beak to burst open a cherry pit. The industrial-strength bill gives grosbeaks their name; *gros* meaning big or thick in French. In the sometimes-confusing and always-evolving world of avian taxonomy, the evening grosbeak isn't actually a member of the grosbeak family, but is classed in the large finch family. True grosbeaks include the northern cardinal, the red-breasted grosbeak and the indigo bunting, among others. But the descriptive name "grosbeak" has stuck to several birds, including the evening and the pine grosbeak.

Grosbeaks stoke their young with plenty of pulverized cherry-stone meal. They also throw in some insects, the only time of year they fall off the vegetarian wagon. They may be plentiful nesters in an area for a couple of years, and then nearly vanish the next. Usually they begin the breeding season around May, as flocks dwindle and birds pair off. Males challenge each other by wrestling with their stout bills locked together, and both sexes sway and posture for each other's attention. Rapturous males seem to sing only directly to their mates during the most climactic moments of pair bonding. The rarity of the song helps perpetuate the fallacy that evening grosbeaks sing only at night, hence their name.

As the heat of first passion cools and relationships solidify, females build nests. The restless birds still frequently forage far from home, however. Females incubate eggs, but males help feed the chicks. After the nestlings fledge, several or more families leave the nesting grounds *en masse* to tour the countryside, descending where they find lots to eat. Come winter, though, the merry band

Food: Cherry pits; conifer, maple, ash, dogwood and sumac seeds; conifer, birch, ash and aspen buds; serviceberries and mountain ash and juniper berries; sap; up to 20% caterpillars and other insects during nesting season

Nest: Usually a shallow bowl of loose twigs and rootlets near branch tips towards tops of spruce or other evergreens

Average clutch: 3–4 peach-pit-sized, blue or turquoise eggs with brown, grey or purple marks

Incubation: 11–14 days

Fledging age: 12–14 days

Lifespan: Adults often live 4–9 years; maximum in captivity 17 years

Range: Just beyond the southern edge of the Canadian Shield to southern James Bay; also in all other provinces

Other birds that have moved into Ontario in the 20th century: Turkey vulture, northern cardinal, house finch

Alien birds introduced into Ontario: Starling, house sparrow, rock dove (pigeon), ring-necked pheasant, gray partridge, mute swan

Also see: Purple Finch, Chokecherry. *Up North:* Red Pine

tends to segregate, with males sticking close to the breeding grounds and females roving farther afield. In years when food is scarce, the mostly female flocks may move into southern Ontario. They return in early spring as melting snow uncovers the fallen maple keys and other seeds on the forest floor, filling woods with a loud racket of "chip-chur" calls. The birds' beaks also shed their whitish coatings to reveal a fresh green shade underneath.

During winters with big crops of conifer seeds, the evening grosbeak's northern finch relatives may arrive to join in the feasting. Because many tree species produce bumper crops erratically, finches that specialize in them are true nomads, moving widely from one region to another where the eatin' is good. When a flock drops out of the sky, it can turn somnolent winter woods into an exotic theatre of song.

Grosbeaks stoke their young

with plenty of pulverized

cherry-stone meal

In particularly bountiful years, crossbills may even nest in the dead of winter. These rugged boreal finches construct large, well-insulated nests for their young. **Red crossbills** use their odd, crossed-over upper and lower beak tips to pry open tough red and white pine cones to get at the seeds. Another species, the **white-winged crossbill**, has a similarly designed but smaller beak suited to flimsier, unopened spruce and tamarack cones. Brown-streaked, loquacious **pine siskins** use their pointy, slightly curved bills to harvest seeds from already-opened spruce, birch and alder cones. Plump, red **pine grosbeaks** mostly eat tree buds. **Redpolls**, with their bright-red caps and black goatees, also migrate from the Arctic tundra to devour birch, cedar and alder cone seeds by the bunch.

COMMON FLICKER
Ground-foraging Woodpecker

TO THE UNTRAINED EYE, this woodpecker, spending so much of its time on the ground probing for ant holes, might be mistaken for some sort of tawny thrush. It is, in fact, the supreme anteater of the avian kingdom, reputed to hoover up as many as 5,000 ants in a single meal. When at a tree trunk, however, the flicker assumes the classic woodpecker posture: head up, feet grasping the bark, stiff tail feathers braced against the tree. And during the mating season, both sexes drum like the rest of their kin, hammering beaks against anything sufficiently resonant, from dead trees to TV antennae, to mark territories or attract mates. In the early 1990s, one fervent flicker even forced the last-minute cancellation of a space-shuttle mission after beating loose the cover of an instrument panel on the multi-billion-dollar craft.

In spring, unabashed flickers also proclaim their presence with repetitive, urgent calls, reminiscent of a car engine turning over without starting. The call also has a junglelike quality that has inspired some birders to dub flickers the "Tarzan bird."

Length: 30–35 cm (12–14 in)
Tongue length: Extends 7.5 cm (3 in) beyond beak
Wingspan: 47–52 cm (18.5–20 in)
Weight: 112–168 g (4–6 oz)
Markings: Dark-brown bands across tan back and wings; tan neck and face with a grey cap and a red patch on the back of the neck (males and females); a wide black bib across the top of the breast and black spots covering a white belly and sides; white rump; blackish-brown pointed tail is yellow on the underside, as are the wings; slightly curved beaks; males have a black "moustache" across cheek
Alias: More than 130 known aliases, including northern flicker, yellow-shafted flicker,

golden-winged woodpecker, antbird, yellowhammer, wood pigeon, wick-up, clape, gaffer, harry-wicket, heigh-ho, Tarzan bird (after its song), *le pic dore, pic flamboyant, Colaptes auratus*

Call: Song a rapid "wick, wick, wick, wick" or "yuck, yuck, yuck, yuck," sounding like a car trying to start, continuing up to 6 seconds; also a "wicka" call, a creaky "clear" call note and several other vocalizations

Name origin: Imitation of "flick-a" call; may also have roots in Old English *flicerian*, meaning "to flutter" or "fluttering of birds"

Drum roll: Loud, even, about 22 beats per second, lasting up to 1.5 seconds

Preferred habitat: Open and patchy woodlands, forest edge, beaver ponds; also seen on lawns, poking for food

Food: Ants (their eggs and larvae make up about half its diet); beetles, grasshoppers, crickets, wasps, wood lice, caterpillars, grubs, worms and flying insects also eaten; acorns, nuts, berries and seeds provide another quarter of its food

Territory: About 300 m (330 yd) across

Nest: Round cavity 5–10 cm (2–4 in) wide and 25–90 cm (10–36 in) deep; bottom lined with fresh wood chips, with entrance usually facing south or southeast; most often 2–5 m high (7–16.5 ft) in dead trees, often aspens; also

In mid-April, males usually return north, a few days ahead of the females. They're the real workers in any flicker marriage. Two females will even face off against each other to win a devoted mate, flaring their wings and tails, bobbing their heads and circling their haughtily upturned beaks in an attempt to intimidate. Contentious males deal with each other in a similar manner. Strangely enough, this pugnacious behaviour between two birds of the same sex becomes seduction between two of the opposite sex. And the only way the lovebirds can actually tell each other's sex is by the male's black moustache. A clever biologist proved this by painting a moustache on a mated female. Hubby quickly rejected the cross-dressed flicker, but took her back when the moustache was removed.

After pairing, males choose a nest site in a soft, rotted tree. Both mates spend one or two weeks excavating with their long, curved beaks, though sometimes they simply renovate an old hole. Occasionally all their work comes to naught as they're evicted by scrappy red squirrels, kestrels or, in more-settled areas, the reviled starling. But even if they lose a clutch of eggs to an interloper, flickers can carve out another nest and lay a second batch. Sometimes they don't show very good manners themselves, taking over the sandbank burrows of kingfishers or bank swallows to secure a place for their young when there are no other options.

Males are the chief incubators and brooders, sitting on the nest through the night and doing most of the feeding by day. Nestlings are fed heaping helpings of regurgitated ants about twice an hour. After they fledge, the raucous young continue to demand food with loud, high-pitched calls. Later they follow their parents to feeding sites, where the whole family may raid a choice ant city together.

At a distance, the flicker seems unprepossessing; but close up, or through binoculars, this bird is beautiful. Its tawny back is intricately barred in darker browns, its white belly is spotted boldly like a leopard and a grey-capped head is highlighted with a splashy red head-band and a long, subtly curved bill. And, of course, males – and the odd unfortunate female – sport the handsome moustache. On the wing, blue jay-sized flickers display a conspicuous white rump patch and an undulating flight. Sometimes a brilliant flash of yellow is seen, particularly at takeoff, as the flicker exposes its exquisite yellow wing and tail undersides.

Males are the chief incubators and brooders, sitting on the nest through the night and doing most of the feeding by day

---

Ornithologists once believed three species of flickers populated North America, but now they've been re-classified as three races of one species. The yellow-shafted flicker found in Ontario ranges east of the Rockies; the red-shafted flicker, with red under the wings and tail, lives west of the mountains; while the gilded flicker flies in the southwest.

uses poles, posts, bankside holes
Average clutch: 5–8 peach-pit-sized, glossy white eggs
Incubation period: 11–16 days
Fledgling age: 25–28 days
Maximum lifespan: 12 years
Predators: Crows, blue jays, chipmunks, red squirrels, bears and weasels all raid nests; sharp-shinned hawks catch adults
Birds that nest in old flicker holes: Wood duck, tree swallow, kestrel, bluebird, saw-whet owl
Flying speed: 33–42 km/h (20–26 mph)
Average population density: 1–10 pairs per km^2 (0.4 sq mi)
Range: Throughout Ontario; also in all other provinces and ter-ritories to the tree line
Average first arrival in central Ontario: Mid-Apr.
Average last departure from central Ontario: Mid-Oct.
Winter whereabouts: Far south-ern Ontario to Central America
Also see: Pileated Woodpecker, Wood Duck. *Up North*: Kingfisher, Tree Swallow

GOLDFINCH
Ontario's Wild Canary

Length: 11–14 cm (4.5–5.5 in)
Weight: 12–21 g (0.7 oz)
Wingspan: 21–23 cm (8–9 in)
Flying speed: 30–62 km/h
 (19–39 mph)
Markings: Males are yellow, with
 black wings, tail and cap and
 a white rump; females have
 olive-green back, dull-yellow
 breast, black wings and tail
 and white wing bars; in
 autumn both sexes turn more
 olive grey
Alias: American goldfinch, wild
 canary, yellow bird, thistle
 bird, shiner, willow goldfinch,
 common goldfinch, *le
 chardonneret jaune, Spinus
 tristis, Carduelis tristis*
Call: Song is a long, musical,
 canarylike series of high,
 squeaky chips, twitters and
 trills; also a flight call in 3
 quick, repeated "per-chicory"
 notes, and a long, springy call
 that drops and rises, sounding
 like a cork twisting in the
 neck of a wine bottle
Name for a group: A charm of
 goldfinches
Food: Seeds of thistles, grasses,
 willow, birch, alder, spruce,
 hemlock, tamarack, goldenrod, aster, burdock, teasel,
 mullein, chicory, evening
 primrose; rarely flower buds
 and small amounts of insects
 and berries
Preferred habitat: Forest
 borders, meadows, shrubby
 river bottomlands, young,
 scrubby woods

BOUNCING THROUGH the air in deeply dipping flights, goldfinches sputter and twitter over tangled riversides and meadows throughout summer. They're often called wild canaries, both for their song and coat of bright-yellow feathers. Real canaries, though, are long-domesticated cage birds originally from the Canary Islands, off North Africa. The European goldfinch was also tamed as a cage bird long ago and widely admired for its beauty; it's often depicted in medieval manuscript illuminations with the child Jesus and was also widely associated with Easter.

Though closely related, Ontario's goldfinch is a separate species from its Old World counterpart. The seed connoisseur was, however, far less common before European settlement greatly expanded the open-area and forest-fringe settings in which it prospers. The goldfinch breeding season does not even begin until the first "weed" seeds of summer start ripening, in late June and July. These pulpy, fresh seeds are more palatable than older seeds for nestlings, who are fed by regurgitation by both parents. Fluffy thistle seedheads are especially favoured, providing down for nest linings in addition to meals for the young. In fact, the scientific name for the goldfinch genus derives from the Latin word for "thistle," *carduus*.

Goldfinches, and the berry-loving cedar waxwings, are among the last breeders of the year, sometimes nesting into September. Like waxwings, goldfinches are also social birds and nest as close as three or four metres (10 or 13 feet). But as territory is the tie that binds for most nesting birds, the lack of an exclusive piece of ground to return to in spring means that goldfinches usually find a new mate every year.

After the young fledge, families forage together for a while. Then, gradually, the drably coloured youngsters drift away and in late September form large, wandering flocks of adolescents. Adults gather in their own groups, seeking out the shelter of streamside thickets and cedar woods while they moult, becoming less buoyant and agile during the transition, like other songbirds. Studies have shown that, once outfitted in their warmer, heavier grey-green winter plumage, goldfinches can withstand temperatures of –70°C (–94°F) for up to eight hours.

Still, as the snow flies in November or early December, most adults head south in large flocks, the females tending to fly a little farther than males. Mobs of juvenile birds, on the other hand, don't seem to know enough to retreat. Goldfinch young stick it out in the land of their hatching for their first winter, finding seeds in conifer cones and the dead standing stalks of goldenrod, mullein and aster. They often form mixed flocks with redpolls and pine siskins, their finch relatives from the north. Adults present in areas south of North Bay during the months of snow are generally goldfinches that have migrated from even colder breeding grounds farther north. More and more adult goldfinches have been braving Ontario winters in recent decades, probably because of all-you-can-eat buffets at birdfeeders across the province. In mid-March, overwintering males put on their bright-yellow spring jackets and become recognizable to those accustomed to the goldfinches of summer.

Nest: Tidy, tightly woven, rounded cone with thick walls of grass and bark strips, lined with thistle and milkweed down, bound with spiderwebs; usually wedged between several upright forked branches in bushes, hawthorns, serviceberries or maple saplings near water; so well made and cosy that they are often taken over as winter quarters for deer mice

Average clutch: 4–6 kidney-bean-sized, pale-blue eggs, often with light spotting

Incubation period: 10–14 days

Fledging age: 11–16 days

Maximum lifespan: 9 years in wild, 13 years in captivity

Origin of canary: According to the Roman writer Pliny, the Canary Islands were called *Canaria*, "Land of Dogs," because of the very large canines reputed to roam the archipelago

Range: South-central Ontario to the southern edge of the Hudson Bay lowlands; also in all other provinces

Average first migrant arrival in central Ontario: Early May

Average last departure from central Ontario: Early Dec.

Winter whereabouts: South-central Ontario to the Gulf of Mexico

Also see: Purple Finch, Evening Grosbeak, Goldenrod. *Up North:* Cedar Waxwing

GRACKLE
The Golden-eyed Blackbird

Length: 28–34 cm
(11–13.5 in)
Wingspan: 43–47 cm
(17–18.5 in)
Weight: Average 115 g (4 oz),
up to 150 g (5.3 oz)
Flying speed: 32–48 km/h
(20–30 mph)
Markings: Males completely
black, with iridescence sometimes shining purple, blue,
green and bronze in the sun,
especially around the head;
females are duller and a
little smaller; juveniles dark
brown till their first autumn,
with brown eyes
Alias: Common grackle, blackbird, bronzed grackle, keel-
tailed grackle, purple
jackdaw, *le quiscale bronze*,
Quiscalus quiscula
Call: High, squeaky screech,
often described as the sound
of a rusty hinge; also clucks
Food: Caterpillars, beetles,
grubs, grasshoppers, ants
and other insects, worms,
spiders, snails, frogs,
salamanders, snakes, crayfish, minnows, mice, bats,
small birds, eggs, nestlings,
seeds, berries, nuts
Preferred habitat: Swamps, open
forests, marshes, woodland
fringes, riversides, wet fields,
open areas
Nest: Bulky, 16–22 cm (6–9 in)
wide, made of sticks, mud,
weeds and lined with grass;
usually 1–4 m (3.3–13.2 ft)
up in evergreens; sometimes
in marshes or tree cavities

PIERCING GOLDEN EYES set grackles apart in a sea of blackbirds. In early spring and again in late summer, grackles are commonly seen in large mixed flocks with red-winged blackbirds and cowbirds. In between, grackles go their own way to raise little grackles. Being able to eat just about anything, they're much more flexible than the largely marsh-bound red-wings in where they choose to raise a family. While grackles frequent swamps, shorelines and other wet sites, they also show up around campgrounds and human habitations, boldly vying with chipmunks and red squirrels for any peanut or piece of scrambled egg falling to the ground or left unattended.

Two items on the grackle's menu that have made them infamous (along with blue jays and crows) are the eggs and nestlings of other birds. The omnivorous birds in black also steal food from ground-foraging birds, especially robins. Grackles, which can be distinguished from other blackbirds in flight by their long, rudder-shaped tails, are blamed for contributing to the decline in songbird populations that has come with the clearing of forests. Settlement and roads create more of the woodland-edge habitat that supports grackles, while exposing songbirds to their raids.

Though classed among the songbirds – possessing the same basic music box in its throat – the grackle has a weak, screechy mating call that has done little to elevate its standing beyond its own kind. Their "singing" begins in earnest in early spring, soon after the arrival of the less-glossy-coated females, who reach the breeding grounds a little later than the mixed male flocks. Cocks call imploringly in front of potential mates, while puffing their feathers up, drooping their wings and raising their long beaks straight in the air. If a female accepts, she then has the task of building a nest, which takes her about five days. Unlike the fiercely territorial red-wings, grackles often settle into small, loose colonies of 10 nests or so, spaced as close as five metres (16.5 feet) from each other.

Females also tend the eggs themselves, though fathers assist in feeding their young. Like most other birds, they usually lay one egg a day and don't begin incubation until they have a full clutch, ensuring all hatch at the same time. In the grackle's case, a full clutch is usually four eggs, but after incubation begins, they often lay a bonus egg, sometimes even more. The later eggs usually contain males and are a little larger than the earlier ones, giving the late-hatching nestlings a better chance to compete with their older siblings at feeding time. A day or two in age can make a huge difference in birds that grow to almost adult size within three weeks. If food (principally insects for nestlings) is in short supply, parents will concentrate on feeding the four oldest birds and let the other youngsters starve.

After the brown-eyed young have fledged, by mid-July, grackles join ever-growing flocks of blackbirds – which can soon reach into the thousands – foraging and roosting together. Older adults usually occupy the best and safest perches in trees at the centre of a large roost, pretty much ensuring that anyone picked off by predators will be the rookies on the periphery. Still, the inexperienced young learn where to find the best grub by sticking with the flock. By the time migrating flocks congregate at traditional winter sites in the southern United States, they can number up to five million in a single roost, and are considered agricultural pests for pillaging grain fields.

Average clutch: 4–5 peach-pit-sized, light-blue-green or brown eggs with dark-brown, black or purple squiggles
Incubation period: 13–14 days
Fledging age: 14–20 days
Maximum lifespan: 16 years
Range: Southern Ontario to the southern Hudson Bay lowlands; also all other provinces and Northwest Territories
Average first arrival in central Ontario: Late Mar.
Average last departure from central Ontario: Late Oct.
Winter whereabouts: Far southern Ontario to Texas
Estimated North American common grackle winter population: About 110 million
Estimated winter population of all North American blackbirds: 400 million
Other species most often in mixed flocks: Red-winged blackbirds, cowbirds, starlings, rusty blackbirds
Largest winter blackbird roost: Up to 50 million, in Texas
Largest-known roosting flocks ever: Billions of passenger pigeons, now extinct
Farthest migrating Ontario blackbird species: Bobolinks, wintering in Argentina
Original blackbird homeland: South America
Number of grackle species nesting in Ontario: 1
Number of grackle species worldwide: 7, all in the Americas
Also see: Northern Oriole. *Up North:* Red-winged Blackbird

GRAY JAY
The Friendly Camp Robber

GRAY JAYS ARE LEGENDARY in the northwoods for their intelligence, industry, and amazing tameness and curiosity. They are the chipmunks of the bird world, complete with cute, beady black eyes, fluffy feathers, and a penchant for frequenting campsites. Gray jays sometimes even land on human hands and shoulders when coaxed with tasty morsels, yet they don't commonly come to call until September.

For native peoples, the plump grey bird was a well-known, whimsical rascal. Wisakedjak, the culture hero of Cree and Ojibway lore, often took the form of the crafty bird. "Whiskeyjack" is still a common name for the gray jay. The bird's familiar presence in winter logging camps, sidling up for dinner along with everyone else, led to stories of the jays as souls of dead lumberjacks, perhaps killed tragically in one of the grisly accidents common to the trade. Even today, the lumberjack staple of baked beans is said to be a gray jay favourite, along with cheese.

Gray jays are compulsive hoarders, as implied by their scientific name *Perisoreus*, Latin for "heap up." They work from June to autumn like feathered beavers, storing away enough food to let them live comfortably through winter. Drawing from unique enlarged saliva glands, the jays cover insects, seeds, berries and mushrooms in gluelike bird spit, then paste them to the trunks and needled branchlets of conifer trees. Stashes are often covered with wispy pieces of lichen or loose flakes of bark. Studies suggest that a gray jay can remember precisely where each of its thousands of hidden snacks is located over its square kilometre (0.4 square miles) or so of turf.

Their food storage system is so efficient that the vast majority of jays easily survive the winter and begin nesting as early as March, the leanest and deadliest time of the year

Length: 25–33 cm (10–13 in)
Wingspan: 38–43 cm (15–17 in)
Weight: 62–82 g (2.2–2.9 oz)
Markings: Both sexes have dark-grey back, wings and tail, lighter-grey undersides, off-white face, crown and throat, black on back of head and neck extending to the eyes; juveniles are a darker, sooty grey
Alias: Whiskeyjack, Canada jay, moose bird, meat bird, grease bird, Labrador jay, carrion bird, Alaska jay, *le geai du Canada, Perisoreus canadensis*
Preferred habitat: Black spruce bogs, coniferous and sometimes mixed forests, beaver meadows, clearings
Call: Often written as "whee-ah," a raspy "chuckle," whistles, squeaks and scolds
Food: Caterpillars, beetles, grubs and other insects, spiders and

for most forest creatures. Native hunters from Labrador to Alaska reported that it was bad luck to see or disturb a gray jay nest. The aboriginal people of northern Scandinavia – the Saami, or Lapps – believed the same about the Siberian jay, probably the gray jay's closest relative.

Only three eggs are usually laid. After a month of happy family life, foraging with their parents, many sooty gray jay fledglings encounter tougher times. Around mid-June, intense sibling rivalry sets in, culminating about 10 days later with one dominant bird driving the others from home. The winner, two out of three times a male, stays with its parents, collecting and storing food through the summer and fall, then living off the stash through the following winter, unless before winter it finds a newly widowed mate in a nearby territory. The ejected offspring are not so lucky. About 80 percent perish before October. Those that survive usually manage by tagging along in the territory of a jay couple without a youngster of their own.

Their food storage system is so efficient that the vast majority of jays easily survive the winter

---

In early autumn, gray jays redouble their food-gathering activities, venturing farther from their coniferous territories and often dipping and gliding into human company. Their buoyant flight is attributed to their long, wide wings and soft, broad feathers. Gray jays don't need the stiff, slim pinions that carry migratory birds through their arduous journeys north and south, because they remain on their territories year round with the same mates for as long as they live.

their eggs; seeds, berries, mushrooms, carrion, birds eggs and nestlings, mice

Average family territory: 0.6–1.7 km² (0.2–0.7 sq mi)

Nest: Deep, bulky bowl with a turned-in top, 14–16 cm (5.5–6.3 in) wide, of sticks, bark and grass, insulated with feathers and fur; usually built 2–7 m (6.6–23 ft) up on a level branch near the trunk of a spruce or other evergreen tree

Average clutch: 2–4 peach-pit-sized, greyish- or greenish-white eggs covered in tiny brownish spots

Incubation period: 18–19 days

Fledging age: 23 days

Maximum lifespan: At least 16 years in wild

Predators: Sharp-shinned hawk, goshawk, merlin

Average annual adult mortality: 17%

Average annual adult mortality of migrating songbirds: Often more than 50%

Range: From Hudson Bay to Manitoulin Island and almost to the southern edge of the Canadian Shield, though sparse south of Algonquin Park and absent in most of Muskoka and eastern Ontario; also found in all other provinces and territories to the tree line

Number of jay species nesting in Ontario: 2

Number of jay species worldwide: 42

Also see: *Up North:* Blue Jay

INDIGO BUNTING
Brilliant Blue Balladeer

THE COLOUR BLUE is rare among Ontario birds, but indigo buntings sport more of the vibrant hue than any other species in the province. Loud, prolonged singing, even through the midday heat of summer, gives away treetop-perching males, coated in resplendent deep blue. Unlike blue jays, male indigos have no real blue pigment; their feathers are actually black, but refract light to produce a brilliant blue. Depending on how the sun hits them, they can sometimes also appear black, grey or even green.

Despite their flashy attire and fervent vocals, male indigos are not widely regarded as particularly tuneful. Yet they're dedicated to their craft and adept at learning new music. Most male songbirds generally pick up a subtly unique tune from their fathers, which they sing for the rest of their lives. An ambitious young indigo arriving in Ontario for his first breeding season may, however, quickly learn and sing his own cover version of the song of an experienced, locally dominant performer. If the knockoff is good enough, local rivals may be fooled into believing that the kid is Big Daddy Blue and give him a wide-enough berth for him to establish a successful breeding territory. Gaining valuable experience their first season, most males find a better territory in a different area the following year, ensuring that one place doesn't become saturated with indigos all singing the same song.

Indigos with only small, inadequate territories can sing all summer long without attracting a mate, but those with large, insect-rich estates may breed with two females. Other brightly coloured, fiercely territorial birds of open habitats – such as yellow warblers, common yellowthroats and red-winged blackbirds – are often polygamous for the

Length: 13–15 cm (5–6 in)
Weight: 12–17 g (0.4–0.6 oz)
Wingspan: 21–23 cm (8–9 in)
Flying speed: 32 km/h (20 mph)
Portion of males that are polygamous: 10–15%
Markings: Males are a completely deep, iridescent blue, with darker wings and tail, moulting to mottled brown in fall with some blue on wings and tail; females are brown with pale, streaked breast; males may not show adult plumage until 2 years old
Alias: Blue finch, indigo canary, indigo bluebird, indigo finch, indigo bird, indigo-painted bunting, *le passerin indigo*, *Passerina cyanea*
Scientific name meaning: In Latin, *passerinus* is "sparrow," and *cyaneus* is "dark blue"
Call: Song a fast, short series of high notes in varied couplets

same reasons. Indigo bigamists can afford the luxury, since females do all the nest-building and incubating and most or all of the nestling care. It may be just as well for hubby to be away most of the time, because sunlight on his bright-blue plumage is a dead giveaway of the nest's location to predators. Females, in contrast, are Plain Janes, with drab-brown backs, beige bottoms and nary a wing bar to distinguish them.

Though indigo buntings don't arrive until late May or early June, if all goes well some mothers nest through the summer, raising two broods. A successful polygamous father may sire four batches of young in a single season. After singing their last refrain in August, much later than most other birds, they begin flying south again for the tropics.

Indigos with large, insect-rich estates may breed with two females

One of Ontario's other blue-feathered celebrities is a thrush, the fabled **eastern bluebird**. Male bluebirds are more of a beautiful sky-blue shade and have contrasting rusty-red breasts. They are less common north of the southern edge of the Canadian Shield. While indigo buntings have benefited from the clearing of forests and subsequent abandonment of marginal farmlands to scrubby growth, bluebirds have suffered with European settlement. With the newcomers came starlings and house sparrows from Europe, aggressive cavity nesters that evicted bluebirds from the tree holes they need to raise their young. Today, bluebirds often nest only where people have built bluebird boxes tailored to their requirements. On their wintering grounds in the southern United States, bluebirds are also susceptible to freak cold snaps. A handful of severe winters in recent decades reduced their population by 60 to 90 percent.

Food: Beetles, caterpillars, grasshoppers, aphids, mosquitoes and flies; seeds of goldenrod, aster, thistles, and grasses; raspberries and elderberries

Preferred habitat: Deciduous and sometimes mixed forest edge and shrubby clearings and thickets

Nest: Shallow cup of grass, stems, twigs, strips of bark and leaves, lined with root fibres, hair and feathers; usually 50–100 cm (20–40 in) high in a tangle of raspberry canes or crotch of a bush or sapling

Average clutch: 3–4 pale-blue or white, pumpkin-seed-sized eggs

Incubation period: 12–13 days

Fledging age: 8–10 days

Maximum lifespan: At least 8 years

Name origin: Indigo is derived from "India," original source of plants yielding a prized blue dye; in English of the 1500s, bunting meant "plump" or "rounded"

Range: Southern Ontario to about Lake Abitibi and north shore of Lake Superior; also in Saskatchewan, Manitoba, Quebec and New Brunswick

Average first arrival in central Ontario: Late May

Average last departure from central Ontario: Mid-Sept.

Winter whereabouts: Southern Florida and Texas to the West Indies and Panama

Average travel time from Central America to Ontario: About a month

Also see: Common Yellowthroat, Wild Red Raspberry. *Up North:* Red-winged Blackbird

KILLDEER
Master of the Broken Wing

Length: 23–28 cm
(9–11 in)
Wingspan: 48–53 cm
(19–21 in)
Weight: 84–92 g (3–3.5 oz)
Flying speed: 40–88 km/h
(25–55 mph)
Running speed: About 8 km/h
(5 mph)
Markings: Brown back, wings
and head; white belly, neck
and between and around
eyes; bold black collar and
breast band separated by
a white band; in flight, a
long white stripe along top
of wings, gold-orange rump
and pointed tail tipped with
black and white are visible;
young sport a single breast
band
Alias: Field plover, chattering
plover, killdee, pasture plover,
killdeer plover, noisy plover,

I F THERE WERE a prize for the most annoyed bird in
Ontario, it would have to go to the killdeer. The
slightly comical bobbing plover with huge orange-
rimmed eyes seems forever ticked off, skittering about or
abruptly launching into the air to call out its name in a
repetitive, shrill "kill-deee, kill-deee, kill-deee." Little
wonder its scientific name is *vociferus*. Yet, if it wasn't for
these loud bursts of displeasure, the cryptically coloured
birds might never be seen, so well do they blend with
their scrubby, open surroundings. Even the killdeer's most
prominent feature, its two black breast bands, help render
it invisible by breaking up the bird's outline.

Distraction is the killdeer's key to survival. Their
sound and fury appears to be aimed at ensuring that other
animals, including humans, don't stumble across their
imperceptible ground nests or young ones. Always nesting
in a wide, open space, such as pastureland or lawns, the
killdeer's view is unobstructed for long distances. Once an
intruder is detected, the bird steals away from the nest
before calling out and drawing attention from the eggs or
chicks. If a predator continues towards the nest, a killdeer

will fly over to the threatening animal and perform its famous broken-wing display. The bird flops on the ground, spreads its tail and drags a quivering, seemingly broken wing, twittering in pain. At the same time it flashes its attention-grabbing, rust-coloured rump. Hobbling along, the crafty killdeer keeps just out of reach until it has lured the assailant a safe distance away. Then it explodes into the air and escapes on swift, bent wings designed for speed. The strategy usually works, though killdeers have been known to overestimate their cleverness. A killdeer pair once nested in the gravel parking lot of a provincial park. Fortunately, an inevitably tragic car-versus-killdeer confrontation was avoided when park wardens roped off the lot around the nest.

More often than not, it's the father who performs the broken-wing act; males are the more dedicated parent in any killdeer couple. As soon as melting snow exposes some ground, males return from the south to stake out their breeding territories, calling persistently from the ground and while circling above. They often reoccupy their previous year's territory. Intruding rivals are berated and repulsed, while visiting females are treated to a zesty nest-scraping demonstration with musical trilling accompaniment. Eventually, a hen chooses one of the ground depressions prepared for her and starts dropping her eggs. The couple takes turns incubating the eggs during the day, but it's the father who usually sits on them through the night. Despite his newfound domesticity, a male killdeer still keeps an eye out for any ladies that happen by. The resident matron tries to intervene before he commits any hanky-panky.

Like many birds that hatch downy and ready to roll, unborn killdeers can peep and listen to the calls of their parents through their shells a couple of days before hatching, becoming well accustomed to the voices of Mom and Dad. The white-bellied, brown-backed chicks leave their exposed nest and trot after their parents as soon as their down is dried, a few hours after hatching. Before long, they're probing the ground for insects. They freeze

le pluvier kildir, Charadrius vociferus

Call: Variations of a loud, high, piercing, repeated "kill-deee, kill-deee" or "dee-kidee," rising up then down; also a rising "dee-ee" and low trills

Food: Grasshoppers, beetles, dragonflies, ants, caddisflies, caterpillars and other insects; spiders, worms, snails and a few seeds

Preferred habitat: Meadows, fields, shorelines, mud flats and forest clearings

Territory: 300–400 m² (375–500 sq yd)

Nest: A shallow, scraped-out ground depression, sometimes lined with smooth stones or a little grass; in fields, gravelly river flats, sometimes even gravel parking lots, pathways and flat roofs

Average clutch: 4 walnut-sized, light-grey or buff, darkly blotched and squiggled eggs

Incubation period: 24–28 days

Fledging age: About 25 days

Maximum lifespan: 11 years

Predators: Foxes, raccoons, hawks, crows

Clutches destroyed by predators and disturbances: 50–80%

Average population density: 1–10 pairs per km² (0.4 sq mi)

Range: Throughout most of Ontario; also in all other provinces and territories

Average first arrival in central Ontario: Late Mar.

Average last departure from central Ontario: Early Sept.

Winter whereabouts: Central and southern United States

Number of plover species nesting in Ontario: 3
Number of plover species worldwide: 63
Also see: *Up North:* Spotted Sandpiper

instantly if their father or mother launches into their distraction strategies. If all else fails, the chicks scatter on their parents' command, sometimes even plunking into the water and swimming submerged to evade a cruising raptor.

The bird flops on the ground, spreads its tail and drags a quivering, seemingly broken wing

Some mothers will lay a second batch of eggs, usually in June, once their first brood has fledged. In fact, if anything happens to their eggs or chicks, female killdeers can lay up to eight replacement clutches. Moms don't always stick around, though, to raise the young fully, leaving the task instead to diligent father birds.

Aside from the killdeer's most common shorebird relative in central Ontario, the spotted sandpiper, its Pinocchio-beaked **woodcock** and **snipe** cousins are seldom seen. Snipes nest and forage low in wetland and mucky shoreline tangles of alder, willow and sweet gale, while woodcocks live amid moist stands of aspen, birch and alder with dense understoreys of dogwood, willow and meadowsweet. Only in early spring, when males solicit female company, is either species generally noticed. Snipes "winnow" loudly during courtship flights over their territory, especially at evening. Chunky male woodcocks perform even-more-spectacular displays, spending about half an hour at dusk and dawn in small clearings, making "beezp" calls and suddenly spiralling straight up in tight circles up to 100 metres (330 feet) in the air, with an audible whirr from their flight feathers. At the height of their ascent, the birds twitter wildly then plummet to the ground to start the "beezp" calls anew. It's one way to get a girl's attention.

EASTERN KINGBIRD
Fearless Lord of Its Realm

T HE KINGBIRD RECEIVED its name, as well as its scientific designation, *tyrannus*, for its imperious insistence on being the absolute ruler of its realm. Even some native groups reportedly called the bird "little chief." The bellicose scrapper is legendary for taking on much larger hawks, crows, jays and foxes at the drop of a hat. Screaming in rage, a kingbird dives and strikes at its opponent, sometimes landing on a larger bird's back and pecking mercilessly, like a crazed Captain Ahab astride Moby Dick. Any known egg robber within sight of their nest can become the target of mobbing by both kingbird parents, their tiny red crowns flared in anger. The indomitable furies have even been documented intercepting low-flying airplanes.

Given their fearless nature, kingbirds are the most conspicuous of flycatchers, hunting from perches over open areas, commonly taking to telephone wires in settled areas. From these stations they periodically dart out to pick off flying insects such as dragonflies and bumblebees, whose stingers they carefully discard. Like other flycatchers, ligaments between their jaws cause the beak to snap on their prey like a sprung trap. In quiet settings, the snap is distinctly audible.

Kingbirds usually return to the previous year's nest site in May. A male is devoted to his partner, escorting her everywhere as she spends about a week gathering materials and building their nest. As she works, he often circles overhead and calls excitedly, in the kingbird's always-agitated-sounding, high-pitch language. Rather than make an effort to conceal their nest, they often place it in the open, on a lone tree with a good view, defying any beast to come near. Though cowbirds sometimes manage

Length: 20–21.5 cm (8–9 in)
Wingspan: 36–38 cm
   (14–15 in)
Weight: Average 43 g (1.5 oz)
Flying speed: 21–37 km/h
   (13–22 mph)
Markings: Dark-grey back, wings and head, white undersides; thin white band across end of tail and a usually hidden small orange-red head crest
Alias: Bee martin, bee bird, field martin, tyrant flycatcher, *le tyran tritri, Tyrannus tyrannus*
Call: Very high, thin, rapid series of harsh, squeaky, "stuttered" pips
Preferred habitat: Forest edge at beaver ponds, lakes and rivers, open bogs, clearings and other open areas
Food: Dragonflies, bumblebees and many other large flying

insects; some seeds and
berries

Nest: Bowl of twigs and stems
lined with grass, rootlets, hair
and feathers; about 14 cm
(5.5 in) wide, usually 2–6 m
(7–20 ft) above ground in a
tree, bush or stump, often in
a branch hanging over water

Average clutch: 3–4 olive-sized,
creamy-white or pinkish eggs,
mottled with brown

Incubation period: 12–18 days

Fledging age: about 12–18 days

Maximum lifespan: At least
6 years

Range: Southern Ontario to
southern James Bay, and
occasionally farther north;
also in all other provinces
except Newfoundland

Average first arrival in central
Ontario: Early May

Average last departure from
central Ontario: Early Sept.

Winter whereabouts: East side
of the Andes in Colombia
and Peru

Also see: Olive-sided Flycatcher,
Chestnut-sided Warbler. *Up
North:* Dragonflies

to sneak in to lay an egg in their clutch, kingbirds usually recognize and disdainfully eject the foreign object.

Ligaments between their jaws cause the beak to snap on their prey like a sprung trap. In quiet settings, the snap is distinctly audible

Kingbird parents are also fiercely dedicated, staying with their young for up to five weeks after they fledge. Oddly enough, after they leave in August or early September and fly back to South America, they seem to change personality, becoming sociable, fruit-eating vegetarians hanging out in large, foraging flocks.

COMMON NIGHTHAWK
High-flying Boom Bird

W AY, WAY UP, against the sparkling stars of a clear summer night, fleet-winged nighthawks feast in the surprisingly bountiful firmament. Hundreds of metres above the earth, they swirl and dip, huge mouths agape, through a virtual soup of flying insects, wind-borne mites and springtails and newly hatched spiders and caterpillars "ballooning" on strands of silk. The presence of countless billions of minute, high-altitude travellers – dubbed "aerial plankton" – was unknown until discovered by airplanes, some as much as 4.5 kilometres (2.7 miles) high.

Ontario's aerial plankton is at its richest mainly from June to August, just long enough for robin-sized nighthawks to reproduce and then return to South America. The alien sound of a soft, low "boom" or "woof" overhead on early-June evenings signals their arrival. The "sonic booms" are caused by air popping through a male's wing feathers as it suddenly pulls out of a deep dive and soars up again during territorial displays. (The boom may be heard at other times during the summer, but is less frequent after mating.) When courting, males land after the daredevil swoops to perform a love-shuffle before

Length: 22–25 cm (8.5–10 in)
Wingspan: 53–61 cm (21–24 in)
Average weight: 70–80 g (2.5–2.8 oz)
Markings: Mottled grey, brown, black and white, with wide white bars under wings; males also have a white chin and bar across underside of tail
Bug nets: A circle of whiskerlike bristles around mouth assists in scooping up flying insects
Alias: Common Nighthawk, bull-bat, pisk, mosquito hawk, moth hunter, burnt-land bird, will-o'-the-wisp, pork-and-beans, l'engoulevent d'Amérique, *Chordeiles minor*
Call: Short, loud, nasal, buzzy sound, usually written as "peent"
Preferred habitat: Rocky shorelines and clearings, logged areas, open woods

Food: Mosquitoes, beetles, flying ants, grasshoppers, moths and other flying insects

Nest: Eggs laid on bare ground, also often on flat-roofed buildings

Average clutch: 2 darkly mottled whitish or olive eggs, about the size of peach pits

Incubation period: 18–20 days

Fledging age: 21 days

Flying speed: 19–56 km/h (12–35 mph)

Average population density: 1–10 pairs per 10 km² (4 sq mi)

Range: Throughout Ontario; also in all other provinces and territories except the island of Newfoundland

Average first arrival in central Ontario: Late May

Average last departure from central Ontario: Early Sept.

Winter whereabouts: South America to northern Argentina

Long-distance migration champs: Arctic terns fly from Arctic nesting grounds across the Atlantic and down coasts of Europe and Africa to islands in the South Atlantic

Also see: Whip-poor-will, Midges.

Up North: Spiders

prospective mates, fanning their tails, puffing up their white throats and swaying like Vegas crooners as they call.

Females incubate their eggs on open ground, even on flat rooftops in urban areas, in the territory marked by their partners' booming flights. There's no nest, and the eggs are often moved around, sometimes into shade or out of pooling water. The birds and their grey-and-brown mottled eggs blend in so well with the surrounding rock and earth that they are virtually impossible to see. Roosting nighthawks also rest lengthwise along logs and branches, because they blend in better with the bark, and because wobbly feet don't allow them to perch easily like other birds.

Downy nighthawk chicks hatch in early summer. They're fed regurgitated bugs by both parents until they're about three weeks old and ready to fly. Within another few days, they, like the adults, take to the air a little before sunset to bag bugs by the hundreds and even thousands before turning in again shortly after sunrise. Insects lured to bright lights such as streetlamps or ballpark floodlamps often attract nighthawks. Occasionally, nighthawks may also be seen at dusk, borne aloft on long, pointy, sharply circumflexed wings. The bold white bar bisecting the underside of each wing clearly identifies the bird. High-flying nighthawk throngs also feast in broad daylight during migration in late summer.

The sky-dining day shift is mainly taken up by the tiny dark **chimney swift**, a swallowlike bird that spends virtually all its waking hours in the air. With extremely long, narrow wings and no tail to speak of, indefatigable swifts are often described as "flying cigars." They chitter incessantly as they flap and glide on bowed wings, often streaking above in small acrobatic squadrons that veer and dip in perfect precision. Named for their penchant for nesting and roosting in chimneys around human dwellings, swifts take to hollow trees in the wild. Like nighthawks, swifts raise their broods on Ontario's bounty of summer bugs, and then, as the skies clear, shoot back in the direction of Peru for the rest of the year.

OLIVE-SIDED FLYCATCHER
Whistling Avian Retriever

QUINTESSENTIALLY Canadian call, "Quick, three beers!" rings out through the north woods. The clear, whistled refrain ordering an urgent round comes from the treetop perch of the olive-sided flycatcher. Like a regular at the local tavern, the bird plants itself at its favourite spot day-in and day-out, usually on a prominent dead branch or spire. Upon spotting a juicy, airborne bug up to 70 metres (230 feet) away, the flycatcher makes straight towards it, picks it off and flies back to its perch to enjoy the meal. If swallows are the hounds of the bird world, tirelessly chasing down insects in the air, flycatchers are the avian retrievers, patiently waiting, erect and alert, then springing into action and promptly returning to their posts.

Flycatchers are really a very large family of tropical birds. Only a relatively small number are bold adventurers, venturing far from their southern homes to find less-crowded conditions in which to raise a family. Most only stay long enough to accomplish the task. Olive-sided flycatchers usually arrive from the Andes in mid- to late May and head south again shortly after their young fledge, in late July or early August. During that time, the stocky

Length: 18–20 cm (7–8 in)
Wingspan: 31–34 cm (12–13.5 in)
Weight: Average 31 g (1.1 oz)
Markings: Dark olive-grey head, back, sides and "vest," with white undersides of belly extending in a narrow band to the throat; white tuft near base of tail
Alias: *La moucherolle à côtes olive, Contopus borealis*
Call: 3 clear, whistled notes, the first abrupt and emphasized, the second and third long and rising, in the rhythm of "whip-whee-wheer!" or "quick, three beers!"; also repeated "pit" notes
Preferred habitat: Evergreen and mixed forests with abundant dead trees and near bogs, beaver ponds, rivers, quiet bays, fens and burned-over areas

Food: Bees, dragonflies and other flying insects, beetles, carpenter ants

Nest: Shallow tray of twigs, grass, rootlets, moss and lichens, usually anchored with cobwebs near tip of thin branch 4–15 m (13–50 ft) up in a coniferous tree

Average clutch: 3 almond-sized, white, buff or pink eggs lightly sprinkled with brown and grey spots

Incubation period: 14 days

Fledging age: 21–23 days

Maximum population density: 1 pair per km² (0.4 sq mi)

Range: Mainly from the southern edge of the Canadian Shield and upper Bruce Peninsula to the Hudson Bay lowlands; also in all other provinces and territories

Average first arrival in central Ontario: Late May

Average last departure from central Ontario: Late Aug.

Winter whereabouts: The Andes, from Colombia to southern Peru

Number of tyrant flycatcher species regularly nesting in Ontario: 10

Number of tyrant flycatcher species worldwide: About 370, mostly in South and Central America

Also see: Kingbird, Barn Swallow. *Up North:* Black Spruce

scrappers fiercely defend their nests, even against humans who get too close.

Half a dozen other flycatcher species are common in central Ontario, but like the olive-sided, they are drably attired and more often heard than seen. The song of the **eastern wood-pewee**, a long, whistled "pee-a-wee," rising at the end, is probably the most familiar, especially in hilly mixed and deciduous forests. The **phoebe** also sings its own name, a whistled phrase similar to the chickadee's song, but raspy and uttered more quickly and with a rising inflection. Phoebes once nested mainly on cliffs, but today usually take up quarters under eaves and bridges.

The stocky scrappers fiercely defend their nests, even against humans

The other flycatchers are less-accomplished singers. **Great crested flycatchers**, with their bright-yellow underside, call from the hardwood forest canopy with a loud-but-simple rising "wheeep!" whistle. The three smallest species are all similar-looking in very plain coats of olive-grey. **Least flycatchers** keep to the mid-levels of deciduous forests, between the top of the understorey and the branches of young trees above. It's a fairly open tier of the forest, heavily used by flying insects. **Alder flycatchers** frequent streamside thickets, and **yellow-bellied flycatchers** mainly haunt black spruce bogs and hillsides.

BALTIMORE ORIOLE
Master Nest Builder

Length: 18–21 cm (7–8.5 in)
Wingspan: 28–30 cm
(11–12 in)
Markings: Males have deep-
orange undersides, shoulders
and lower back, and a black
head, throat, upper back and
wings, with diffuse white wing
bar and orange-bordered
black tail; females and juveniles are olive brown above,
yellow with orange tinge
below and have 2 thin white
wing bars
Alias: Northern oriole, hang
nest, hammock bird,
Baltimore bird, fire-hang-
bird, golden oriole, pea-bird,
*l'oriole du nord, Icterus
galbula*
Call: Song a jumble of deeply
whistled notes, sounding a bit
like the squiggle of a thick
Magic Marker on cardboard;
also a loud, harsh "check,
check" call note
Preferred habitat: Deciduous
forest edge, especially riversides; also open woodlands
and fields with scattered trees
Food: Caterpillars, beetles,
grasshoppers, ants, aphids,
spiders, snails, seeds,
berries, buds
Nest: Baglike structure,
10–15 cm (4–6 in) deep,
of finely woven strips of
bark, plant fibres, grass and
hair, hanging from upper,
outer branches of hardwood
trees; string and wool commonly used around human
habitation

WHEN THEY FIRST catch the attention of lucky observers, Baltimore orioles seem to explode into view like miniature fireballs of intense orange flame and jet-black smoke. Males use the stunning contrast to maximum effect when courting the opposite sex. Urgently bowing up and down before prospective mates, they flash their deep-orange breasts, black heads and orange rumps in a testosterone-powered strobelike sequence. Fiercely territorial, like most brightly coloured birds, the sartorially splendiferous males also announce themselves with a flourish of song at forest-edge and riverside treetops in May. "A golden chord and flute, where the throat of the oriole swells," as Canadian poet Archibald Lampman put it a century ago.

While the males strut, the drab females reveal their own brilliance in a more refined manner. Clad in sensible olive green, female orioles are masters of avian engineering. Their nest-building skills combine advanced architecture with delicate needlecraft. They begin by weaving long strands of stringy stems or other plant fibres around and between twigs at the tips of thin, flexible, outer branches in the crown of a tall hardwood tree. Gradually,

Average clutch: 4–6 olive-sized, greyish or blue-white eggs mottled dark brown and black

Incubation period: 12–14 days

Fledging age: 12–14 days

Maximum age: At least 7 years in wild, 14 years in captivity

Predators: Crows and squirrels sometimes raid nests

Maximum flying speed: 42 km/h (26 mph)

Range: Southern Ontario to about Temagami and Wawa; also in all other provinces except Prince Edward Island and Newfoundland

Average first arrival in central Ontario: Mid-May

Average last departure from central Ontario: Early Sept.

Winter whereabouts: Southern Mexico to Colombia and Venezuela

Number of oriole species nesting in Ontario: 2

Number of oriole species worldwide: 30

Namesake: Named in honour of George Calvert, 1st Baron Baltimore (died 1632), whose armorial shield was orange and black. King James I first granted the English nobleman the Avalon peninsula in Newfoundland, but his efforts to colonize the area failed. The king then gave him land that eventually became Maryland

Also see: *Up North:* Red-winged Blackbird, Blue Jay, Red Squirrel

they add slender shreds of bark, long, dry grass, hair and even wool and string where humans are handy, needling each piece into the mass and then pulling it through from the other side. After four to 14 days, they've created a strong purselike structure suspended from the branch tips, which may hang snug for several years. The bouncy sack easily holds an incubating mother and all of her eggs, and its location on thin, pliable branches keeps it out of the reach of heavier predators such as raccoons. Both parents assail any lighter nest robbers, such as red squirrels or jays, that venture too close.

The intricate nests are often visible after the tree's shielding foliage has dropped. The Ojibway said that orioles learned the secret of nest-building from the sun, which also granted the males glowing coats like its own in return for their sunrise serenades.

Drunk with song when courting, males know enough to clam up considerably to keep nest locations secret once they find mates. Unpaired males, though, may continue their serenades through June and July; many are year-olds that must wait another season before acquiring the black-and-orange uniform of experienced males. A lucky few of the olive-and-yellow bucks, however, may succeed in mating. Later in the summer, after nestlings fledge and parents lie low to moult, even older males assume the mottled-olive colours of camouflage. Adult males are on their own by that point, while females and juveniles flock together by the dozen. August evenings gradually carry most away to the tropics where, after having gorged on Ontario's caterpillars and bugs, they turn to the sweet nectar of flowers for part of their winter sustenance.

Long known as the northern oriole, the orange bird was recently given back its original name, Baltimore oriole, after leading ornithologists finally agreed that it is a species distinct from the western Bullock's oriole, with which it was previously grouped.

PILEATED WOODPECKER
Monarch of the Tree Whackers

Meaning of pileated: "Crested" or "capped"
Length: 41–50 cm (16–20 in)
Wingspan: 69–76 cm (27–30 in)
Weight: 240–340 g (8.5–12 oz)
Markings: Mostly black, with a large, red triangular head crest, long beak, wide black-and-white stripes on face and neck, white underwings bordered with black flight feathers; males sport a red "forehead" and moustache; on females these are black
Alias: Log-cock, cock-of-the-woods, black woodpecker, carpenter bird, black log, king-of-the-woods, stump breaker, laughing woodpecker, johnny-cock, Indian hen, wood kate, cluck-cock, *le grand pic*, *Dryocopus pileatus*
Call: Loud, startling, repeated cackle, rising, then falling in pitch, variously rendered as "kyuk-kyuk-kyuk" or "wicka-wicka" or "wok-wok-wok," often lasting for many seconds; also several other "waaa" and "wuk" calls
Territorial drumming: Short bursts, often repeated every 40–60 seconds for an hour or more by males; females also drum occasionally
Drum beats per second: 14–17
Firing of a machine gun per second: Up to 17
Preferred habitat: Stands of mixed or deciduous forests, covering at least

T HE CROW-SIZED PILEATED woodpecker bares a dagger bill longer than an eagle's beak and a bold red crest sticking straight up in the air. Surely the model for Woody the Woodpecker, the big bird seems to have stepped right out of a cartoon. It's the monarch of its kind, and is indeed sometimes attended by downy and hairy woodpeckers picking insect leftovers from the havoc wreaked by the pileated's giant beak. Pileated woodpeckers actually listen for the hustle and bustle of a carpenter ant colony deep inside a tree, then tear through the hard outer layers of wood to reach the rotting, ant-infested heart. Once found, the colony is ravaged by the woodpecker's barbed, sticky and ultimately deadly tongue, which extends many centimetres beyond the bill.

Unfortunately, the square-shouldered, thin-necked regal woodpecker is rather retiring and seldom grants an audience. But it often leaves signs of its whereabouts. Piles of crayon-sized splinters and wood chips as big as a hand accumulate below pileated snack trees. The holes themselves may be 30 centimetres (one foot) long and 10 centimetres (four inches) wide. A row of holes is sometimes joined together, forming a gash more than a metre

40 ha (100 acres), with large,
dead standing trees and water
close by
Food: Carpenter ants, ground
ants, beetles, cluster flies,
moths, mosquitoes, caterpillars and other larvae; berries,
nuts, acorns and cherries
about 25% of diet
Territory: 40–80 ha
(100–200 acres)
Nest: In tree cavity 25–76 cm
(10–30 in) deep, about
18–20 cm (7–8 in) cm wide,
with vertical oval opening
9–12.5 cm (3.5–5 in) wide;
usually 3.5–27.5 m
(12–90 ft) up on south or
east side of dead deciduous
tree trunk, sometimes in a
large branch or in living trees
Average clutch: 4 chestnut-sized,
white eggs
Incubation period: 15–18 days
Fledging age: 26–28 days
Maximum lifespan: 13 years
Predators: Sharp-shinned hawks,
Cooper's hawks, goshawks
Species that use old pileated
woodpecker holes: Flying
squirrels, red squirrels,
martens, fishers, owls, wood
ducks, hooded merganser,
common mergansers, blue-
birds, kestrels, starlings, mice
Range: All of Ontario to southern James Bay; also in all
other provinces except
Newfoundland
Also see: Downy Woodpecker,
Wood Duck

(three feet) long. The birds also rip away and discard large sheets of bark from dead trees while searching for beetles and grubs, and tear apart rotten stumps and logs on the ground.

Loud, hollow-sounding, resonant "drum" rolls, heard as much as a kilometre (half a mile) away, also announce the pileated woodpecker's presence. Although they may perform year round, to mark their territories and keep in touch, they're especially active before breeding. In late winter and early spring, single males drum as often as twice a minute and fly above the trees, flashing their white underwings and calling loudly for female company. Like the rest of the spring bird-song orchestra, this percussion section performs most often in early morning and late in the day.

Once paired off, most pileateds stay close together for life, staying year round on the same territory. Though quite often they use the same dead tree in which they nested the previous year, they usually excavate a new cavity, wary of parasites left over in the old hole. Both mates spend up to a month chiselling out their nesting chamber, starting in late March or April. Pileated woodpeckers are one of the few bird species known to actually pick up and carry their eggs to an alternate nest site if their chosen tree ever becomes unstable or falls.

In May and June, the birds take turns through the day incubating the eggs and brooding the noisy hatchlings, with males taking sole nest-sitting duties at night. Mothers sleep in roosting cavities nearby. Young woodpeckers begin sticking their heads out of the nest hole when about two weeks old, and continue to be fed by regurgitation for a while after fledging, usually around late June. They then start following their parents, and after watching Mom or Dad rip open a tree full of ants, they take over. Families stay together till September, when the young disperse, flying up to 30 kilometres (19 miles) before stopping and digging out winter roosting holes for themselves.

PURPLE FINCH
Wide-ranging Winter Wanderer

KNOWN AS WINTER wanderers, often showing up at birdfeeders, purple finches also turn out in force to nest in a particular area for several springs running. Drawn in small flocks to a spot where conifer seeds are abundant during the winter, young purple finches usually settle there for their first breeding season. Since these bumper crops occur at best every second year, leaner winters take the birds farther afield, even as far as the Gulf of Mexico. But always they nostalgically return in April to that magic spot where they mated for the first time. With their offspring growing up to breed in other areas, however, the local nesting population gradually dwindles as the first generation dies off. Eventually, travelling winter finches may come across another local cone-seed bonanza and the cycle will begin anew.

A newly arrived generation of young purple finches may not be recognized by human observers familiar only with the male's "sparrow-dipped-in-raspberry-juice" look. Males don't take on the red plumage before their second breeding season, till then resembling plain, striped sparrows, as do the females.

Length: 14–16 cm (5.5–6.3 in)
Wingspan: 23–27 cm (9–10.5 in)
Markings: Males are mostly dull wine-red, brighter on head and rump, with brown-streaked wings and tail and a white belly; females are brown on top, with brown-streaked white undersides and long beige stripe above and behind eye; both have a notched tail
Alias: Eastern purple finch, purple grosbeak, red linnet, purple linnet, grey linnet, *le roselin pourpre*, *Carpodacus purpureus*
Genus name meaning: *Carpodacus* is Latin for "fruit-biting"
Call: Song a fast, budgie-like jumble of high notes, lasting many seconds; also a dull metallic "tick" call

Preferred habitat: Coniferous and mixed forests

Food: Conifer, ash, red maple, grass and weed seeds; maple, birch and aspen buds; raspberries, mountain ash, honeysuckle and other berries; caterpillars and beetles when nesting

Nest: Shallow cup of small twigs, grass and rootlets lined with moss and hair; usually in dense foliage near top of tall, mature fir, spruce, pine or cedar

Average clutch: 4–6 almond-sized, darkly spotted light-blue-green eggs

Fledging age: 14 days

Portion of population living more than 6 years: 1.5%

Maximum lifespan: 12 years

Range: North central shore of Lake Erie to southern James Bay; also in all other provinces and territories

Winter whereabouts: From about Sault Ste. Marie and Pembroke to eastern Texas and northern Florida

Also see: Evening Grosbeak, Goldfinch, Mountain Ash.
Up North: Red Pine

Whatever their colour, males initiate the breeding season by singing frequently from treetop posts around mid-May. When wooing a particular female, they puff out their breasts and drag their wings while hopping about. They then rise in the air 18 to 36 centimetres (seven to 14 inches) on rapidly vibrating wings, tail cocked high and softly singing, sometimes with nesting material clasped in their beaks. If chosen, a male must make good on his promise and help build a nest and feed his spouse while she's incubating the eggs. The seed eaters turn to insects to help feed their nestlings, who remain dependent on their parents for about three weeks after they fledge.

In recent years, the purple finch's California cousin, the **house finch**, has begun moving into central Ontario, though still in small numbers. Slightly smaller, and with red feathers restricted to its head, breast and rump, house finches have spread phenomenally in the east since 1940, when, so the story goes, New York's Macy's department store released its caged "Hollywood finches" on Long Island after learning it was illegal to sell the birds.

If chosen, a male must help build a nest and feed his spouse while she's incubating the eggs

The **warbling vireo**'s song is slightly less upbeat than that of the house finch, and on the Canadian Shield is the one most often confused with the music of the purple finch. One of the plainest of birds, solid grey-green above, with a white breast and eye stripe, the warbling vireo lives in the high branches of open maple or aspen forests. So fervent a singer is the male of the species, he often croons while taking his turn at the nest, an extremely rare habit among songbirds.

RAVEN
Commanding Ancient Respect

Length: 55–68 cm (22–27 in)
Wingspan: 1.2–1.3 m
   (4–4.3 ft)
Weight: 1–1.5 kg (2.2–3.3 lb)
Beak length: Average 8 cm
   (3 in)
Markings: Adults are glossy
   black all over; juveniles are
   duller, with some brown in
   wings and tail
Colour origin: In Greek mythology, Apollo turned his snow-
   white raven messenger black
   in a fit of rage when it told
   him his girlfriend was unfaith-
   ful. British Columbia native
   peoples said higher spirits
   changed Raven black because
   of his mischief. The Siberian
   Voguls said the raven was
   turned from white to black as
   punishment for eating corpses
Alias: Northern raven, common
   raven, corby, *le grand
   corbeau, Corvus corax*
Name for a group: An unkind-
   ness of ravens
Call: Wide repertoire, including
   loud, resonant, croaking
   "oook, oook, oook," deeper
   and less raspy than the "caw"
   of a crow; also a deep, bell-
   like "crong," a metallic "tok,"
   and a buzzing burble like an
   electrical current; males have
   deeper voices
Mimicry: Able to imitate many
   sounds, including human
   words
Preferred habitat: Coniferous
   and mixed forests
Food: Carrion, birds' eggs and

F ROM THE TIME spear-bearing humans fanned out from Africa some 100,000 years ago, they have undoubtedly been intimates with the raven. The bold black bird commonly forms close associations with northern big-game hunters, scavenging at wolf kills and following polar bears out onto Arctic pack ice to clean up seal carcasses. It has a wide vocabulary, and often works in pairs, flushing out and ambushing prey. The raven's size, smarts, grace and longevity, as well as its close association with death, must have made a profound impression on people's minds and imaginations. European cave paint-ings apparently investing birds with mystical significance date back as far as 32,000 years, and many authorities believe the magical avian beings are likely ravens.

Northern cultures around the world had taboos against killing ravens, which figure prominently in their cos-mologies. They play a role in most of the nearly universal flood stories. Among Ontario natives, the bird is some-times named as the first of several animals that after the deluge tried to gather mud to form a new world. In the Bible, the raven is also the first sent by Noah to seek dry

nestlings, crayfish, insects, mice, voles and other small rodents, berries, seeds; wolf droppings when all else fails

Nest: 50–150 cm (1.7–5 ft) wide, thick, bulky collection of sticks, twigs, clumps of grass and soil, with 15–30-cm-wide (6–12-in-wide) central depression lined with moss, lichens, bark shreds and fur; usually on conifer treetop or cliff ledge, also in hydro and water towers

Telltale nesting signs: Piles of fallen sticks and streaks of white droppings on or below cliff or tree

Average clutch: 3–5 plumb-sized, greenish eggs with dense brown and olive spotting or blotches

Incubation period: 18–21 days

Fledging age: 35–44 days

Age at sexual maturity: 3–4 years

Predators: Raccoons and bears occasionally raid nests; great horned owls may possibly take roosting adults

Maximum lifespan: 29 years in captivity

Raven play: Sometimes seen frolicking together in the sky, apparently playing tag and dropping sticks and other objects for each other to catch

Honours: Official bird of the Yukon; battle standard of Danish Vikings and William the Conqueror; most frequently depicted figure on West Coast totem poles

Odin's ravens: Hugin and Mumin ("Thought" and "Memory") flew over the world every day

land. For the native peoples of British Columbia and Alaska, the raven is not only the chief player in the flood tale, but the bringer of the sun, moon, stars and fresh water, as well as the creator of people. The Inuit said the raven, by flicking sparkling flakes of mica into the sky, created the Milky Way.

Early North Americans, Siberians, Chinese, Greeks and Scandinavians thought ravens controlled or at least influenced the weather. Norse and Celtic gods and semi-divine warriors often took the form of ravens or employed them as their messengers. Early Irish and Anglo-Saxon literature is also rife with references to ravens following armies to feast on the spoils of the battlefield. The Vikings embraced the gruesome association, hoisting the image of the black scavenger on their standards.

Christian lands pillaged by the hardy northmen came to associate the raven with pagan religions, death and ill omen. The raven was said to "shake contagion from her sable wing," and was blamed even for the pestilence that spread in the aftermath of war. Ravens seen scavenging from dead livestock and wild game were held responsible for their deaths. European settlers brought their persecution of the great bird to North America with guns, traps and poison. Ravens retreated with the wolf from settled areas, falling back into the fastness of the Canadian Shield.

In recent decades, ravens have made a comeback, becoming common again as far south as the edge of the Shield and returning to the Bruce Peninsula. In 1993, one wayward male even nested with a crow in Toronto, the first-ever confirmed case of the two species cross-breeding. Though almost identical, crows are only about two-thirds the size of ravens, have a sleeker bill and lack the shaggy throat feathers of the larger bird. The best way to tell the two apart is to look for the raven's rounded, paddle-shaped tail in flight; the back of a crow's tail is straight-cut. Ravens also tend to soar and flap their wings less than their smaller, adaptable cousins, and have a much deeper, hoarser voice.

Ravens also don't migrate like crows; mates remain together on the same territory for life. They spruce up their relationships early each year, performing breathtaking courtship flights in the bitterly cold, clear skies of February. Soaring males call frequently and make sudden steep dives, often somersaulting at the end before pulling out of the fall. Couples also fly synchronized manoeuvres, their wing tips virtually touching as they circle over their nest sites. Males usually fly slightly above their partners in the sky dance. Upon landing, they often nuzzle beaks together, and may preen and caress each other's breast and head feathers.

An ideal cliffside or treetop nesting spot may be used off and on by successive generations, some for up to 100 years. Old raven nests are also often used by hawks and owls. A couple usually spends two or three weeks building a new nest or renovating an old one, breaking off large, dead sticks from trees and piling them up. Both mates quieten down once egg-laying begins, in mid-March to April, the female tending the nest while hubby brings home the bacon.

Things become noisy again when the nestlings hatch and start begging for food, though they fall silent at their parents' command when an outsider approaches the area. As they grow, the young cry out in a muffled crow-voiced "caw." For about the first 18 days, fathers continue to be the main providers, while females brood their families. The males sometimes carry water in their throats for the nestlings to drink. After spending several days learning to fly, the young follow their parents over wide spaces for three or four months in search of food. Then they drift off on their own, sometimes forming small winter flocks with other adolescents, though ravens are generally not nearly as gregarious as crows. A young bird may meet its future life mate in these groups, but may also strike up a relationship with a widowed raven eager for a new partner.

and related all they saw and heard to the ruler of the Norse gods, giving him universal knowledge

"Raven's knowledge": Irish term meaning to see and know everything

Ravenstone: An old English name for the site of executions

Tower of London ravens: After the Great Fire of London, in 1666, ravens were persecuted for scavenging, but King Charles II was warned to keep them at the Tower of London or disaster would strike the monarchy. Six ravens have been kept at the Tower castle ever since

Notable deeds: Ravens fed Elijah in the Jordanian desert, and a raven released from a wayward Viking ship flew west without returning, leading the way to the settlement of Iceland

Name origin: From the ancient German *khraben*, an imitation of the raven's harsh croak

Average population density: 2–10 pairs per 10 km^2 (4 sq mi)

Range: Southern edge of Canadian Shield, Bruce Peninsula and Manitoulin Island to Hudson Bay; also in all other provinces and territories north to Ellesmere Island

Also see: *Up North:* Crow, Snowshoe Hare, Wolf

RED-BREASTED NUTHATCH
Spike-nosed Conifer Hopper

Length: 11–12 cm (4.5–4.7 in)
Wingspan: 20–22 cm (8–8.7 in)
Weight: 8–13 g (0.3–0.4 oz)
Markings: Blue-grey back and
 wings; rusty-red undersides;
 black eye stripe and crown;
 white cheeks, neck and
 stripe above eyes
Alias: Canada nuthatch, red-
 bellied nuthatch, topsy-turvy
 bird, devil-down-head,
 la sittelle à poitrine rousse,
 Sitta canadensis
Call: Oft-repeated, high nasal
 beeps, written "ank, ank
 ank"; song, less often heard,
 is a rapid staccato like a high-
 pitched puttering of the lips
Preferred habitat: Evergreen
 forests, especially with
 mature trees
Food: Conifer seeds, nuts,
 berries, beetles, grubs, caterpillars, moths, wasps, crane

NUTHATCHES ARE MUNCHKINLIKE birds with oversized beaks and feet, which they use to good effect. A strong grip with long, curving claws enables them to scamper along in any direction, up, down and around tree trunks and branches. By poking into bark fissures and crevices from an upside-down position, the stubby-tailed birds find bugs and grubs missed by brown creepers and downy woodpeckers working the same spots from the other direction. Often, they even follow foraging woodpeckers to snap up the rattled insects left in their wake.

Red-breasted nuthatches also spend a lot of time at flimsy branch tips, especially in winter, using their long, needlelike bills to pick seeds out of open evergreen cones. Whenever the sprites come upon other shelled morsels too hard to crack, they steady them in a bark crevice and then drive their spikes into the shells until they "hatch" the nuts or seeds.

The pointy beaks also come in handy for chiselling out nesting quarters in dead trees when an old woodpecker hole or natural cavity can't be found. Once a red-breasted nuthatch couple finishes the excavation, they collect wads of sap oozing from wounds in surrounding spruce, pine and fir trees and smear them thickly around the rim of the entrance. Some authorities speculate that the sticky goop may prevent or discourage predators, such as tree-climbing snakes, from entering the nests. Others believe it is aimed primarily at keeping out pests and parasites, such as ants, mites and ticks. In deciduous and mixed forests, **white-breasted nuthatches**, the red-breasts' cousins, decorate their portals with the squashed bodies of insects containing defence chemicals, which may work in the same way as sap from evergreens. It has also been found that many hawks and some songbirds continually supply their nests with cedar bark and green leaves that contain natural pesticides.

flies, spiders, insect and spider eggs
Nest: Twigs, bark strips and grass lining a conifer tree cavity, with sticky pitch around entrance; usually 2–12 m (6.6–40 ft) high
Average clutch: 5–6 raspberry-sized, reddish-brown-specked white eggs
Incubation period: 12 days
Fledging age: 14–21 days
Maximum lifespan: 7 years
Range: Central shore of Lake Erie to southern James Bay; also in all other provinces and extreme south of the territories
Number of nuthatch species nesting in Ontario: 2
Number of nuthatch species worldwide: 31
Also see: Brown Creeper, Downy Woodpecker. *Up North:* Red Pine, Trembling Aspen

---

They drive their spikes into the shells until they "hatch" the nuts or seeds

---

After the nesting season, red-breast mates often remain on the same territory, though roosting in separate tree holes. They stow away seeds and nuts beneath bits of bark to help get them through the winter. In years of poor conifer-cone crops, many pick up and leave for birdfeeders and natural food sources in southern Ontario and the United States. Some find southern living to their liking and end up nesting in their new domain rather than returning north in spring.

RUBY-CROWNED KINGLET
Energetic Big-voiced Mite

T INY, WINGED BUNDLES of energy, ruby- and golden-crowned kinglets are beaten out only by the ruby-throated hummingbird for the prize of Ontario's smallest feathered creature. They're almost as manoeuvrable as hummingbirds, too, hovering at evergreen branch tips and flitting constantly from one spot to another, catching a bug every five or six seconds. On occasion, ruby-crowned kinglets follow yellow-bellied sapsuckers to their treeside drill holes to wash the bugs down with oozing sap. In general, their activities in the dense upper storeys of spruce and other conifers make them hard to see, but male ruby-crowns make their presence known by frequently opening their pencil-tip beaks to blast out remarkably loud, spirited songs.

The little bird with the big voice was fancifully proclaimed a kinglet for the red crown at the top of his head. The crown is only visible, however, when the feathers are raised for regal occasions, such as courting a potential queen or confronting enemies of the realm. Males face-off over territory by dropping their heads to display their royal signatures while uttering threats and hopping menacingly. Actual combat is usually avoided. When flaring their crest before females, they call more gently, spreading their wings, lifting their tails and nervously flitting here and there.

One reason kinglets are such busy birds is the number of offspring they raise. Within a two-week period, females may lay up to 11 eggs. To hold and warm such a clutch, weighing far more than the mother herself, the miniature monarchs construct a 15-centimetre-wide (six-inch-wide) sphere of moss and lichens deep within a jumble of dense spruce or fir boughs. The nests are so well hidden that only a handful have ever been found in Ontario. A

Length: 9–11 cm (3.5–4.5 in)
Wingspan: 17–19 cm
  (6.7–7.5 in)
Weight: 5–6 g (0.2 oz)
Weight of a loonie: 7 g (0.25 oz)
Markings: Olive back; black
  wings with 2 white bars;
  grey undersides; short, dark
  tails; white eye rings; thin,
  pencil-point bills; males have
  red crown, usually hidden
  from view
Alias: Ruby crown, ruby-crowned
  wren, ruby-crowned warbler,
  le roitelet à couronne rubis,
  Regulus calendula
Call: Loud, rapid, high twittering,
  interspersed with repeated,
  distinctive up-and-down
  call notes
Preferred habitat: Spruce bogs
  and evergreen and mixed
  forests
Food: Aphids, wasps, ants and
  other insects; spiders; insect

small opening at the top leads to a warm chamber lined with a thick, cushiony-soft layer of feathers. After their cricket-sized young hatch, parents scurry to feed them more than 20 times an hour, 16 hours a day.

Ruby-crowned kinglets need such big families because winters take a sizeable toll on their numbers. Though they migrate south in autumn, many go no farther than the northern United States, and many, if not most, die every year. Milder winters, however, lead to sudden population increases. It's during spring and fall migrations to and from these wintering grounds that kinglets are most often seen, foraging by day in mixed flocks, characteristically flicking their wings constantly, often unheedful of human observers only a few metres away.

The nests are so well hidden that only a handful have ever been found in Ontario

Golden-crowned kinglets are also widespread across central and northern Ontario, but being high-rise inhabitants of tall, mature evergreens, and weaker singers to boot, they are much less noticed than ruby-crowns. Slightly smaller than rubies and similarly coloured, they have more visible black-trimmed crowns, which are yellow on females and yellow topped with orange on males. They also bear a black eye stripe instead of the ruby-crown's white eye ring.

Both kinglets are notable for being among only three species of North American birds that belong to the Old World warbler family. Unlike the colourful wood warbler family of the Americas, the unrelated warblers of Eurasia and Africa are mostly drably attired birds. Though kinglets have nested in North America since before Europeans arrived, they must have immigrated some time in the distant past.

and spider eggs; small amounts of sap, berries and seeds

Average territory: 1–2 ha (2.5–5 acres)

Nest: 6–10-cm-wide (2.4–4-in-wide) ball of moss, lichens, twigs, leaves and shreds of bark bound with spiderwebs; walls about 2 cm (0.8 in) thick, plushly lined with feathers, with small entrance at top; usually well concealed, 3–8 m (10–27 ft) up in an evergreen, squeezed between forked branches

Average clutch: 7–9 baked-bean-sized, white or cream-coloured eggs, sparsely specked with brown

Incubation period: About 2 weeks

Fledging age: About 12 days

Range: About the southern edge of the Canadian Shield, Bruce Peninsula and Manitoulin Island to Hudson Bay, with a sparse scattering south of the Shield; also in all other provinces and territories

Average first arrival in central Ontario: Mid-Apr.

Average last departure from central Ontario: Mid-Oct.

Winter whereabouts: Northwest shore of Lake Erie to Guatemala

Number of kinglet species nesting in Ontario: 2

Number of kinglet species worldwide: 4

Also see: Kingbird. *Up North:* Ruby-throated Hummingbird, Yellow-bellied Sapsucker, White Spruce, Black Spruce

SCARLET TANAGER
Raspy-voiced Treetop Dazzler

Length: 17–19 cm (6.7–7.5 in)
Wingspan: 28–30.5 cm
(11–12 in)
Markings: Males have bright-red
body, black wings and tail,
whitish beak; females and
juveniles are dull green
above, yellowish below, with
dark wings
Alias: Firebird, black-winged
redbird, *le tangara écarlate,
Piranga olivacea*
Call: Song a loud, deep, musical
whistle of raspy up-and-down
notes; also a quick, sharp
"chick-burr" call
Preferred habitat: Large tracts of
upland deciduous forest
Food: Caterpillars, beetles,
grubs, dragonflies, spiders,
some berries, seeds and buds
Nest: Loose, shallow tray, 9–13
cm (3.5–5 in), of twigs,
grass, stems and rootlets
Average clutch: 4 olive-sized,
speckled, blue or green eggs
Incubation period: 12–14 days
Fledging age: 9–11 days
Range: Southern Ontario to the
southern edge of the boreal
forest; also in Manitoba,
Quebec and New Brunswick
Average first arrival in central
Ontario: Mid-May
Average last departure from
central Ontario: Late Sept.

LIKE A PINT-SIZED superhero, the black-and-red-clad scarlet tanager seems to streak from nowhere upon any evildoer nearing his nest or territory. Once the intruder is foiled, the brave defender melts back into the shadows of the canopy high above, where he lurks with measured, subtle movements. He is heard more often than seen, whistling a pleasant, raspy song that is commonly described as "a robin with a sore throat."

Wearing considerably less-conspicuous dull-green coats, female tanagers tend to hunt for insects near the treetops, a little higher up than their brilliantly attired husbands. If they moved higher, the males would present glaring targets for cruising sharp-shinned and Cooper's hawks. While the female's wardrobe is designed to blend with the leaves as she sits on the nest, the male's flashy outfit is calculated to impress. A full red coat shows he's an experienced bird, at least two years old, which is in itself a significant accomplishment for short-lived migrants. In late summer, as soon as he's finished helping raise his family, a father begins moulting back into drab green, improving his chances of evading predators and surviving to breed another year.

SHARP-SHINNED HAWK
Diminutive Songbird Nabber

A SUDDEN, DEADLY swoop has ended many a songbird lover's moment of finch- or warbler-viewing bliss. The "tragedy" of a small bird suddenly snatched in the talons of a sharp-shinned hawk, bolting in from nowhere, has likewise befuddled outdoor instructors introducing the beauty of nature to schoolchildren at nature-trail birdfeeders. Yet for many, even children, it's an exhilarating rush to witness this pure force of nature.

A diminutive hawk about as big as a blue jay, the sharp-shin is an exquisitely designed small-bird nabber. It cruises silently at treetop level, scanning for feathered meals, then darting down upon them. Relatively short, rounded wings and a long, rudderlike tail make the hawk very agile for ducking through tangled branches to capture its prey. As its victims are most often inexperienced young or sick or injured birds, the sharp-shin plays the same role as the wolf and other predators in permitting only the fittest prey to survive and reproduce.

With large waves of migrant sparrows and other songbird suppers arriving in Ontario in April under cover of night, sharp-shinned hawks soon follow, coming in on

Length: 25–35 cm (10–14 in)
Weight: Males 85–110 g (3–4 oz), females 170–225 g (6–8 oz)
Wingspan: 51–69 cm (20–27 in)
Flying speed: 45 km/h (28 mph)
Distance travelled per day in migration: Up to 180 km (111 mi)
Average number of migrating sharp-shins counted in autumn over Holiday Beach, Lake Erie: About 14,000
Maximum density of visual cells in the average hawk's eye: About 1 million
Maximum density of visual cells in the human eye: About 200,000
Markings: Both sexes have grey back and upper wings, rust-coloured horizontal bars on breast and belly, grey-and-

white barred outer under-
wings, long, narrow tail
(fanned when gliding)
banded black and grey on top
and grey and white on underside; immature birds have a
brown back and streaked
white breast
Eye colour: Young have yellow
eyes, turning orange when 1
year old and blood red at
age 4
Alias: Bird hawk, sharp-shin,
sparrow hawk, little blue
darter, bullet hawk, slate-
coloured hawk, pigeon hawk,
l'épervier brun, Accipiter
striatus
Call: Rapid, high, shrill "kik, kik,
kik," something like a
flicker's call; also a long,
thin squeal
Food: Warblers, sparrows, woodpeckers and other small birds;
rarely small rodents, frogs,
insects
Preferred habitat: Moist
coniferous and mixed
forests and bogs
Nest: Dense mass of twigs, lined
with flakes of bark, 50–65 cm
(20–26 in) wide, usually
built across sturdy branches
close to trunk of an evergreen
tree, sometimes in an old
crow's nest
Average clutch: 4–5 apricot-
sized, white or blue-tinted
eggs with brown blotching
Incubation period: 30–35 days
Fledging age: 24–27 days
Age at sexual maturity: 2 years
Maximum lifespan: At least
12 years
Predators: Larger hawks, such as
harriers, Cooper's, red-tails
and goshawks, possibly also

day flights from points south. Adult sharpies, at least two years old, arrive first, intent on securing good breeding territories. Veterans usually return to the same area they occupied before, performing courtship flights and wooing with shrill squeals. They normally build a new nest every year, usually towards the margins of dense evergreen stands. They're largely silent and seldom seen around the nest site, going farther afield to hunt.

Fathers must nail six to ten hapless sparrows and warblers a day to keep the brood fed

About two weeks after returning, females begin laying their eggs. The remarkable size difference between the mates reflects their duties. Females are almost twice as heavy as their partners, and settle their warming, protective bulk onto the eggs for the duration of the incubation. Meanwhile the little males, who have higher voices than their wives, provide for the egg-sitting big mamas. Using their sleek build to their advantage, males can get in at the more plentiful smaller birds. Once the downy white hatchlings emerge, fathers must nail six to ten hapless sparrows and warblers a day to keep the brood fed. They present the catches to their hefty spouses, who then feed the nestlings. After about two weeks, females begin hunting as well, catching larger birds such as woodpeckers and jays.

Parents continue feeding their young for four or five weeks after they fledge in early summer, gradually reducing their rations. Then, as the family wanders away from the nest area, it gradually breaks up. Though adolescents aren't skilled hunters, as they become independent in August the pickings are relatively easy. At that time the first southbound songbirds are passing through and are more vulnerable on unfamiliar ground than are birds on their nesting territories. Immature female sharp-shins soon follow this bounty south, their numbers on the migration route peaking along the north side of Lake Erie a little past mid-September. The number of juvenile males peaks about a week later, as the males are smaller and able to hold out on less food in the north a little longer. The same pattern holds for adults, with female migration hitting full stride in late September and males trailing them in early October.

Tens of thousands of sharp-shinned hawks pour from forests in Eastern Canada and the northeast United States every year. Being smaller and lighter than all other Ontario hawks except falcons, sharp-shins flap their wings more in migration, rather than simply soaring from one rising column of warm air to another. They don't migrate over large bodies of water, but join other raptors along the seasonal hawk highways following the shores of the Great Lakes and the Atlantic, as well as along the Appalachians. The traffic seems to bring out the worst in sharp-shins, who are known for diving at each other as well as larger hawks.

The **Cooper's hawk** looks very like a sharp-shin, but is a little larger and has a round-tipped tail rather than the straight-cut or slightly notched tail of the sharpie. Cooper's are far less common in central Ontario, concentrated mostly in the hardwood forests of Shield-edge areas such as Muskoka and the Rideau Lakes. They catch larger songbirds, such as flickers and thrushes, as well as lots of chipmunks and squirrels. The sharp-shin's other close relative, the large and powerful **northern goshawk**, cruises thick forest settings in scattered areas across the region. It is central Ontario's only really non-migratory hawk, though the pale-bellied raptor sometimes moves farther south when its main prey – hares and ruffed grouse – are at a low in their population cycles.

great horned owls; raccoons raid nests
Average population density: 1–2 pairs per 10 km^2 (4 sq mi)
Range: Most of Ontario, though sparse in the north; also in all other provinces and territories
Average first arrival in central Ontario: Early Apr.
Average last departure from central Ontario: Mid-Oct.
Winter whereabouts: Southern Ontario to Panama
Mixed-forest raptor species: Broad-winged hawk, goshawk
Forested river bottomland species: Red-tailed hawk
Open-area species: Red-tailed hawk, northern harrier, kestrel
Marshland species: Northern harrier, osprey
Also see: *Up North:* Broad-winged Hawk, Snowshoe Hare

SONG SPARROW
Virtuoso with a Wide Repertoire

Fair little scout, that when the iron year
Changes, and the first fleecy clouds deploy,
Comest with such a sudden burst of joy.

ARCHIBALD LAMPMAN,
"The Song Sparrow"

Length: 13–17 cm (5–7 in)
Wingspan: 10–23 cm (4–9 in)
Weight: Average 21–22 g
  (0.8 oz)
Flying speed: 27 km/h (17 mph)
Markings: Streaky brown back
  and streaked white breast with
  a telltale large, dark spot in
  the middle; tan eye stripe with
  reddish-brown band above
Alias: Ground sparrow, bush
  sparrow, hedge sparrow, silver
  tongue, everybody's darling,
  marsh sparrow, bround-bird,
  swamp finch, red grassbird,
  le bruant chanteur,
  Melospiza melodia
Call: Songs are highly variable,
  but mostly in pattern of first
  note or phrase repeated 2 or 3
  times, followed by a complex
  string of buzzy trills, twitters
  and whistles, often in the
  rhythm of "maids, maids,
  maids, put on your tea kettle-
  ettle-ettle," lasting 2 or 3
  seconds; first 3 notes of song
  said to be similar to
  Beethoven's Fifth; also a nasal
  "tchep" call note

SONG SPARROWS, in Latin *Melospiza melodia*, are fully deserving of their name. Peals of exuberant song sparrow melodies, breaking late winter's still silence, are one of the first clear signs of the turning of the year. Males in particular belt it out for hours on end, each bird drawing from a repertoire of eight to 10 songs – sometimes as many as 20 – to create kaleidoscopic medleys. The females, for their part, sing short, soft tunes once they in turn arrive from the south. The most vocally versatile males command the most attention from the opposite sex and respect from rivals. They must also be good listeners, learning to recognize dozens of different songs performed by next-door neighbours in order to distinguish them from transient sparrows.

As the cacophony of red-winged blackbirds drops off in early summer, and warbler choruses begin to thin, song sparrow refrains rise to the fore and continue through the hot days ahead. Song sparrows stay in top form because they hold on to nesting territories long enough to raise two broods of future songsters. Females usually spend four to 10 days in April or early May building their first nests on the ground, hidden amid shrubs and the previous year's long, dry plant stems. Later, after the leaves open, they turn to the cover of bushes to locate a home for their second clutch.

Fathers help feed their offspring and take primary charge of them soon after they fledge, when mother birds are working on their second nest. Despite the equal amount of care given to the second brood, sparrows born in the first clutch have better chances for survival, because they have more time to gain experience in their first summer. When about three or four weeks old, they break their link with their parents. Males spend the next couple of months learning the craft of their species, listening intently to the songs of surrounding adults. Adding their own improvisations, they begin singing their own ditties by autumn. By the time they begin their first breeding season the following spring, they've developed an expansive songbook that they'll follow for the rest of their lives.

Song sparrows return each spring to the same general locale where they hatched. Since they learn to sing in a particular milieu, generations of birds perpetuate distinctive musical styles in an area. Song sparrow enthusiasts estimate the birds may have developed up to 900 local "dialects" across the continent. The sparrows are abundant throughout North America – their range stretching from the Aleutian Islands to Newfoundland and south to Florida – but are especially fond of cottage-country lakesides. Gifted soloists frequently provide the musical accompaniment for morning or afternoon tea down by the dock or by a campsite rockface.

In less shrubby, more open areas such as meadows and fields, apparent song sparrows often have a markedly different, high-pitched buzzing call. These are, in fact, **savannah sparrows**, which also have streaky undersides but lack the, or have a less-distinctive, central breast spot of the famous songster. Savannahs also usually sport yellowish "eyebrows" and a white strip along the top of their heads. Arriving in spring about a month later than song sparrows, they build their nests in small ground depressions obscured by tall grass.

Preferred habitat: Shrubby forest edges and clearings near lakes and rivers; small islands, thickets, marshes and swamps

Food: Grass and weed seeds, berries, beetles, grasshoppers, ants, flies, wasps

Territory: 0.2–0.6 ha (0.5–1.5 acres)

Nest: Neat cup of grass, stems, bark strips, leaves and rootlets, on ground in early spring or in shrubs or trees later in season

Average clutch: 3–5 light-green or pale-blue eggs covered in brown spots

Incubation period: 11–15 days

Fledging age: 9–12 days

Percentage of eggs laid that produce surviving fledglings: 40

Lifespan: Up to 11 years, though adults average 2.5 years

Predators: Sharp-shinned and Cooper's hawks; crows and blue jays raid nests

Nests parasitized by cowbirds: About 23%

Number of song sparrow subspecies: 31; a highly variable bird across North America

Percentage of songbird species that sing 2 or more songs: About 75

Range: Southern Ontario to the tree line; also in all other provinces and extreme south of territories

Average first arrival in southern Ontario: Late Mar.

Average last departure from southern Ontario: Late Oct.

Winter whereabouts: Southern Ontario to Mexico, mostly in the United States

Also see: Chipping Sparrow. *Up North:* White-throated Sparrow

VEERY
The Rippling-voiced Thrush

Length: 16–19 cm (6.5–7.5 in)
Wingspan: 29–32 cm
  (11–12.5 in)
Weight: 24–39 g (0.9–1.4 oz)
Markings: Russet brown on top
  and white below, with faded
  brown spots on breast
Alias: Willow thrush, *la grive
  fauve, Catharus fuscescens*
Call: Song a flutelike tremulous
  spiral of descending notes;
  also a call that seems to
  say "view"
Preferred habitat: Young, damp,
  low-lying hardwood and
  mixed forests and swamps
  with dense understoreys,
  willow-choked streamsides
Food: Beetles, grubs and other
  insects, spiders, slugs,
  worms, berries
Nest: Bulky cup of grass, bark
  shreds, twigs, stems, moss
  and rootlets, lined with
  leaves; usually on ground at

THERE ARE THINGS that render an Ontario forest magical in the dwindling daylight hours, such as the rich, golden light that paints the woods in a warm, glowing chiaroscuro. Another is the ethereal song of the veery, rippling through the trees in a gentle, fluted nocturne. The veery's voice seems unreal partly because it sounds like two birds harmonizing, repeating their own names in a descending "vee-ur, vee-ur, veer, veer." The truth is that a veery can sing two notes simultaneously. Like most other mellifluous thrushes, it sings most often in early evening and morning, but some-times lets loose at other times of day as well.

Veery serenades usually don't begin until early June, about two weeks after the birds start arriving at their breeding grounds in thickety woods. As with most song-birds, rival males who ignore the melodic warnings and trespass into foreign territory are confronted violently by the proprietor. Females, meanwhile, build the nest and incubate the eggs, generally at a well-hidden address amid dense ferns and shrubs on the forest floor. Young veeries are introduced quickly into the world. The passage from new egg to fledged youngster takes about three weeks.

Seldom venturing out of their thick, moist, understorey haunts, the plainly attired, slender thrushes are among those elusive "dickey birds" that can drive birders nuts. It's often difficult to get a fix on them as they scamper through the underbrush. The first sighting is usually out of the corner of the eye. In the split second it takes to turn for a better view, the veery disappears like a forest sprite. Then peripheral vision picks up the bird's trail again . . . and then it vanishes once more. Other than by their song, veeries reveal their whereabouts mostly by their habit of kicking up fallen leaves, looking for tasty insect morsels. They also hunt from low perches, pouncing on both passing crawlies and fliers. Later in summer, with their offspring fully grown, they turn more to the woods' ripening berries. By mid-August they seem to have had their fill of Ontario and begin taking off for the faraway tropical tangles of the Amazon jungle.

Veeries reveal their whereabouts by kicking up fallen leaves, looking for tasty insect morsels

---

Like many other tropical migrants, veeries have suffered from forest-clearing, both in their southern homes and here in the north. Although the veery is still the most common forest thrush in much of central Ontario, its numbers have declined by more than 50 percent in recent decades. In some areas, veeries are only one-fifth as common as they once were. And those remaining may sing less often, because lower population densities put less pressure on territorial boundaries, causing fewer encounters. One can only imagine the volume of the divine chorus in better times.

base of a bush or other vegetation, sometimes on a stump or low in a shrub
Average clutch: 4 olive-sized, light-blue eggs
Incubation period: 10–12 days
Fledging age: 10 days
Maximum lifespan: 10 years
Predators: Foxes, skunks, raccoons; blue jays and crows raid nests
Upland deciduous forest thrush: Wood thrush
Spruce forest thrush: Swainson's thrush
Mixed forest thrush: Hermit thrush
Range: Southern Ontario to Lake Abitibi and Hearst; also in all other provinces
Average first arrival in central Ontario: Mid-May
Average last departure from central Ontario: Early Sept.
Winter whereabouts: Central America to Brazil
Number of thrush species nesting in Ontario: 7
Number of thrush species worldwide: 30
Chiaroscuro: The technique of using light and shade in paintings, practised most famously by Caravaggio (1573–1610, Italian) and Rembrandt (1606–69, Dutch)
Also see: Beaked Hazel, Willows. *Up North:* Wood Thrush

WHIP-POOR-WILL
Incessant Night Caller

Length: 22–25 cm (9–10 in)
Wingspan: 41–49 cm
  (16–19.3 in)
Average weight: 63 g (2.25 oz)
Call: A loud, rapid, rhythmic
  3-syllable cry, often endlessly
  repeated, described as "whip-
  poor-will" or "purple-rib,"
  with emphasis on first and
  last syllables; if close, a quiet
  "cluck" may be heard
  between each call
Noted repetitions: Canadian naturalist R. D. Lawrence once
  counted 569 consecutive
  "whip-poor-wills" without
  pause; others report more
  than 1,000 repeated calls
Average cruising altitude: Under
  8 m (26 ft)
Markings: Mottled brown, grey
  and black, with grey streaks
  over the eyes and a black
  throat with a white neck band

NORTH AMERICA'S fondly remembered birding guru, Roger Tory Peterson, said it best: the whip-poor-will is "a voice in the night woods." For most, that's all this fabled, robin-sized bird will ever be. Whip-poor-wills are seen about as often as nuns at a hockey game. The vociferous nocturnal insectivores (the birds, not the nuns) sleep by day, perfectly camouflaged amid dead leaves on the ground. They don't venture out until well into dusk, catching insects on the wing and stopping to rest at favourite spots along their regular hunting circuits. They often repeat their whimsical name more than 100 times in a row, the call ringing out through the woods and across wilderness lakes.

While the whip-poor-will's insistent cry has greeted human ears for thousands of years, the bird is so hard to see that it was not identified by modern science until the early 1800s. Before that, its song credit went to the similarly attired but higher-flying nighthawk. Both birds are members of the bizarrely named goatsucker family (also called nightjars), inconspicuous insect eaters with tiny beaks and very short legs. Goatsuckers were tagged with their unflattering label by farm workers in England who believed the whip-poor-will's relatives swooped down to suckle from goats in the night. The belief probably sprang from the birds' habit of flying low amongst livestock to pick off insects disturbed from the ground by the animals' hooves.

But whip-poor-wills *are* somewhat peculiar birds. Although they roost and nest on the ground, their weak legs and claws don't allow them to walk or hop far. When resting on a tree, they sit, like the nighthawk, lengthwise along the branch, rather than perched across it like other birds. They also have cute little whiskers that help scoop insects into their mouths as they fly. Deceptively small bills actually conceal huge mouths – held vastly agape as they hunt – extending back past their eyes. Like nighthunting owls, whip-poor-wills also sport especially soft feathers that allow for silent flight.

They time their mating to ensure their young hatch around the time of the full moon

---

Ontario's spring explosion of insects, so reviled by humans, lures whip-poor-wills all the way from the sunny winter climes around the Gulf of Mexico. After migrating at night for six weeks or more, they arrive here in May and start carving out breeding territories and looking for significant others. Those lucky enough to have viewed the secret whip-poor-will love ritual report that courting males make strange, guttural clucking sounds and do an urgent little dance. Females respond with low, buzzing grunts of consent. They touch bills and walk, entranced, side by side. With seemingly incredible forethought, they time their mating to ensure their young hatch around the time of the full moon, ensuring maximum light for

(more narrow and buff-coloured on females); black bristles around the mouth; tiny, curved beak; rounded wings; long, rounded tail with white trim on males and buff on females visible in flight

Alias: *L'engoulevent bois-pourri, Caprimulgus vociferous*

Preferred habitat: Dry, open or broken rocky forests of red oak, jack pine, juniper and bush honeysuckle, with lots of clearings

Food: Moths, mosquitoes, caddisflies, crickets, grasshoppers, ants, beetles, worms

Whip-poor-will floral footwear: The Iroquois call moccasin flowers "the whip-poor-will's shoes"

Nest: Eggs laid on top of fallen leaves and needles or on bare ground, often under or near a tree, bush or fallen branches at the forest edge or in a small clearing free of green herb cover

Average clutch: 2 peach-pit-sized, white eggs, covered with brown and grey splotches and spots

Incubation period: 19–21 days

Fledging age: About 20 days

Range: Southern Ontario to Kapuskasing

Average first arrival in central Ontario: Early May

Average last departure from central Ontario: Late Aug. to mid-Sept.

Winter whereabouts: From the Carolinas south along coast to Honduras

Number of goatsucker species in Ontario: 3

Number of goatsucker species
worldwide: 67
Also see: Nighthawk, Barn
Swallow. *Up North:* Moccasin
Flower

catching the full bounty of night-flying insects needed for growing nestlings.

Whip-poor-wills sing through the spring and early-summer nesting season, proclaiming their domain. Occasionally, they may belt out a refrain in late August or early September.

Expectant mothers lay their eggs on the ground, without the pretence of making a nest, and stick doggedly by them. Relying almost entirely on their camouflage, becoming one with the forest floor, they flush only at the last second, sometimes faking injury to lure intruders from their eggs or young. Baby whip-poor-wills, true to form, are also covered in grey or brownish down, blending with their surroundings. They go long periods between big regurgitations of bug stew from their parents, which minimizes activity at the nest and thus helps keep them hidden.

Unfortunately, the ideal habitat for whip-poor-will reproduction and concealment has become scarce in many parts of Ontario. Agriculture and development rob them of the broken forest cover they need, and in other parts, dense, maturing forests shut whip-poor-wills out from sites that once offered a more open canopy in the wake of past logging operations. For many campers and cottagers, the whip-poor-will's wild, rising voice in the night has become a rare echo from the past.

WOOD DUCK
The Backwater Beauty

ANDS-DOWN WINNER of the Ontario-wide waterfowl beauty pageant, the wood duck is a stunning scene-stealer whenever spotted. Unfortunately, that's not very often, since the web-footed wonder generally keeps to out-of-the-way beaver ponds and small, swampy lakes. Grazing the shallows near water's edge, it's usually obscured by thick vegetation. The woody is also a truly odd duck, the only one of its kind in Canada to perch in trees, thanks to special clawed extensions to its feet. Able to fly swiftly through tangled branches, the arboreal fowl is an acorn connoisseur.

Wood ducks also nest in trees, often in old pileated woodpecker or flicker holes. Paired mates usually return to the lake of the female's ducklinghood during the latter half of April in search of suitable nesting quarters. The plain grey hen does most of the tree-cavity inspecting while Mr. Goodlooking stands by. With large, unoccupied holes sometimes unavailable, females resort to depositing eggs in the nest holes of other wood ducks. It's not hard, since wood ducks spend little time at home until they start incubating, after laying most of their eggs. The eggs are dropped at a rate of one a day. Even if they have a nest of their own, hens often leave a few extra eggs with their neighbours as insurance against predators finding their main clutch. Sometimes the foster home belongs to a hooded merganser, another cavity-nesting duck of the same backwater areas. The hoodies return the favour in wood duck holes.

With all the dumping, nests often have 20 eggs, 50 in extreme cases. A week or so before the mob hatches, fathers jump ship, disappearing to moult to a drab summer coat of grey. Mothers manage, however, because precocious little wood ducklings can feed themselves. A

Length: 43–51 cm (17–20 in)
Markings: Males have green-crested head, black face and neck trimmed with white; white chin, spotted chestnut-brown breast, tan sides, white belly, dark, iridescent wings, dark back and tail, orange bill at the base trimmed with yellow, and red eyes; females are mostly grey, with blue and white patch on dark wings and white eye and chin patches
Alias: Tree duck, acorn duck, Carolina duck, *le canard branchu, Aix sponsa*
Scientific name meaning: *Aix* is classical Greek for "water," *sponsa* is Latin for "bride"
Call: Usually silent, occasionally utter squeals, whistles and cheeps
Food: Aquatic vegetation, seeds, acorns, nuts, berries; less than

10% of food aquatic insects, crustaceans and tiny fish

Preferred habitat: Beaver ponds, swamps with large, mature trees, temporary forest ponds and other wetlands surrounded by woods

Nest: Down-lined tree cavity, usually an old pileated woodpecker or enlarged flicker hole; at least 28 cm (11 in) wide and 30 cm (1 ft) deep

Average clutch: 10–15 plum-sized, white or tan eggs

Incubation period: 27–37 days

Fledging age: 8–10 weeks

Predators: Raccoons, skunks, mink eat eggs; snapping turtles, pike eat ducklings; goshawks sometimes kill adults

Average population density: 2–10 pairs per 10 km^2 (4 sq mi)

Other cavity-nesting Ontario ducks: Common merganser, hooded merganser, common goldeneye and bufflehead

Other ducks of small, boggy lakes: Black duck, ring-necked duck, hooded merganser

Range: Southern Ontario to southern edge of the Hudson Bay lowlands; also in all other provinces except Newfoundland

Average first arrival in central Ontario: Mid-Apr.

Average last departure from central Ontario: Mid-Oct.

Winter whereabouts: Northern Kentucky to Mexico and Cuba

Total number of duck species nesting in Ontario: 26

Also see: Black Duck, Pileated Woodpecker. *Up North:* Common Merganser, Beaver

day after hatching, they follow their parent out of the tree, falling as much as 18 metres (60 feet) to the ground. Bouncing, sometimes a little stunned but seldom hurt, they gather themselves up and trail Mom as much as a kilometre (half a mile) or more to the nearest beaver pond or secluded lake.

Their beautiful feathers were popular for trout-fishing flies

Hens shepherd their broods for about five weeks, often amalgamating with one or more other wood duck families on the lake. Then, after the mothers leave to moult in small groups, the young are on their own for another month before fledging. Once airborne, in late summer, they venture into the world, joining groups of adults in marshes and other feeding areas. There, males are already undergoing their second moult back into their flashy breeding plumage, which is complete by mid-September. For about three weeks, while changing their feathers, wood ducks are unable to fly.

For all their reclusiveness during the breeding period, wood ducks are renowned for the ease with which they can be approached later in the year. The timing was perfect for early shotgun-bearing hunters, coming across freshly decked-out males, spectacular sitting ducks, crying out for taxidermy. Their beautiful feathers were also popular for trout-fishing flies. "The warfare against this sort must be considered a slaughter, rather than a sport," wrote one appalled observer of Upper Canada's wood duck hunting in the 1830s. Swamp drainage and logging contributed to bringing the species close to extinction by the beginning of the 20th century. Only with a hunting ban from 1918 to 1941, and the building of thousands of nest boxes, did wood duck numbers recover. Today the population is healthy, despite being the second most commonly shot duck in Ontario.

CREEPY-CRAWLIES

M ORE THAN ONE MILLION *insect species are known to science, and at least several times that number are undoubtedly yet to be studied. The small sample of the insect world we feature here does include the beetle order, which accounts for more than one-third of all known kinds of insects. We also look at mayflies, which are strongly identified with the "up north" experience, and midges, one of the most important groups of bugs in the aquatic food chain. Two of the region's most commonly seen butterflies are added, along with grasshoppers, perennial favourites of children large and small. Together, they offer a few examples of how insects interact with and influence nature at large.*

BEETLES
Greatest of the Animal Orders

I NSECTS ACCOUNT FOR three-quarters of all known animal species on Earth. The bulk of this planet-dominating army is an armoured corps of beetles, the greatest order in the animal kingdom. With hundreds of thousands of varieties to choose from, it's little wonder Charles Darwin began his career in natural history as a beetle collector. Amid the intellectual tumult sparked by Darwin's theories of evolution, one scientist commented that the one thing that can be known about the Creator, if one exists, is that God had a particular interest in beetles.

Employing a design patented more than a quarter-billion years ago, virtually all beetles are shielded by hardened wing covers, called elytra, resembling shiny coats of armour. The elytra lift forward to free the wings for flight. Whether hunters, scavengers, vegetarians, fungus eaters, parasites or pollinators, beetles and their segmented, wormlike larvae, known as grubs, sport sharp, biting mandibles for munching their meals.

Perhaps the most popular of all beetles, ladybugs (illustrated) are themselves divided into more than 3,000 species around the world. Named for deities in some 50 languages, they've been honoured since ancient times for their services in eating aphids and other crop-damaging insects. In medieval England, they were associated with the blessings of the Virgin Mary – "Our Lady" – and are still greeted with delight upon landing on a human hand. Like many brightly coloured beetles, their pretty black-spotted orange or red attire is thought to serve as a warning to predators of their bitter taste. Most huddle together in dormitories beneath fallen leaves or bark for the winter and may be seen well into autumn and soon after the snow melts in spring.

Number of known beetle species worldwide: 300,000–370,000

Number of known Ontario beetle species: 3,843

World's biggest insect: Goliath beetle of central Africa, up to 15 cm (6 in) long, 10 cm (4 in) wide, weighing 100 g (3.5 oz)

World's smallest beetles: Hairy-winged beetles, 0.25 mm (0.009 in) long

Top beetle running speed: 2 km/h (1.2 mph)

Clutch: 1–10,000 eggs; most species lay eggs singly

Lifespan: 3 days to 15 years; most species 1 year

Predators: Skunks, raccoons, foxes, shrews, moles, snakes, woodpeckers and many other birds; also spiders, fish and other insects

Alias: *Les scarabées, Coleoptera*

Among other widely recognized beetles, June bugs make their presence known on hot summer nights when they're drawn to lights, often whacking into lanterns and cottage screen doors. The hefty, reddish-brown bombers spend their first two or three years of life initially as white, subterranean, root-gnawing grubs, then as resting pupae on their way to becoming adults. In agricultural areas, they're among the choicest morsels snatched up by gulls and blackbirds following farmers' ploughs. Emerging as adults in late spring, June bugs sleep beneath the ground by day and fly up to snack on tree leaves after dark.

June bugs are part of the scarab beetle family, whose members include a vast assortment of shiny, round sanitation workers known as the dung beetles. From rabbit pellets to moose muffins, dung beetles set to whatever falls their way. They not only feed on the waste but roll small balls of it into little burrows, then lay their eggs in it so that upon hatching their offspring find a ready food supply. It may not be a pretty way to make a living, but it was well appreciated by early agricultural societies, which recognized the vital job the beetles did in cleaning up and in fertilizing the soil. In ancient Egypt, the scarab was a sacred and much-reproduced symbol of resurrection and the sun. Its practice of rolling balls of dung was a reminder of the way the sun was rolled across the sky. After dying, the scarab apparently rose again from the mud in great numbers every year. Its dung-nursery constructions may even have been the inspiration for Egyptian tomb-building and mummification in preparation for rebirth.

Carrion beetles are similarly intriguing insects working in a grim milieu. Members of the family known as sexton beetles actually bury deceased beasts as large as mice or chipmunks, though they themselves are only one to 2.3 centimetres (0.4 to one inches) long. Working in pairs and driving others off, the usually black and red or orange undertakers either dig beneath the corpse where it lies or drag it up to a metre (three feet) away to a prepared shallow grave. Females of some species, after laying eggs in the burial chamber, stay to tend and feed their young.

Meaning of *Coleoptera*: From classical Greek words *koleos*, meaning "sheath," and *pteron*, meaning "wing," in reference to hard wing shields

Word origin of beetle: From Old English *bitula*, meaning "biter"

Biggest bites: Though they are mainly sap drinkers, male stag beetles have huge, horn-like mandibles capable of painful bites. Blood-sport gamblers in tropical lands pit stags with mandibles several cm (at least 1 in) long against one another

Beetle defences: Some predatory, nocturnal ground beetles produce foul odours when threatened. Others, called bombardier beetles, make a popping sound as they release toxic liquids that can irritate human skin or create diversionary puffs of vapour

Love potions: The Mediterranean blister beetle is the fabled "Spanish fly," whose body secretions are used to make the aphrodisiac of the same name (there's no scientific proof it works). The beetles were collected since Roman times to extract the substance, called cantharidin, which is toxic and causes skin blisters and was used in medicine. It also promotes hair growth

Clickers: Family of flattish bugs, called click beetles, are unable to roll over when on their backs; instead, they snap their bodies, producing an audible "click," which flips them right-side up

Black or dark-brown water scavenger beetles provide their own cleanup services in ponds and still inlets. The big bugs, up to four centimetres (1.6 inches) long, dine on decomposing organic material in the murky depths.

Similar in size and look, but far more ferocious, are diving beetles, which swiftly tackle live prey as large as tadpoles, minnows and spring peepers. By trapping air beneath their wing covers, they are able to remain under water for up to 36 hours at a time. At night, they may fly from pond to pond looking for mates. Diving beetle larvae, called water tigers, are every bit as carnivorous as their parents.

The surface of still waters is the domain of whirligig beetles. Resembling steely oval beads, they often appear in large groups soon after the ice melts, rising from muddy winter quarters. By swimming in high-speed circles, shiny black whirligigs create radiating waves that they use like radar signals to detect prey, usually other aquatic insects or fliers that have fallen onto the water. Where currents run faster, water penny beetles find their niche by clinging to plants and debris. The beetle is named for its flat, round, copper-coloured larvae, which stick to submerged rocks like suction cups and feed on algae.

Just as picking rocks from swift streams may turn up water pennies, large dead branches strewn over the forest floor often reveal evidence of quite a different, arboreal group of beetles. Called engraver or bark beetles, most are only about three millimetres (0.1 inch) long. They burrow unseen between a tree's inner bark and sapwood, eating as they go and leaving squiggly tunnels in their wake. After females lay their eggs in a long central chamber, larvae hatch and tunnel away from it in all directions, leaving intricate designs, revealed on the surface of debarked limbs. Each species creates its own unique pattern, further evidence of the immense diversity within beetledom.

GRASSHOPPERS
Meadow Jumpers of Summer

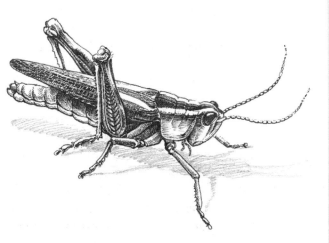

Maximum jumping distance:
2.6 m (8.5 ft)

Adult length: Most species
1.5–3 cm (0.6–1.2 in); females
up to twice as big as males

Largest Ontario species:
American grasshopper, up to
9.4 cm (3.7 in) long

Smallest Ontario species: Under
1 cm (0.4 in)

Markings: Most are brown or
grey, often with varying
yellow, green, red or black
features

Alias: Short-horned grasshoppers, grigs, locusts,
les sauterelles, Acridids

Wing: Hard front pair cover back
pair when folded

Number of eyes: 2 compound,
3 simple

Ears: Tympanum located on sides
of first abdominal segment

Preferred habitat: Meadows,
fields, forest paths and edges,
clearings, bare rocky places
and bogs

Food: Grass and other plants

Clutch: Usually a number of
separate pods, up to 20 for
some species, each holding
8–100 eggs

Age at moulting to become an
adult: 40–60 days

Lifespan: Up to 6 months

Predators: Garter and smooth
green snakes, skunks, raccoons, foxes, leopard frogs,
toads, spiders, killdeer,
herring gulls, ravens, red-
winged blackbirds and many
other birds; fly and beetle
larvae eat eggs

ALWAYS A FAVOURITE with bug-catching children, grasshoppers are also one of humankind's most feared scourges. The Chinese even had a god of grasshoppers, Pa Ch'a, who was venerated in hopes of persuading him to keep the swarms of his ravenous charges away from crops. Needing open areas in which to bask, grasshoppers are mostly limited in Ontario's forest regions to meadows, clearings, roadsides and shorelines. However, large numbers of the huge, crop-threatening American grasshoppers – closely related to two locust species – sometimes fly to southern Ontario in summer migrations from as far away as Florida.

Many grasshoppers use their wings only to glide once they've sprung into the air. Some can jump up to 20 times their own length, a feat achieved by more than muscle power alone. A protein, called resilin, in a grasshopper's long back legs releases an explosive burst of energy with each leap. It's so efficient that the insect can virtually hop forever without tiring.

Most grasshoppers hatch from overwintering eggs in spring or early summer. Called nymphs at this stage, they can already jump and look like tiny, wingless versions of

Winter whereabouts: Adults of most species die, leaving only eggs behind

Cereal crop losses during grasshopper outbreaks: Often 5–10%

Locusts: About a dozen species (none in Canada) of normally solitary grasshoppers that grow larger wings in crowded conditions and form huge flying swarms wandering over vast areas, sometimes consuming every day enough grain to feed 50 million people

Largest recorded locust swarm: Estimated 250 billion, covering 5,200 km² (2,000 sq mi), crossed the Red Sea in 1889

Human response to locust plagues: In Africa and Asia, beleaguered populations eat the locusts

Word origin of locust: Latin for "a burned place"

Grasshopper range: Throughout Ontario; also in all other provinces and territories

Age of oldest grasshopper fossils: More that 190 million years old

Number of Ontario Acridid grasshopper species: About 51

Number of grasshopper species worldwide: More than 11,000

Number of Ontario cricket species: 15

Number of Ontario katydid species: 26

Also see: Smooth Green Snake.
Up North: Grasses

adults, but with disproportionately large heads, like a puppy or kitten. They go through five or six moults on the way to adulthood, taking cover after each shedding until their new, pale exterior hardens and colours. Fully grown two-striped grasshoppers (illustrated) and other species start appearing in July, when dozens may fly up with each footstep taken through meadows of long grass. Many varieties flash bright yellow or red as they expose their underwings in flight, which may startle predators and attract mates.

When ready to mate, males of some but not all species crank out daytime love songs by running saw-toothed back legs along the hard, sharp edges of veins in their folded wings. Band-winged grasshoppers also attract mates with loud clicking sounds made by snapping their wings while they fly. When a female comes around, the eager hopper jumps on her back and holds on during her initial attempts to throw him. If he proves a steady rider and she is ready, she accepts his packets of sperm, called spermatophores, released from the curled tip of his abdomen into hers. Mating lasts about 45 minutes for many species, though some may couple for a day and a half. Some fertilized females store their sperm packets internally until late summer or early fall, when most lay several batches of eggs in bare patches of soil. Each clutch has a frothy coating that hardens into a pod.

Crickets are closely related to grasshoppers, but are creatures of the night, and so are usually darkly coloured. The males' nocturnal chirping, sweeter and more musical than the daytime efforts of grasshoppers, is achieved by rubbing the vein ridge of one wing along the hard edge of another. Their chirp rate rises with the temperature. Crickets also have much longer antennae than grasshoppers, and long forked tails. Most lay overwintering eggs late in the season, injected singly into the ground or into twigs. Higher up, green grasshoppers called **katydids**, which also have very long antennae, often chirp from tree branches.

MAYFLIES
Rising to Fleeting Glory

T HE SUDDEN APPEARANCE of countless millions of bizarre, fairylike insects filling the sky is a spectacular event at lakesides across the province. Seeming to materialize from nowhere, thick swarms of big-eyed, long-tailed mayflies flutter across open spaces and gravitate towards lights at evening, sometimes covering the sides of cottages, triangular wings held together upright over their backs. Yet, within 24 hours of their arrival, they may be gone again, or lying lifeless in thick heaps along the shore and on the water.

Mayflies generally swarm in June and July. Smaller numbers appear earlier and later, though they are noticed by few, save for avid anglers. The large, delicate insects are usually missed because they spend virtually all their lives beneath the water as aquatic "nymphs," emerging to fly, mate, lay eggs and die all within a day or two. Some do it all in 90 minutes. "Nature holds a couple of draughts from the cup of love to be fair payment for the pains of a lifetime," said German writer Johann Goethe of the fated fliers. Since the time of Aristotle, their evanescence has been taken as a metaphor for human life. Fittingly, the scientific name of their family, *Ephemeroptera*, means "living for a day with wings."

Mayflies are one of the most primitive and ancient groups of living flying insects. With little time for wide dispersal, a species tends to be geographically limited, which has made comparison of mayfly types an important aid in piecing together the history of continental drift.

Offspring of many varieties hatch in lakes, rivers and streams within a few weeks of their parents' passing. The eggs of others may lie dormant for months. The vaguely

Length: 3–30 cm (1.2–12 in)
Markings: Most species are various shades of brown or dusky yellow, some are black or reddish
Alias: Shadflies, fishflies, dayflies, duns, spinners, lake-flies, drakes, trout flies, quills, cocktails, sailors, dotterels, mackerels, willow flies, cisco flies, river flies, cob flies, salmon flies, June bugs, *les éphémères, Ephemeroptera*
Feather fishing flies imitating mayflies: Blue wing olive, quill Gordon, March brown, royal coachman, dark Cahill, white-gloved howdy, Hendrickson
Habitat: In and around lakes, rivers, streams, ponds and marshes
Food: Most eat algae and bits of decaying vegetation

Clutch: 50–1,000 eggs
Lifespan: 3 months to a year for most species; some live 2 years
Predators: Trout, pickerel, bass, suckers, frogs, salamanders, swallows and other birds, crayfish, dragonflies, diving beetles, stoneflies, water striders and spiders; snails and caddisfly larvae eat eggs
Range: All of Ontario; also in all other provinces and territories
Age of oldest fossils: 300 million years
Number of mayfly species in Canada: 300–411
Number of mayfly species worldwide: 2,100
Also see: Midges. *Up North:* Brook Trout

crayfishlike nymphs have sets of gills along the sides of their distinctly segmented abdomens. They crawl along the bottom with sharply bent, pointy legs, hiding beneath rocks, amid weeds and in the mud to avoid fish and other predators. Nymphs that survive may moult up to 50 times as they grow larger through the year.

The year's first mayflies are smaller species, emerging from snowmelt-swollen rivers usually on sunny days in early May. Later in the summer, many continue appearing well past dusk. Mass emergences ensure that feasting trout, pickerel and other fish will not be able to get all of them while they are most vulnerable.

Congregating at shallow plateaus and near the shore, transforming nymphs rise up as their old skin splits. Bursting from the top of their larval shells as they hit the surface, they appear as dull-brown air cadets, called duns. In as little as 10 seconds, as they drift along, their wings unfold, dry and lift them up in clumsy maiden flights to the nearest landfall, usually waterside trees and shrubs. They then spend up to another day moulting again, the only insects known to do so after they've received their wings, and appear afterwards in shiny, full flying colours and clear, intricately veined wings. Also known as spinners, adult mayflies have been models for fishing lures for hundreds of years.

Unlike most insects, adult mayflies have soft bodies; developing a tough shell isn't worthwhile for their short time left on Earth. Neither do they eat. Instead, groups of eligible bachelors emerging from lakes fly courtship patterns over the water, repeatedly rising and floating back down. At the first opportunity, a male uses his outstretched front legs to grab a female that wanders into the swarm, mating with her in midair. The female lays her eggs in small batches on the water surface within an hour or so of mating, and then, spent, lays herself down on the waves. Her lifeless mate soon joins her in the watery grave.

MIDGES
Pesky but Harmless Swarms

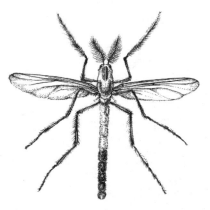

ONLY AN EYE-LEVEL SCAN during a cool summer swim can truly reveal the busy traffic on the surface of a dark, rocky lake. In the right light, on a calm day, multitudes of the tiniest bugs are visible floating on the water, touching off and buzzing just above. They draw swallows by day and bats by night, both swooping low to feed. Though the surface crowds are cosmopolitan, their greatest components are usually newly transformed midges up from the watery depths.

They don't get all the headlines like blackflies and mosquitoes, but midges are more numerous than both and absolutely vital to aquatic ecosystems. Fortunately, the vast majority – all true midges – don't bite. Though some sip flower nectar, most don't even eat during their brief life as winged adults, which usually lasts several days. Resembling tiny, light-model mosquitoes, midges are most often noticed when swirling in a small cloud, light as air, around someone walking down a path or standing by the waterfront. Unlike their biting colleagues, the midges flying around people are males, sporting huge bushy antennae, rather than females. They are only interested in humans as beacons in an open space around which they can swarm to attract the opposite sex. They're just looking for a place to hang out and meet girls.

Midges spend most of their lives in the mud as wiggly worms smaller and thinner than grains of rice. They live by the thousands in almost every square metre of submerged ground in Ontario. Much of their food is sunken bits of dead algae and the microscopic animals found in the deepest, darkest waters, where little else lives. Because they can capture and recycle so much decaying matter, midges often make up more than half of a lake's or river's non-microscopic invertebrates. As such, they are the main fare for most larger bottom-feeders.

Number of wing beats per minute: Up to 63,000, the fastest animal movement on Earth

Larvae per m² (1.2 sq yd) of lake or river bottom: Commonly several thousand, up to 50,000

Maximum swarm populations: 50 million

Length: 1–13 mm (0.04–0.5 in)

Largest species: *Chironomus plumosus* (illustrated)

Mature larvae length: 1–30 mm (0.04–1.2 in), most under 10 mm (0.4 in)

Markings: Most black or brown, others green, blue, yellow or red; larvae can be red, orange, yellow, green, blue, purple, brown, white or translucent; pupae are yellow, gold, brown, grey or clear

Alias: Lake flies, harlequin flies, chironomids, gnats (really another kind of fly), *les moucherons, Chironomidae*

Preferred habitat: In and around any body of water or wetlands; some larvae found living more than 300 m (1,000 ft) deep at bottom of Lake Superior, in icy pools beneath glaciers and inside pitcher plants

Winter whereabouts: Most larvae dormant, often in cocoons, at water's bottom

Average number of midge species in a lake: Usually more than 50, each occupying a different niche; scientists judge habitat types and ecosystem health by finding out which species are present

Environmental services: Larvae are essential to biological processes in sewage-treatment ponds

Best wind speeds for midge swarming: 0.8–15 km/h (0.5–9 mph)

Food: Larvae eat algae, microscopic animals and bits of decaying organic matter; some prey on the larvae of mosquitoes and other midges

Eggs: Most laid or dropped in globs or long strings of sticky jelly on the surface of the water; some attached to aquatic vegetation

Incubation period: Several days for most species

Lifespan: 1 or 2 generations a year for most species

Predators: Swallows, chimney swifts, bats, suckers, lake trout and other fish, spiders, dragonflies, water beetles

Range: All of Canada, including the high Arctic

Oldest midge fossils: Entombed in 130-million-year-old amber

Number of known Canadian midge species: More than 500

Number of known midge species worldwide: More than 5,000

Many midge larvae at first swim or drift freely after hatching. Tiny, writhing clouds of deep-red, lace-thin wigglers, known as bloodworms, can sometimes be seen near the edges of ponds and other still waters, where they may be attracted to light. Their colour is caused by haemoglobin, bubbles of oxygen that make human blood red and permit midge larvae to live in stagnant, poorly aerated habitats. After their initial wandering stage, they and many other species spend the rest of their larval lives on the bottom, in protective cases of sand and other fine particles stuck together with silken saliva.

After metamorphosing, midges rise to the surface and take 10 to 30 seconds to burst from their pupal case, which they then use as a raft while their wings expand and harden. Though mating swarms occur at midday during cooler months, the greatest activity comes in June and July, when swarms build from late afternoon till the last light of dusk, when many are attracted to lights. Weak fliers, they need a slight breeze or warm air rising in thermals to give them lift. If the wind is any stronger, they are forced either to the leeward side of a tree or other shelter, or are grounded. Each species has its own favoured terrain, altitude and characteristic group movements – often rising up and falling – that identify them for females of their own kind watching from the sidelines.

The innocuous swarmers get a bad name from a few members of a completely different family commonly called biting midges. Also known as **no-see-ums**, they are mere black specks and can pass through screen doors and administer burning bites that often leave red dots. They often strike at midsummer, just when it seems as if the mosquitoes are settling down a little.

MOURNING CLOAK BUTTERFLY
First Flutter of Spring

ON A BRIGHT, beautiful March day, when the mercury rises above freezing and everything radiates with the glow of the strengthening sun, thoughts of spring can materialize on the dark wings of a mourning cloak butterfly. Cold winds and more snow invariably drive this protospring away and send the yellow-fringed butterfly back to bed for several weeks more. But the mourning cloak, with its first foray, will have claimed the forest for the coming spring.

Named for their sombre, dark wings, likened to a funeral cape, mourning cloaks are one of only a small number of butterflies that hibernate as adults. They're usually the first kind to appear in spring. In preparation for the climax of their lives, rousing mourning cloaks fortify themselves for the first plunge into spring air by revving up their flight muscles, causing their wings to shiver and their internal temperature to rise 60 to 80 percent. Then, stepping from winter dens in narrow tree cavities and rock or log crevices, they press their furry bodies against sun-warmed surfaces to absorb radiant heat. At the same time, they spread their dark, heat-absorbing wings to bask in the direct sunlight. Evolutionary theorists speculate that insect wings may have evolved from what were initially solar panels.

While most of their brethren are too chilled even to fly on overcast summer days, hardy mourning cloaks, through all their efforts, can raise their body temperatures to up to 25°C (77°F) above the air around them. That ability, combined with a wandering tendency, has made them one of the most widespread butterflies in the world. They fly in the enduring summer sun of the Mackenzie

Wingspan: 8–10 cm (3–4 in)
Caterpillar length: Up to 5 cm (2 in)
Markings: Dark-brown wings bordered by a black band with light-blue spots and yellow trim; dull underwings look like a dead leaf or bark when closed; fuzzy brown body and white-tipped antennae; caterpillars are spiny and black, covered with white specks and with a row of orange-red spots along back, also have red feet
Alias: Camberwell beauty, yellow edge, antiopa butterfly, willow butterfly, yellow-bordered butterfly, grand surprise, antiope vaness, trauermantel, white border, spiny elm caterpillar, *le morio, Nymphalis antiopa*
Preferred habitat: Deciduous and mixed forests and meadows

Food: Caterpillars eat leaves of willows, birch, poplars and elm; butterflies sip sap, nectar, fruit juice and moisture from mud

Clutch: Up to 250 ridged, whitish eggs in a long, neat cluster around twigs near tips; eggs turn tan before hatching

Chrysalis: Dark grey or light tan with pink-tipped points, hanging from twigs, often many close together

Lifespan: Up to 1 year

Minimum butterfly body temperature needed to fly: 27°C (81°F), usually over 33°C (91°F)

Range: Throughout Ontario; also in all other provinces and territories

First appearance of butterflies: Probably 80–100 million years ago

Other butterflies that hibernate as adults: Milbert's tortoiseshells, Compton tortoiseshells, question marks, gray commas, green commas, hop merchants, satyre angle wings, occasionally black swallowtails and red admirals

Number of butterfly species resident or regular migrants in Ontario: 138

Number of butterfly and skipper species worldwide: About 4,500

Also see: Willows. *Up North:* Yellow-bellied Sapsucker

River delta, Siberia to the northern reaches of Europe, and occasionally Britain, where they're highly prized by collectors and called Camberwell beauties. Mourning cloaks journey up to 70 kilometres (43 miles).

The butterflies come out of hibernation for good around late April or early May. Their prime directive during their one or two remaining months of life is to seek each other out and mate. Eggs are commonly laid around the twig tips of willows, where the butterflies gather to sip catkin nectar, and on aspens and birch, where they lap up sap from holes bored by yellow-bellied sapsuckers.

Insect wings may have evolved from what were initially solar panels

Mourning cloak caterpillars hatch in June, just in time to munch upon fully unfolded new leaves, around which, working together, they build protective webs. They're so gregarious that when threatened the spiny-backed grazers rise together on their hind prolegs and do a menacing Watusi. Even after they enter the pupal stage, if a metamorphosing mourning cloak perceives danger outside its chrysalis, it begins swaying inside, setting off its siblings encased nearby until they are all rattling their shells against the branches and the neighbourhood is rocking with the sound and furry of the shaking pupae.

The band breaks up when the butterflies burst free in July. Many butterfly species live just a matter of days or weeks once they spread their wings. But most northern mourning cloaks must fly through a whole summer and sleep through winter before they're ready to breed. If summer is hot and dry, they go dormant, but resume fluttering through September and into October, building up fat for the winter. Their unique yellow wing trim, bright when freshly transformed, fades with time to white, becoming worn down to almost nothing by the end of their long lives.

CANADIAN
TIGER SWALLOWTAIL
Yellow Beauties of June

I N CULTURES AROUND the world, the ethereal beauty of butterflies has stirred the imagination. The ancient Greeks used the same word, *psyche*, for both the soul and butterflies. The fluttering insect represented immortality because it was transformed and resurrected from a deathlike state in its chrysalis. An Ojibway story says butterflies were created after the first humans were born – a pair of twins. The children showed no interest in learning to walk, so the Great Spirit told their benefactor, Nanabush, to collect a pile of colourful stones in the western mountains and throw them in the air. The stones became butterflies, followed Nanabush back to the twins and, by staying just beyond their grasp, enticed them to sit up, walk and run for the first time.

Among North America's most familiar butterflies, the tiger swallowtail has always cheered observers with its black-striped yellow wings and double-pointed rear fins. It was one of the first creatures recorded by the English in the New World, painted during a 1587 expedition to the ill-fated Roanoke Island colony off North Carolina. In Ontario woodlands, the tigers appear from late May through early July, everywhere there are open spaces and

Wingspan: 6.5–8 cm (2.5–3 in)
Wingspan of Ontario's largest butterfly: 10–15.5 cm (4–6 in) giant swallowtail
Wingspan of world's largest butterfly: Up to 30 cm (12 in), New Guinea's Queen Alexandra's birdwing, member of swallowtail family
Wingspan of world's smallest butterfly: 1–2 cm (0.4–0.8 in), pygmy blue butterfly
Tiger swallowtail markings: Yellow wings with partial black stripes and borders, blue and orange spots along border near tail; body dark brown or black on top, yellow with black stripe on sides; caterpillars are lime green with a pair of large yellow or orange "eyespots" with black "pupils"
Caterpillar length: Up to 5 cm (2 in)

Alias: Canadian tiger swallowtail, Canadian swallowtail, *le papillon tigre du Canada, Papilio canadensis*

Preferred habitat: Meadows and edges of deciduous and mixed forest

Food: Caterpillars eat leaves of yellow birch, aspen, black cherry; butterflies drink nectar of milkweed flowers, day lilies and other flowers, and fluids from carrion and animal droppings

Eggs: Laid scattered apart, green at first, turning greenish yellow with reddish-brown specks

Chrysalis: Light brown with blotches of green and black, up to 3 cm (1.2 in) long

Lifespan: Up to 13 months

Predators: Birds, mice, shrews, spiders, ants, parasitic wasps and flies

Range: Throughout Ontario; also all other provinces and territories

Number of Ontario swallowtail species: 6

Number of swallowtail species worldwide: 534, mostly in tropics

Also see: Yellow Birch, Chokecherry, Twinflower. *Up North:* Snowshoe Hare

forest edges. Like their largely tropical swallowtail kin, they characteristically flutter their wings while drinking nectar from flowers, which they sample first with taste buds on their feet.

Groups of swallowtails are often seen sipping water from muddy puddles and wet ground, especially near roadsides, to obtain salt. They also visit animal droppings and corpses to suck up amino acids. Most of the imbibers are males, who concentrate salt and proteins into their sperm capsules, or spermatophores. Upon fluttering behind a butterfly maid and convincing her to land and join abdomens, the yellow charmers provide, with their sperm, a rich nutrient loading for her fertilized eggs. Females then look for suitable nursery sites, usually leaves up to 2.5 metres (eight feet) high on the south side of yellow birch, aspen or black cherry trees.

Producing only one generation a year, the butterflies unfortunately die after early summer, leaving only their crawling or dormant young behind. Hatching soon after the eggs are laid, swallowtail caterpillars are at first disguised as tiny black-and-white bird droppings. As they grow, they turn green, blending with the leaves, save for two black-dotted orange or yellow spots on the high hunch behind their tiny heads, giving the impression of the face of a green snake. If that doesn't fool predators, the future tigers pull out their secret weapon, a forked appendage, called the osmeterium, that pops out from behind the head and emits a smell that ants, spiders and parasitic wasps find most disagreeable.

In their later youth, the caterpillars keep mostly out of sight, often spinning silk pads over the upper sides of leaves to make them curl up, creating solar-heated homes up to 3.5°C (5.4°F) warmer than the surrounding air. The warmth speeds their development, and sometime between mid-June and early July, they turn brown and become inactive as they begin to pupate. They remain entombed inside their chrysalis for 10 or 11 months, until emerging as butterflies in the latter half of May.

FISH
(AND AQUATIC COMPANIONS)

S INCE THE GLACIERS *receded about 10,000 years ago, the Canadian Shield has been a land of cool, dark lakes and streams. From the time humans first ventured into the region, the waterways have been the focus of life, providing a means of travel, sustenance and recreation. Today, pickerel and pike are still practically cultural institutions in central Ontario. From the resplendent sunfish of the shallows to the whitefish and burbot of the deep, the watery world holds a host of fabled and fascinating inhabitants. Average weights and sizes of species featured here are given for Ontario's inland waters, rather than for the Great Lakes or farther south, where the fish tend to be larger. We've also included entries on freshwater clams and mussels, and on the vast array of plankton which, as in the sea, forms the base of the food chain in lakes, rivers and streams.*

BURBOT
Ontario's Freshwater Cod

THE BURBOT is an Ontario fish after a wayward Maritimer's heart. It's the only cod to forsake the sea and live permanently in fresh water. Inland anglers are thrown off by its unusual eel-tailed appearance, slimy smooth feel and the classic cod barbel hanging from its chin. They traditionally shun the fish – despite accidentally catching large numbers while ice fishing – in the old days even stacking their unwanted corpses to form windbreaks. The waste is considerable, since burbot is actually quite tasty and contains cod liver oil, high in vitamins D and A.

Like other cod, burbot are denizens of cold water. In summertime, they keep to deep lake waters by day, mingling with lake trout and whitefish. At night, they swim to the shallows to binge on crayfish, perch and even fish their own size to satisfy their widely renowned appetites.

In the frozen stillness of winter nights, beneath the ice just offshore, burbot throng for their most important engagement of the year. Any time between January and March, males begin congregating nightly in sandy or gravel-bottomed bays and rivers in 30 to 120 centimetres (one to four feet) of water, or over slightly deeper shoals. Females join them a few nights later, sparking mating free-for-alls of up to a dozen fish in a single swirling, orgasmic mass. The fertilized eggs fall to the bottom and hatch between late February and June, depending on the temperature.

Average adult length: 30–70 cm (12–28 in)

Average adult weight: 0.9–3.1 kg (2–7 lb)

Largest ever caught: 1.2 m (47 in) long, 34 kg (75 lb)

Markings: Usually brown, tan or yellow on top, with sides mottled dark brown or black; sometimes completely dark brown or black

Alias: Freshwater cod, ling, lawyer, maria, methy, lush, American burbot, eelpout, *la lotte, Lota lota*

Preferred habitat: Deep lakes

Maximum depth inhabited: 213 m (700 ft)

Food: Mayfly nymphs and other aquatic insects, crayfish, molluscs, perch, sculpins, sticklebacks, deep-water chubs, ciscoes, whitefish, pickerel

Clutch: 45,000–2 million eggs

Age at sexual maturity: 2–4 years

Maximum lifespan: 15 years

Range: Throughout Ontario; also in western provinces and the territories, Quebec, New Brunswick and Labrador

BROWN BULLHEAD CATFISH
Super-sensitive Air Gulper

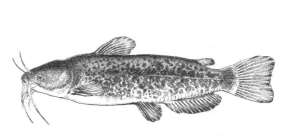

IF ITS UNNERVINGLY scale-less skin, sharp spines and sour puss aren't enough to throw you, the brown bullhead has the ability to croak in distress when pulled from the water. The enigmatic, sedentary catfish of murky shallows also sometimes breathes air, eats anything and is a devoted family fish. Hiding by day beneath rocks, overhanging banks or inside hollow logs, it hunts and scavenges at night. Its tiny dim eyes are of little use in a dark, weedy world. Instead, the slimy bottom-feeder feels its way about and probes the silty sediments for food with highly sensitive fleshy barbels that sprout from its face like the long whiskers of a wise old cat.

While it might not be the most charming occupant of the water, the catfish certainly has the most taste. Several hundred thousand taste buds line its entire body, especially concentrated along the barbels, making the bullhead's very existence a continuous taste sensation. The fish, snapping up food from the water as well as on the bottom, can pinpoint the source of flavours flowing to it from more than five metres (16 feet) away. At the same time, the bullhead's highly sensitive nostrils pick up the individual scents of every other catfish in the neighbourhood, identifying them as friend or foe, mate or rival.

Relationships are important in the sophisticated ways of the catfish. Like few others in Ontario waters, bullhead mates maintain a close bond and make very caring parents. Waiting for the water to warm to about 21°C (70°F), they usually mate during daylight in June, after one or both partners sweep out a rounded nest depression in the mud with their fins. They spawn many times, first running their barbels over one another, mutually stimulating half a million taste buds, then releasing eggs and

Average adult length: 20–36 cm (8–14 in)
Average weight: 340–450 g (12–16 oz)
Maximum length: 48 cm (19 in)
Call: Croaks loudly, when threatened, by vibrating internal gas bladder, a gas-filled sac used to regulate buoyancy
Markings: Almost black to olive or yellowish-brown back, lighter and mottled on sides, white or pale yellow below
Weaponry: Single sharp spine on each of the side, front top and front bottom fins
Alias: Common catfish, common bullhead, northern brown bullhead, mudcat, hornpout, minister, *la barbotte brune*, *Ictalurus nebulosus*
Preferred habitat: Warm, weedy, mud- or sand-bottomed shallows of small lakes, quiet bays, slow streams, ponds
Food: Aquatic insects, plankton, crayfish, snails, small fish, eggs, leeches, worms, carrion, organic waste, algae, vegetation, seeds

Nests: Rounded depression, a little wider than length of fish, in mud, sand or between roots, 15 cm (6 in) to about a metre (3.3 ft) beneath surface, most often shaded and sheltered by or beneath a large rock, stump or tree along calm lakeshore pockets and creek mouths; also sometimes inside hollow logs, stumps, stream banks or dockside tires

Clutch: 1,000–13,000 pale-yellow eggs, in a large, sticky, gooey mass

Incubation period: 6–10 days

Age at sexual maturity: Usually 3 years

Maximum lifespan: 8 years

Predators: Pike, pickerel, muskies, sauger, bowfins (dogfish), osprey, otters

Electric catfish: An African species, sacred in ancient Egypt, can stun humans with shocks of up to 800 volts

Catfish Godzilla: Japanese folklore attributes earthquakes to the thrashings of a giant catfish held down by a magic rock in mud below the Earth

Catfish Row: Nickname for poor black neighbourhoods in southern United States; catfish once commonly caught by slaves and poor whites, now a major item in Southern cuisine, source of phrase "There's more than one way to skin a cat"

Range: Southern Ontario to Wawa and Kapuskasing; also in Saskatchewan, Manitoba, Quebec, New Brunswick and Nova Scotia

Number of catfish species native to Ontario: 7

sperm into the nest. For a week or so afterwards, they guard, fan and frequently rearrange the clutch.

Even after the eggs hatch, bullheads stay with their rice-grain-sized young, which remain for about seven days in the nest, absorbing their yolk sacs. Then, for several weeks afterwards, parents herd their huge families around in dark, fluid swarms that are often clearly visible in the shallows. Siblings split up after their parents leave, but catfish may gather in schools throughout their lives.

While they're still quite small, the black catfish fry, with their wide heads, look like tadpoles. This is appropriate, given their almost-amphibious nature. Thriving in warm, sometimes even stagnant water, where oxygen levels are low, bullheads can gulp air if needed. They can stay alive out of water considerably longer than other fish, and are far more tolerant of pollution than most. The walking catfish of Asia, an exotic pet that has spread into the wild in southern Florida, can squirm overland for up to 12 hours from one stream or pond to another or burrow into the mud during dry seasons.

Though there are many catfish species, only brown bullheads are common throughout central Ontario. Two much-smaller catfish found on the periphery of the Canadian Shield, the stonecat and tadpole madtom, are no larger than nine centimetres (3.5 inches) long and notable for being the only fish in the province with venom glands at the base of the fin spines behind their gills. Their prick is as painful as a wasp or bee sting. Bullheads, too, erect fin spikes when threatened. Though lacking poison, their coating of bacteria-laden slime can cause burning pain. Native peoples used the spines as awls for hides and as sewing needles, which have been found at 3,000-year-old archaeological sites on Lake Huron.

CLAMS & MUSSELS
Sedentary Filter-feeders

WHILE CLAMS and mussles evoke images of briny seashores, Ontario's lakes, rivers, creeks and wetlands have their own smattering of the hard-shelled filter-feeders. Mussels are the more conspicuous, with the largest of central Ontario's half-dozen common species reaching up to 16 centimetres (6.4 inches) long. Most live at depths between 30 centimetres (one foot) and two metres (6.6 feet), though the high-domed shells of fat mucket mussels (illustrated) are common in finger-deep water just off riverbanks.

The region's more than two dozen clams, on the other hand, are much smaller, most just a centimetre (0.4 inches) long or less. They dwell anywhere from a few centimetres to many metres beneath the water. One group, called fingernail clams – which actually look more like toenails – live amid the submerged vegetation or sediments of rivers, lakes or ponds, while the even-smaller pea clams generally keep to the mud and fine sand of lake bottoms.

Lying half-buried underwater, mussels and clams set up shop by simply opening their shells slightly and flushing water through their systems, siphoning oxygen to breathe and bits of plankton for food. Two strong muscles attached to each shell near the rear hinge contract to snap the protective covers shut whenever needed. The molluscs dig themselves down or, rarely, move short distances by extending a central muscular lobe, called a "foot," forward into the mud and then contracting the rest of their body so that it's pulled towards the foot.

Mussels and clams do most of their real travelling when they are very young. Developing for up to nearly a year inside a special brood pouch within their mother's gills, microscopic mussel young are called glochidia, from

Mussel word origin: From Latin *musculus*, "little mouse," because the dark, hunched shells beneath the water reminded early observers of crouching mice

Bivalve sex: Males release sperm into the water to be filtered out by any female nearby; some species produce both eggs and sperm

Mussel markings: Outer shells of most usually a shade of off-brown, but may be yellowish, greenish to almost black; inner shells can be white, pink, purple, bluish or yellow

Best buttons: Smooth, colourful, often iridescent inner lining of freshwater mussel shells, called "mother-of-pearl," once commonly used to make shiny buttons

Clam markings: Outer shells off-white, yellowish or brown

Smallest Ontario freshwater clam: Perforated pea clam, maximum length 1.7 mm (0.07 in)

Largest Ontario freshwater

mussel: White heal-spitter,
19 cm (7.5 in) long
Food: Planktonic algae, protozoa, bacteria, organic waste
Growth rings: The thickest,
peaked portion is the oldest
part of a shell. Periodic secretions of liquid calcium carbon-
ate harden along the edges,
forming new layers that show
up as distinct ridges on the
exteriors of many species
Mussel lifespan: 6–100 years
Fingernail clam lifespan: Up to
8 years
Pea clam lifespan: Most just up
to 1 year
Predators: Otters, raccoons,
mink, muskrats, sunfish,
trout, whitefish and other
fish, ducks, ravens, gulls
Edibility: Freshwater mussels are
edible but accumulate any
pesticides and other pollutants
Appearance of first clams: More
than 400 million years ago
Clam and mussel range:
Throughout most of Ontario;
also in all other provinces and
territories
Number of freshwater mussel
species native to Ontario: 40
Number of freshwater clam
species native to Ontario: 31
Number of species introduced to
Ontario: 3 clams, 2 mussels
Zebra mussels: Native to Caspian
and Black Sea area, discovered in Lake St. Clair in 1988,
probably released from
foreign freighter bilge water,
has spread to the Muskoka,
Kawarthas and Rideau lakes;
free-swimming microscopic
hatchlings become tiny clams,
sticking *en masse* to any hard
surface

the Greek for "arrow point," because of their shape when their tiny shells are agape. The mussels leave home in the stream of their mother's waste water when most are still microscopic, and within a few days must clamp onto the fins or gills of a passing fish or die. The lucky few take up residence as parasites in the fish's gills. Usually after several weeks of steady blood-nutrient meals and travelling far and wide with their hosts, the mini-mussels bail out and settle down to adult life in the muck.

Fingernail and pea clams also hitch rides, but as accidental tourists rather than parasites. They're so small after leaving their mother's brood pouch that they're picked up on the feathers or muddy feet of water fowl or even the legs of large insects, such as dragonflies. Freshwater clams are so easily spread that many Ontario species are found as far away as Australia and Hawaii. Ontario's most common, the aptly named ubiquitous pea clam, is the world's most widespread mollusc, found on every continent. One species, Harrington's fingernail, is so used to air transport that it specializes in small bodies of water that dry up for part of the year.

The white shell of another tiny clam, the megis, was the symbol and source of power of the Ojibway's sacred Midewiwin Society. It is said to have appeared on a number of occasions as a brilliant light in the water. Though a marine clam of the East Coast, its shells were brought inland through trade, as were quahog shells, used to make the cylindrical beads of widely prized wampum belts. Clam shells are, in fact, one of the world's oldest items of trade and have been used for human ornamentation for at least 30,000 years. The abundance of shell piles excavated at sites of human activity up to 120,000 years old also attests to the importance of molluscs as a staple for early bands of people living along coasts and rivers.

PICKEREL
Ontario's Favourite Game Fish

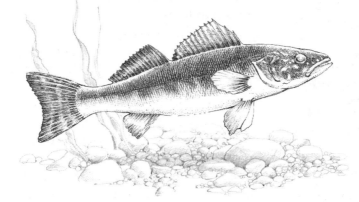

A T INNUMERABLE SHINDIGS across most of central and northern Ontario, usually on the first exuberant night of the Victoria Day weekend, angling celebrants cast off at midnight to inaugurate the much-anticipated pickerel fishing season. It is the most commonly caught game fish and, therefore, the most loved. Pickerel thrives on deep Canadian Shield lakes like nowhere else and is an eager biter. Best of all, for those of the rod and reel, the golden-hued whoppers are as tasty as perch but considerably larger, and put up a spirited fight before surrendering to fate as a fillet.

Pickerel are, in fact, really gargantuan perch, the biggest members of the family, though they're sometimes confused with a couple of similarly named pike species. Indeed, the word "pickerel" means "little pike." The name was probably bestowed on the predatory fish because of their fair size, ample jaws and big canines, which they love to sink into their smaller relatives.

When the sun sets, loose schools of pickerel go on roving picnics, searching out yellow perch and other fish slumbering amid underwater debris and weeds. They scan the darkness with large, light-sensitive eyes that shine orange-red in the beam of a flashlight, like those of a deer

Average adult length: 35–51 cm (14–20 in)
Average weight: 450–2,500 g (1–5.5 lb)
Largest caught in Ontario: 107 cm (42 in) long, 10.6 kg (23 lb, 9 oz), on the Moon River, Parry Sound District
World record: 104 cm (41 in) long, 11.2 kg (25 lb), caught in Tennessee
Markings: Variable, most often back and sides olive to dark brown flecked with yellow, with dark vertical bands on smaller fish; bottom white, sometimes tinted yellow; lower tail fin tipped white, black spot on spiny dorsal fin; cloudy silver eyes
Alias: Walleye, wall-eyed pickerel, yellow walleye, yellow pickerel, pike-perch, yellow pike, walleye pike, dory, glass eye, marble eye, *le doré jaune, Stizostedion vitreum*
Peak activity periods: Sunset to 11:00 P.M. and 3:00 A.M. to sunrise

Preferred habitat: Usually around 15 m (50 ft) deep in lakes and rivers, often on shoals, venturing to both shallower and deeper waters to feed at night

Maximum depth found at: 21 m (69 ft)

Home range: Usually wander over 5–10 km (3–6 mi) in schools, but migrate much farther to spawn

Food: Perch, sunfish, suckers, ciscoes, minnows, whitefish, burbot, bass, catfish, darters, rock bass, sticklebacks, crayfish, frogs, mudpuppies, snails, mayflies and other insects, rarely small rodents; eat each other when other fish wanting

Clutch: 25,000–600,000 eggs

Incubation period: 12–18 days

Hatchlings: 6–9 mm (0.02–0.04 in) long

Fry mortality: Up to 99%

Age at sexual maturity: Males 2–4 years, females 3–6 years

Lifespan: Usually about 7 years for adults, up to 20 years

Predators: Pike, muskies, osprey, otters; young eaten by perch, sauger, older pickerel and other fish

Range: Throughout Ontario, but mostly absent from highland areas, such as Algonquin Park; also in the Prairie provinces, Quebec, New Brunswick and the Northwest Territories

Number of Ontario perch-family species: 15

Recent extinctions: Blue pickerel, once one of the most widely caught fish on Lake Erie, unseen since the 1960s

Number of perch-family species worldwide: 150–160

Also see: Pike, White Sucker, Plankton. *Up North:* Perch

or a cat. Up close, the eyes have a smoky look, responsible for the pickerel's other common name, "walleye." In traditional rural parlance, a blind animal was called walleyed because its cloudy eyes stare outward in different directions – the opposite of cross-eyed.

Pickerel are usually caught at dusk and dawn, or on an overcast day or in murky waters. Sunlight drives them to the shade of thick vegetation or sunken logs or rocks, where they themselves may be vulnerable to predation by their chief nemesis and competitor, the northern pike.

Throughout the winter, pickerel continue to prowl through near-blackness beneath the ice. Once the ice breaks apart on rivers in April, males cruise upstream to boulder-strewn riffles, rapids, waterfalls and dams. The opposite sex gradually joins them, and night spawning begins when water temperatures reach 7° to 9°C (45° to 48°F). Pickerel-runs on tributaries of large lakes may last three weeks, peaking with hundreds of thrashing, spawning fish visible along a single stretch of frothy white water. Females, noticeably larger than their partners, usually release all their eggs in one night and leave, while males stick around to mate again, lying low during the day just downstream from spawning grounds.

The sticky fertilized eggs settle downstream on rocky beds or sand, kept clear of vegetation by the fast current. Some eggs also develop on shallow lake shoals, where pickerel also spawn. Tiny fry hatch a couple of weeks later, but stay put to absorb their yolk sacs, swimming towards the surface to dine on plankton after another 10 to 15 days. Perch take the opportunity to pick off as many of the potential menaces as possible while they're still small and vulnerable. By autumn the survivors are about 10 centimetres (four inches) long and are back near the bottom, eating aquatic insect larvae and other invertebrates.

PIKE

Stuff of Fishy Stories

COMMANDING FEAR and respect in the aquatic world, the mighty pike is the big game icon of clear, weedy waters across most of Canada to the Arctic Circle. With treacherous teeth set in a huge pair of jaws, the long, lunging, barrel-chested beast takes the last bite in the proverbial chain of big fish eating littler fish. Ducklings, snakes and young muskrats are also snapped up for good measure. Though the fearsome fish commonly weighs in at a couple of kilograms, a few wily old codgers can reach eight kilograms (18 pounds).

Monster-pike-and-angler duels are the stuff of fishy stories stretching back into the reaches of time. Native groups of the Yukon and Alaska told tales of remote demon lakes where giant pike could swallow a man whole, along with his canoe. Pike are also native to Asia and Europe, which were rife with stories of 45-kilogram (100-pound) alligatorlike pike pulling mules and maidens into watery graves. Angling guides of a few centuries ago claimed that pike lived up to 200 years and were spontaneously formed from aquatic vegetation and ooze heated by the sun.

For much of the time, pike do seem to be one with their weedy surroundings. Largely sedentary creatures, they hide in lairs within shallow beds of submerged plants, pickerelweed or sedges, where they wait in ambush. When

Average adult length: 45–75 cm (18–30 in)

Average weight: 1–2 kg (2.2–4.4 lb)

Ontario record: 19 kg (42 lb), caught near Kenora

World record: 23.8 kg (53 lb), 129.5 cm (4 ft 3 in), caught in Ireland

Ontario muskie record: 29.5 kg (65 lb), 147 cm (4 ft 10 in)

World muskie record: 31.5 kg (70 lb), 1.6 m (5 ft 4 in) long, caught in St. Lawrence River

Markings: Green, olive or almost brown on top, shading to lighter green on sides, lined with yellowish spots and flecked with gold; white or creamy belly; gold, squiggly lines on cheeks; bright-yellow eyes; green or yellow fins with dark splotches; young have wavy white or yellow vertical bars

Alias: Northern pike, great northern pike, Canadian pike,

jackfish, jack, great northern pickerel, *le grand brochet, Esox lucius* and some 40 other local names

Pike name origin: Originally pikefish, from Old English *pic*, meaning "pointed thing," also the origin of "peak" and tool "pick"

Preferred habitat: Weedy, warm, clear waters, from shallows to 4.5 m (15 ft) deep, in quiet bays, small lakes and slow rivers

Greatest depth found at: More than 30 m (100 ft)

Food: 90% fish, including perch, catfish, shiners, bass and pickerel; also frogs and crayfish, occasionally ducklings, snakes, mice and young muskrats

Clutch: Average 32,000 sticky, clear, amber eggs, maximum 595,000; each about 2.5 mm (0.1 in) wide; about half are infertile

Portion of eggs yielding fry that survive more than a few weeks: 0.2% in one study

Incubation period: Usually 12–14 days

Hatchling length: 6–8 mm (0.2–0.4 in)

Length by end of 1st summer: Most about 15–20 cm (6–8 in)

Age at sexual maturity: Males 2–3 years, females 2–4 years

Maximum lifespan: 13 years in southern Canada, 26 years in far north; females live longest

Predators: Osprey, eagles and bears take small adults, usually while spawning; herons, kingfishers, loons,

something comes within reach, they thrust out with lightning speed, just as the similarly built and sharp-toothed barracuda hunts in the sea. With a fish clamped in its jaws, a pike returns to its private quarters to swallow the meal headfirst. Fish approximately one-third of a pike's own length are preferred, though pike are found with more than two dozen perch in their stomachs.

Pike move a little deeper during the peak of summer heat and also for the winter, when they stay active but eat a little less. As soon as the ice starts melting from shorelines, they begin journeys to spawning grounds, usually just a couple of kilometres (about a mile) upstream. Hundreds of pike may make a single run, which lasts about a week. Mating takes place during the day in 10 to 45 centimetres (four to 18 inches) of water, often over spring-flooded banks of grass and shrubs or on marshy lake margins. Females may spend several days periodically releasing batches of five to 60 eggs as they vibrate alongside one or two milt-spewing partners, all thrashing their tails after each episode to scatter the roe.

Sticking to submerged branches and stalks of grass, eggs and immobile hatchlings are at the mercy of receding waters, late cold spells and caviar-loving predators. Surviving fry leave spawning areas several weeks after hatching, quickly switching from a diet of waterfleas and insect larvae to attacking baby fish hatched around the same time as them, such as white suckers. A three-centimetre (1.2-inch) pikelet will even fratricidally dine on one of its own just a half-centimetre smaller.

Because they hatch about two weeks earlier, pike fry also tend to eat and out-compete **muskellunge** young. Grownup muskies, however, average about half as long again and at least twice as heavy as northern pike. The two fish occasionally interbreed, producing offspring called tiger muskies.

Sporting dark vertical bars along their sides, muskellunge are most abundant in the Kawarthas, and are found along the rest of the Trent-Severn Waterway, the Rideau Lakes, Lake Nipissing, and the Ottawa, French and Mattawa rivers. They mostly lurk towards the edge of the weeds or along rocky shoals. The water wolves are revered as the greatest of freshwater fishing challenges. In waters where either fish is common, experienced rod-handlers catch an average of three pike every two hours. The average muskie comes with a hundred hours of quasi-religious perseverance. One storied metre-long muskie, nicknamed Moby Dick, eluded anglers on the Trent River throughout the 1950s and '60s, winning epic battles that lasted up to seven hours.

Ontario's greatest fish of all, however, is the **lake sturgeon**, which can reach up to 2.4 metres (eight feet) long and weigh 140 kilograms (308 pounds). Sturgeon are ancient fish, whose kind first appeared some 138 million years ago. With a scaleless, armoured body of pointy, dinosaurlike ridges, the grey or olive behemoths may be the source of most lake-monster stories across Canada. They are scavengers, feeding off deep-water bottoms with vacuumlike mouths and short barbels on their snouts, like catfish. Though caught commercially by the millions in the 19th century, they are rare today, largely limited to the Great Lakes, the Trent-Severn, Lake Nipissing and the Ottawa River. Growing slowly, sturgeon don't spawn until they are 14 to 23 years old, and can live more than 150 years.

mergansers, otters, mink, snapping turtles, perch, minnows, dragonfly nymphs, water tigers and pike themselves eat young; silver lamprey parasitize but rarely kill adults

The Mannheim Hoax: The famous Emperor's Pike, whose skeleton was long held at Mannheim Cathedral in Germany, was 5.8 m (19 ft) long. When caught in 1497 it reportedly weighed 247 kg (545 lb) and bore a ring on its gills stating it was released by Emperor Friederick II 267 years before. The skeleton was later discovered to contain the vertebrae of half a dozen fish joined together

Privy etiquette: Studies show fathead minnows produce "alarm pheromones" to alert their fellows to danger, and which show up in the waste of pike that have eaten minnows. Evolution may have favoured fastidious pikes that dump their loads off-territory, thereby not giving their lairs away

Age of oldest pike-family fossil: 62 million years

Range: All of Ontario, but rare in headwater regions such as the Haliburton and Algonquin highlands and in the Kawarthas; also in all other provinces and territories except the Maritimes

Pike fishing season: Third Saturday in May to Mar. 31 in most of central Ontario, virtually year round north of Lake Nipissing and the Spanish River

PLANKTON
Vast Realm of Tiniest Creatures

Number of rotifers per litre
(0.9 qt) of lake water:
Commonly up to 1,000,
rarely up to 5,000

Plankton word origin: From the
Greek *planktos*, meaning
"drifting"

Protozoa word origin: From the
Greek *protos*, meaning "first,"
and *zoia*, meaning "animals"

Waterflea length: 0.2–18 mm
(0.008–0.8 in)

Copepod length: Less than
0.5–3 mm (0.01–0.12 in)

Rotifer length: 0.05–3 mm
(0.002–0.12 in)

Protozoan length: Vast majority
microscopic, some ocean
species up to 15 cm (6 in)

Largest planktonic animals: The
North Atlantic jellyfish *Cyanea
arctica* can be more than 1.8
m (6 ft) wide, with tentacles
up to 36 m (118 ft) long

Freshwater jellyfish: About 2 cm
(0.8 in) wide, almost transparent; very rare in Ontario
but has been found in shallow
waters of Lake Nipissing, the
French River and Parry
Sound, probably introduced
from China

Rotifer swimming speed:
12–150 cm/min (5–59
in/min), some can "jump" 5
cm (2 in) in a second

Protozoan swimming speed: 1–6
cm/min (0.4–2.4 in/min)

Rotifer lifespan: Average 8 days
at 20°C (68°F), up to about
25 days

Copepod lifespan: 1 to several
months

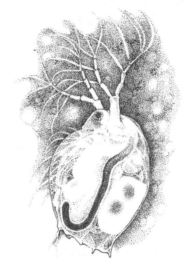

A DARK, MOONLESS night on a perfectly calm northern lake is the ideal setting for beholding the sky's limitless multitude of heavenly lights. It's also the best time to gaze downward and, in the beam of a flashlight, witness the incredible array of life teeming just below the surface of the lake. With sunset on summer evenings, clouds of waterfleas (illustrated) and other planktonic animals rise up to feed on microscopic algae, bacteria and protozoa floating near the top of the water. The darkest evenings afford the most protection from fish and other predators, emboldening the tiny creatures to come very close to the surface, where the eating is best. Though just barely visible, waterfleas are among the largest of untold billions of organisms that support almost everything else in every lake, river, pond and stream.

Like oceans, though not to the same degree, bodies of fresh water abound with plankton, which includes any free-floating or weak-swimming aquatic life-form largely at the mercy of the current. It's virtually impossible to fill a canteen with lake water without taking in many of the little beasts and microscopic plants, though they're much less numerous farther from shore. The comparatively large waterfleas, or *Cladocera*, are rarely more than four millimetres (0.2 inches) long and usually possess transparent shells, shaped like squat Frisbees. Related to crayfish and shrimp, they "jump" like a flea through the water with each sweep of their long, branched antennae, and use their four to six pairs of spindly legs, beating about five times per second, to draw algae, known as phytoplankton, to their mouths. With a single compound eye, they detect light, colour and movement. Mixed liberally with waterfleas are many narrow micro-crustaceans called copepods, measuring a millimetre or two (0.04 to 0.08 inches), with long, whiplike antennae and tails.

Rotifers can reproduce when as young as two days old

Predatory waterfleas and copepods feast on even tinier planktonic animals called rotifers, most only a tenth to a half of a millimetre (0.02 inches) long. Sometimes accounting for half or more of the zooplankton (planktonic animals) in a lake, slow-swimming rotifers are one of the most important foods for baby fish, insect larvae and other invertebrates. Living no more than a few weeks, usually eaten even sooner, rotifers can reproduce when as young as two days old. Rising water temperatures trigger population explosions among the transparent bag- or cylinder-shaped micro-creatures. Two rings of constantly beating, hairlike fibres around gaping rotifer mouths appear to rotate, giving the animals their name. The fibres, called cilia, flush water through the rotifer's body – up to 1,000 times its total volume every hour – allowing it to filter out algae, bacteria and other microscopic bits of food. During the day, when more fish and other predators are active, the rotifers fan out a metre or two (3.3 to 6.6 feet) farther down.

Included on the rotifer menu are members of the vast realm of protozoa, multicellular life-forms that feature

Rotifer age of sexual maturity: As little as 2 days

Waterflea clutch: Depending on species, 1 to hundreds of eggs laid within mother's shell. Young hatch and leave shell just before mother moults and starts another set of eggs in newly formed carapace

Copepod clutch: 2–50 eggs

Planktonic sex: Waterfleas and rotifers are usually female, laying eggs without mating. As daylight grows shorter or if food becomes scarce, they produce males, which mate with females to create genetically invigorated, fertilized eggs that can remain dormant for years, even freezing or drying out, until favourable conditions return

Platonic sex: By definition impossible

Transportation: Dormant eggs and protozoan cysts may fall to water's bottom, float with the current, become airborne in the wind, stick to birds' feet or animal fur or be eaten and passed through an animal's digestive system unharmed

Protozoan cysts: Protective coverings formed by many species during food digestion, cell division or at times of food shortage

Protozoan weaponry: Some can shoot up to 8,000 "darts," others have poisonous tentacles or can release toxic substances

Protozoan sex: Some species exchange genetic material before cell division, sometimes achieved by two special "gamete" protozoa first fusing together

Protozoan predators: Aquatic insect larvae, micro-crustaceans, rotifers, other protozoans and possibly fish fry

Micro-crustacean predators: Fish, aquatic insects and their larvae, leeches

Protozoan-caused diseases: Malaria, dysentery, African sleeping sickness, beaver fever

Discovery of protozoa: 1674, by Dutch microscopist Antony van Leeuwenhoek, father of protozoology and bacteriology

Number of known waterflea species worldwide: About 400

Number of known copepod species worldwide: More than 7,500, mostly in salt water

Number of known freshwater crustacean species worldwide: About 4,000

Number of known crustacean species worldwide: About 32,000

Number of known rotifer species worldwide: About 2,000

Number of known protozoa species worldwide: More than 30,000

Also see: Mayflies, Midges, Clams & Mussels, White Sucker. *Up North:* Algae, Lakes

organisms as different from each other as a duck is from a jellyfish. They are neither plants nor animals, though many protozoa move about with tail-like "flagella" *and* capture energy through photosynthesis. Others, called amoebas, are little more than blobs, oozing their bodies in one direction or another. Unlike most multicellular animals, or "metazoans," protozoans largely reproduce by splitting in two rather than sexually reproducing. Species colonizing masses of algae and bacteria are thought to have evolved into the first metazoans between a billion and 800 million years ago.

Protozoans eat by enveloping their food and absorbing its nutrients. As the biggest consumers of bacteria in their ecosystem, protozoa are a vital link in passing on vast amounts of carbon and nutrients in the aquatic food chain. Depending on its size, a protozoan eats anywhere from dozens to hundreds of thousands of bacteria an hour. Bacteria-eating protozoans are also the workhorses of sewage treatment plants. The larger species tend to be either algae grazers or predators of smaller protozoans. Others are carrion feeders, parasites or even harmless organisms living inside human digestive systems.

In open waters where it's too deep for rooted plants, most planktonic life exists in the top several metres, where there's enough light for phytoplankon to photosyn-thesize. Most nutrients, however, come from lake-bottom sediments, which are stirred up only twice a year, during the spring and autumn turnovers, when a lake's waters reach a uniform temperature and circulate freely. During the summer, the upper layer warms significantly, but the bottom remains cold and ceases to mix with the heated water above. During winter, ice cuts the water off from the wind, minimizing circulation. After flourishing on nutrients brought by the spring and fall turnovers, plank-tonic algae, and most other micro-organisms with it, dwindle in numbers through winter and summer.

WHITE SUCKER
Big, Lumbering Bottom-dweller

"LOOK AT THE SNOUT on that sucker!" The expression is apropos for the big, lumbering fish that scours lake and river bottoms, vacuuming up its meals. Fleshy, overhanging lips and a jowly face give the white sucker the look of a portly, bewigged aristocrat at the court of King George III. With its toothless mouth placed at the bottom of its ample snout, the fish simply drops its lips and sucks in minute bloodworms and micro-crustaceans by the tens of thousands. Comblike teeth in its throat shred the food with each gulp.

Bottom-feeding being a little-respected profession, suckers are generally looked down on by anglers, some-times even wrongly accused of depleting trout popula-tions by eating their eggs. In truth, the broad-bodied suckers are good eating fish, if a little bony. They're easy to catch, and seldom show up with trout eggs in their stomachs. And if it weren't for suckers feeding off the dense concentrations of life on the water bottom, over much wider areas than shallows-loving catfish, there would likely be far fewer game fish around; as it is, white suckers are often the most abundant species in many lakes and streams, feeding a good many pike and pickerel.

Average adult length: 30–51 cm (12–20 in)

Average weight: 450–900 g (1–2 lb)

World record: 3.3 kg (7.2 lb), caught in Wisconsin in 1978

Markings: Olive-brown, bronze or black backs, silver-grey sides, white or creamy belly, smoky fins

Alias: Sucker, common sucker, mullet, coarse-scaled sucker, fine-scaled sucker, black mullet, carp, *le meunier noir*, *Catostomus commersoni*

Preferred habitat: Shallow lakes and bays or rivers and small streams flowing into large lakes, usually at depths of 6–9 m (20–30 ft)

Greatest depth found at: 46 m (151 ft)

Greatest depth longnose sucker found at: 183 m (600 ft)

White sucker adaptability: Happy

109

in clear or cloudy waters; populations fall in acidified lakes

Food: Usually about 50% midge larvae (bloodworms), but 60–90% bottom-living waterfleas in summer; also snails, caddisfly larvae, worms and vegetation

Most important senses: Taste and touch

Average clutch: 20,000–50,000 yellow eggs

Incubation period: About 2 weeks

Fry mortality in first 2 weeks: Up to 97%

Age at sexual maturity: Males 2–3 years, females 3–4 years

Adult mortality: At least 20% live to spawn a second year, 10% a third year

Maximum lifespan: 17 years; females live longest

Predators: Pike, muskies, pickerel, burbot, osprey; otters, bears and other mammals at spawning time; bass and trout eat young

Slang: A "sucker" is someone who's as naive and easy to fool as an unweaned toddler

Range: All of Ontario; also in all other provinces and territories except Prince Edward Island and the island of Newfoundland

Number of Ontario sucker species: 12

Number of sucker species worldwide: About 65, mostly in North America

Also see: Midges, Brown Bullhead Catfish, Pike, Pickerel, Plankton. *Up North:* Lakes, Black Bear

Most active at dusk and dawn, suckers are nearly invisible from above, even in low water, because of their darkly shaded backs. On spring spawning runs, though, when their silvery sides break the surface in shallow, gravelly streams, creeks and lake margins, they're hard to miss. Some runs involve thousands, with as many as a hundred passing by every minute in a writhing mass. In May, the thronging, spawning fish were so easy to catch that the Ojibway called it the month of the Sucker Moon. Stumbling upon a sucker run can also mean a hearty breakfast for bears recently roused from hibernation, or for ospreys just in from Mexico.

Breeding males take on a golden tint and sport a temporary red, black or cream racing stripe down their sides. For 10 to 14 days, especially at dusk and dawn, the male contestants occupy spots where the currents are fast, and intercept fertile females venturing from their own gatherings just downstream. Two to four males, usually, close in alongside a streaming feminine bomber, the whole group thrashing and vibrating as they release eggs and milt in spurts of a few seconds, anywhere from half a dozen to 40 times an hour. Eventually, the sated female returns downstream until she's ready to spawn again.

When the party's over, the fish migrate back to their regular haunts in lakes and deeper water. The hundreds of thousands of eggs left behind on the gravel bottom begin hatching within two weeks, with a sucker born every minute. Upon digesting their egg sacs, fry join adults downstream, but initially feed on plankton near the surface close to lake edges. When the young are almost two centimetres (0.8 inches) long, their mouths move from the front to the bottom of their faces, and they start feasting in weedy shallows. Suckers reaching 20 centimetres (eight inches) become too hefty for most predatory fish and commonly mingle with schools of pickerel.

PUMPKINSEED SUNFISH
Glimmering from the Shallows

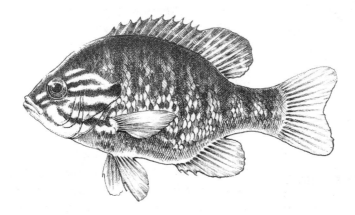

NEVER WAS THERE a better-named fish than the flat, yellow-bellied dazzler of warm, weedy waters. Probably the most vibrantly hued swimmer in the province, the two-dimensional pumpkinseed sunfish glistens iridescent like "a brilliant coin fresh from the mint," in the words of famed naturalist and philosopher Henry David Thoreau. Indeed, it's only when the sun shines that its namesake fish ventures forth. The brief shadow of a passing cloud is enough to send schools of sunfish to deeper water. "Pumpkinseed" alludes to the fish's pointed oval shape, though its numerous oval spots are also reminiscent of the seeds.

Like other sunfishes and bass, many pumpkinseed males are hardworking homebodies, while females are absentee moms. When shoreside waters warm to near room temperature around late June or early July, robust male stalwarts, usually six or seven years old, begin sweeping away debris with their tails and pulling out roots from weed beds to form circular nests about twice their own length. Nurseries of 10 to 15 nests, about a metre (three feet) or more apart, are often established by groups of the maternally inclined bruisers.

Average adult length: 18–23 cm (7–9 in) in lakes, 10–15 cm (4–6 in) in brooks and ponds
Adult weight: 28–340 g (1–12 oz)
Maximum size in Ontario: 25 cm (10 in), 480 g (17 oz)
Markings: Gold sides in alternating shades forming vertical bars, most noticeable on females, and covered with oval spots of olive, orange and red; golden-brown to olive top, bright-yellow, bronze to reddish-orange bottom; wavy blue-green lines on orange cheeks, distinct bright-red spot on gills; spiny fins, big golden eyes, small mouth; colours intensify in spawning territorial males
Alias: Common sunfish, yellow sunfish, sunny, punky, sun bass, pond perch, ruff, kivry, *le crapet-soleil, Lepomis gibbosus*

Winter whereabouts: Largely inactive at bottom of deep water early Sept. to early May
Preferred habitat: Shallow, warm water of marshes, muddy brooks and pickerelweed-choked or water lily-covered rivers, ponds, bays and small lakes
Food: Dragonfly and mayfly nymphs, bloodworms and other insect larvae, snails, small crustaceans, salamander tadpoles, fish eggs and fry, clams, leeches, worms, algae
Nest: Shallow, saucer-shaped clearing in weeds and debris, 10–40 cm (4–16 in) wide, in 30–150 cm (1–5 ft) of water
Clutch: Females lay 600–5,000 light-amber eggs, each 1 mm (0.04 in) wide
Incubation period: 3–10 days
Age at sexual maturity: 2 years for "sneaker" males, 5–6 years for territorial males, 4–5 years for females
Maximum age: 10 years
Predators: Pike, pickerel, sauger, muskies, osprey and kingfishers; bass, perch, catfish, other sunfish and older pumpkinseeds eat young or eggs
Range: Southern Ontario to about Lake Temiskaming and Sault Ste. Marie; also in New Brunswick, Quebec, southeastern Manitoba and introduced in southern British Columbia
Number of Ontario sunfish species (including bass): 9
Number of sunfish species worldwide: 30
Also see: Pickerel, Brown Bullhead Catfish. Up North: Smallmouth Bass, Belted Kingfisher

Many male sunfish are young turks with no taste for the settled life. At least a third smaller than the established pumpkinseeds, they are fast-living, cheating scoundrels. They stand back and observe as members of the opposite sex come to inspect nest colonies. The females are chased about by the eager residents until convinced by one to come back to his place. As a couple slowly circle around the nest, her body inclined towards his in the act of spawning, a young sneaker will dash in close and squirt a stream of his own milt into the mix and then try to make off before being detected.

The sneak-and-squirt strategy is a successful one. Nest-tending fathers often unknowingly raise more offspring of other fish than their own. Most of their real sons remain celibate until later in life, when they're big enough to hold down a good nesting spot and drive others away. Foster sons, however, mainly grow up to be shiftless, promiscuous cheaters like their daddies, sexually active by the time they are two. Putting more of their internal resources into sperm production, they never grow as big as the territorial males. All the fast living and being chased from one nest to another also burns them out more quickly. Few live more than five years. Many die from fungal infections of fin wounds inflicted by jealous homesteaders.

Often mating with several partners, territorial males can accumulate piles of more than 15,000 eggs. They fan them constantly, to keep them aerated in the warm water, and fiercely attack any other fish that intrudes, even biting human fingers. After the minuscule, transparent fry hatch, fathers watch over them in the nest for up to another 11 days, until the young swim off on their own. Some males then mate again and raise a second batch.

Bluegill sunfish are almost as common in central Ontario. Pumpkinseeds sometimes either mate with bluegills or take over their nests. The two fishes are similar in most ways, with the bluegill having blue-green or olive colouring reflecting a purple iridescence.

LAKE WHITEFISH
Shoal-spawned Fish of the Deep

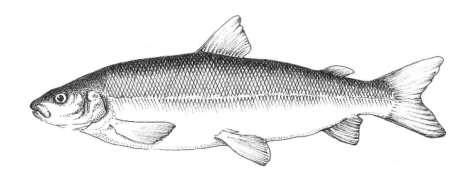

WHITEFISH PLACE NAMES across north and central Ontario and the rest of Canada attest to the importance of the deep-water dweller to past generations. Places where whitefish congregated near shore every autumn and spring were important seasonal gathering points for the Ojibway, Ottawa and other peoples coming to harvest the year's greatest bounty before and after the lean days of winter. When the French first reached Sault Ste. Marie in the 1600s, they found at least 16 nations meeting there to trade and to catch lake whitefish, which is also known as Sault whitefish. In Ojibway legend, the whitefish was one of Spirit Woman's three most faithful children, with the life-sustaining hare and ruffed grouse.

A sun-warmed burst of life and food in shallow waters is what brings schools of whitefish in from the deep at springtime. Near-shore zones provide by far the highest concentrations of aquatic insect larvae and other invertebrates in any lake. Rising water temperature, however, forces bottom-feeding whitefish back into the depths in early summer, along with lake trout and other cold-water species. They wait until the water drops again to a frigid

Average adult length: About 38 cm (15 in)
Adult weight: 450–1,800 g (1–4 lb)
World inland record: 6.5 kg (14.4 lb), caught in the Big Head River, near Meaford
Great Lakes record: 19 kg (42 lb), caught in Lake Superior
Markings: Silvery sides with light-greenish to pale-brown back and silver-white bottom
Alias: Common whitefish, Sault whitefish, eastern whitefish, inland whitefish, Great Lakes whitefish, humpback whitefish, grizzard fish, *le grand corégone, Coregonus clupeaformis*
Preferred habitat: Usually 15–45 m (50–148 ft) deep in lakes or large rivers
Greatest depth caught at: 128 m (420 ft)
Food: Mayfly nymphs,

113

bloodworms, caddisfly and other aquatic insect larvae, snails, clams, leeches, water mites, scuds (flealike crustaceans) and small fish and eggs; plankton and surface insects sometimes eaten; young eat micro-crustaceans called copepods and water-fleas (see pages 106–108)
Average clutch: 15,000–22,500 eggs, each 2–3 cm (0.8–1.2 in) wide; sold as caviar
Age at sexual maturity: 2–7 years
Maximum lifespan: 28 years
Predators: Pickerel, lake trout, pike and burbot; perch and ciscoes eat hatchlings, whitefish eat each other's eggs
Peak Great Lakes whitefish catch: 7.9 mil kg (17.5 mil lb) in 1948
Peak Lake Erie cisco catch: 21.6 mil kg (48 mil lb) in 1918
Range: All of Ontario; also in all western provinces and the territories, Quebec, New Brunswick and Labrador
Number of Ontario whitefish species: 7
Number of threatened or vulnerable species: 4
Number of whitefish species worldwide: 20
Also see: Mayflies, Plankton. *Up North:* Brook Trout, Roughed Grouse, Lakes

8°C (46°F) in October or November before returning to spawn above rocky reefs and shoals between the shore and depths of eight metres (26 feet). Starting at sunset, for seven to 10 nights, mating whitefish thrash about at the surface, sometimes jumping out of the water. Each female releases small batches of roe over several nights.

Settling over rocks and gravel, whitefish eggs hatch when the ice melts in spring. Fry rise to the surface and are carried inshore, gathering with burbot, cisco and sculpin hatchlings off steep rockfaces in about 30 centimetres (one foot) of water. After feeding on plankton near the surface, they move farther out from shore by late May.

A sun-warmed burst of life brings schools of whitefish in from the deep at springtime

---

Central Ontario's only other common whitefish species, the **cisco**, is a smaller, sleeker fish with a pink or purple iridescence to its silvery sides. Not swimming as deep as lake whitefish, it dines on plankton, and is itself a staple of lake trout. Also known as lake herring, ciscoes were once caught in the millions by commercial fishing boats in the Great Lakes. By the 1960s, overfishing, pollution and invading parasitic sea lampreys had cut cisco, whitefish and lake trout populations on the big lakes to a fraction of what they once were. While ciscoes are now pretty much left alone, lake whitefish remain the most important commercially netted catch in large water bodies across Canada.

MAMMALS

T HOUGH CENTRAL ONTARIO *has more than 50 native species of mammals, many are nocturnal or mostly subterranean and therefore not often encountered. Flying squirrels are, in fact, as common as red squirrels, but swoop about like bats in the night. Ontario's most diverse group of carnivores, the weasel family, includes fishers, martens and other species that are seen by few but trappers. Yet they are around, and play a part in the natural order. Fortunately, the largest and perhaps most intriguing member of the family, the otter, can be observed by many visiting wilderness lakes in the latter part of summer. The lynx, on the other hand, is one of the province's most elusive hunters. Though few of us ever cross paths with the big-footed cat, we feel its place in the north woods warrants recognition in these pages.*

ERMINE
Winter's White Weasel

"WEASEL" USUALLY has a negative connotation, while "ermine" invokes royalty – yet they are one and the same. When the little short-tailed weasel changes into its winter coat of dense white fur, it's called an ermine. The silky feel of ermine was favoured for the trim of native ceremonial headdresses and robes for European royalty. Close to 50,000 ermine pelts figured in the coronation pageantry of King George VI in 1937, most of them from Canada, though the weasels are also native to Europe.

Weasels are most commonly described as bold, blood-thirsty gluttons, "wandering demons of carnage," in the words of early Canadian nature writer Ernest Thompson Seton. The enmity probably arises from the slinky predators' considerable skill at infiltrating chicken coops, and it's true that long-necked, agile ermine are frighteningly efficient predators, wrapping themselves around their prey like a snake with claws. They often do kill more than they can eat, but they store away leftovers for leaner times. And with good reason. Though accused of killing for pleasure (by a species brimming with sport hunters), most of the small-faced animals end up starving to death.

Deer mice and voles – also known as meadow mice – are at the centre of a short-tailed weasel's life. Competing in a field of foxes, coyotes and other skilled mousers, the weasel, itself resembling an elongated mouse, chases the squeaking quarry right into their tunnels and burrows. The long, slim build required to fit down a two- to three-centimetre-wide (0.8- to 1.2-inch-wide) tunnel creates a large surface area for such a small creature to keep warm in winter. To stay alive, an ermine must stoke its internal furnace much more frequently than do stouter animals. A fiery metabolism wears the body out quickly, and slowing down means the end. When voles and mice

Adult body length: Females 12–18 cm (5–7 in), males 14–22 cm (5.5–9 in)

Average weight: Females 45–75 g (1.6–3 oz), males 80–180 g (3–7 oz)

World's smallest carnivore: Least weasel, 35–90 g (1.2–3.2 oz), a northern hunter, rare in central Ontario

Ermine markings: In summer, dark or reddish-brown back and sides, creamy-white neck, chest, belly and inner legs, black tail tip; all white in winter except for tail tip

Alias: Short-tailed weasel, stoat, *la hermine*, *Mustela erminea*

Meaning of *Mustela*: From Latin *mus*, meaning "mouse," and *telum*, meaning "spear"

Calls: Shrill shrieks, squeals, hisses and a quiet, trilled "tuk, tuk, tuk"; young squeak and purr

Preferred habitat: Mixed and evergreen forest edges, especially near streams, shrubby areas of new growth, wet meadows, marshes

populations crash, even healthy weasels fail to catch what they need.

Hard times in the mouse-catcher ranks turn many predators against each other, the larger eating the smaller. The smallest of all are ermine, normally too ferocious and too stinky to bother with. Whenever threatened, they release an odious musk from a gland beneath the tail, also used to mark their territories. The tail's black tip is probably an anti-predator device as well, especially in winter, drawing the aim of a striking hawk or owl away from the snaking body.

The weasel chases squeaking quarry right into their tunnels and burrows

Ermines are generally loners, except when mating or raising young. Their lives usually begin in April, in renovated vole burrows or hollow logs. Though mothers have to provide for their young by themselves, they can rustle up a storm of grub, as they need far less for themselves than do twice-as-big males. On top of everything else, mothers mate again within weeks of giving birth. Newborn females also invariably mate before the end of the summer. It's common, in fact, for males to mate not only with new mothers but with each of her unweaned daughters as well.

Their eyes newly opened, young weasels emerge from the nest in late May and June. Though they may soon accompany their mother on nightly forays, they don't need to be taught to hunt. Young males, already up to 50 percent larger than Mom when they stop nursing in early summer, are soon able to wrestle chipmunks and squirrels bigger than themselves. The young scatter by autumn, often travelling many kilometres before finding good hunting territory not occupied by another weasel. Those that succeed are rewarded with their first white winter coat, grown in November in response to decreasing daylight.

Average home range: Females 10–15 ha (25–37 acres), males 20–25 ha (49–62 acres)

Homes: Old rodent burrows, hollow logs and stumps, rock or wood piles and crevices, several maintained throughout territory; ermine seldom stray more than 200 m (220 yd) from a home

Food: Usually more than 50% voles, followed by mice, shrews, chipmunks, young hares, squirrels, bird nestlings, frogs, snakes, fish, carrion, worms and other invertebrates

Gestation period: About 11 months

Average litter: 6–8

Average birth weight: 2 g (0.07 oz)

Lifespan: Most 2 years or less, maximum 7 years

Predators: Goshawks, great horned owls, snowy owls; more rarely foxes, coyotes, lynx, mink, martens, fishers and long-tailed weasels

Heartbeats per minute: 360–390

Jumping ability: Up to 2.5 m (8 ft) high

Tracks: Prints less than 2.5 cm (1 in) diameter, in pairs 2.5–5 cm (1–2 in) apart; stride 15–90 cm (6–36 in) long, with back feet landing in the tracks made by front

Scats: Black or dark brown, with lots of fur, sometimes bits of bone, usually less than 3 cm (1.2 in) long, noodle-thin

Population density: 4–11 per km^2 (0.4 sq mi)

Range: Throughout Ontario; also in all other provinces and territories

FISHER

Prickly Prey a Forté

Adult body length: 48–67 cm (19–26 in)

Average weight: Females 1.3–3.2 kg (3–7 lb), males 2.2–5.4 kg (5–12 lb)

Height: Males average 23–26 cm (9–10 in) at shoulder, the hunched back a little higher

Maximum weight: More than 9 kg (20 lb)

Markings: In winter, mostly dark brown, sometimes almost black; in summer, grey-brown; black legs, rump and tail; often small white patches on throat and between legs; black eyes shine bright, light green in lights at night

Alias: Fisher marten, black cat, fisher cat, wejack, black fox, Pennant's cat, *le pekan*, *Martes pennanti*

Calls: Growls, hisses, chuckles, soft trills

Preferred habitat: Dense mixed forests, often in coniferous woods and swamps in winter

Average home range: Females 7–20 km² (3–8 sq mi), males 25–40 km² (10–16 sq mi)

Homes: Tree cavities, hollow logs, ground burrows, rock and brush piles, old muskrat and beaver lodges

Food: Hares, porcupines, mice, voles, red squirrels, flying squirrels, chipmunks, shrews, ruffed grouse, carrion, occasionally smaller birds and their eggs, frogs, fish, ermine, martens, young beavers, insects, berries and nuts

EACH MEMBER of the weasel family has a slightly different specialty. Confusingly, the fisher's is not to catch fish. The stocky mustelid was probably named for its resemblance to the European fisher, also called a polecat. Sometimes as big as a fox, with shorter, more powerful legs, fishers commonly clamber up dead trees and rip away at nest holes to reach flying squirrels or other occupants. Hunting day or night, they also take larger prey – especially snowshoe hares – far more often than does their closest relative, the diminutive marten. On occasion, they'll even go after raccoons, which are generally too ornery for larger predators.

But what fishers do better than anything else in the world, save for speeding cars, is dispatch porcupines. With a swiftness and agility second to none, they run circles around the big pincushions, dodging the swishing tail while repeatedly biting their victim's face until, after a half-hour or more, the porcupine succumbs. Then it's merely a matter of flipping the porcupine on its back to feast on the soft, unquilled underside. By stashing a good-sized porky beneath leaves or snow, a fisher has enough meat to keep it going for a couple of weeks.

Fishers also stick close to winter-killed deer or wolf leftovers whenever they find them. Deep snow limits their movements considerably, and extreme cold or storms can keep them denned up for days. Come late March and April, however, males venture far and wide off their usual territories in search of the opposite sex. Females, often just a week after they've given birth, strike up liaisons with visiting suitors that may last several days, during which they may mate for one to five hours in a single stretch.

Though often just half the size of adult males, mothers keep their callers well away from the tree-cavity dens where they keep their young. When the kits are eight to 10 weeks old, the single mothers bring them down to a ground borrow. By midsummer, when the young stop nursing and are learning to hunt for themselves, tempers start running short amongst siblings and their parent. A month or so of family squabbles finally sends the nearly full-grown young off on their separate ways in August or September.

Fanning out to establish large individual territories, fishers have always been far less numerous than mink, martens and other smaller weasels. Logging, poison wolf baits and a particularly high demand after the First World War for their lustrous pelts brought the animals close to extinction by the 1930s. Only strict regulations, such as assigning trapping licences based on watersheds rather than townships, turned things around for both fishers and martens in the early 1950s. Draftees from a strong remnant population in Algonquin Park have since been used to reintroduce the fisher in the Ottawa Valley, Georgian Bay hinterlands, Manitoulin Island and the Bruce Peninsula. As a result, dense populations of tree-destroying porcupines have declined, going some way to restoring the natural balance.

Gestation: 11–13 months
Average litter: 2–3
Birth weight: 40 g (1.4 oz)
Age at sexual maturity: 1 year, but males and many females don't mate till 2 years old
Maximum lifespan: About 10 years in wild, 18 years in captivity
Predators: Young under 2 years old most commonly killed by older fishers; adults possibly taken by great horned owls, lynx and bears
Tracks: Pawprints 5–10 cm (2–4 in) long and 5–7.5 cm (2–3 in) wide, bigger when fishers run and back feet land in prints made by front
Scats: Usually 2.5–5 cm (1–2 in) long, thin, black or dark brown, containing hair, sometimes quills or berries
Peak activity periods: Around dusk and dawn
Population density in untrapped areas: 1 per 6.5 km^2 (2.5 sq mi)
Number of fishers trapped annually in Ontario, 1985–95: 2,300–4,700
Range: Northern Ontario to the southern edge of the Canadian Shield, Manitoulin Island and the Bruce Peninsula; also in all other provinces and territories except Prince Edward Island and island of Newfoundland
Also see: Marten. *Up North:* Big Dipper, Porcupine

NORTHERN
FLYING SQUIRREL
Gliding through the Nightshift

Adult body length: 14–19 cm
(5.5–7.5 in)
Tail: Almost as long as body,
resembling a flattened bottle-
brush, serves as a rudder and
air break during glides
Average weight: 70–140 g
(2.5–5 oz)
Markings: Light greyish-tan
to reddish-brown back,
light-grey undersides, large
black eyes shine red in
lights at night
Alias: *Le grand polatouche,
Glaucomys sabrinus*
Calls: Chucks, squeaks, sharp
squeals, birdlike chirping
and calls beyond human
hearing range
Habitat: Coniferous and mixed
forests with mature trees
Homes: Old woodpecker holes
or natural cavities lined with
shredded leaves, moss,
lichens, grass, bark strips, fur
or feathers; in summer, also
build spherical nests of sticks,
bark, moss, leaves and
lichens in forked branches,
usually of an evergreen,
and in witch's broom tangles
at tops of black spruce,
occasionally in a covered-
over bird nest; each squirrel
usually has several nests
Food: Mushrooms, raspberries,
serviceberries, acorns and
other nuts in summer and
fall; lichens and conifer seeds
in winter; maple sap and
buds of aspen, alder and

L IKE INHABITANTS of a fairy realm, northern
flying squirrels are unseen nocturnal creatures that
sail through the air and visit hidden places where
mushrooms flourish. Though the fur-caped aerialists are
little known, they're as plentiful as the bigger red squirrels
that chatter vociferously through the day. Night-gliders
sleep through the sunlit hours in tree holes or in spherical
bark nests, and rise for the nightshift soon after the can-
tankerous reds and chipmunks call it a day.

Just as regular squirrels use well-worn routes that allow
them to flash through the branches with hardly a thought,
flying squirrels navigate along regular flight corridors,
with takeoff spots marked by their urine and other body
scents. Tossing themselves into the air, they spread their
legs to unfold a continuous furred flap of skin reaching to
each of their four feet, turning themselves into flying
carpets. They can remain airborne for several seconds,
swiftly gliding down to the lower branches of their target
tree, up to 48 metres (160 feet) away. Upon landing, they
climb up and up until attaining a sufficient height to
launch off again. The mouse-eyed sprites can also drop
straight down by spinning in a tight spiral.

Like so much that rarely meets the eye in the wild, flying squirrels may play an important role in the forest ecosystem. It's a role that's only starting to be studied. The night-gliders are true mushroom fanatics, sniffing out and digging up even subterranean fruiting fungi. Such mushrooms, called false truffles, may be largely spread in the droppings of their animal nibblers. A great variety of trees and plants in turn form close symbiotic relationships with these types of organisms, known as mycorrhizal fungi. Tree roots entwine with the fungal threads and provide them with sugars created through photosynthesis in return for nutrients and water collected from the ground by the extensive network of fungal fibres.

Flying squirrels may play an important role in the forest ecosystem

In winter, northern flying squirrels also eat lots of hanging tree lichens, a low-nutrition food on which few other animals, save caribou, can get by. The night-gliders also become quite social during winter, in contrast to the fierce individualism of daytime squirrels. On cold days, as many as nine flying squirrels will curl close together in tree cavities for warmth. As the sun rises higher in the sky and mild days foreshadow spring in mid- to late March, the velvet-furred rodents develop a keen romantic interest in one another. New litters result in May. Little Rockies leave the nest to learn to glide in summer, remaining with their mothers until August or September.

In mature hardwood forests as far north as Muskoka and Ottawa, **southern flying squirrels** can also be found. They're a little smaller than their northern brethren and have white, rather than grey, undersides. The southern fliers' diet is centred on more traditional squirrel fare, such as acorns and beech and hickory nuts, which nevertheless are collected unseen after nightfall.

willow in spring; also flowers, bird eggs and nestlings, beetles, moths, mayflies, insect larvae, carrion; said to be the most carnivorous of squirrels
Gestation period: 37–42 days
Average litter: 2–4
Birth weight: 4–6 g (0.14–0.2 oz)
Weight of a nickel: 4.5 g (0.16 oz)
Age at sexual maturity: 9 months for females, later for males
Lifespan: Most less than 4 years, up to 13 years in captivity
Predators: Owls, hawks, ravens, martens, fishers, raccoons, weasels, foxes, lynx, wolves and coyotes
Rate of gliding descent: Averages out to 1 m (3.3 ft) down for every 3 m (10 ft) forward
Peak activity periods: For 2 hours after sunset and 1 hour before sunrise
Range: All of Ontario except extreme south and above tree line; also in all other provinces and territories except island of Newfoundland
Number of Ontario flying squirrel species: 2
Number of flying squirrel species worldwide: 38
Also see: Fisher. *Up North:* Fungi, Lichens, Red Squirrel, Black Spruce

LYNX
Ontario's Premier Wild Cat

Adult body length: Females
78–84 cm (31–33 in), males
82–88 cm (32–35 in)
Average height at shoulders:
48–61 cm (19–24 in)
Average weight: 7–13 kg
(15–29 lb)
Maximum weight: 19 kg (42 lb)
Claw length: 3 cm (1.2 in)
Markings: Reddish-brown to
brownish-grey back and sides;
greyish-white to light-beige
chest, chin, legs and undersides
with faint spots
Visual capabilities: Can see mice
75 m (250 ft) away and hares
at 300 m (985 ft)
Alias: Canada lynx, wood ghost, *le
loup-cervier, Lynx canadensis*
Calls: Growls, shrieks, yowls, hisses
Preferred habitat: Coniferous
forests with dense underbrush
mixed with shrubby clearings,
willow thickets, conifer swamps
and bogs
Average home range:
16–20 km² (6–8 sq mi)
Food: At least 60% hares in
winter, 40% in summer; also
grouse, songbirds, mice,

A LYNX IS ROUGHLY twice the size of a house cat, with enormous paws and extra long legs. Exceedingly fluffy, with a feline face framed by long-tuffed ears and trailing white mutton chops, the oversized tabby is a cat person's fantasy. But very few people ever see Ontario's premier wild cat; it's a silent night-prowler of dense, tangled bush, keeping well away from any sign or scent of human habitation.

Even to the Ojibway, the reclusive cat was a fierce, rarely encountered spectre of great mystique. The feared underwater and underground manitou, Mishipizheu, is shown in pictographs in the form of a great lynx with horns of power rising from its head. The supernatural cat claimed many lives at rapids and in storms whipped up by its heavy tail. People travelling by canoe made offerings of appeasement, and Midewiwin Society members sought Mishipizheu's power, often held in nuggets of copper from cliffsides on Lake Superior said to be its lair.

Stories of Mishipizheu feasting on the eyeballs of its victims to gain their power may allude to the ordinary lynx's piercing night vision. Glaring out from amber peepers that shine green in the moonlight, the cat has retinas packed full of reflective rod cells, maximizing its ability to see in the dark. Europeans long believed that their own native lynx could even see through walls. The name "lynx" comes from the Greek *lugx,* believed ultimately to be based on the Indo-European word *leuk,* which spawned "light, lunar, luminous" and "lucid."

First and foremost, the wild cat uses its night-penetrating vision to find snowshoe hares. It often conceals itself at the crossroads of busy bunny trails, waiting for dinner to come hop, hop, hopping along. The lynx also stalks in the classic cat fashion, tensely crouching ever closer to prey and suddenly springing when within a few bounds of the target. Some can cover more than four metres (13 feet) in a single jump. Paws often wider than a human fist are mittened with thick fur, even on their undersides in winter, allowing the sprinting cats to stay on the surface of the snow.

Dependence on snowshoe hares means lynx fortunes are bound to the hares' roughly 10-year population cycle. When the population of the long-eared prey crashes, most lynx offspring starve to death and females either produce only one kitten afterwards or don't mate at all until more hares start popping up again. Lynx populations can drop by two-thirds in just a couple years.

Though the cats were once common in southern Ontario, most now reported south of the French and Mattawa rivers are believed to be lynx that either migrate during lean years or wayward adolescents in search of good hunting territories. First-years usually set off on their own after their mothers leave them in mid-March or early April to breed again. Mates find each other with blood-curdling caterwauls that ring through the forest. Mothers give birth two months later in dens beneath uprooted trees, rock piles or low, dense evergreen branches. When about three months old, kittens start tagging along with their hunting mother.

The lynx's southern cousin, the **bobcat**, also reaches into Ontario, scattered mainly in a band running from Lake Nipissing to Sault Ste. Marie. Some occasionally turn up farther north or south. Easily mistaken for a lynx, the bobcat tends to be slightly smaller, with shorter legs, smaller ear tufts and a darker, more spotted coat. Lacking its near-twin's wider, fur-soled paws, the southern cat keeps to areas where the snow isn't as deep, close to the shores of Lake Huron's North Channel.

voles, red squirrels, flying squirrels, chipmunks, muskrats, frogs, invertebrates and carrion; rarely foxes, porcupines and ambushed fawns and moose calves

Average hunting success: 2 hares every 3 days

Chase success rate: 9–42%

Gestation: 9 weeks

Average litter: 2–3

Age at sexual maturity: Females either 10 or 22 months, males 22 months

First-year mortality: 65–95%

Annual adult mortality: About 7% when hares plentiful, 38% after hare population crashes

Maximum lifespan: 15 years in wild, 18 years in captivity

Predators: Occasionally wolves; adults sometimes kill young

Maximum running speed: Probably about 30 km/h (18 mph)

Tracks: Prints 8–10 cm (3–4 in) wide, with peripheral fur edges, up to 15 cm (6 in) apart

Scats: Usually 2–10 cm (0.8–4 in) long, 1–2 cm (0.4–0.8 in) wide, with lots of fur

Range: Northern Ontario to the southern edge of the Canadian Shield and eastern Ontario; also in all other provinces and territories

Number of native Ontario cat species: 2

Ontario cougar status: Disappeared in 1860s, hundreds of unconfirmed sightings in recent years

Number of cat species worldwide: About 37

Also see: Willows. *Up North:* Snowshoe Hare

MARTEN
Taking to the Big Trees

Adult body length: Females 35–38 cm (14–15 in), males 41–43 cm (16–17 in)
Tail: 18–23 cm (7–9 in)
Average weight: Females 410 g (14.5 oz), males 670 g (23.6 oz)
Markings: Most often golden- to yellowish-brown, sometimes reddish-, light or dark brown; darker on legs and tail; greyish face, ears trimmed grey or white, throat and chest orange or yellow
Alias: Pine marten, American marten, Canadian sable, pussy marten, Hudson Bay sable, *la martre, Martes americana*
Call: Growls, snarls, hisses, clucks
Preferred habitat: Mature coniferous and mixed forests with lots of deadfall
Average home range: About 1 km² (0.4 sq mi) for females, 3.6 km² (1.4 sq mi) for males
Homes: Tree cavities, hollow logs, ground burrows or rock crevices, lined with grass, moss and leaves
Food: Red-backed voles, mice, hares and ruffed grouse most important; also red squirrels, chipmunks, flying squirrels, smaller birds and their eggs, frogs, snakes, weasels, mink, fish, insects, carrion, berries, nuts, conifer seeds
Gestation period: About 7–9 months
Average litter: 3–6
Average birth weight: 28 g (1 oz)
Age at sexual maturity: 1 year

T HE MOST ARBOREAL members of the weasel clan, martens are probably better suited to mature forests than any other predator. The cat-sized prowlers can sail through the trees with the speed and dexterity of squirrels. They spend most of their time, however, on damp, mossy ground, pouncing on voles and mice. During winter, they frequently tunnel beneath the snow while hunting bunnies, as suggested by their Cree name, *wabachis*, meaning "hare chaser."

They move swiftly and silently,
preferring to bound from one
fallen log to another

Though martens are widely reputed to be squirrel catchers, the rodents make up only a very small portion of their diet in Ontario. Up in the trees, most healthy resident red squirrels are usually too sure of their territories and regular escape routes through the tangle of branches to be captured by even the fastest assailants. But ailing or injured squirrels, or dispersing young on unfamiliar turf, are occasionally captured.

Martens work fairly small territories and can be quite abundant in mature stands with plenty of deadfall, especially when their prey populations are at the peak of their cycles. Never able to resist bait, martens were once nearly trapped to the point of extinction in central Ontario, but have made a considerable comeback since the 1950s. Still, the slightly foxy-faced predators are so stealthful, they're almost never seen. They move swiftly and silently, preferring to bound from one fallen log to another, frequently marking them with droppings and scent from their musk glands.

Seeking each other out during the warm days of summer plentitude, marten mates may stay together for a few days before going their separate ways. Both sexes may have more than one tryst during the breeding season. Like most of their weasel relatives, though, pregnant martens hold their fertilized eggs in a state of suspended animation until late winter, so that the young, born the following April, have a full warm season to grow. Mothers often keep their charges high up in tree cavities until after their eyes open and they become active, usually in June. Families then relocate to ground nests, where they stay together for a couple more months before the full-grown offspring venture up to 80 kilometres (50 miles) away in search of good hunting territories.

Maximum lifespan: 14 years in wild, 17 years in captivity

Average annual adult mortality in untrapped, unlogged areas: 10–20%

Predators: Fishers, lynx, foxes, coyotes, great horned owls

Tracks: Usually in 7.5–12-cm-wide (3–4.8-in-wide) pairs, each print about 5–7.5 cm (2–3 in) long and 3–7 cm (1.2–2.8 in) wide, with back feet landing in marks made by front; strides averaging 38–84 cm (15–33 in); occasionally walks more slowly with each foot sometimes leaving a separate print

Scats: Usually several cm (1 or 2 in) long, less than 1 cm (0.4 in) wide, black or dark brown with fur, bits of bone and sometimes seeds

Population density: 0.5–2 per km^2 (0.4 sq mi)

Number trapped annually in Ontario, 1985–95: 30,000–80,000

Range: Northern Ontario to the southern edge of the Canadian Shield and Manitoulin Island; also in all other provinces and territories except Nova Scotia and Prince Edward Island

Also see: Ermine, Fisher. *Up North*: Deer Mouse, Red Squirrel

OTTER
Playful Master Fish Catcher

QUIET WILDERNESS LAKES and rivers are animated by the arrival in August of otter families from backwater natal retreats up small streams and remote beaver ponds. Moving through the water in an undulating train of sleek dipping and rising bodies, appearing like one long, snaking lake monster, they often venture within clear reconnoitring distance of passing canoes. Looking beaverlike when just breaking the surface, their heads rise on long, weaselly necks as they stop, snort and turn to get a good look at their paddle-flapping companions on the water.

Otters are creatures of boundless enthusiasm and famed curiosity. They're said by some to be one of the few animals besides man known to engage in play even as adults. Dispassionate biologists caution that many otter antics, such as playing tag and diving for pebbles, serve as practice for hunting, and that instances of groups repeatedly using mud or snow slides are fairly rare in the wild. Still, the aquatic animal's intelligence, hyperactivity and keen interest in all things are universally acknowledged. The otter is sacred to many native groups throughout North America. It was one of the Ojibway Midewiwin Society's most important spirit guides and protectors. Otter pelts, the most durable of all furs, were used for medicine bags, quivers, bow casings, hats and robes.

For their part, otters have every reason to be upbeat creatures. They're largely impervious to the weather, have few if any predators and enjoy a food supply so plentiful and easily caught that they have lots of time to lounge and amuse themselves. Insulated by a layer of fat and by air bubbles trapped within their fur, otters glide stealthily underwater, taking fish unawares with lightning strikes. Though streamlined like seals, they're actually one of the

Adult body length: 53–82 cm (21–32 in)
Weight: 5–15 kg (11–33 lb)
Markings: Dark-brown to light-chestnut back, lighter brown with some grey on sides; appear black when wet; young born black
Alias: River otter, land otter, common otter, *la loutre de rivière*, *Lontra canadensis*
Calls: Coughing snorts, sniffs, grunts, chirps, growls, hisses, humming and high whistles
Habitat: Quiet wilderness lakes, rivers, creeks and beaver ponds, interspersed with marshes and swamps and in water with lots of submerged fallen trees and logjams
Home range: 24 km (15 mi) or more of shoreline in summer, 2 or 3 times as big in winter
Home: Old bank burrows or lodges of muskrats and

largest members of the weasel family. Special flaps close tight within their ears and nostrils while submerged. Long, prominent, highly sensitive whiskers help otters probe darkened waters at night and beneath the ice of winter, picking up waves fanned by their prey. Their eyes, too, are so specialized for scanning the submerged nocturnal world that in the surface realm otters seem actually near-sighted.

Even in winter, otters have little trouble going about their business. They use the snow to their advantage, alternately running and sliding while journeying overland several kilometres from one body of water to another. To get into the water, they break through the ice at weak points around rocks, logs and stumps, keeping several openings clear in a given area. Otters can also catch a breath at air pockets left beneath the ice by changing water levels. They also frequently slip through open spots at the spillways of beaver dams. With beavers creating ideal habitat for otters, peaceful co-existence between the two species is generally the rule.

In late April and May, male otters often join females that have recently given birth at dens on or near small beaver ponds. Taking time out from maternal duties, mothers join their visitors to mate in the water for 15 to 25 minutes at a time. After repeated performances, males usually depart, though some apparently return to lend a helping paw after the pups first leave the den and are taught to swim, when about two months old. Several weeks later, when the young are adept, families troop out to larger bodies of water where food is more plentiful. Here the otters may wander along many kilometres of shoreline, and become a common sight of late summer.

beavers, uprooted trees, eroded root tangles, hollow logs and stumps, rock crevices, dense thickets of willow and alder; old groundhog burrows; lined with grass, leaves and sticks

Food: Mostly slower-moving fish 7–13 cm (3–5 in) long, including minnows, sunfish, catfish, suckers, perch and sculpins; less often bass or trout; also crayfish, frogs, salamanders, mussels, water beetles, stonefly nymphs, worms and snails, occasionally ducklings, muskrats, mice, water snakes, ground-nesting birds and their eggs; some grass, blueberries, algae and aquatic vegetation

Gestation: 11–13 months

Average litter: 2–3

Dispersal: Mothers leave young when 8–11 months old; siblings together till 12–13 months old

Maximum lifespan: 15 years in wild, 25 years in captivity

Peak activity periods: Predawn to midmorning, late afternoon to midnight

Maximum time under water: 4 minutes

Normal swimming speeds: 5–10 km/h (3–6 mph)

Running and sliding speed over snow: Up to 30 km/h (18 mph)

Scats: Small piles of often greenish scattered fish scales and reddish bits of crayfish shells

Range: Northern Ontario to the north shore of Lake Ontario; also found in all other provinces and territories

REPTILES

GENERALLY WARM-*weather creatures, reptiles are represented by fewer species than most other classes of animals in Ontario. Snapping and painted turtles, garter and water snakes account for the vast majority of those encountered. Closely related to garters, ribbon snakes are more limited in distribution, tied closely to the moist margins of streams, lakes and wetlands. There are plenty of ringneck snakes, but being strictly night-prowlers, they keep out of sight. Green snakes, too, are so well camouflaged and speedy, they're usually a surprise to spot.*

Among the scattering of Ontario's other shelled reptiles, the Blanding's turtle, though not widespread, is locally common in some areas. The five-lined skink is also not observed by a lot of people, but is notable for being Eastern Canada's only lizard.

BLANDING'S TURTLE
Yellow-necked Bottom-walker

A VERY LONG, deep-yellow neck sets the Blanding's turtle apart from all other northern terrapins. With just its head breaking the water surface, the shelled reptile can look like a thick yellow-bellied water snake (of which there are none in Ontario). Blanding's turtles spend most of their time walking the bottoms of shallow, weedy bays and marshes. They use their long necks to reach between and beneath rocks and driftwood to get at crayfish and snails, which they vacuum into their mouths. They are most often found scattered across Muskoka, Haliburton, eastern Algonquin Park and east along the southern edge of the Canadian Shield.

A good time to see Blanding's turtles is after they rise from hibernation in late April or early May, around the same time as painted turtles. On sunny days for about the next month, when the air warms above 15°C (60°F), they spend long stretches basking either at the water's surface or on logs or low alder branches, attempting to get their metabolism up and running at full throttle. They are, however, quite shy, and plunk into the water at the slightest disturbance.

Average adult shell length: 15–25 cm (6–10 in)
Maximum shell length: 27 cm (10.8 in)
Markings: Highly domed black or dark-brown shell with faint yellow or tan spots, more noticeable on younger turtles; very dark-brown or blue-grey head and limbs with deep-yellow chin and throat; yellow plastron with dark splotches; males have a longer tail, females have a yellow upper jaw
Alias: Semi-box turtle, *la tortue mouchetée, Emydoidea blandingi*
Call: Sometimes hisses when threatened
Preferred habitat: Marshes and shallow, quiet lakes and bays with lots of vegetation and mucky, silty bottoms

Winter whereabouts: Submerged in weeds, partially buried by mud, occasionally waking to move to different sleeping spots

Food: Crayfish, mayfly larvae, dragonfly nymphs, beetle grubs and other aquatic insects, snails, slugs, leeches, tadpoles, frogs, fish, carrion and some berries and plants

Average home range: 0.4–2.3 ha (1–5.7 acres)

Adult females becoming pregnant each year: About 50%

Nest hole: About 18 cm (7 in) deep, 18 cm (7 in) wide at bottom, in exposed, sandy ground

Average clutch: 6–11 dull-white, plum-sized eggs

Incubation period: 73–104 days

Consistent temperature at which eggs produce all males: 22.5–26.5°C (73–80°F)

Consistent temperature at which eggs produce all females: 30–31°C (86–88°F)

Average hatchling carapace length: 3 cm (1.2 in)

Age at sexual maturity: 12–20 years

Maximum lifespan: May exceed 77 years

Clutches found by predators: 43–93%

Predators: Raccoons, foxes, skunks, herons, large fish and snapping turtles eat eggs or soft-shelled young

Namesake: Dr. William Blanding, early-19th-century Philadelphia herpetologist

Herpetology: Study of reptiles and amphibians, from the Greek *herpein*, "to creep"

The early days of sun-seeking is also a time of turtle romance. Though Blanding's, like other turtles, may mate at any time in the summer and fall, the most intensive breeding is in the first weeks out of torpor. Males search out and chase domed damsels to the bottom of the water. Wooing then begins, with the pursuer climbing onto the female's back, clasping the edge of her carapace with his four clawed feet and imploringly caressing her head with his chin, nibbling her neck and swinging his head from side to side. If, after up to 70 minutes, she decides he's the one she's been waiting for, she lets her tail slip from her shell to entwine with his, and they consummate their brief union. Their reptilian rapture lasts 15 to 30 minutes before they depart one another for good. They are quite promiscuous, however, and the eggs in most clutches are suspected to have been fertilized by more than one father.

From mid-June to early July, both sexes may boldly venture onto land

From mid-June to early July, both sexes may boldly venture onto land. Males sometimes travel more than a kilometre (half a mile) from one body of water to another over a two-day period, resting under cover along the way. Most female forays are egg-laying missions, often taking them 100 to 200 metres (110 to 220 yards) away from the water. Setting out under the falling veil of dusk, pregnant terrapins head to open, sandy sites, where they spend up to three and a half hours digging a hole with their back feet and laying and burying their clutch. Most return to the drink by 11:00 P.M.

Blanding's turtles have a special hinge across their bottom plastron that allows them to close the front of their shell tighter than any other native Ontario species. The added protection equips them for both their long journeys and short foraging around shorelines for berries, leaves, worms and grubs. They're also the only pond turtles that don't need to submerge their heads in water in order to swallow food.

Hatchlings burrow out from the ground in September. Their shells are yet to harden, so they keep low in the mud, sedge and alders to avoid being eaten by all manner of beasts, including their own kind. For their part, adult Blanding's turtles begin slowing down in late summer, eating little, and finally lapsing into hibernation around mid- to late October.

While Blanding's turtles are most active in the morning, the ignobly named **stinkpot turtle** wanders over the same marshy lake bottoms and on the bed of slow streams after dark. The diminutive stinker, just eight to 13 centimetres (three to five inches) long, is named for its habit of releasing a musky odour when picked up. Despite being fairly common, the dark, beak-snouted turtle is very rarely seen, sleeping beneath logs or lily pads by day. Even when laying eggs, it usually goes no farther than a muskrat lodge or pile of rotting vegetation along the water's edge to dump its load. It nibbles mostly on aquatic plant seeds, insects and soft, young crayfish.

The stinkpot's distinction of being Ontario's smallest hard-shelled reptile is shared with the **spotted turtle.** Protected by a yellow-dotted black carapace, spotted turtles occupy the shallows of bogs, marshy channels and muddy lake edges along the periphery of the Shield and Georgian Bay's hinterland, but they are fairly rare. **Map turtles**, living along the same zone in the deep water of large, slow rivers and lakes, have flattened black shells with yellow swirls and may grow up to 25 centimetres (10 inches) long.

Range: Scattered pockets in southern Ontario to Manitoulin Island, Sudbury and northern Algonquin Park; also in southwestern Quebec and southern Nova Scotia
Number of turtle species native to Ontario: 8
Number of turtle species worldwide: 257
Also see: *Up North:* Painted Turtle, Wood Turtle, Crayfish

SMOOTH GREEN SNAKE
Beauty in the Grass

A SNAKE-IN-THE-GRASS that's a true beauty, the smooth green snake, with its bright, brilliant mantle, blends completely with its surroundings. When climbing low shrubs, it even sways the leading part of its body to give it the appearance of just another green stem moving in the breeze. On the rare occasions it is detected, the startled crayon-thin snake moves so swiftly and smoothly it quickly becomes impossible to make out amid the grass. In the unlikely case that a green snake is caught, its glistening skin feels satiny smooth, bearing scales that lack the slightly ridged "keel" found on rougher snake skins.

Green snakes strike terror into the hearts of only the smallest creatures – caterpillars, spiders and other invertebrates – which they hunt by day. Accordingly, they don't come out of hibernation until bugs are plentiful, around early May, later than other snakes. Pregnant females incubate their eggs internally, for more than a month, by basking in the sun. Then, in late July or August, they lay their clutches on moist ground beneath flat stones, logs, bark or stumps. Occasionally they give birth to live young. Dark-olive to bluish-grey baby snakes usually hatch within two weeks, soon moulting to bright green.

Unfortunately, green snakes are probably affected wherever their insect prey are poisoned by pesticides. Some also fall to the blades of lawnmowing-obsessed cottagers, especially down near the waterline.

Average adult length: 40–50 cm (16–20 in)

Maximum length: 66 cm (26 in)

Markings: Back and sides range from bright green to light yellowish-green; belly white or yellowish

Alias: Green snake, grass snake, la couleuvre verte, Liochlorophis vernalis, Opheodrys vernalis

Preferred habitat: Wet meadows, clearings, fields, forest margins, open woods, often around ponds and marshes

Winter whereabouts: In ground below frost line

Food: Spiders, caterpillars, grasshoppers, crickets, beetle grubs, snails, slugs, centipedes, millipedes

Average clutch: 6–7 capsule-shaped, leathery, white eggs, about the size of peanut shells

Incubation period: 1–4 weeks

Range: Southern Ontario to a little north of Sault Ste. Marie and Sudbury; also in Saskatchewan, Manitoba, Quebec and the Maritimes

RIBBON SNAKE
Streak of Yellow Lightning

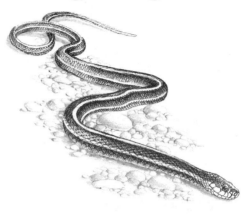

THE RIBBON SNAKE is a garter in a slicker, sleeker guise – a "warp-nine" streak of yellow light tracing through the ferns and grass. Its passage perhaps reminded the Ojibway of the lightning caused by thunderbirds casting their enemies, the snakes, to Earth. Long veins of white quartz were said to mark the serpents' landfalls and are sometimes sites of centuries-old rock paintings depicting snakes and other animal manitous.

More slender and distinctly lined than the closely related common garter, the ribbon snake has a noticeably narrowed neck and large eyes. It also has a strong predilection for water. Ribbon snakes are never far from and are often in marshes, swales and shrubby watersides. Unlike often submerged water snakes, they prefer to swim across the surface, though when threatened can dive to the bottom and stay under for several minutes.

Being probably less tolerant of cool temperatures than the hardy, adaptable garter, the ribbon snake hibernates a little longer, rising in anticipation of late May's return of tasty treefrogs to the branches around breeding ponds. After sometimes-aquatic courtships, most mothers give birth to live young in August, just in time for a feast of green, leopard and tree froglets in the awkward stage of metamorphosis. The snakes commonly hunt and bask in the branches in or above the water.

Average length: 45–64 cm (18–25 in)
Maximum length: 102 cm (40 in)
Markings: Black, brown or olive above, with a bright-yellow stripe along each side and down middle of back; dark-brown borders below side stripes; white belly with greenish or yellow hue; curved white spot in front of eyes; sharply defined yellow lips
Alias: Eastern ribbon snake, northern ribbon snake, *la couleuvre mince, Thamnophis sauritus*
Preferred habitat: Thickets and brush around streams and ponds, marshes, bogs, swamps, weedy lakeshores and wet meadows
Food: Mostly small frogs and tadpoles, also salamanders, toads, minnows, fish fry, mice, insects and spiders
Average litter: 9–12
Range: Southern Ontario to Renfrew County, Haliburton, the Georgian Bay hinterlands and Manitoulin Island

RINGNECK SNAKE
Secretive Salamander Stalker

Average adult length: 25–35 cm
(10–14 in)
Maximum length: 62.5 cm
(25 in)
Markings: Bluish-grey or slate-coloured top, bright-yellow neck ring and yellow belly
Alias: Northern ringneck snake, eastern ringneck snake, corkscrew snake, *la couleuvre à collier, Diadophis punctatus*
Preferred habitat: Dense, moist forests with rocky outcrops around bogs and marshes on hillsides
Winter whereabouts: Below frost line in rock crevices and other natural cavities, also in old mouse burrows
Food: Salamanders, especially redbacks and their eggs; worms, spring peepers, wood frogs, toads, young snakes and adult redbelly snakes, slugs, beetle grubs, sowbugs and other insects, spiders
Average clutch: 3–4 white, grape-sized eggs, the capsule shape often curving with expansion after being laid
Length of hatchlings: 9–14 cm (3.5–5.5 in)
Age at sexual maturity: 2–3 years
Predators: Great horned owls, broad-winged hawks, raccoons, skunks, milk snakes and other large snakes
Range: Southern Ontario to about Wawa and Temagami; also in southern Quebec, New Brunswick and Nova Scotia

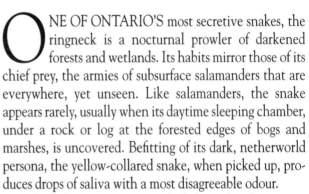

ONE OF ONTARIO'S most secretive snakes, the ringneck is a nocturnal prowler of darkened forests and wetlands. Its habits mirror those of its chief prey, the armies of subsurface salamanders that are everywhere, yet unseen. Like salamanders, the snake appears rarely, usually when its daytime sleeping chamber, under a rock or log at the forested edges of bogs and marshes, is uncovered. Befitting of its dark, netherworld persona, the yellow-collared snake, when picked up, produces drops of saliva with a most disagreeable odour.

When the time comes to bed down for the winter, from October through late April or May, ringneck snakes can be gregarious, often hibernating in small groups. Like garter snakes, they use the opportunity to mate both when arriving at and departing from the winter dorms. Several females may also lay eggs together in late June or July in a favourite spot used from one year to the next. It's usually under the bark of a rotting log or stump. For most of the summer, though, ringnecks keep to themselves beneath the forest litter, in mossy rock crevices and inside partially buried, pulpy fallen trees. They become inactive during hot, dry spells. The young hatch in late August or September, their backs, bellies and ringed necks even more vividly contrasting than on adults.

FIVE-LINED SKINK
Ontario's Only Lizard

LIZARDS ARE STAGGERINGLY successful creatures, with more species filling more niches around the world than any other group of reptiles. Yet all of Eastern Canada boasts but one of the fabled serpents, a reclusive lizard known by few. Those who do see the five-lined skink may assume it's a salamander. Unlike its amphibian look-alikes, however, the skink has dry scales, claws and ear openings. It was probably once found throughout much of southern Ontario, but now holds out in scattered pockets, most of them across the southern foot of the Canadian Shield.

Young, inexperienced skinks – with gleaming yellow lines set against a polished black back and a royal-blue tail – are more often seen than their secretive elders. The vibrant colour of their tails distracts the jaws of predators away from vital organs. Like many other small lizards, as well as salamanders, a skink can lose its tail with the slightest tug, leaving it to wriggle for up to several minutes afterwards while the reptile makes good its escape. The wound is clean, almost bloodless and heals quickly. A new tail, with only cartilage and lacking any bone, miraculously grows back afterwards, one or two millimetres a week. Losing a tail in late summer or in fall can doom a skink, however, because the appendage stores fat reserves needed as winter fuel during hibernation.

Skinks are among the toughest of the world's handful of cold-hardy lizards. They move about at temperatures as low as 6°C (43°F). Once things are a little warmer, the tiny-legged creatures skitter like quicksilver over the ground and under rocks and logs, following microscopic particles of insect scent picked up on the tips of their constantly flicking tongues. They are extremely agile, twisting and winding their long, sleek bodies like snakes.

Average adult length: 12–17 cm (4.7–6.7 in)
Maximum length: 21.5 cm (8.5 in)
Weight: Normally about 10 g (0.4 oz); pregnant females up to 16 g (0.6 oz)
World's largest lizard: Komodo dragon of Asia, up to 3 m (10 ft) long
World's smallest lizard: Monitio gecko, 3.4 cm (1.4 in) long
Markings: Shiny black body with 5 creamy-white or yellowish stripes running from snout to solid-blue tail; vibrant colour contrast fades with age, the body bronzing and tail turning grey
Alias: Blue-tailed skink, blue devil, red-headed lizard, *le scinque pentaligne*, *Eumeces fasciatus*
Senses: Hunts by tasting scent; eyes highly sensitive to movement and hears very well
Preferred habitat: Sunny, open forests on bare bedrock outcroppings with juniper, red oak and pine, close to water; also

135

on broken, rocky shores, sometimes on islands and in rock piles in open spots
Winter whereabouts: Below the frost line in crevices and under rock piles as deep as 3 m (10 ft), also in old stumps and large logs, sometimes in groups of up to 8
Home range: 2.7–8.1 m² (30–87 sq ft), overlapping with other skinks
Food: Beetles, spiders, worms, flies, millipedes, crickets, grasshoppers, caterpillars, moths, snails
Double endowment: Like snakes, male skinks have 2 penises
Average clutch: 6–10 white, chickpea-sized eggs with thin, leathery shells
Incubation period: 30–40 days
Length at birth: 5–6 cm (2–2.4 in)
Age at sexual maturity: Almost 2 years
Maximum lifespan: At least 6 years
Predators: Snakes, broad-winged hawks, crows, raccoons, skunks, shrews
Most active time: Late morning and in the afternoon
Range: Around Georgian Bay, including the Bruce Peninsula, and across Muskoka, Haliburton and the southern edge of the Shield to north of Kingston; also in spots along Lake Huron and Lake Erie
Skink capital of Ontario: Point Pelee, on Lake Erie, with estimated population of 1,000
Number of lizard species in Canada: 5
Number of lizard species worldwide: About 3,750

Great leaping lizards, they also occasionally snatch bugs from the air.

In late May and June, males also take up feminine skink scent trails, following them for as far as 100 metres (330 feet) if fresh. Though the bright-blue tails of their youth have faded to grey, mature males develop a brilliant orange-red throat and mouth during the breeding season. Females accept callers with the healthiest glow, entwining with them after a preliminary chase. Rival bucks coming across one another are hostile, and one is either chased away at once or after several minutes of jaw-snapping combat. Novices usually lose out to battle-scarred veterans and don't breed until their third year.

Skinks become harder to find after the mating season. Even when basking, they can remain out of sight in the slimmest of exposed cracks and crevices. Around late July, females begin looking outside of their normal haunts for pockets beneath flat rocks and logs where they can lay their eggs. They're fiercely maternal, curling around and guarding their eggs closely. Two mothers sometimes tend their clutches under the same rock, doubling the garrison's defences against mice, snakes and other nest robbers. Scarcely even eating until the eggs hatch in August or September, they leave soon afterwards, lest their appetites get the better of them at the sight of their own squirming young. The hatchlings keep close to the nest at first, but are able to catch their own food. They don't have long to put on weight and grow before going into hibernation in late September or October.

Ontario researchers believe some populations of the rare reptiles are also preyed upon by human poachers, collecting soon-to-hatch eggs for pet stores. Selling any native wild animal to the pet trade is illegal in Ontario, as is collecting reptiles for personal use.

PLANT KINGDOM

PLANTS

THERE ARE HUNDREDS *of native plants in the region covered by this book. A great many, though, are rare or limited in distribution. We've concentrated on the most common and generally conspicuous species encountered throughout the southern Canadian Shield. Of the 30 entries in this section and 18 entries in Up North, some – such as goldenrods, asters, violets and grasses – cover whole groups of plants, each with a dozen or more very similar species. Several single-species entries also include information on other plants (their names appearing in* **bold***) that are either related or have certain features in common. While most general wildflower guides seem to give most of their space to field and meadow species, many of them non-native, our emphasis is on the woodland plants found along trails and around campsites and cottages in the region's predominantly forested landscape.*

As in the first book, the entries feature the lore surrounding the various plants and note some of their traditional uses as food or medicine. We strongly recommend, however, consulting detailed medicinal references and wild-food guides before experimenting. The same active ingredients that have curative powers in many plants can also be toxic in high concentrations or if not prepared properly.

ASTERS
Frost Flowers of Autumn

The scarlet of the maples can shake me like a cry
Of bugles going by.
And my lonely spirit thrills
To see the frosty asters like smoke upon the hills.

BLISS CARMAN, "An Autumn Song"

ASTERS PUT ON the last display of the year's flowering revue. Taking over from the goldenrods of late summer, aster blooms explode in purple and white across meadows in September and October. The galaxies of flowers are aptly named: *aster* means "star" in ancient Greek, a reference to the starlike bursts of rays spreading from their flowerheads. In past ages, when fate was commonly believed to be guided by the stars, an ill-starred event was literally a "disaster." In Greek mythology, asters were created when Virgo, the celestial virgin, wept tears of stardust that fell to Earth. The Greeks used these sacred flowers to make altar wreaths for festivals.

But the Old World's handful of relatively drab asters pale in comparison to North America's huge array of brightly coloured species. There are more kinds of asters on the continent than any other genus of flowers. Not surprisingly, asters are members of the highly evolved and successful composite family, the world's largest, accounting for about 10 percent of all known flowering plants. Unlike plants that retain the older design of a single, large-petalled blossom, composite flowerheads are composed of many individual miniature flowers. The long, petal-like rays surrounding each aster flowerhead are sterile flowers that have evolved primarily to catch the attention of pollinating insects with their colour.

Height: 20–244 cm (0.7–8 ft)
Alias: Michaelmas daisies, starworts, frost flowers, *les asters*, Asteraceae
Flowers: Composite flowerheads 1–4 cm (0.4–1.6 in) wide, composed of light-blue, violet, reddish-purple, pink or white rays around a usually yellow centre of tiny, tubular fertile florets, which turn brown, red or purple after pollination
Seeds: Very light and tiny, attached to silken fibres, with many together forming spheres of fluff, spread by the wind
Leaves: 1–20 cm (0.4–8 in) long, narrow and grasslike on most meadow asters; somewhat heart-shaped, up to 15 cm (6 in) wide and 25 cm (10 in) long, with widely toothed edges on woodland asters

Numerous minute fertile flowers form the asters' yellow centres, together pooling much nectar.

By massing so many flowers so closely together, asters guarantee a large portion of their population will be fertilized. As hardy late bloomers, they virtually monopolize the services of pollinating bumblebees and other diehards making their last rounds for the year. The huge number of flowers also helps ensure great genetic variability and adaptive potential.

Each tiny, pollinated floret produces a single seed, with long, wispy fibres, a few weeks after fertilization. As the colour fades from the landscape and the first snow falls, the fluffy aster seedheads are broken up by the wind. The dead stalks often remain standing into winter. Dispersed far and wide, the seeds of most species germinate in spring. They first form small ground-hugging whorls of leaves, called rosettes, and then flowering stalks. However, frost asters – species with small, white-rayed flowerheads, including central Ontario's calico aster – have seeds that germinate and produce rosettes in the autumn before going dormant.

Once established, an aster persists for years, its large, tough rhizome continually spreading and sending up numerous new stalks. But unlike most colonially spreading forest plants, asters can develop flowers and seeds in their first year.

Several varieties of asters also grow in forests where the overhead cover is not too dense. Woodland asters maximize their light-gathering ability with much bigger, broader leaves than those of their meadow relatives. They grow in large, lush patches, usually not too deep into the forest. Just those growing close to the edges of woods get enough sunlight to send up flowering stalks, which display only a small number of light-blue flowerheads.

Roots: Long, thick rhizomes

Flowering period: Purple-stemmed and flat-topped asters may begin blooming in late July; most others start in Aug. and continue into Oct.

Meadow species: Flat-topped aster, panicled aster, Lindley's aster, calico aster, New England aster

Deciduous and mixed forest species: Large-leaved aster (illustrated), heart-leaved aster, Lindley's aster

Wetland species: Bog aster, panicled aster, purple-stemmed aster, flat-topped aster

Shoreline species: Purple-stemmed aster, flat-topped aster, panicled aster

Common visitors: Bees, butterflies, mice, chipmunks, hares, moose, deer, ruffed grouse, chickadees, goldfinches, swamp and tree sparrows

Native uses: Ojibway hunters camouflaged their human scent by smoking aster rootlets, said to resemble the smell of the scent glands in the clefts of deer hooves

Range: Throughout Ontario; also in all other provinces and territories

Number of asters native to Ontario: More than 30

Number of aster species worldwide: At least 250, most in North America

Number of composite-family species worldwide: 19,000–25,000

Also see: Goldenrod, Virgo, Goldfinch. *Up North:* Bees

BEDSTRAW
Aid to Sweet Dreams

Height or length: 20–200 cm
(8–78 in)
Alias: Catchweed, goose grass,
cleavers, stick-a-back, maid's
hair, gravel grass, cheese
rennet, *le gaillet*, *Galium*
Leaves: Narrow, pointed, 1–9 cm
(0.4–3.6 in) long, in whorls of
2–6, often raspy on bottom
Stems: Green, thin, four-sided,
most lined with bristles
Flowers: White or greenish white,
2–3 mm (0.08–0.11 in) wide,
usually 4 petals, in small clusters on slender stalks from leaf
whorls; most bloom in summer
Seeds: 1 per tiny capsule, which
appears in pairs, most shiny,
but some with hooked hairs
Origin of word "straw": From the
ancient Germanic word
strawam, meaning "strewn,"
in reference to dry grain stalks
or grass spread on the earthen
floors of huts
Range: Throughout Ontario; also
in all other provinces and
territories
Number of bedstraw species
native to Ontario: 14

THE STUFF OF DREAMS lies in mats strewn in great abundance beneath the trees and open skies. Countless bushels of long-stemmed bedstraw were once gathered for stuffing the homemade mattresses of Ontario's pioneer past, when self-reliance and improvisation were imperative for "roughing it in the bush." A variety known as fragrant bedstraw (illustrated) was favoured because, when dried, it gave the bed a pleasant vanilla scent. The plant's bristly seeds were dried and roasted as a backwoods coffee substitute. In fact, bedstraw is in the same family of mostly tropical plants that includes true coffee, native to east Africa.

When boiled in water, the roots of northern and wild bedstraw provided a red dye, used in native porcupine quill work and early Québécois sashes and clothes. The root of a southern European plant in the same family, madder, was the biggest source of red dye from the days of ancient Egypt right up to the 19th century. Other important family members include the South American species that yield quinine and ipecac, the 17th-century wonder drugs that for the first time effectively treated malaria and dysentery respectively.

While certainly not the first plants one notices in the wild, bedstraws are actually quite distinctive, with whorls of leaves encircling long, square stems at regular intervals. They're perhaps most frequently encountered as long, ankle- to waist-high whips hindering progress through thick bush as they cling to clothing. The clinging is caused by small bristles lining the stems of most species, most notably on rough bedstraw. The bristles help the weak, falling stems hold on to other plants, and stick to the fur of passing animals, thereby spreading their seeds.

BLUE BEAD LILY
Lush Leaves of Summer

THE BLUE BEAD lily, with its lush, tuliplike leaves, stands out in the heart of the summer forest like few other woodland plants. In patches receiving the most sunlight, sturdy green stems rise from between the glossy, rubbery leaves. Each stem bears several smooth, round berries, like navy-blue beads, giving the lily its name. The plant's other common name, yellow clintonia, is more applicable in June, when its greenish-yellow flowers nod from the stem tops. Though the sharply pointed, flaring petals turn more purely yellow as they mature, they are far less striking than the single berry produced by each flower.

Some authorities say the attractive berries are mildly poisonous. One tale, passed down from the Ojibway and others, held that dogs poison their teeth with the berries before a hunt. Forest-food enthusiasts, however, praise the cucumber taste of the newly sprouted leaves.

The "*clintonia*" part of the blue bead lily's scientific name commemorates De Witt Clinton, an early 19th-century naturalist and governor of New York, who organized the building of the Erie Canal and advocated the export of the forest herb mayapple as a cash crop. The man who bestowed Clinton with floral immortality was a decidedly more obscure naturalist named Samuel Rafinesque, a pioneering absentminded-professor type at a university in Kentucky, whom fellow Frenchman John James Audubon described as a bit of an "odd fish."

Height: 15–40 cm (6–16 in)
Alias: Yellow clintonia, corn lily, northern lily, dogberry, wild corn, *la clintonie jaune, Clintonia borealis*
Flowers: Pale to greenish yellow and loosely bell-shaped, 3–8 per plant at top of stem, each 2 cm (0.8 in) wide, with 3 petals and 3 petal-like sepals, 6 golden stamens and a long green pistil
Berries: Navy blue, shiny, 8–10 mm (0.4 in) wide, each containing 6–10 seeds
Leaves: Up to 30 cm (1 ft) long, 4–9 cm (1.6–3.6 in) wide; thick, glossy, bright green above, downy on bottom, with bluntly pointed tip and parallel veins; usually 3 arch from base of the flowering stem, occasionally 2, 4 or 5
Roots: A thin, knotted, branching rhizome near surface
Habitat: Moist coniferous and mixed forests
Range: Throughout Ontario; also in Manitoba, Quebec and Atlantic provinces

BOG LAUREL
Spring-action Pollination

Height: 15–60 cm (6–24 in)
Alias: Pale laurel, swamp laurel,
le kalmia a feuilles
d'Andromede, Kalmia polifolia
Flowers: Pink, saucer-shaped,
10–15 mm (0.4–0.6 in)
wide, with 5 lobes, 10 prominent dark-tipped stamens surrounding long, pink pistil;
clustered at top of stems
Seeds: Many held in roundish
brown capsule, up to 5 mm
(0.2 in) wide, with a long
thread projecting from its tip;
appearing in summer
Leaves: In pairs, 1–4 cm
(0.4–1.6 in) long, 6–12 mm
(0.2–0.5 in) wide, pointed at
both ends, smooth edges
curled downwards, glossy,
dark green on top, powdery
white and hairy below
Stems: Woody, dark brown,
two-sided, usually with
several branches
Preferred habitat: Peaty ground
in bogs and coniferous
swamps
Companion plants: Bog rosemary, leather-leaf, Labrador
tea, pitcher plants, sundew,
tall meadowrue, cranberry,
sedges, three-leaved false
Solomon's seal, winterberry,
mountain holly
Legendary attributes of true
laurel: Divine purification,
protection from lightning and
evil; symbol of triumph and
merit, especially merit in
poetry
First poet laureate to the British
royal court: Ben Jonson,

O F THE MANY spring-flowering wetland plants, bog laurel is one of the prettiest. Its bunches of bright-pink, saucer-shaped blossoms sprinkle the shrubby sections of bogs in May and June with colour and fragrance. Pollen-seeking insects attracted to bog laurel are co-opted by an entertaining design into becoming sexual partners with the flower. Each of the small, dark dots circling the flower's interior is the pollen head, or anther, of a stamen, held tightly within a pit in the petal's surface. When an insect alights on the flower, its weight triggers one or more of these stamens to spring forward like a mini-catapult and shower the bug with pollen. Moving on to a flower on another plant, the pollen-bearing visitor becomes the agent of cross-fertilization.

Farther back from the bog's open spaces, among the black spruce and tamarack on its fringes, the closely related **sheep laurel** displays much larger clusters of similar but somewhat darker-pink flowers. Its flowers, unlike the bog laurel's, appear a little below the top of the stem. It blooms in late June and early July. Sheep laurel also grows in dry, acidic soil on rocky hilltops.

Both of Ontario's laurels were so named because their dark, shiny evergreen leaves are reminiscent of true laurel, an unrelated fragrant Mediterranean shrub. Still a symbol of honour today, laurel represented triumph to the ancient Greeks and Romans and was especially sacred to Apollo, god of light and healing. Greek oracles ate laurel leaves and seeds to help them see into the future. In Rome, religious sacrifices were always burned with laurel and juniper. Earlier, in ancient Mesopotamia, laurel resin was burned as sacred incense. Today, it is familiar in spice racks as the common bay leaf.

Unlike those of their Old World namesake, bog and sheep laurel leaves are decidedly bad choices for flavouring soups and sauces. They are, in fact, quite poisonous to humans and livestock, though deer and snowshoe hares seem to have no problem nibbling them. Native peoples reportedly used the leaves if they wanted to kill themselves, just as despairing Europeans turned to the hemlock herb in their homelands. Native healers also knew how to make very dilute solutions from the dangerous plant to act as a sedative and treat inflammations.

Bog, sheep and mountain laurel's poisonous properties were first reported to science by pioneering Swedish botanist Pehr Kalm, who in 1749 scoured Quebec's forests for new species. His return to Sweden with a bevy of unnamed New World plants sparked his mentor, Carl Linnaeus – who had been down in the dumps – to complete his revolutionary work of scientifically naming all the world's known species. Linnaeus's practical taxonomic system of Latin and Greek names quickly became the international standard for all plants and animals, and is still used today. Linnaeus rewarded his young friend by naming bog laurel's genus, *Kalmia*, after him.

The Swedish government had originally funded Kalm's mission to the New World to look for new northern plants that could be grown commercially in Scandinavia. While Labrador tea and wild sarsaparilla never did catch on as cash crops in Sweden, Kalm's book about his travels became a classic on life in the closing days of New France.

1572–1637, charged with composing verse for the king's birthdays and state occasions

Range: Throughout Ontario; also in all other provinces and territories

Ontario's most poisonous plant: Spotted water hemlock

Other poisonous plants: Doll's-eyes, jack-in-the-pulpit, purple iris (roots), columbine (roots and seeds), red-berried elder, cardinal flower, Dutchman's breeches, milkweed, buttercup, Queen Anne's lace

Number of *Kalmia* species native to Ontario: 2

Number of *Kalmia* species worldwide: 8

Also see: Labrador Tea, Twinflower. *Up North:* Wetlands, Juniper

CANADA MAYFLOWER
Unsung Floral Emblem

Height: 5–25 cm (2–10 in),
  usually under 15 cm (6 in)
Alias: False lily-of-the-valley,
  wild lily-of-the-valley, Canada
  maianthemum, May lily,
  beadruby, *le muguet,*
  maiantheme du Canada,
  Maianthemum canadense
Scientific name meaning: From
  the Latin *Maius,* meaning
  "May"; the Romans named
  the month after Maia, the
  goddess of growth and spring;
  anthemum means "flower"
Anglo-Saxon name for May:
  Thrimilcmonath, "three-milk-
  month," referring to cows'
  ability to produce enough to
  be milked three times a day
  in mid-spring
Flowers: Many minute white
  blossoms, 4–6 mm (0.2 in)
  wide, on an erect spike,
  1.5–5.5 cm (0.6–2.2 in)
  long, above the leaves; each
  flower has 4 jutting stamens
Berries: About 4 mm (0.2 in)
  wide, initially hard, whitish
  and translucent, turning
  green, speckled with purple
  and finally completely red
  when ripe in autumn; each
  contains 1 or 2 seeds
Leaves: 2–10 cm (1–4 in) long,
  1.5–5 cm (0.6–2 in) wide,
  shiny, pointed, smooth-edged,
  with notched base that hugs
  around stem; 2 or rarely 3 on
  flowering plants, just 1 on
  sterile plants; turn brown
  and wither back from tips in
  autumn

CANADA MAYFLOWER is often not given its due, being passed off with names such as "false lily-of-the-valley," implying secondary significance to a refined garden import. In fact, Canada mayflower is a true lily and perhaps the most common plant found in the mixed and evergreen forests that cover most of central Ontario. The sheer ubiquity of its lacy white spires of blossoms, in multitudes throughout the country, could easily make it Canada's national flower.

But Canada mayflowers are tiny and bloom early. The vast majority produce no flowers at all, just a single leaf that rises a few centimetres above the ground. They are so commonplace that they seem to go virtually unnoticed. Pre-formed in underground shoots during the previous growing season, tightly curled, pointed mayflower leaves burst straight up through the rotting leaves of the forest duff soon after the snow is gone. But unlike trout lilies in hardwood stands, which disappear from view in June, mayflower plants persist until the frosts of autumn.

Spreading in colonies by connected underground stems, each single-leaved mayflower plant is part of a team, sending energy to a number of more select confrères growing in the best light and soil conditions. These lucky few are the breeders, producing two or, less often, three leaves along a flowering stalk, which usually blooms in late May and June. Up close, the flowers resemble little globes with long, white antennae, and give off a strong, sweet perfume. Bending down to sample the fragrance comes with a warning, however: there is an old English superstition that smelling lilies can cause freckles.

About a month after starting to bloom, the flowers give way to hard, little, speckled green berries that ripen through the summer, becoming soft and red by fall. They're feasted upon by an assortment of birds and animals. The Ojibway called the plant *gunkisaehminuk*, "chipmunk berry." The bittersweet berries are edible to humans, but have been known to cause frequent trips to the latrine.

> *Each single-leaved mayflower plant is part of a team, sending energy to a number of more select confrères*

Another lily that can be mistaken for the Canada mayflower at first glance is **three-leaved false Solomon's seal**. With longer, more upwardly pointing leaves and a sparser spike of flowers, it most commonly grows amid the sphagnum of open or partially forested bogs and cedar swamps.

Stem: Usually changes angle where it joins with leaves on flowering plants
Roots: Long, white rhizomes with many fine tan-coloured rootlets ending in rounded swellings in fall
Preferred habitat: Acidic humus soil of forests
Companion plants: Bunchberry, moccasin flowers, violets, wintergreen, twinflowers, goldthread, red baneberry
Common visitors: Chipmunks, mice, hares and grouse eat berries
Pests: Slugs, leaf miner caterpillars
Range: Throughout Ontario; also in all other provinces and territories
Also see: Trout Lily, Solomon's Seal. *Up North:* Chipmunk

COLUMBINE
Tailor-made for Hummingbirds

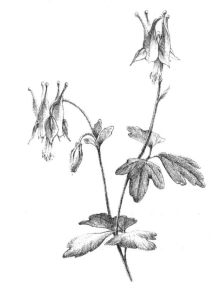

Height: Usually 30–60 cm
(1–2 ft), sometimes up to
100 cm (3.3 ft)
Alias: Canada columbine, wild
columbine, red columbine,
rock-lily, rock-bells, Jack-in-
trousers, cluckies, meeting-
houses, American columbine,
honeysuckle, *l'ancolie du
Canada, Aquilegia canadensis*
Flowers: Bright-red petals and
sepals form 5 erect, narrow
tubes, 3–4 cm (1.2–1.6 in)
long, bent at their peaks.
Petal tips and stamens
are yellow and face the
ground. Each plant blooms
for about 3 weeks
Seeds: Tiny, black, shiny; many
released from a 5-chambered
capsule, 1.5–2 cm (0.6–
0.8 in) long, which splits
open in midsummer
Leaves: Compound, with 3 delicate leaflets, each with 3
lobes, with upper leaves
varying in shape; a new
rosette of leaves forms at the
ground in late summer and
fall and remains through the
winter
Stem: Thin, smooth, purplish,
branching into arching flower
stalks; several flowering
stems and leaf stalks often
joined at the ground; all
wither and collapse in late
summer
Roots: Slender, twisting tap root
Preferred habitat: Thin soil
around outcrops, cliffs, ridges
and other rocky sites in open

A RUBY-THROATED hummingbird buzzing about its business always adds an exotic touch to the north woods. So, too, does a beautifully intricate flower closely allied to the hummingbird, helping make its presence in Ontario possible. With elaborate hanging blossoms of red spires joined at a frilly yellow centre, wild columbine sets itself apart where sunbeams reach patches of thin soil on rocky outcrops. Hummingbirds are quick to take notice of the flowers, red being their biggest head-turner. Blooming from late May to July, the flowers reserve rich caches of nectar at the apex of their long spires for the hummingbird's long, probing beak. Hummers also pick up and spread pollen as they poke from one plant to the next.

Catharine Parr Traill reported in the early days of Upper Canada that columbine grew near every settler's home. Admirers soon took to incorporating the tame wildlings in their gardens. Wild columbine was also carried across the Atlantic to European gardens, where it was deemed to represent "anxiousness and trembling" in the popular floral lexicon of Victorian times. Though related species of columbine also grow in Europe, the lack of hummingbirds in the Old World caused the flowers there to evolve differently. European columbines have shorter tubes, or "spurs," which allow insects to reach their nectar and pollinate them. The five nodding spurs of the European plant are said to resemble doves in a circle with their heads bent, once a popular motif on dishes. This notion is the source of the flower's name, from the Latin word for dove, *columba*. The Old English name for the flower was *culverwort*, meaning "pigeon plant."

Catharine Parr Traill reported that columbine grew near every settler's home

---

Columbine also took the fancy of North American natives, especially those of the eastern prairies, who used it as a love charm. Young men who rubbed columbine seeds between their hands were said to become irresistible to the next pretty woman with whom they shook hands. The seeds are actually poisonous, as are the roots, and all parts of the plant are carcinogenic. The Ojibway, however, called columbine *misudidjeebik*, "stomach root," because they somehow used it to treat stomach problems without causing harm.

As the last columbine petals fall, another made-to-measure red tubular flower comes into bloom just in time for hummingbirds. The numerous scarlet blossoms of the **cardinal flower** brighten riversides, marsh margins and the moist edges of low-lying forests in late summer and early autumn. Topping prominent stems, 50 to 150 centimetres (20 to 60 inches) high, cardinal flowers' long, outreaching petals and sweet scent also attract humans. Picking has made them rare in many areas.

forests, especially towards edges, along paths, hillsides and clearings

Companion plants: Rock polypody ferns, grasses, strawberry

Pollinators: Hummingbirds, long-tongued moths

Pests: Bees and wasps sometimes chew through the top of flower to get nectar without pollinating plant; also larvae of leaf miner fly

Range: Throughout most of Ontario; also found in all provinces east of Alberta except Prince Edward Island

Close relations: Columbine is a member of the buttercup family. The common tall buttercup of meadows is an alien flower, but central Ontario has more than half a dozen native species, kidneyleaf buttercup of hardwood forests being perhaps most common. Baneberry, goldthread and the less abundant marsh marigold, hepatica and anemone are also family members

Number of columbine species native to Ontario: 1

Number of columbine species worldwide: About 70

Also see: Jewelweed, Doll's-eyes.

Up North: Ruby-throated Hummingbird, Goldthread

DOLL'S-EYES
Poison Berries with
Striking Allure

SCATTERED THROUGH HARD-wood forests of maple, beech and yellow birch, bunches of doll's-eyes stare boldly out from deep-red stalks in August and September. The large, white, black-eyed berries command attention wherever they ripen. Yet, for all their allure, doll's-eyes are reputed to be deadly poisonous. They're also known as white baneberries, from the Old English word *bona,* meaning "killer."

Authorities don't agree on just how poisonous doll's-eyes are to humans. Few want to take the test themselves. A single berry is said to be so bitter it would discourage anyone to try another. Other reports put fatal dosages at two berries for a child and something above six for a pre-viously hale and healthy adult. Mice, ruffed grouse and other animals seem to snap up the white fruits happily.

Ojibway women drank a tea made from doll's-eyes roots, also considered poisonous, to reduce heavy men-strual bleeding and cramps, while the men ate the root for stomach problems. They called the plant *weekizgum,* meaning "that which extracts." It may be that, as with other plants and fungi known to be deadly, native practi-tioners using careful preparations distilled just enough toxin and turned it to beneficial use.

A close relative of doll's-eyes, **red baneberry** has large, bright-red berries and is also said to be poisonous. It grows in small colonies, rather than singly, in mixed as well as deciduous forests. Both varieties of baneberry are peren-nial herbs, with purplish shoots rising from overwintering roots each spring.

FIREWEED
Rising from
the Ashes

F IREWEED IS THE EMBODI-
ment of the earth's regenerative
powers, rising from the ground's
blackened wounds after devastating forest
fires. Downy wisps of seeds released by the
plant throughout summer and fall are
always in the air, holding the potential to
sprout and thrive in the exposed mineral
soil and full sunlight left by fire. Many also
grow in older fields and along lakeshores and trails,
forming dense patches of bright-pink flowering spires.

Scores of flowers bloom along the length of each fireweed spire from July to September. Starting at the
bottom, each blossom lasts only two days. On the first, it
produces only sticky pollen; on the second, it has no
pollen, but becomes receptive to fertilization, and to
attract pollinators, especially bumblebees, gives off a
strong fragrance from its rich pool of nectar. After a bee
drains the nectar from one flower, it buzzes up to the one
above, usually finding a younger pollen-laden blossom
with little nectar. It then gives up on the plant and flies to
a receptive flower at the bottom of a nearby spire. The
flowering sequence, combined with the bee's systematic
work habits, usually ensures cross-pollination rather than
self-fertilization.

After pollination, blunt, upward-pointing purple
spikes form in place of the flowers, so that each spire
usually has spikes at the bottom, blossoms in the middle
and unopened flower buds at the top. As they mature, the
spike pods curl and split open, releasing silken-fibred
seeds to the wind. A single plant sheds about 45,000 seeds
a year, ensuring good odds that a few will find their way to
just the right sites to put down roots. Several plants can
rapidly colonize a newly opened area by spreading underground rhizomes, though in a few years they are usually

Height: 50–200 cm (20–80 in)
Alias: Great willow-herb,
rosebay, firetop, purple
rocket, willow-weed, blooming sally, Indian wickup,
French willowherb, herb
wickup, Indian pink, pigweed,
wild asparagus, *les épilobe à
feuilles étroites, les bouquet
rouges, Epilobium angustifolium*
Scientific name meaning:
Epiobon is Greek for "upon
pod," *angustifolium* means
"broad-leaved" in Latin
Flowers: About 100 blossoms per
plant, each 1.5–2.5 cm
(0.6–1 in) wide, with 4
rounded, bright-pink petals
and 4 thin, reddish-purple
sepals. Flower centre features
8 long stamens and an even
longer white pistil divided
into 4 at tip
Seeds: Wisps of fluff released
from tubular purple-pink pods
3–8 cm (1–3 in) long; from a
distance, many blown by the
wind can look like rising
smoke

Leaves: 3–20 cm (1–8 in) long, narrow, dark green on top, dull green beneath, pointed at both ends, with wavy edges outlined by prominent veins; often turn bright red in autumn

Stem: Stiff, smooth, dark pink or green, standing through winter

Roots: Long, many-branched rhizome

Preferred habitat: Burned-over areas, open places, lakeshores, wide portages and trails

Companion species: Grasses, orange hawkweed, goldenrod, aster

Common visitors: Bumblebees, honey bees, wasps, moths, butterflies, hummingbirds

War service: In the days of the Blitz, desolate bombsites in the heart of London transformed into stunning wild gardens of teaming pink fireweed

Food value: Honey bees produce a very sweet, highly regarded white honey from fireweed nectar. Spring shoots, high in vitamin A and C, have been used in salads, steamed or stir-fried

Range: Throughout Ontario; also in all other provinces and territories

Number of *Epilobium* species native to Ontario: 9

Number of *Epilobium* species worldwide: 215

Also see: Pickerelweed, Largetooth Aspen. *Up North:* Bees

overtaken and shaded out by pin cherry, aspens, poplars, wild raisin and other fast-growing tree saplings.

Still, feathery-light fireweed seeds are so successful at finding a place in the sun that they have spread throughout the world's fire-dominated northern boreal forest zone. The flowers, providing vast concessions of nectar, make possible an abundance of species of butterflies, moths and bees in these otherwise lean environments. In tribute to its vibrant spires, glorying in the long daylight hours of northern summers, fireweed is designated the official flower of the Yukon.

Northern peoples once stripped long, stringy fibres from fireweed stems to make into twine and fishing line and ate the soft pith from inside the stems. Russian peasants boiled the pith with poisonous fly agaric mushrooms to make a psychotropic ale and, even more commonly, brewed the plant's willowlike leaves for tea. Canadian voyageurs esteemed the leaves as a pot herb and used the fluffy seed pods to start their fires. The Ojibway called the plant *zhoshkidjeebik*, meaning "slippery root," because the outer coating of its roots lathered up when they moistened it and pounded it into a poultice for bruises, boils and sores.

Note: Fireweed is similar in colour and appearance to the invasive alien **purple loosestrife**. Those seeking to rid their property of the purple pest should take care to make a positive ID. Loosestrife has six narrow petals, rather than four rounded ones as on fireweed. Loosestrife also grows in marshes, wet meadows or along wet shorelines, while fireweed usually grows on drier ground.

GOLDENROD
Multi-tiered Insect Cities

*And she's bound his wounds with the goldenrod, full fast in
  her arms he lay
And he has risen hale and sound with the sun high in the day.*

ARCHIE FISHER, "The Witch of the West-Mer-Lands"

ALIEN PLANTS OFTEN dominate Ontario fields and meadows, having arrived as part of the package with European settlers, agriculture and the clearing of forests. But come August, in the same open spaces, native goldenrods steal the scene. Though they are composites – sporting tiny flowers on each flowerhead, like many aliens such as dandelions and daisies – goldenrods are as Canadian as Beaver McGee at centre ice. They spread rapidly by both roots and seeds, forming large colonies that hold their ground against foreign upstarts.

Yet, as with many wholesome native species, goldenrod has been denunciated, persecuted and uprooted. It is widely, and erroneously, reviled as a hay-fever-causing weed. In truth, goldenrod produces large, sticky grains of pollen that are picked up by insects rather than the wind. The real great hay-fever culprit is ragweed, a

Height: 20–200 cm (8–80 in)
Tallest foreign goldenrod: Subtropical species in Florida reach 5.5 m (18 ft)
Alias: Woundwort, Aaron's rod, blue mountain tea, *la verge d'or, bouquets jaunes, Solidago*
Flowers: Each tiny yellow flowerhead has numerous female ray flowers around its edge and at least 20 disk flowers at its centre with both male and female organs; numerous flowerheads form a plume, with those on top blooming first
Blooming period: Late July to late Sept.
Seeds: Minute, with fluffy fibres that carry them on the wind; emerge from split, dried flowerheads through fall and winter; eaten by many birds and mammals
Leaves and stem: Many different forms, depending on species; both die back in autumn, though remain standing through winter
Roots: Some of the deepest taproots of any native herb, the Canada goldenrod reaching 3.3 m (11 ft) below ground in prairies; also spreading horizontal rhizomes
Development: Usually no flowers produced in first year. In second autumn, 4 or 5 rhizomes spread beneath ground from stem base, each sending up new stalks the following spring. Colonies of

clones may grow to several metres in diameter

Lifespan: More than 100 years for some colonies in the prairies

Dry meadow species: Canada (illustrated), gray, early and tall goldenrod

Wetland and wet meadow species: Marsh, bog, rough-stemmed, grass-leaved and Canada goldenrod

Shoreline species: Tall, Canada, grass-leaved and early goldenrod

Open forest species: Large-leaved and sharp-leaved goldenrod

Forest edge species: Late, early and Canada goldenrod

Ontario's only non-yellow goldenrod: Silverrod, with white flowers

Non-medical uses: Leaves brewed as tea substitute; flowers long used for home-made yellow dyes; rich, golden honey produced by goldenrod-addicted honey bees; diviners once used stems to find water

Common visitors: Honey bees, bumblebees, monarch butterflies, paper wasps, syrphid flies, long-horned beetles, soldier beetles, praying mantises, *Formica* ants, downy woodpeckers, juncos, sparrows and finches

Common residents: Ambush bugs, goldenrod beetles, goldenrod spiders, and the larvae of flies, moths, midges and tree-hoppers

Number of known gall-causing insects: About 2,000, 75% wasps or gnats

small, inconspicuous plant that also blooms in late summer and sends out vast clouds of dry, tiny, windborne pollen that finds its way to many an unhappy nose.

The castigation of goldenrod as a noxious weed is especially misguided given that its scientific name, *Solidago*, means "make whole" or "solid" in Latin, a tribute to its ancient use in healing wounds. The Ojibway called it *geezisomuskiki*, meaning "sun medicine." They, as well as many other native nations and settlers after them, brewed the flowers into a tea for a wide assortment of ailments, from fevers and chest pains to ulcers, kidney problems, even excessive flatulence. The Ojibway also added the flowers to a pipe blend that was smoked to bring success in hunting, and applied the boiled roots as a poultice for burns and sprains. Many modern herbalists still consider it a panacea.

Wherever they grow, goldenrods are of vital importance to an incredible assortment of tiny inhabitants

---

In recent years, goldenrod has even been used to heal the earth. It is planted, along with species such as poplar, arrowroot and duckweed, in polluted habitats, because it has enzymes that break down organic toxins contaminating the soil and water.

Wherever they grow, goldenrods are of vital importance to an incredible assortment of tiny inhabitants, forming veritable multi-tiered cities. Offering vast quantities of nectar and pollen, the flowers dominate the attentions of bees, butterflies, flies and other pollinating insects during late summer. Meanwhile, goldenrod beetles and their larvae eat the plant's leaves, and tree-hoppers siphon off sap. Amid all the activity, predators such as ambush bugs, crab spiders and even praying mantises select from the bounty of inhabitants, like lions on the Serengeti.

The offspring of at least one species of tree-hopper, however, enjoys the protection of organized bands of *Formica* ants, who in return sup on the waste sap exuded by the larvae.

Even in winter, when goldenrod stalks stand dry and lifeless, the young of many insects lie sleeping within the plant's derelict tissues. These winter quarters are created when small flies use their pointy ovipositors to inject eggs into goldenrod stems during the growing season. When a maggot hatches and begins nibbling at its natal chamber, the plant responds by rapidly constructing new tissue around the irritant, resulting in the characteristic spherical bulges, called "galls," found on many goldenrod stems. More oval-shaped galls are caused by minute moth caterpillars, while midge larvae create black blister-galls on leaves and bunchy, flowerlike galls at branch tips. Ambush bugs, as well, leave their eggs in the overwintering leaves and stem.

To top it all off, gall-causing larvae often have company. Many other insect species specialize in taking advantage of the little gall forts created by others. These insects are called "inquilines," meaning literally "lodgers" in Latin. But before both homeowner and freeloader are ready to chew their way out of the gall and transform into adults, they may be joined by the worst lodgers of all, the parasitic larvae of ichneumon wasps and beetles, which feed upon the occupants themselves. Their world can also be shattered by the gall-probing beaks of downy woodpeckers in search of fresh grubs in the dead of winter. Ice fishers in need of bait sometimes resort to galls as well.

Other gall causers: Mites, nematodes, fungi, bacteria and viruses

Portion of plant galls that appear on leaves: 95%

Oldest fossil galls: More than 100 million years old

Gall ink: Aleppo galls from the Middle East have been used to make high-quality ink and dyes for more than 1,000 years, still used both for printing paper money and for tattoos

Common meadow alien species: Ox-eye daisy, dandelion, common buttercup, bird's-foot trefoil, silvery cinquefoil, toadflax, common St. John's wort, orange hawkweed, chicory, viper's bugloss, purple vetch, heal-all, mullein, knapweed, tansy

Common native composite meadow flowers: Asters, Joe-Pye weed, yarrow, fleabane, pearly everlasting, black-eyed Susans, pussy-toes, beggar's ticks, boneset, wild lettuce

Other common native meadow flowers: Milkweed, fireweed, evening primrose

Goldenrod range: Throughout Ontario; also found in all other provinces and territories

Number of goldenrod species native to Ontario: 28

Number of species worldwide: About 100, most in North America

Also see: Asters, Beetles, Midges, Downy Woodpecker. *Up North:* Bees

HORSETAIL

Spore-bearing Stalks
of Silica

WHEN PASSING a dense stand of horsetail, it's easy to imagine the plants below as forest trees, with broadly sweeping limbs and pointed peaks, as seen from an air-craft. Tree-sized horsetail actually did exist some 400 million years ago, in primitive, steamy tropical jungles inhab-ited by giant salamanders, crocodiles and scorpions during Earth's Devonian Age. Together with huge ferns and club-mosses, horsetails dominated the land, until cone-bearing trees appeared and eventually succeeded them. As conditions changed, most of the primitive trees that survived were those that allowed their trunks to shrivel and grow sideways beneath the ground. The ridged, hollow stalks of today's horsetail, which pull apart in segments, are really the branches of these submerged stems, called rhizomes, which survive unseen through the winter.

Like ferns, clubmosses and mushrooms, horsetail repro-duces the old-fashioned way, by spores rather than seeds. In fact, it's the first order of business every year, with conical spore-bearing heads, known as "strobilus" cones, on leafless stalks rising up from the ground as soon as frost has left it. With field horsetail (illustrated), sepa-rate green leafing stems follow later, but by the time most spring wildflowers are in full bloom, the strobilus cones have already released their yellow spores to the wind and shrivelled away.

Successful spores germinate within a week, produc-ing a tiny "gametophyte" plant that takes about a month to form a millimetre-wide leaflike "plate," called a pro-thallus. By the end of the summer, it may have grown to a centimetre (0.4 inches) wide. Male structures on the prothallus produce sperm that travel in the moisture on damp ground to receptive female organs of other prothalli. Once fertilized, the plants develop rhizomes that spread and continually send up new horsetail stalks.

Horsetail also differs from most other plants in not only relying on carbon, the basic building material of all life-forms, for its structure. Its stiff, ridged stem walls are reinforced with silica, an inorganic element that is the prime component of granite. Their rows of silicon crystals give field horsetail stems an abrasive edge, used by native groups to polish surfaces smooth. Similarly, another species, called scouring rush, cleaned the pots and pans of pioneer families. It's also been used to polish both wood and metal.

Though somewhat uncommon in Shield country, scouring rush is distinctive, lacking branches and looking like high, thick, jointed grass stalks. Water horsetail, growing in shallow bays, river edges and wetlands, has a similar look, often lacking branches and reaching up to a metre high.

But by far the most common species, in Ontario and throughout the world's northern temperate regions, is field horsetail. Growing both in meadows and open forests, it's usually about 25 centimetres (ten inches) tall and has many branches. After a forest fire or other disturbance, it often becomes the dominant initial ground cover, because its deep roots allow it to survive. Woodland horsetail is also plentiful in the Shield, differing from field horsetail in having branches that subdivide into smaller branchlets.

Finally, the smallest species, dwarf scouring rush, usually grows in matted tufts of twisted, threadlike stems, three to 20 centimetres high (one to eight inches), on mossy ground. These rough, dark-green, unbranched tangles persist through the winter, rather than withering with the autumn frosts like most other horsetails.

Branches: Soft, green, needle-shaped, up to 15 cm (6 in) long, growing in whorls around the stem

Spores: Fine, yellow, dustlike, released from a conelike strobilus, 1–4 cm (0.4–1.6 in) long in most species

Roots: Strong, thin, long horizontal rhizomes can be as deep as 1 m (3.3 ft)

Foul fodder: Horsetail contains a chemical called aconitic acid, which breaks down vitamin B, poisoning young horses and cattle

Range: Throughout Ontario; also in all other provinces and territories

Number of horsetail species native to Ontario: 8

Number of horsetail species worldwide: 15

Also see: Fireweed. *Up North:* Ferns, Granite

INDIAN PIPE
Ghostly Plant without Chlorophyll

Height: 10–20 cm (4–8 in),
rarely up to 30 cm (1 ft)
Alias: Ghost flower, ice plant,
corpse plant, fairy-smoke,
convulsionroot, fitroot, eyebright, Dutchman's pipe, con-
vulsionweed, *le monotrope
uniflore, Monotropa uniflora*
Flowers: White, waxy-looking,
bell-shaped, 1.5–2 cm
(0.6–0.8 in) long, formed by
5 overlapping petals, with 10
yellow stamens surrounding
round white pistil inside;
scentless
Seeds: Brown, dustlike, released
from large, upright capsules
at top of stem
Stems: White or pale pink,
translucent; turning brown
and woody in autumn
Roots: Small, dense ball of brittle
brown rootlets covered by
matted fungal fibres

DEEP IN THE DARKEST forest shade, where nary
a green plant dares to venture, one may encounter
a bowed, stunted ghoul. Appearing in small
groups of what look like bizarre, emaciated fungi, Indian
pipe is the custodian of the forest's inhospitable nether
regions. Amazingly, it's actually a flower, though one that
seems to have defected to the ranks of mushrooms. It survives by subversive means, getting the sun's energy denied
other forest-floor plants by stealing it from the roots of the
light-hogging trees. Accordingly, it has no need for leaves
and chlorophyll, the green matter that allow plants to
capture sunlight and turn it into energy.

Indian pipe, however, is no welcome convert in a col-
legial world of mushrooms. Rather than obtaining nourishment directly, its dense rootlets cluster around and
parasitize fungal fibres that themselves feed off tree roots.

The roots of plants in the closely related wintergreen
family, such as shinleaf, pyrola and prince's pipe, maintain
close, symbiotic bonds with certain kinds of fungi, sending
them photosynthesized energy in sugar compounds in
return for moisture and soil nutrients collected by the

fungi. It may be that Indian pipe's ancestor somehow acquired the ability to tap into tree-root fungi as well. Finding life easier as a parasite than as a symbiont, it discarded its green attire, today bearing only tiny, gauzy vestiges along its stem of what were once real leaves. Seeming to enter a realm of shades between plant and mushroom, Indian pipe acquired its strange, not-quite-mortal aspect. As if its pallid, waxy appearance weren't enough, the plant bruises black when handled. If picked, it bleeds a thick, gooey liquid. The whole business seriously creeped-out many 19th-century botanical writers, who denounced Indian pipe as "weird," "ghostly" and "degenerate."

Others saw dignity in the ghost flower. They noted that once fertilized, it slowly, solemnly raises its head to stand straight up. The motion is noted in the plant's scientific name *Monotropa*, which means "one turn." Once out of its "pipe" posture, the plant becomes hard, tough and woody as it darkens to dusty brown. From late summer through to spring, it remains standing, though now lifeless, gradually releasing dustlike seeds from slits in the pipehead capsule. But even as the plant lets its stem dry out, its roots form new flower buds, which push up as translucent, silvery sprouts early the following summer.

Preferred habitat: Rich humus or mossy soil of pine and hardwood forests
Companion plants: Wintergreen, bunchberry
Range: Southern Ontario to northern boreal forest; also in all other provinces
Only other monotrope species: Pinesap, also found in Ontario
Also see: *Up North:* Fungi, Moccasin Flower, Beech

The plant bruises black when handled. If picked, it bleeds a thick, gooey liquid

---

Native healers embraced the plant. They mixed its thick juice with water to use as an eye lotion and for colds and fevers. The dried root was also enlisted by 19th-century doctors to help cure fainting and epileptic fits and nervous disorders.

Indian pipe's sister plant, **pinesap**, is more rare, growing mainly in pine and evergreen woods, where it, too, parasitizes tree-root fungi. It is similar to Indian pipe, but is pale yellow, orangish or sometimes tinted red, and has several nodding flowers at the top of a stem, rather than just one.

Another, completely unrelated, plant that thrives without chlorophyll is, amazingly, an orchid, the **spotted coral-root**. Hoisting a spike of small and inconspicuous tubular flowers, coral-root's slender stem, up to 50 centimetres (1.6 feet) tall, is often a striking deep purple-red. Like Indian pipe and pinesap, it has densely clustered, coral-like roots, deriving all their energy and nutrients from fungi. However, the fungal victims get their food from decaying leaf mould rather than tree roots.

There are, as well, parasitic, non-green plants that live off tree roots without the help of fungi. Calling little attention to themselves amid the crumpled fallen leaves at the foot of beech trees are slim, knobby, reddish-brown "twigs," growing about 30 centimetres (one foot) high. They're called **beechdrops**, and they attach themselves directly to the trees' roots. With a few, purplish-lined, ascending branches, they bloom fleetingly around late September with tiny, tubular brownish-purple-striped flowers. **One-flowered cancer-root**, a close relative parasitizing roots in southern Ontario forests, produces a single, yellow-centred flower with five white petals in June. It usually appears in small batches, on a leafless, fuzzy pink stem six to 25 centimetres (2.4 to 10 inches) high.

WILD IRIS
Flower of Myth and Majesty

DISPLAYING ONE of the largest and most resplendent flowers in the wild, iris commands attention and captures the imagination wherever it blooms. Irises carry a long tradition in both myth and majesty. Egyptian pharaohs topped their sceptres with an iris design, its three petals representing wisdom, faith and courage. In ancient Greece, Iris was the name of both the female messenger of the gods and her bridge to Earth, a rainbow. Because she was usually the bearer of ill tidings (Hermes got to carry all the good mail), rainbows were a sign of foreboding. According to one story, Iris was yet another of Zeus's illicit girlfriends, and to save her from the wrath of his wife, Hera, he changed her into a flower. Other accounts hold that irises got their name because the various species come in most colours of the rainbow. The pigmented part of the eye is called an iris for the same reason.

A white iris was adopted as the symbol of French royalty by the 12th-century king Louis VII and became known as the *fleur-de-Louis*, later shortened to *fleur-de-lis*. An old legend relates that an earlier king, Clovis, won a great victory in 496 A.D. after irises on a section of the Rhine river pointed the way to a ford where his army could cross and outflank an invading German horde. The *fleur-de-lis* continues to fly on Quebec's flag. Yet strangely, the province's official floral emblem is the madonna lily, a non-native plant whose white petals resemble the stylized flower on the flag. Québécois, however, call wild purple iris *fleur-de-lis*, and many associate it with their national symbol. Admirers have called for it to be recognized as the true official flower.

Humans are far from the only devotees of wild iris. Bumblebees, butterflies, flies and other insects actively seek

Height: 20–90 cm (8–35 in)

Alias: Blue flag, purple iris, wild blue flag, larger blue flag, wild blue iris, American fleur-de-lis, liver lily, poison flag, water flag, snake lily, flag lily, dagger flower, dragon flower, flower de luce, *la fleur-de-lis*, *Iris versicolor*

Flower: 2 or more per plant, each 6–8 cm (2.4–3.2 in) wide, with 3 violet true petals standing erect and 3 larger, down-curving sepals, which are violet with white-and-yellow bases veined with deep purple

Seeds: Light brown, triangular, many held in 3-chambered, ridged pod 4–5 cm (1.5–2 in) long, maturing by late summer

Leaves: Bright green and shiny, grasslike, 20–80 cm (8–31 in) long, 0.5–3 cm

159

(0.2–1.2 in) wide, standing upright. Plant maximizes energy intake in dense colonies by absorbing light on both sides of leaf, rather than on just one like most other plants

Stem: Bright green, glossy

Roots: Thick, spreading rhizomes with many fibrous rootlets

Habitat: Moist ground and shallow water of shorelines, marshy sites, bog fringes, swamps, fens

Common visitors: Bumblebees, skipper butterflies, moths, flies

Native uses of leaves: All parts of the plant are poisonous, but leaves were used for making green dyes, baskets and mats

Range: All of Ontario except far north; also in Manitoba, Quebec and Atlantic provinces

Number of iris species native to Ontario: 4

Number of iris species worldwide: 150–200, mostly in Asia

Also see: Fireweed. *Up North:* Bees, Rainbows, Wetlands

out its ample pools of nectar, guided there by the prominent veins lining the flower's large, purple sepals. As an insect scurries inwards, bearing pollen from the last flower it visited, its back brushes against and fertilizes the petal-like purple stigma arching above the sepal. Farther inside, another set of stamens replenish the pollen on the bug's back. After drinking, the insect leaves by way of the open space between the arch of the stigma and the sepal.

Fed by the abundant nutrients of its marshy habitat – the richest of Ontario's natural settings – wild iris serves up steady meals for its pollinating helpers all summer long. Each plant produces many large, nectar-brimming flowers, with several blooming at any given instant. After pollination, the flowers wilt, giving way to fruiting pods that in time slowly split to let seeds fall one by one to the water below. In spring, the seeds germinate and send up leaves. It takes at least another year, more often two, before the roots have stored enough energy for the plant to produce flowers.

Insects seek its ample pools of nectar, guided by the prominent veins lining the flower's large, purple sepals

---

Though highly poisonous, even deadly, iris roots are valued for a variety of uses. They were used in small doses by both natives and settlers to induce vomiting, relieve constipation and increase urine flow, perhaps giving rise to its Ojibway name, *weekaehn*, meaning "that which extracts." In later times, diuretic drugs called irodin and blue flag were made from the rhizomes. The roots of various kinds of irises are also a source of black dyes, ink and a substance called orris root, which is extremely good at drawing in and then gradually giving off the scents of other things, making it an important fixative for perfumes, soaps and cosmetics.

JACK-IN-THE-PULPIT
The Transsexual Preacher

I N THE FOREST cathedral, jack-in-the-pulpit is a silent preacher, ministering to the more brightly coloured spring ephemerals. Wearing simple vestments of striped green, it may easily be overlooked at first. But the elegant, shade-loving flower holds secrets which, upon close inspection, prove to be as intriguing as its name.

The name comes from the plant's likeness to a figure, "Jack," standing in an antiquated church pulpit with a canopy (which was designed to project the preacher's voice). A modified leaf forms the hood-shaped canopy enclosing Jack, a thick column that pokes its head out from the top of the pulpit. The plant's name may actually mix the sacred and profane, since "Jack" was once a common nickname for the penis, while another name for the flower was priest's "pintle," an Old English word for the male member.

Jack-in-the-pulpit's flowers are very tiny, growing in clusters hidden down in the pulpit around the base of the column. Overhead, the drooping canopy keeps rain from pooling in the pulpit and drowning the dwarfish flowers.

The pulpit's stately lines may guide flying insects to its centre. Small fungus gnats are common visitors, perhaps mesmerized by the preacher's perfumed homily into

Height: Usually 30–40 cm (12–16 in), up to 91 cm (3 ft)
Alias: Woodland jack-in-the-pulpit, Indian turnip, marsh turnip, pepper turnip, wild turnip, bog onion, brown dragon, starchwort, dragon root, devil's ear, cuckoo plant, priest's pintle, *le petit prêcheur, Arisaema atrorubens*
Flower: Green or purplish-brown hood, called a "spathe," often striped, about 4–8 cm (1.5–3 in) long, surrounds a thick green or purple, club-shaped "spadix," 3–6 cm (1.2–2.4 in) long, which bears many tiny yellow male or green female flowers near its base. Blooms May to June
Leaves: Dark-green compound leaves, 1 on male plants and usually 2 on females, each with 3 wavy-edged, pointed

leaflets, on separate stems from flower; pale-green undersides

Berries: Scarlet, waxy, corn-kernel shaped, about 1 cm (0.4 in) long, in a tight, dense, oval cluster of up to more than 2 dozen. Each berry has 1–3 seeds

Roots: Bulbous, starchy rhizome up to 6 cm (2.4 in) thick, with root filaments trailing from it. New rhizomes often form at the ends of roots, sending up clones of the parent plant, forming colonies

Preferred habitat: Rich, moist soil of forests; swamp and bog edges

First sign in spring: A green or purplish pointed shoot pushes up from the ground, unfolding its leaves when 20–30 cm (8–12 in) high

Maximum lifespan: At least 20 years

Range: Southern Ontario to the southern boreal forest; also in Manitoba, Quebec, New Brunswick and Nova Scotia

Close Ontario relatives: Water arum, sweet flag, skunk cabbage, green dragon, arrow arum

World's largest arum: *Amorphophallus titanum*, with a spathe and spadix up to 3 m (10 ft) long

Number of arum species worldwide: Probably more than 3,500, mostly in tropics

Number of *Arisaema* species worldwide: More than 100

Also see: Round-leaved Sundew, Striped Maple, Doll's-eyes, Pickerelweed

believing the plant is a mushroom on which they can lay their eggs. But once inside, the gnats are trapped by slippery, narrowing walls, forcing them down onto the floor of the pulpit. If they're lucky, it is a male plant and they can escape, covered with sticky pollen, by crawling out through a passage at the bottom of the pulpit. If they make the same mistake twice, though, and the next stop is a female plant, they find no way out, and must remain there to pollinate the flowers. The sexual strategy leads some evolutionary entomologists to speculate that the plant may eventually evolve into a meat eater, like pitcher plants or sundew.

Jack-in-the-pulpit begins life as a male, with pollen-bearing flowers. But as soon as it stores up enough nutrients and energy, often when about three years old, the preacher has a sex change. Jack becomes Jill, with all-female flowers. While the jack and pulpit of a male plant withers with its flowers, the female pulpit remains, protecting the fruits developing on the spadix until late summer. Then the hood falls away to reveal a cluster of bright-green berries. Later turning scarlet, the berries flag hungry birds, who serve as flying seed-dispensers. But if a jack-in-the-pulpit is damaged or conditions change somehow to diminish the nutrients needed to produce berries, the plant may become male again.

While its flowers, leaves and stems wither and die with autumn's frosts, the plant survives winter by storing supplies in its rhizome, a small, bulbous underground stem just beneath the surface. This bulb also contains another of the jack-in-the-pulpit's secrets: minute, needle-shaped calcium oxalate crystals that if eaten immediately burn and blister the mouth severely. Jack-in-the-pulpit is, in fact, a member of the arum plant family, whose name derives from the Arabic word for fire. All other parts of the plant are also toxic, though wood thrushes and other birds eat the berries. Even sap from handling jack-in-the-pulpit can cause skin irritation. Antihistamines and topical ointments or creams help relieve the irritation, while milk, cold liquids or ice in the mouth provide some soothing if the root or leaves are eaten.

SPOTTED JEWELWEED
Unique Flower Relieves an Itch

DANGLING LIKE DELICATE orange earrings, sparkling in the dew, jewelweed flowers are the highlight of an exceptional plant. To start with, their colour, orange, is one of the rarest in the wild, outside of autumn. The plant's succulent stems and its leaves also seep a watery, orange-tinted juice when crushed. Native peoples and others have long used the liquid on the skin for quick relief from insect bites, poison ivy, nettle stings, athlete's foot and general itching. Jewelweed juice has also been used to make yellow dye.

Unlike most forest plants, jewelweed lives only one year. Growing in dense patches on mucky ground, the plants' water-filled stems shoot up more than a metre (three feet) in the space of a few weeks. They begin to bloom around mid-July, and continue until the first frosts in September, when expanding ice crystals destroy the tender stems from within. While they flourish, their flowers' uncommon colour is perhaps key in flagging jewelweed's principal partner in survival, the ruby-throated hummingbird. Storing nectar deep inside conical spurs, the flowers are ideal vessels for the hummingbirds' needlelike bills and long, probing tongues. With its nose in the flower, a tiny hummer picks up pollen on its forehead and then cross-fertilizes the next receptive plant it visits. Bees and wasps also seek out jewelweed nectar, though they usually cheat the flowers by biting holes through the back of the spur and bypassing the sexual organs.

But plants robbed of all their nectar, without receiving another's pollen, can still produce seeds. Jewelweed, like a number of other Ontario species, has a backup system. Later in the summer, on its lower branches, it grows many very tiny flower buds that never open.

Height: 50–150 cm (1.6–5 ft)
Alias: Spotted touch-me-not, snapweed, silver leaf, *l'impatiente du cap, chou sauvage, Impatiens capensis*
Ojibway name: *Muklkeebug,* meaning "frog petal"
Flowers: Intricate hanging, horn-shaped structures, 2.5–3 cm (1–1.2 in) long, orange, sometimes yellowish, speckled with rust red; top of flower cavity shows white pollen during male stage and pointed green pistil during female stage; cleistogamous buds just 1–2 mm long (0.04 in)
Seeds: Pop out from green pods that are 1.5–2 cm (0.6–0.8 in) long
Stem: Shiny light green, sometimes mauve, succulent and translucent
Leaves: 3–9 cm (1.2–3.6 in) long, thin, light green, with

pointed ends and large-toothed edges, appearing particularly silvery when glistening with dew; temporarily wilting in hot weather
Roots: Short, thin, pink and clawlike
Preferred habitat: Along creeks, ravine bottoms, shorelines, beaver meadows, hardwood and cedar swamps, marshes and low-lying soggy clearings
Companion plants: Ostrich ferns, sensitive ferns, marsh marigolds, blue marsh violets, goldthread, jack-in-the-pulpit, raspberry, black current, sweet flag, grasses
Common visitors: Hummingbirds, bees, wasps, hawkmoths, hares, mice, ruffed grouse
Range: Most of Ontario, almost to the tree line; also in all other provinces
Number of *Impatiens* species native to Ontario: 2
Number of *Impatiens* species worldwide: 500–600, mostly in tropical Asia and Africa
Also see: Columbine, Violets. *Up North:* Ruby-throated Hummingbird

Instead, they pollinate themselves internally. Called cleistogamous – "hidden marriage" – flowers, they have no nectar and require less energy for their production. Their seeds are genetic clones of a single parent, without the variation that makes cross-pollinated seeds more adaptable. But they ensure another generation will get a chance at life. It is an important contingency given that jewelweed is only an annual. Where conditions are drier or otherwise more difficult, the plants produce greater numbers of closed flowers. In Britain, where jewelweed became widespread after being imported from North America, there are no hummingbirds to cross-pollinate the plants. Charles Darwin found only one in 20 in his country that produced regular flowers.

A mere touch or even a strong wind will burst the ripened pods open

However they are pollinated, fertilized jewelweed flowers develop small seed pods that perform the best known of all the plant's tricks. About a month after fertilization, a mere touch or even a strong wind will burst the ripened pods open, their seeds flying as far as two metres (seven feet). Seeds landing in water can be transported long distances to spread the plant. Mice and grouse eat any they find on the ground.

The pods' hair-trigger action is the source both of jewelweed's other common name, touch-me-not, and of the scientific designation for its genus, *Impatiens*. The species name, *capensis*, actually refers to South Africa's Cape Province, mistakenly identified as the plant's place of origin by the confused European botanist who first named it in 1775. Despite the gaff, the sacrosanct International Code of Botanical Nomenclature decrees that the first species name entered in the tomes of science can never be changed, no matter how wrong.

LABRADOR TEA
Canada's Backwoods Beverage

FOR CENTURIES, Labrador tea has been one of the unifying features of Canadian backwoods culture. Easily obtainable year round across the country, often when real tea and other substitutes were not, the woolly evergreen leaves of the wiry shrub were brewed into a comforting beverage by natives, voyageurs, fur traders and settlers alike. In the late 1700s, David Thompson, the great unsung explorer of much of Western Canada, sipped it with his native guides to cure dysentery after they lost their canoe and supplies to a treacherous set of rapids.

Little wonder Labrador tea was so widely regarded as both refreshing and as a herbal remedy. It is extremely high in iron, as well as in vitamin C and protein. It is still commonly taken by many northerners, usually with a little sugar or honey. Care must be taken, however, not to brew too strong a pot or to drink too much at a time. Like other members of the heath family, the plant also contains a compound called andromedotoxin, high levels of which can cause sickness and vomiting.

Its distinctive leaves, with edges that curve inwards towards furry undersides, make Labrador tea easy to

Height: Up to 1 m (3 ft)
Alias: Common Labrador tea, Hudson Bay tea, *le ledon du Groenland, Ledum groenlandicum*
Leaves: Distinctive rust-coloured, woolly undersides; dark green, leathery on top; young leaves have white wool and light-green tops; smooth edges curling towards undersides; 2.5–6 cm (1–2.4 in) long, narrow, thick and stiff; aromatic when crushed
Flowers: Small, white, star-shaped, with 5 petals, on long stalks, blooming in small clusters at branch tips
Seeds: Minute, many contained in brown oval capsule 5–6 mm (0.2 in) long, with a long, curved hair at its tip, maturing late July or Aug.
Branches: Covered with curly brown hairs

Roots: Small rootlets reach down along a thin, creeping underground stem

Preferred habitat: Edges of bogs and swamps, shorelines and wet clearings in coniferous forests

Companion plants: Sphagnum moss, bog rosemary, leather leaf, bog laurel, sweet gale, meadowsweet, pitcher-plant, sundew, rose pogonia, cottongrass, cranberry

Common visitors: Nashville warblers, mourning warblers, rusty blackbirds, Lincoln's sparrows

Iron content per 100 g of leaves: 184 mg

Vitamin C content per 100 g of leaves: 98 mg

Protein content per 100 g of leaves: 4.2 g

Range: All of Ontario south to about Hamilton and Sarnia; also in all other provinces and territories

Number of *Ledum* species in Ontario: 2

Number of *Ledum* species worldwide: 5–10

Also see: Bog Laurel, Round-leaved Sundew. *Up North:* Wetlands, Moss

identify for beverage fanciers. These features are part of a design that allows the plant to live in difficult conditions. With little recycling of nutrients in bogs, most inhabitants retain their leaves rather than dropping them at the end of every growing season. These evergreen leaves survive the winter thanks to their sugary natural antifreeze, a leathery exterior and a thick blanket of insulating snow. But Labrador tea, being taller than most other bog dwellers, is usually exposed to cold, drying winds for at least part of the winter while its roots are still unable to draw water from the frozen ground. Therefore, the undersides of its leaves, through which it breathes, are specially clothed and protected to minimize water loss, a design that is also found on many desert plants.

When winter finally does depart, the bog stirs from dormancy and puts on a floral show. Dense swathes of **leather-leaf** usually bloom first. Like Labrador tea, it is one of the taller bog plants, and its white flowers, resembling tiny hanging bells, appear soon after the snow vanishes in early May. The wide, pink petals of bog laurel, and bog rosemary's white or pinkish nodding flower clusters, quickly follow. **Bog rosemary** leaves somewhat resemble those of Labrador tea, with rolled edges and fuzzy white undersides. They are, however, more slender, sharply pointed and, more importantly, poisonous.

Frothy white Labrador tea blossoms eventually join the show around late May, and may continue to bloom into early July. Only afterwards does the plant concentrate its energy and nutrients on growing new leaves at the base of these flower clusters. Then in autumn, it reverts to flower production, forming pink buds that will yield another explosion of spring blossoms after a long winter's sleep.

MEADOWSWEET
Garland of the Ancients

I N ANCIENT GREECE, where garlands were eminently popular, one plant with closely packed flowers and leaves along a flexible stem was so ideally suited for the purpose, it was christened *spiraea*, Greek for "garland." In Ontario, a near relative of the same plant forms dense, wild hedges that brighten shorelines with profusions of fuzzy white blossoms throughout the summer. Known both as white spiraea and meadowsweet, the tall plant is a member of the rose family, with its small flowers resembling miniature bleached roses.

Not just an adornment, spiraea was used in beverages on both sides of the Atlantic. Many native peoples, and later the Québécois, brewed it as a readily available tea. In England, it was originally called "mead-wort," because it was added to a wine made from honey known as "mead," one of northern Europe's oldest alcoholic drinks. Before it became more widely available, mead was the drink of kings and was originally taken during sacred rituals to commune with the gods. In addition to meadowsweet, mead was also brewed with hemp and other mind-altering herbs.

Meadowsweet's pink-flowered relative **steeplebush** was also used by natives for tea. It, too, grows along shorelines, though it is a little shorter and less dense than meadowsweet. Steeplebush is named for its slender, steeple-shaped clusters of flowers, which can also be rose-red.

Height: 60–180 cm (2–6 ft)
Flowers: 5 tiny white petals and long, outstretching stamens; many blossoms appearing together in creamy plumes
Alias: White spiraea, narrow-leaved meadowsweet, *la spirée blanche, Spiraea alba*
Seeds: Several in each small, smooth, shiny sheath, which appear in bunches of 5–8
Leaves: Narrow-leaved variety 3–6 cm (1.2–2.4 in) long, 1–2 cm (0.4–0.8 in) wide, with sharp-toothed edges, pointed at both ends, falling in autumn; broad-leaved variety up to 3 cm (1.2 in) wide
Stem: Shiny yellowish to reddish brown; woody with purple-grey, papery, peeling bark on older plants
Roots: Long rhizome with branches
Preferred habitat: Moist, rocky and sandy shorelines, wetland margins, damp forest edges
Range: All of Ontario except far northwest; also in all other provinces

PICKERELWEED
Watery Beds of Purple Beauty

NOTHING TOPS OFF lazing by the riverside on a sunny midsummer's day like the visual feast of a vast, purple swathe of pickerelweed in bloom nearby. Rising in dense jungles from quiet, shallow, muddy waters under full sun, the aquatic beauty is a joy for human and beast alike. The Ojibway called pickerelweed *kinozhaeguhnsh*, "the pike's plant," because the great-fanged fish often lurks amid the plant's submerged tangled stems, waiting to ambush its prey. The English version became the plant's common name, pickerel originally being another name for pike, as well as for walleye.

Though colonies of pickerelweed may cover hundreds of square metres, they are often populated by clones of the same plant, replicating itself by rapidly spreading rootstocks rather than by setting seed. In fact, the tens of thousands of flowers in such a colony cannot even fertilize each other. Pickerelweed has three kinds of flowers, distinguished by the lengths of their female pistils and male stamens. To prevent plant incest, pistils are only receptive to pollen from a stamen of corresponding length, which is never present in the same flower or in any of its clones. Each blossom has two different lengths of stamens, so that it can fertilize either of the other two varieties of pickerelweed. Nectar-seeking insects, often bumblebees, nose their way from one fragrant bed of pickerelweed to another, ensuring genetic vigour through cross-pollination.

Pickerelweed's multiple-flowered spire gives bees lots of opportunity to do their job. Though blossoms remain open just for a single day, they take turns, gradually blooming from bottom to top between July and early September. The finished flowerheads droop down to let their seeds fall to the water. Those not eaten by ducks or muskrats may find

Height: 30–120 cm (1–4 ft) high, usually reaching 30–60 cm (1–2 ft) above water
Alias: *La pontederie condée, Pontederia cordata*
Flowers: Small, bluish-purple, vase-shaped, many densely clustered on a vertical spike
Seeds: 1 per flower, covered by a ridged jacket about 6 mm (0.25 in) long
Leaves: Large, arrow-shaped, succulent, glossy, on separate stems attached at base of plant underwater
Stems: Green, thick, erect, though often snaking, filled with air chambers
Preferred habitat: Shallow water of muddy-bottomed streams and sheltered lakesides; often around outlets or inlets

their way to another ideal spot where they can sink into the muck and generate a new colony. New leaves emerge on the surface around late May or early June, and many are munched upon by deer and muskrats. In autumn, they wither and die back, to be replaced the following spring by new growth sent up by overwintering roots.

To an untrained eye, another purple beauty might be mistaken for pickerelweed in a growing number of wetlands. Blooming around the same time, **purple loosestrife** shares many similarities, including pickerelweed's trilogy of flower types, a relatively uncommon cross-pollination strategy in the plant world. But it is the differences between the two plants that are significant, and ominous.

The magenta-coloured purple loosestrife is an alien invader, which first infiltrated the continent in the early 1800s, probably arriving in loads of ship ballast and in livestock feed and fur from Europe. With tough roots, woody stems and salt-grain-sized seeds, it offers little food for wildlife and quickly forms dense mats that choke out edible vegetation, turning shorelines and marshes into a vast single-species monopoly. Producing up to 2.7 million seeds per plant, loosestrife spreads far and wide by wind, water and the muddy feet of birds. With few enemies here to keep it in check, it has infested at least half of Ontario's wetlands south of Sault Ste. Marie and Kirkland Lake. It is extremely hard to eradicate once established, although, in the early 1990s, government researchers began experimenting with releasing European beetles and weevils that specialize in feasting on loosestrife.

Another plant similar to pickerelweed is sometimes crowded out by loosestrife. **Broad-leaved arrowhead** is, like pickerelweed, an aquatic species with arrow-shaped leaves, though they are much more pointed, rather than rounded, at their base. The plant's white, three-petalled flowers bloom through summer.

Companion plants: Arrowhead, water lilies, cattails
Common visitors: Pike, ducks, kingbirds, turtles, bullfrogs, muskrats, deer
Edible portions: New leaves can be eaten with salads or boiled and taken with butter; raw seeds also nutritious
Scientific name meaning: *Pontederia*, after early-18th-century Italian botanist Guilio Pontedera, and *cordata*, Latin for "heart-shaped," referring to leaves
Range: Southern Ontario to about Temagami; also in Quebec and Atlantic provinces
Number of *Pontederia* species native to Ontario: 1
Number of *Pontederia* species worldwide: 25
Number of vascular plants native to Ontario: About 2,000
Number of non-native vascular plants growing wild in Ontario: About 700
Also see: Pike, Fireweed. *Up North:* Cattail, Wetlands

WILD RED RASPBERRY
Summer's Sweet Bounty

Height: 60–150 cm (2–5 ft)
Alias: *Le framboisier, Rubus idaeus, Rubus strigosus*
Genus name meaning: *Rubus* from the Latin *ruber*, meaning "red"
Berries: Deep red, about 1 cm (0.4 in) wide, very sweet and fragrant
Calories per half-litre (2 cups) of raspberries: About 100
Flowers: About 1 cm (0.4 in) wide, with 5 thin white petals, blooming in clusters of 2–5 at branch tips
Leaves: Compound, usually composed of 3–5 leaflets in first year and 3 in second year; each leaflet 5–10 cm (2–4 in) long, sharply toothed and pointed, with crinkled surface, dark green above and silvery with down below; turn deep purple-red in autumn
Stems: Arching, covered with bristles and prickles; turn brownish or golden and streaked in second year
Roots: A knotted rhizome with many rootlets
Preferred habitat: Forest fringes, clearings, thickets, open woods and burned-over areas, usually on dry, sandy ground
Common nesters: Song sparrows, indigo buntings, chestnut-sided warblers, mourning warblers
Common visitors: Robins, crows, blue jays, cedar waxwings, ruffed grouse, grackles,

SWEET RASPBERRIES, embodying summer's bounty, are among the best known and most abundant of wilderness fruits. Indeed, the Ojibway called July the month of the Berry Moon because of the rich harvests of that time of year. That raspberry seeds are found so frequently at excavated Neanderthal encampments attests to their age-old popularity.

Like many other small, fleshy fruits, raspberries grow mostly in open places and are packed with sugar. Their sweetness and protein attract large numbers of birds, bears, foxes and many other animals, which spread the tiny seeds with their droppings, sometimes in new clearings created by treefalls in the forest, where berry-producing plants thrive.

While raspberry plants attract wildlife with their fruit, they arm themselves for protection, as any raspberry picker knows. Like many other members of the rose family, the stems, or "canes," of most raspberry species have sharp prickles, which also help support them. Yet, somehow, hares manage to gnaw away at canes rising above the snow in winter. Raspberry is also one of the few ground plants porcupines bother with; they seem to enjoy the leaves.

Raspberry roots are perennial, but each cane they send up lasts just two years. During its first growing season, the cane shoots straight up and produces only leaves; the following spring, it grows branches that bear flowers in June and July and raspberries from July to August.

Wild red raspberry is widespread across North America and Eurasia, and is essentially the same species as the cultivated raspberry. There are, however, many other raspberry species, a few of which are sometimes called blackberries. **Common blackberry** grows even higher than red raspberry, reaching two metres (6.5 feet) or more. **Dwarf raspberry** is also very common, reaching about 30 centimetres (one foot) high on herbaceous canes that have hairs but no prickles. Another small relative, the **swamp dewberry**, has sour berries and grows in bogs and other swampy places with sandy soil. All feature white blossoms, except for **purple-flowering raspberry**, which blooms along rocky forest edges and openly wooded ravines during the summer. Displaying five-centimetre-wide (two-inch-wide) rose-pink flowers with yellow centres, it is often mistaken for a wild rose. However, it has maple-shaped leaves and produces dry, seedy, acidic fruit.

An assortment of summer-ripening wild **currants** and **gooseberries** also have maplelike leaves. Most reach up to about one metre (three feet) high or less and are found in a variety of habitats, from forests to meadows and swamps. Skunk currant gets its name from the vaguely skunky smell of its leaves when crushed. Its red berries are covered in bristles, as are swamp black currants. Reddish-purple prickly gooseberries are even more formidably armed, with small, stiff spikes. Native harvesters burned the spikes off by putting baskets of the berries over glowing coals. They, along with the other currants, were dried for winter provisions if not eaten fresh.

flickers, phoebes, red-eyed vireos, northern orioles, veeries, wood thrushes, catbirds, kingbirds, white-throated sparrows, grosbeaks, chipmunks, mice, porcupines, hares, foxes, bears, deer, moose, martens, fishers

Rude associations: The indecorous sound known as a raspberry (also called a Bronx cheer) comes from the 19th-century cockney rhyming slang code, in which "raspberry tart" referred to a fart

Medicinal uses: Tea made from leaves, high in magnesium, proven to guard against miscarriage and ease labour if drunk during pregnancy

World's biggest commercial raspberry producer: British Columbia

Range: Throughout Ontario; also in all other provinces and territories

Prickly berried relatives: Swamp black currant, skunk currant (red berries), prickly gooseberry (reddish-purple to black berries)

Smooth berried relatives: Red currant, wild black currant, smooth gooseberry (bluish-black berries)

Number of bramble (*Rubus*) species native to Ontario: 19

Number of bramble species worldwide: About 120

Also see: Serviceberry, Indigo Bunting. *Up North:* Blueberry

RED TRILLIUM
Pretty, but Not So Sweet

Height: 15–40 cm (6–16 in)
Alias: Wake robin, purple trillium, birthroot, stinking benjamin, ill-scented trillium, wet-dog trillium, red benjamin, Indian balm, beth root, beth-flower, nosebleed, true love, ground lily, bumblebee root, trinity lily, herb trinity, lamb's quarters, squaw flower, *le trille dresse, le trille rouge, Trillium erectum*
Flower: 3 reddish-purple or maroon petals, each 2–4 cm (0.8–1.6 in) long, tapered to a point; straight edged
Berries: Reddish black, oval, with 6 ridges, 1 per plant, containing many seeds
Leaves: 1 whorl of 3 per plant, each 4–19 cm (1.6–7.6 in) long, very broad in middle, pointed at tip; smooth-edged
Roots: Brown rhizome up to 3 cm (1.2 in) thick

T HE WHITE TRILLIUM, Ontario's floral emblem, is probably the best-known wildflower in the province, but its dashing purple-red cousin is really more common on the acidic soil of the Canadian Shield. Standing out in a show of mostly white and yellow spring forest flowers, the red trillium is a sexual maverick in the woodland plant world. Rather than attracting insects with sweet-smelling nectar in a bid to get them to spread pollen from one plant to another, red trilliums emit an odour that smells faintly of rotten meat and produce no nectar at all. The smell appeals to green carrion flies, which are tricked time and again into visiting the trilliums, cross-pollinating them in the process. Red trilliums may also have evolved their butcher-shop colour to assist in this conceit.

After blooming for a few weeks, red trilliums fade. Those that are pollinated develop a large, six-sided, berrylike capsule containing many seeds. The seeds of all trilliums – like those of violets and many other spring flowers – each have a small handle, convenient for ants to grab hold of and drag back to their colonies, sometimes as far as nine metres (30 feet) away. After feasting on the tasty, oily handles, ants discard the seeds, whose coats are too hard for them to penetrate, thus spreading them far from the parent plant.

Native healers associated the red trillium's colour with blood, and used its root in preparations to stop bleeding, especially in childbirth. They also relied on the root as an antiseptic, to treat heart palpitations, fight gangrene and, when chewed (despite a horrible taste), as an antidote to snake venom. Modern herbalists debate the medicinal value of the plant, though some say merely smelling a freshly dug root can stop a nosebleed.

Occasionally, red trilliums bear streaks or patches of green on their normally solid reddish-purple petals. This is not a colour morph, but rather caused by a microbial disease. Aberrant yellow trilliums appear in rare instances as well.

Preferred habitat: Upland hardwood forests and swamps
Companion plants: Trout lilies, wild sarsaparilla, true and false Solomon's seal, spring beauty, violets, rose twisted-stalk, Canada mayflowers, foamflowers, woodferns
Common visitors: Carrion flies, ants, squirrels, deer
Range: Southern Ontario to the southern Shield; also in Manitoba, Quebec, New Brunswick and Nova Scotia
Portion of spring forest wildflowers producing seeds spread by ants: About 30%
Number of trillium species native to Ontario: 4
Number of trillium species worldwide: About 40
Also see: Trout Lily, Violets. *Up North:* White Trillium

Native healers associated the red trillium's colour with blood, and used its root in preparations to stop bleeding, especially in childbirth

---

Painted trilliums also grow in the southern portions of the Canadian Shield, sometimes with red trilliums in hardwood forests or venturing into mixed and coniferous woods. They have daintier flowers than their better-known relatives, with narrow, wavy-edged white petals and streaks of red joining at their centres. The Iroquois called the flower *o-je-genstah,* or "radiant forehead." Though it emerges from the ground later than other trilliums, the painted trillium develops very quickly, its buds opening when the plant is only about 10 centimetres (four inches) high. It may grow up to six times as big, but as soon as it is pollinated, the plant stops growing and the flower fades and withers. All the plant's energy is then devoted to nourishing its seeds.

WILD SARSAPARILLA
The Original Backwoods Root Beer

Height: 30–60 cm (1–2 ft)
Alias: American sarsaparilla, false sarsaparilla, wild licorice, rabbit root, small spikenard, *l'aralie à tige nue, la salsepareille, Aralia nudicaulis*
Flowers: Tiny, white, spiky, usually in 3 spherical clusters branching from a stem rising from the base of the plant, separate from leaf stem; sometimes 2 or up to 7 clusters
Berries: Purple-black, each usually containing 5 seeds, edible but disagreeable
Leaves: Compound, with 3 groupings of 3–5 broadly pointed leaflets, each 5–12.5 cm (2–5 in) long, with finely serrated edges, purplish brown at first, deep green in summer, yellow or bronze in fall

"SARSAPARILLA" CONJURES UP images of 19th-century soda fountains and old country doctors dispensing tried and true natural tonics. The aromatic, nutritious root bark of the wild plant was the prime ingredient of homemade root beer and medicinal pioneer teas. The tea was adopted from the natives, who also dug up the root as an emergency food when travelling. The Ojibway, Hurons and other native peoples also pounded, crushed or chewed the root into a poultice for wounds, burns and sores.

Perhaps not surprisingly, wild sarsaparilla is in the same family as ginseng, the priceless wonder root of Chinese herbal medicine. Ginseng's discovery in 1718 by a Jesuit in Quebec set off a North American ginseng-hunting frenzy that nearly wiped it out. Dwarf ginseng, which looks vaguely like wild sarsaparilla, grows in hardwood forests in central Ontario, though it is not very common.

Certainly, there's no scarcity of wild sarsaparilla in Ontario forests. Its outstretched leaves are legion, forming a second storey of growth and shading woodland ground-cover plants. Sarsaparilla's own tiny white flowers are also hidden beneath those leaves. Blooming in small spherical clusters in June, they have no trouble attracting a wide assortment of flies and other pollinating insects with their heavily perfumed scent. By August the clusters of flowers are transformed into globes of purple-black berries that are eaten by foxes, skunks, bears, chipmunks, thrushes and white-throated sparrows.

Few sarsaparilla plants, however, actually flower and produce berries. Like most forest herbs, sarsaparilla puts relatively little of its resources into sexual reproduction, which demands a great deal of energy to produce the necessary nectar, pollen and seeds. Instead, with sun-supplied energy in relatively short supply on the tree-shaded forest floor, sarsaparilla spreads mostly by underground rhizomes that establish colonies of self-supporting clones.

Like most forest herbs, sarsaparilla puts relatively little of its resources into sexual reproduction

In more dry, sandy, open places, such as rocky shorelines and forest edges, the closely related **bristly sarsaparilla** is also common. Its somewhat larger spheres of flowers and berries are considerably more striking because they are borne on prickly, reddish, woody stems well above the plant's leaves.

Roots: Long, tough, woody horizontal rhizomes
Preferred habitat: Deciduous and mixed forests
Companion plants: Trilliums, true and false Solomon's seal, trout lily, spring beauty, violets, rose twisted-stalk, twinflowers, foamflowers
Reputed medicinal uses of root: Skin diseases, rheumatism, syphilis, general aches and pains. Once a tonic for purifying blood. Also used as a stimulant and diuretic
Name origin: Named after the unrelated Central American sarsaparilla plant, long exported as a medicine and later as a root extract used to flavour soft drinks; the Spanish *sarza* means "bramble," and *parilla* is "little vine"
Range: Throughout Ontario; also in all other provinces
Number of ginseng family species native to Ontario: 6
Number of ginseng family species worldwide: About 700, mostly tropical trees and shrubs

SOLOMON'S SEAL
Mystically Decreed Herbal Healer

Height: 50–100 cm
(1.6–3.3 ft)
Alias: Hairy Solomon's seal,
true Solomon's seal, conquer-
John, *le sceau-de-Salomon a
deux fleurs, Polygonatum
pubescens*
Ojibway name:
Nauneebidaeodaekin,
meaning "those which grow
together hanging"
Flower: Greenish white or
white, bell-shaped,
1–1.5 cm (0.4–0.6 in) long,
hanging in pairs, sometimes
single, beneath arching stem
Berries: Bluish black, containing
several seeds
Leaves: 5–15 cm (2–6 in)
long, 1.5–7.5 cm (0.6–3 in)
wide, pointed at both ends,
pale bottoms with conspicuous veins, stalkless, turning
yellow in autumn

EARLY GREEK WRITERS named the Solomon's
seal of the Old World after the mysterious circular
marks resembling Hebrew letters on its thick root-
stock. Legend held that they were from the ring of King
Solomon, marking the root for its medicinal powers. A
long tradition esteemed the wise King Solomon as the
first learned botanist because the Bible mentions his fasci-
nation with trees of all kinds. Judging from the fabled
number of great cedars of Lebanon used to build his
temple in Jerusalem, around 950 B.C., his interest in trees
might well have stemmed more from an enthusiasm for
construction.

In truth, the "Hebrew letters" are scars, marking where
each year's stem has risen from the lily's perennial root.
The rhizome, though, has indeed long been used for
treating bruises, stomachaches, broken bones and trou-
blesome complexions. Similarly, many native groups
on this continent employed roots of the closely related
North American Solomon's seal as a poultice for bruises,
sores, wounds and black eyes. The Ojibway brewed the
roots into a tea to treat coughs and inhaled the steam

from a preparation that was placed on hot stones. The Iroquois ate the root raw, cooked or pounded into flour.

Solomon seal's graceful, arching stems rise from the ground in May, their pointed leaves unfolding to reveal tiny pairs of bell-like flowers dangling in a long row below them. After they are pollinated by bees, the flowers yield bluish-black berries later in the summer. The berries are eaten by birds, who spread the seeds in their droppings.

Another native lily, though in a separate genus, **false Solomon's seal** looks very similar to its distant relative, with the same zigzag, arching stem and alternating pointed leaves. The two plants sometimes grow side by side and bloom around the same time. False Solomon's seal is easily distinguished by its prominent plume of frothy, tiny white flowers at the end of its stem – hence its other name, Solomon's plume. The flowers have a disagreeable odour and produce pale, purple-dotted green berries, which weigh down the tips of the arching stems. By late summer, the berries soften, shrink somewhat and turn bright red.

False Solomon's seal is easily distinguished by its prominent plume of frothy, tiny white flowers

---

Rose twisted-stalk also bears a strong resemblance to both true and false Solomon's seal. But unlike the other two plants, its wavering stem actually divides into several arching branches. In late May and June, it blooms with small, flared, pink flowers hanging from beneath its leaves. Soft, translucent red berries ripen in summer. It, too, is a member of the lily family.

Roots: Deep, 1–2 cm (0.4–0.8 in) thick, knotted, white rhizome

Preferred habitat: Upland hardwood forests, often mixed with white pine; hardwood swamps

Companion plants: Trout lilies, Canada mayflowers, blue bead lilies, violets, rose twisted-stalk, wild sarsaparilla, evergreen wood ferns, foamflowers

Scientific name meaning: *Polygonatum* is Latin for "many kneed," in reference to the zigzag joints of the stem; *pubescens* means "hairy," after the fine hairs lining veins on the leaf bottoms

Range: Southern Ontario to Lake Temiskaming and Batchawana Bay; also in Quebec, New Brunswick and Nova Scotia

Number of true Solomon's seal (*Polygonatum*) species native to Ontario: 2

Number of true Solomon's seal species worldwide: About 20

Number of false Solomon's seal (*Smilacina*) species native to Ontario: 3

Number of false Solomon's seal species worldwide: About 20

Also see: Canada Mayflower, Wild Sarsaparilla

SPRING BEAUTY
Dainty Ephemeral of
the Hardwoods

DOTTED IN THE CARPET of green trout lily leaves that briefly dominates the snowmelt-moistened forest floor, tiny bouquets of spring beauties offer pink and white greetings to the new season. But the greeting is a quick one. Spring beauty's appearance every year is a fast-paced, precision operation. First, one to several small leaves sprout and open close to the ground, collecting sunlight to power the rise of the flowering stem that soon follows. By the time the flower blooms, these basal leaves have usually died. After pollination – often by ladybug beetles, emerging from hibernating colonies in the litter below – spring beauty quickly forms its seeds. Upon releasing them, the stem and its two remaining leaves wither away as the trees begin to leaf out above.

After the show's over, however, spring beauties do not rest. Deep beneath the ground, the plant's root bulb, called a corm, continues to work, fired on the energy sent down by its leaves' brief time in the sun. It sends out new runners, which push upwards to just beneath the soil surface, ready to sprout early the following spring. Spreading runners also snake through the ground to start new bulbs that will eventually send up their own flowers. All this energy packed into the succulent white tissues of the corms made them a worthwhile vegetable to dig up for many native gatherers.

The genus name for spring beauty, *Claytonia*, honours John Clayton, an 18th-century county clerk in Virginia with an interest in wildflowers. The collection of plants from newly settled lands was all the rage at the time, and Clayton sent specimens he came across to the National Herbarium in England for classification. Many species with the scientific designation *Virginica* were originally found by the plant-loving clerk.

.Height: 10–20 cm (4–8 in)
Alias: Carolina spring beauty, *la claytonie de Caroline, Claytonia caroliniana*
Flower: 12–14 mm (about 0.5 in) wide, with 5 white or light-pink petals with dark-pink stripes
Seeds: Black, shiny, 3–6 per small, drooping capsule; ejected up to 60 cm (2 ft) away when ripe
Leaves: 4–8 cm (1.6–3 in) long, 1–2 cm (0.4–0.8 in) wide, pointed, smooth-edged, 1 pair per stem, situated halfway up; 1 or more basal leaves also appear before stems
Stem: Pale green or pinkish, thin, smooth
Roots: Deep, rounded, light-brown corm, up to the size of a walnut
Preferred habitat: Hardwood forests
Range: Southern Ontario to southern Shield; also in Quebec and Atlantic provinces
Also see: Trout Lily, Beetles

STARFLOWER
Shining in June Woods

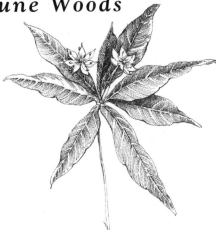

STARFLOWER'S SINGLE SET of sharp-tipped leaves, spreading from a central point on its stem, make it easy to pick out. The leaves are very thin, almost transparent, revealing a branching-vein pattern that forms a border along the leaf edges.

Blooming in June, starflowers have white blossoms, like many spring forest plants, and attract various kinds of polli-nating flies. They put most of their energy below the ground. The surface portion of the plants is really just branches of buried horizontal stems, which spread out in early summer. As the plant detects that the days are shortening, around mid-July, it starts forming a new tuber at the leading end of the subterranean stem. With their nutrients drawn down to fuel the growth, starflower leaves start to yellow by late July, and either fall or turn brown by September. About one in five plants develops two new tubers, and a few can make three, which continue to grow well into autumn, storing all the energy and materials needed to send up new shoots in the coming spring.

The only Ontario plant that resembles starflower is **Indian cucumber root**, a member of the lily family scattered through hardwood and mixed forests. It, too, has a whorl of leaves around its stem, but flowering plants also spread a second tier of three smaller leaves at their crest, making them stand up to 50 centimetres (20 inches) tall.

Blooming around the same time as starflower, Indian cucumber's tiny yellow-green blossoms are markedly different, their stalks leaning downwards from the junction of the uppermost leaves in clusters of three to nine. Dark blue or purple berries develop later. The plant was named for its crisp, edible white tuber, three to eight centimetres (two to three inches) long, which tastes like cucumber and was eaten by natives and early settlers.

Height: 5–25 cm (2–10 in)
Alias: Anemone star, chickweed wintergreen, American starflower, la trientale boreale, Trientalis borealis
Flowers: White, star-shaped, 8–15 mm (0.3–0.6 in) wide, with 5–9 petals and a tiny green centre; 1–3 (usually 2) per plant, each on a 2–5 cm (0.8–2 in) long, threadlike stalk rising from centre of leaf whorl
Seeds: Tiny, black, with white coating; several in small rounded pod, ripening in July
Leaves: 4.5–10 cm (1.8–4 in) long, slender, pointed at both ends, smooth-edged, thin; 5–10 of differing lengths in a whorl around stem
Roots: Tuberous, white, up to 6 mm (0.2 in) thick, with thin horizontal rhizomes running from them
Habitat: Mixed and coniferous forests
Range: All of Ontario except far north; also in all other provinces and the Yukon

ROUND-LEAVED SUNDEW
The Sticky-leaved Carnivore

Leaves: Round, light green, 4–10 mm (0.1–0.4 in) long, covered with "dew"-tipped purple-red bristles

Number of bristles per leaf: Up to 400

Flowers: 3–15 blossoms along the top of a long, thin stalk, each with 5 tiny white or pink pointed petals, opening one at a time July to Sept. at midday if sunny

Flower stem: Light green or reddish, 5–35 cm (2–14 in) long, arching downwards

Seeds: Minute, dark, numerous, in a 3-chambered capsule about 3 mm (0.1 in) long

Roots: Small mass of thin, tiny rootlets

Alias: *Rosa solis*, red rot, lustwort, eyebright, youth wort, moor grass, *le rossolis à feuilles rondes*, *Drosera rotundifolia*

EEP IN A DAMP, quaking bog, or low by the sandy edge of a quiet, backwater bay, carnivores silently lie in wait, ready to kill when unsuspecting prey wander their way. While predators may come in all shapes and sizes, these are perhaps the most surprising, being red not in tooth and claw, but in leaf and flower. The Venus flytrap of North and South Carolina is probably the most famous rooted insectivore, a plant Charles Darwin called the "most wonderful" in the world. But Ontario harbours several bug-eating veggy species of its own. Perhaps the most common, the round-leaved sundew is in the same family as Darwin's favourite.

One has to look closely to find the tiny, ground-hugging sundew plants. Their diminutive circles of leaves are covered in bright-red bristles tipped with tiny beads of "dew," which glisten in the sun and attract small insects, usually flies. Upon landing, the bugs discover the shining little gems are actually deadly globs of sticky gel that ensnare their legs and wings. The highly sensitive bristles bend inward like tentacles once an insect makes contact, pulling the whole leaf around the struggling victim. Sundew goo blocks the bug's breathing pores, bringing death by suffocation. The drama may last just a minute or many hours.

Enzymes in the goo, produced by glands in the red bristles, gradually digest the insect's soft innards. When the meal is finished, the leaf unfolds again, and the bug's drained, lifeless shell blows away in the wind. To add insult to injury, sundew's summer flowers are usually pollinated by the same unsuspecting flies that they devour.

Such decidedly unvegetarian habits develop among plants living where they cannot obtain the nutrients they need through their roots. Sundew thrives where few other plants can grow, in bogs and in sterile, acidic patches of ground near still, somewhat stagnant water. Stagnant water doesn't contain enough oxygen for bacteria to prosper and break down plant matter. Bacterial decomposition normally contributes the nitrates in soil moisture that are taken up and used by new plants to produce proteins and other compounds. Carnivorous plants beat this problem by trapping insects, a much richer source of nitrogen and other vital chemicals.

Scientific name meaning: *Drosera*, Greek for "dewy," and *rotundifolia*, Latin for "round-leaved"

Preferred habitat: Wet, open, sandy shores of still inlets, bogs, beaver ponds, acidic swamps, floating logs

Companion plants: Grass, moss, club-spur orchids

Pests: Caterpillars of plume moths

Range: Throughout Ontario; also in all other provinces and territories

Number of sundew species native to Ontario: 4

Number of sundew species worldwide: About 100, mostly in Australia and southern Africa

Also see: Jack-in-the-pulpit. *Up North:* Wetlands, Soil, Moss

---

Enzymes in the goo gradually digest the insect's soft innards

---

Sundew is, in fact, so successful in acquiring nutrients that it has more vitamin c than oranges and other citrus fruits. Found in northern regions around the world, it has long been used in herbal teas and medicines, for colds, asthma, bronchitis, hypertension, hardening of the arteries and for lowering blood sugar. Juice from the leaves has also been pressed into service against pimples, warts and corns. Since at least the 1500s, sundew was distilled with wine to make a liquor, called *rosa solis*, famed for its nourishing qualities. Country folk also held that cattle became filled with wanton desire after grazing on sundew, which they called lustwort.

The true carnivorous nature of sundew's sticky leaves

was not understood by modern science until 1875, however, when Darwin published his book on insectivorous plants. Yet, in Ontario, the Ojibway seem to have known the plant's secret; they called it *wawiaeneegaeguhnsh*, meaning "round setting-a-trap plant."

Other perils await insects lured by the sweet nectar of the larger, but somewhat less common, **pitcher plant**. Found in and around bogs across Canada, and serving as Newfoundland's provincial flower, pitcher plants have stiff, purple-veined leaves, up to 25 centimetres (10 inches) high, curving in on themselves to form upright vessels that actually hold water. Insects landing on the slippery surface on the inside of the leaves slip into a pool of rainwater at the bottom and drown. The leaves absorb the victim's juices after releasing digestive enzymes into the water that make it more acidic than vinegar. This vitriolic soup, however, actually is a whole ecosystem unto itself, with the larvae of pitcher plant mosquitoes, flesh flies and midges, as well as microscopic organisms and bacteria living off the debris of drowned insects. In return, these tiny tenants pay a rent with their waste products: carbon dioxide and high-nitrogen ammonia.

The mats of rootless, floating **bladderworts** are yet another deadly plant design. They may be seen with their small yellow, sometimes red or purple, flowers bobbing on erect stems in shallow water from mid- to late summer. Most of the plant is a mass of lacy, submerged branches with hundreds of tiny round bladders. When mosquito larvae or smaller aquatic creatures touch one of the bladder's sensing hairs, a trapdoor suddenly opens, drawing a gush of water and the unhappy wanderer into the empty dining chamber.

TRAILING ARBUTUS
Blooming Ground Vine of Spring

LEGEND HAS IT that trailing arbutus, blooming just after the snow shrinks away, was the first flower the Pilgrims saw after their December landing and winter of death and privation at Plymouth. It's often called mayflower, like the Pilgrim's ship, and is venerated throughout New England and the Maritimes. It is Nova Scotia's official flower. The old tradition of picking the sweet-smelling blossoms and bringing them home as a spring greeting made them almost endangered in some parts of the United States. Luckily, they still flourish in Ontario.

In Ojibway legend, trailing arbutus is the gift of Hope, a beautiful pink-cheeked maiden, with white moss covering her hair and with pussy willows on her feet. She came to Earth long ago to grant a wish for an old man who wanted to be remembered for giving something lasting to his people. At his passing, she covered him with leaves and the white and pink blossoms that have since returned to inaugurate each spring.

Trailing arbutus is really a short ground vine, its creeping stem often covered by fallen leaves and pine needles.

Height: 2–5 cm (0.8–2 in)
Alias: Mayflower, ground laurel, Plymouth mayflower, winter pink, mountain pink, gravel plant, shadflower, crocus, *la fleur de mai, Epigaea repens*
Name origin: *Arbutus* is the Latin name of the European strawberry-tree, which also has evergreen leaves and pinkish-white flowers
Flowers: 5 waxy-looking white or light-pink petals join to form a tube 1–2 cm (0.4–0.8 in) long; several bloom together in a tight bunch; "heterostyled," meaning a flower can only be fertilized by pollen from another with slightly differently structured organs, ensuring cross-pollination
Seeds: Minute, dark brown, numerous, held in rounded

5-chambered capsule; mature in late summer
Leaves: Evergreen, 2–10 cm (0.8–4 in) long, 1–4 cm (0.4–1.6 in) wide, with rounded tips, smooth edges, shiny green and rough on top, hairy on bottom
Stem: Woody, covered by bristly, reddish-brown hairs, up to 30 cm (1 ft) long
Preferred habitat: Acidic sandy or mossy ground around coniferous and mixed forest edge and clearings
Companion plants: Wintergreen, bunchberry, northern blue violets, Canada mayflowers, bearberry, bracken ferns
Common visitors: Ruffed grouse, voles, chipmunks, ants, slugs
Medicinal uses: Iroquois and set-tlers treated kidney stones and blood problems with leaves
Range: Southern Ontario to the southern edge of the Hudson Bay lowlands; also in Manitoba, Quebec and Atlantic provinces
Home of the only other *Epigaea* genus member: Japan
Number of heath species native to Ontario: At least 25
Number of heath species world-wide: 1,300
Also see: Pickerelweed, Twinflower. *Up North:* Bears

Its genus name, *Epigaea*, means literally "on the Earth" (*Gaia* is the Greek name for Mother Earth). *Repens* is Latin for "creeping." Because the stem is woody, trailing arbutus is considered a shrub, despite its low stature. Like most other northern forest heath shrublets, it keeps its tough, leathery leaves through the winter. Each year's new set of leaves appears around June, after the flowers have already set their seeds, which are eaten and spread by chipmunks, voles and other animals.

Like most other northern forest heath shrublets, it keeps its tough, leathery leaves through the winter

There are a number of other common creeping ever-green heath plants with similar approaches to life. Sometimes growing in the same rocky clearings and sandy jack pine stands as trailing arbutus, **bearberry** spreads its shredded-bark stems and branches along the ground for up to several metres. As bearberry's name suggests, it's visited by Yogi and Booboo when its pitted red berries ripen in August. Tart, red **cranberries** also ripen on viney stems, lined by very tiny, dark-green leaves, lacing through the spongy sphagnum moss of bogs in late summer. Just as a heath flower reportedly greeted them in their first spring, the Pilgrims are said to have celebrated their first harvest with brimming bowls of cranberries on their Thanksgiving table.

TROUT LILY
Early Spring's Green Mantle

The old year's cloaking of brown leaves, that bind
The forest floor-ways, plated close and true –
The last love's labour of the autumn wind –
Is broken with curled flower bud white and blue
In all the matted hallow, and speared through
With thousand serpent-spotted blades up-sprung,
Yet bloomless, of the adder-tongue.

ARCHIBALD LAMPMAN, "April"

I N EARLY SPRING, about the first signs of growth on
the hardwood forest floor are the pointed, tightly
rolled, purple leaves of trout lily, also called adder's
tongue, poking up *en masse* through the previous year's
brown fallen leaves. With patches of snow still on the
ground nearby, the scene resembles a rolling medieval
battlefield with countless thousands of Lilliputian spears
hoisted high. As they unfurl, the leaves – mottled like the
skin of a brook trout – transform the ground into a transi-
tory sea of green, speckled here and there with yellow
clumps of trout lily flowers. The glory is short-lived. As
soon as green spreads to the treetops, it drains from the

Height: 10–25 cm (4–10 in)
Alias: Dogtooth violet, yellow
  adder's tongue, fawn lily,
  yellow lily, yellow bells, yellow
  snowdrop, rattlesnake tooth,
  rattlesnake violet, yellow
  snake's tongue, lamb's tongue,
  snake root, *l'ail doux*,
  Erythronium americanum
Ojibway name:
  Numaegbugoneen, meaning
  "sturgeon leaf"
Flowers: 3–3.5 cm (1–1.4 in)
  wide, nodding, with 3 back-
  ward-curving yellow petals
  with a purple stripe on the
  back of each; 3 petal-like,
  deeper-yellow sepals curve
  back even more; 6 orange or
  yellow stamens and a green
  pistil at centre
Seeds: Contained within oval
  green pod
Leaves: Shiny, green, mottled
  with purple-brown or grey,

10–20 cm (4–8 in) long, 2–4 cm (0.8–1.6 in) wide, tapered at top and bottom, smooth-edged, parallel veins, cool to touch; just 1 on non-flowering plants, 2 growing from the base of flowering stems

Stem: Light green, slightly leaning, extending 10–23 cm (4–9 in) straight below ground to bulb

Roots: Older corms are brown and scaly; young ones are white, thin and pointed, like a dog's canine tooth

Preferred habitat: Deciduous and sometimes mixed forests

Companion plants: Spring beauty, red trilliums, true and false Solomon's seal, wild sarsapar-illa, jack-in-the-pulpit, starflowers, violets

Number of trout lilies per m² (11 sq ft) in hardwood forests: 400 common, up to 1,100

Plant biomass created by trout lilies each spring: Up to 165 kg/ha (146 lb/acre)

Other plants whose seeds are spread by ants: Trilliums, violets, fringed polygala

Past medicinal uses: Poultice from leaves used to treat skin disease, ulcers and tumours; parts of plant also ingested to induce vomiting

Range: Southern Ontario to about Wawa and Lake Temiskaming; also found in Quebec, New Brunswick and Nova Scotia

Number of *Erythronium* species native to Ontario: 2

Number of *Erythronium* species worldwide: About 22

Also see: Spring Beauty, Red Trillium. *Up North:* White Trillium

ground, the lily leaves fading and dying as they are cut off from the sun.

In truth, many trout lily colonies are as old as the same arboreal giants that crowd them out every June. After its leaves crumble, a trout lily plant resumes its life deep underground, May's captured sunlight fuelling it for the next 10 months. Its bulb, or corm, is the plant's power-house and factory. After taking a summer siesta, it kicks into operation in late August. The next spring's leaves and flowers are formed in tightly packed buds on shoots that push towards the surface through autumn and winter. Trout lilies also spread runners up to 25 centimetres (10 inches) through the soil to create new bulbs. These cloned corms send up their own leaves in spring. The process repeats itself year after year, decade after decade, forming extensive subterranean networks that help hold the soil together. Some are up to 300 years old.

Many trout lily colonies are as old as the arboreal giants that crowd them out every June

---

More than 99 percent of trout lily corms produce just one leaf. As the colony spreads randomly, eventually some bulbs grow in choice spots with enough light, mois-ture, nutrients and shelter to support flowers. Still, it takes a seed or new corm in a good location at least five years to flower, producing bigger leaves each growing season and pushing deeper in the soil until the bulb is 10 to 20 centimetres (four to eight inches) below the surface. Flowers often bloom in small patches, usually about two weeks after first sprouting enclosed within two curled leaves. The blossoms nod towards the ground, protecting their nectar and pollen from rain. The backward curving petals also close at night and during showers.

Only a small percentage of the flowers are fertilized,

developing green pods holding a few seeds. Like trilliums and many other spring flowers, the seeds are spread by ants. Enticed by a nutritious, oily appendage attached to each seed, the insects carry the seeds back home, feast on the attachments and discard the rest.

Trout lily also plays a vital role in the forest ecosystem that goes beyond its brief spring appearance. Because it dominates so thoroughly immediately after the snow melts, it draws up to almost half of all nutrients – such as nitrogen and potassium – accumulated from the breakdown of fallen leaves by bacteria working beneath winter's insulating snow. Without the trout lily's quick action, much of these nutrients would be washed away in spring runoff before the dormant roots of trees and other plants begin to stir. This enormous nutrient load, combined with abundant snowmelt and unobstructed sunlight, creates the incredible burst of trout lily leaves. When opening tree buds shade out the ground in late May, whatever nutrients not drawn into the trout lily corms are released by the plants' rapidly decaying leaves into the soil and absorbed by the rest of the forest vegetation.

TWINFLOWER
Dainty, Paired Bells

Height: 3–10 cm (1.2–4 in)
Alias: Deer vine, twin sisters, ground vine, *la linnée boreale*, *Linnaea borealis*
Flowers: Pink and white, 10–15 mm (0.4–0.6 in) long, hanging in pairs from very thin stalks like dainty, flared bells
Seeds: 1 per tiny, dry capsule covered by a bristly bract
Leaves: In pairs, rounded, 1–2 cm (0.4–0.8 in) long, evergreen, with tiny bristly hairs
Stems: Very slender, hairy, running along the ground, becoming woody with age, sending up erect, slender stalks with leaves and flowers
Roots: Thin, hairlike tufts at intervals along ground-creeping stem

DELICATE AND DIMINUTIVE, twinflower is easily missed beneath the layers of herbs, shrubs and saplings crowding the forest's lowest levels. But once discovered in early to midsummer, perhaps under overhanging sarsaparilla leaves, the dainty, lightly scented, paired bells may suddenly seem to be everywhere, like specks of pink frosting across the forest floor. The process of discovery, keying the eyes to something that is all around, is similar for many flowers, mushrooms and other wonders of the woods.

Close inspection reveals twinflower to be a ground vine, with the thinnest of woody stems trailing for two or more metres (six feet), sending down hairlike roots every few centimetres to hold itself in place. In some locations they form large colonies, creating a dense carpet of interlacing vines creeping over mossy rocks and decaying logs. Their resinous evergreen leaves, which are also paired and borne on stalks rising from the prostrate stem, are often browsed by deer. Bristly coated seeds, appearing in August and September, are spread by getting snagged in the fur of passing animals.

Twinflower is a member of the large honeysuckle family, though it has few close relatives. It grows in northern forests around the world. Carl Linnaeus, the 18th-century father of modern taxonomy, found it growing in his native Sweden and adopted it as his own, holding it in portraits of himself. It was Linnaeus who came up with the brilliantly adaptable system of scientific binomial classification, in which all plants and animals are given surnames, denoting their genus, followed by their individual species name. His good friend and fellow botanist Johann Gronovius did Linnaeus the favour of naming the twinflower's tiny genus after him. In later reference to the plant, Linnaeus described it as "lowly, flowering for but a brief space – [name derived] from Linnaeus, who resembles it." The 19th-century American poet Ralph Waldo Emerson paid tribute to the botanist and the flower with the lines:

He saw beneath dim aisles, in odorous beds,
The slight Linnaea hang its twin-born heads;
And blessed the monument of the man of flowers,
Which breathes his sweet fame through the northern bowers.

Like the Europeans, the Ojibway called the flower "the twins," *neezhodaeyun.* Cultures the world over have always been fascinated with the idea of twins, giving them prominence in their lore, from the Greek Gemini to Dylan and Lleu, personifying the powers of light and darkness in Celtic mythology. Similarly, Iroquois cosmology has Mother Earth giving birth to the primal twins of good and evil, named Sky Holder and Flint respectively. Ojibway tradition says that Earth was created on the back of a turtle, amid a great flood, so that Sky Woman, *Geezhigo-Quae,* could give birth to twins, who subsequently spawned the human race.

Preferred habitat: Coniferous and mixed forests, mossy clearings and bogs
Companion plants: Canada mayflowers, wintergreen, bunchberries, blue bead lilies, moccasin flowers, goldthread, starflowers, northern white violets, wild sarsaparilla, wood sorrel, false Solomon's seal
Medicinal uses: Native groups made tea from leaves for insomnia and applied a pulpy preparation for inflamed limbs; herbalists used the plant as a diuretic
Range: All of Ontario except extreme southwest; also in all other provinces and territories
Linnaeus's lifespan: 1707–1778
Taxonomy word origin: From Greek, *taxis,* meaning "arrangement," and *nomos,* meaning "law"
Number of *Linnaea* species native to Ontario: 1
Number of *Linnaea* species worldwide: 2
Also see: Red-berried Elder, Bog Laurel, Gemini. *Up North:* Painted Turtle, Muskrat

VIOLETS
Sweet, Nutritious Flowers of Love

Height: 2.5–45 cm (1–18 in)
Alias: *Les violettes, Violeae*
Flowers: 0.3–3 cm (0.1–1.2 in) wide, 5 petals, with nectar held in enclosure – called a spur – formed by the lowest petal
Seeds: Released from dividing, 3-chambered, beige capsules, 4–12 mm (0.2–0.5 in) long
Leaves: Usually heart-shaped (notable exceptions being lanced-leaved and kidney-leaved violets), pointed at tips and curled at base, with toothed edges, 1–10 cm (0.4–4 in) long, 1–12.5 cm (0.4–5 in) wide
Roots: Species with leaves and flowers on separate stalks have numerous thin roots and runners; species with leafy flower stalks have thick, branching woody roots

CHERISHED BY LOVERS, prophets and generals, violets come not just in purple but in varying shades of white, blue, pink and yellow as well. The colour violet was actually named after one of the purple varieties. In central Ontario, there are at least 16 species, adapted to a wide assortment of habitats. Those of late-April's leafless hardwood forests are the first to bloom, including the woolly blue violet (which, to add to the confusion, is really violet in colour). Wetland fringes, meadows and evergreen forests soon brighten with their own violets, with the greatest profusion of bloomings coming in June.

In their highly varied colours and sizes, violets everywhere share a very similar design and layout. All feature a specialized lower, central petal that forms an organ- and nectar-bearing tube stretching towards the back of the flower. The front of this petal also serves as a landing platform for incoming flying insects, complete with runway markings in the form of brightly coloured veins. Drawn by the flower's delicate scent, flying insects follow the veins straight to the rich payload of nectar. Violets also display (appropriately enough) ultra-violet patterns, visible to bees and other pollinators but not to humans, which must make the veined petals even more striking in appearance.

The attributes that attract insects – alluring colours, structure and sweet scent – have also long endeared violets to humanity. They flourished in the gardens of ancient Greece and served as a symbol of Athens, the most cultured city of the classical world. Indeed, the word *viola* is the Latin rendering of *Io*, the Greek name both for the flower and for the daughter of the river god Inarchus. According to one story, the Olympian philanderer Zeus, after casting his affections on Io, turned her into a white cow to save her from his significantly ticked-off other, Hera, queen of heaven. As consolation, he created violets to provide sweet fodder for his beloved cow goddess.

Mortals also enjoy the sugary violet. The petals have been added to jams, syrups and liqueurs and used both as a dye and as flavouring in many candies. The flower decorations topping cakes today imitate the old practice of placing sugar-coated violets on desserts. Crystallized violets were also once commonly sold in drugstores as a sweet cough drop known as violet plate. And the sweet essential oils of Mediterranean violets are one of the oldest sources of perfumes.

Violet leaves are used in salads and added to soups and omelettes, though they are somewhat more bitter than the flowers. What they lack in sweetness is, however, more than compensated in nutrition. The leaves of some species have five times more vitamin c than oranges and more than twice the vitamin A content of spinach. Many violets also contain salicylic acid, the same active ingredient in willow bark that led to the development of Aspirin. Not surprisingly, violets have been used for centuries by both Europeans and North American natives for ailments ranging from insomnia to epilepsy and sore throats to heart problems. The Romans considered violets excellent hangover remedies and covered their banquet tables with the flowers, both for decoration and as a prudent nibble.

Violets are probably more highly regarded, however, for their symbolic value than for any practical benefit. Equated with modesty, chastity, love and loyalty, they

Deciduous forest species: Sweet white violet, Canada violet, downy yellow violet, woolly blue violet

Coniferous forest species: Northern blue violet (illustrated), northern white violet, sweet white violet

Wetland species: Marsh blue violet, sweet white violet, downy yellow violet, woolly blue violet, northern white violet

Shoreline and forest edge species: Lance-leaved violet, blue marsh violet, northern white violet, northern blue violet, dog violet, shore violet, Canada violet

Wet meadow species: Northern white violet, marsh blue violet

Meadow species: Dog violet, Canada violet, smooth yellow violet

Common visitors: Bees, butterflies, mice, grouse, juncos, woodcocks, mourning doves

Pests: Cut-worms, caterpillars of fritillary butterfly, slugs

Official flower of New Brunswick: Blue marsh violet

Number of parma violets needed to produce half a kg (1 lb) of essential oils for perfume industry: 2 million

Napoleon's nickname: Corporal Violette

Name for someone who studies ant–seed relationships: Myrmecochorigist, from the Greek words *myrmex*, meaning "ant," and *chore*, meaning "farm"

Range: Throughout Ontario; also in all other provinces and territories

Number of violet species native

to Ontario: About 23 (much hybridization and much debate as to what to label species or subspecies)
Number of violet species worldwide: About 500
Birthplace of violet genus: The Andes of South America
Also see: Willows, Red Trilliums.
Up North: Bees

have been worn by brides or carried in their bouquets since the days of Helen of Troy. The garden pansy, developed from a small European violet, derives its name from the French *pensée*, meaning "thought" or "remembrance," after the custom of offering violets as a courting gift aimed at turning the admired one's thoughts towards love. Violets were also said to be the favourite flower of the prophet Muhammad and of Napoleon, who, when being sent into his first exile, said, "I shall return with the violets in spring." Unfortunately, he returned to Waterloo.

For all the fame and glory of their blossoms, most violet species actually reproduce mainly without them. These species are colonial, spreading thin underground runners that send up many clones of the original seed-propagated plant. In addition, while cold weather or other mishaps often prevent insects from pollinating many violets, the plants still produce seeds with a second set of smaller flowers that never actually bloom. These "cleistogamous" buds are usually formed near or below the ground in summer and pollinate themselves without opening, eventually producing even more seeds than the conventional flowers.

Seeds developed in both conventional and above-ground cleistogamous flowers are shot a metre (three feet) or more into the air with the pressure released by the splitting of their pods, which gradually contract as they dry. Those not eaten right away by mice and birds are picked up by ants, which also collect seeds from the subterranean buds. Known to cache these loads in colonies up to 60 metres (200 feet) away, the ants eventually eat fatty, oil-filled knobs, called elaisomes, attached to the seeds. Unable to break through the main shell, they simply toss the rest in with their rubbish, thus both spreading the seeds and providing them excellent conditions for germination the following spring.

WINTERGREEN
Little Leaf with Bubblegum Flavour

THE TASTE THAT FLAVOURS chewing gums, toothpaste and cough drops is not hard to find in the woods. Simply plucking a stiff, shiny little wintergreen leaf and giving it a quick chew yields instant *essence du bubblegum*. Growing on mossy or sandy ground in mixed and coniferous forests, wintergreen was long used – from northern Cree country to the tilled lands of the Iroquois – to flavour food, drink and tobacco. The Ojibway tied up bundles of the leaves, which remain green through the winter, with stringy strands of basswood bark to brew as an aromatic tea. Adopted by early settlers, wintergreen tea later became quite popular in rebel cups after the Boston Tea Party.

A chemical substance known as oil of wintergreen is also found in other plants and extracted from them commercially for food flavourings and perfume. Early manufacturers found it easiest to obtain large quantities from the bark of "sweet" or cherry birch, which doesn't grow north of the Niagara Peninsula. Today the flavour is widely synthesized. Because it soothes irritations, the oil was also used in medicine. It yields methyl salicylate, similar to the active ingredient in Aspirin, also found in willow bark. One of its greatest uses, however, was as an ingredient to cover the taste of "miracle formulas" – comprised largely of alcohol – peddled by 19th-century snake-oil salesmen.

Still, wintergreen's real powers as a mild stimulant and astringent seem to have been well known to Ojibway and Algonquin paddlers, who said they chewed the plant's leaves during portages and other exhausting activities to increase their endurance. They also credited the plant's red berries, which they ate fresh or preserved, with aiding digestion. Herbalists warn, however, that too much wintergreen oil can cause allergic reactions in some, especially children, who should be discouraged from eating

Height: 10–15 cm (4–6 in), rarely up to 20 cm (8 in)

Alias: Checkerberry, teaberry, spring wintergreen, Canada tea, partridgeberry, grouse berry, creeping wintergreen, spicy wintergreen, chinks, ground-berry, one-berry, spice-berry, red pollom, box-berry, deer-berry, mountain tea, *le thé des bois*, *Gaultheria procumbens*

Flowers: White, waxy-looking, barrel-shaped, 5–10 mm (0.2–0.4 in) long, hanging beneath leaves

Berries: Scarlet, about 1 cm (0.4 in) wide, containing capsule with seeds inside

Leaves: 1–5 cm (0.4–2 in) long, oval, fragrant, shiny, flexible in first season, becoming dark green, stiff and leathery, turning reddish with age, always pale on undersides; 3–4 per stem

Stem: Short, bare, woody, topped by several leaves; is actually one of many stalks, or branches, rising along length of rhizome

Roots: A thin, woody rhizome running on or just below the ground, with many rootlets along its length, hence the scientific name *procumbens*, Latin for "prostrate"

Preferred habitat: Acidic, mossy or sandy soil in mixed and coniferous forests and clearings

Companion plants: Goldthread, blue bead lilies, moccasin flowers, Canada mayflowers, bunchberry, wood sorrel, twinflowers, trailing arbutus

Common visitors: Mice, chipmunks, deer, bears, ruffed grouse, bumblebees

Medicinal uses: Preventing tooth decay, soothing aching muscles, treating colds, stomachaches, toothaches

Namer of species: 18th-century Swedish botanical explorer Pehr Kalm first described wintergreen for science after chumming around on field trips with Quebec naturalist Jean-François Gaultier

Wintergreen family: A small group of plants, some of which contain the oil of wintergreen. However, the species wintergreen, *Gaultheria procumbens*, is not a member of the family

Range: All of Ontario except extreme southwest; also in Manitoba, Quebec and Atlantic provinces

Number of *Gaultheria* species native to Ontario: 2

Number of *Gaultheria* species worldwide: About 200

Also see: Labrador Tea, Yellow Birch, Willows

the leaves and berries. The pitted berries are, reportedly, most palatable after they have spent a winter mellowing on the vine, hanging beneath the plant's evergreen leaves deep in the snow. Perhaps that's why, though they're eaten by mouse and bear alike, they're not snapped up as soon as they ripen in autumn.

Ojibway paddlers chewed the leaves during portages to increase endurance

Wintergreen is sometimes called **partridgeberry**, which is more properly the name of a small, mat-forming forest ground vine, also a member of the health family, which produces pairs of similar, winter-persistent red berries. Both provide a ready food source for early migrant birds returning to their breeding territories in spring before insects become abundant.

Snowberry, wintergreen's closest relative in Ontario, also sounds the wintery theme, though its name actually alludes to the plant's white berries. Like wintergreen, it has tiny, waxy white bell flowers, but they're borne on vinelike, hairy branchlets forming mats over the ground in coniferous forests and sphagnum bogs. Its leaves are also very tiny, just two to 10 millimetres (0.08 to 0.4 inches) long, lining the length of the branchlets.

Both wintergreen and snowberry have the scientific surname *Gaultheria*, a genus named after Jean-François Gaultier, who served as the king's physician to New France from 1742 to 1756. The position was sort of that of a surgeon-general and chief scientist for the colony rolled into one. It was Gaultier's job to catalogue and investigate the great stream of newly discovered Canadian plants, which outpost commanders were ordered to collect for him. Canadians, often described as a weather-obsessed people, can also look to him as the founder of the country's first meteorological station.

WOOD SORREL
Far-flung Shamrocks of Mossy Realms

E
VEN WHEN NOT in bloom, wood sorrel is very distinctive, its three glossy, smooth-edged leaflets forming three perfect hearts joined together at their pointed tips. The plant, which also grows in Europe and Asia, is sometimes hailed as the original shamrock, a sacred symbol of the ancient Celtic druids used by St. Patrick to explain the concept of the Holy Trinity to the pagan Irish. There are, however, several other leading shamrock candidates, including common clovers.

Growing happily in some of the deepest shade of Canada's northern evergreen forests, wood sorrel is a lonely adventurer, boldly striking out like a coureur de bois, far from its own ken and kind. Most of the little plant's large family warm their leaves in Africa and South America, and only one other close relative is native to Ontario. The family must have emerged before the two southern continents separated, about 80 million years ago, with only a handful of its offspring fortifying themselves to survive the northern climes.

Indeed, the dainty wood sorrel of the Canadian Shield is tougher than it looks. Like many other plants growing under coniferous trees, it is an evergreen, bolstered by

Height: 5–10 cm (2–4 in), rarely up to 15 cm (6 in)
Alias: Common wood sorrel, upright wood sorrel, white wood sorrel, true wood sorrel, shamrock, sleeping beauty, cuckoo flower, sour trefoil, hearts, *l'oxalide de montagne, Oxalis montana, Oxalis acetosella*
Word origin of shamrock: From Irish *seamróg,* meaning "little clover"
Flowers: 1.5–2 cm (0.6–0.8 in) wide, 5 small white, sometimes light-pink, petals with thin, dark-pink stripes and a tiny yellow dot at the base of each petal; 1 per plant, on a separate stem from leaves
Seeds: Have white ridges, shot out from small pod when ripe
Leaves: Like tiny, distinct, smooth-edged, glossy clovers, 1–3 cm (0.4–1.2 in) wide

Stems: Light green or pink, several joined together at ground

Roots: Slim, scaly vertical rhizome with slender connecting runners

Preferred habitat: Mossy, acidic ground in coniferous and mixed forests, often beneath hemlocks and yellow birch, or in bogs

Companion plants: Canada mayflowers, goldthread, bunchberry, gay-wings, moccasin flowers, northern blue violets, twinflowers, wintergreen, blue bead lilies

Frequent visitors: Hares and deer graze leaves; chipmunks, ruffed grouse, juncos and sparrows eat seeds; pollinated by beetles, flies and moths

Folk remedies: Once used by Europeans for heart problems because leaves are heart-shaped; also a popular spring tonic and medicine for heartburn, liver ailments, fevers and mouth ulcers; Algonquins considered it an aphrodisiac

Scientific name meaning: *Oxalis* comes from the Greek word for a sour, sharp or acid taste

Age of oldest-known flowering plant fossils: 120 million years

Range: Southern Ontario to about Kapuskasing and the northeast shore of Lake Superior; also in Quebec and Atlantic provinces

Number of *Oxalis* species native to Ontario: 2

Number of *Oxalis* species worldwide: 800

Also see: Violets, Yellow Birch. *Up North:* Goldthread

sugary antifreeze compounds that allow its leaves to persist, dormant but alive, beneath the snow. The leaves also contain salts that make them taste quite sour, hence the name sorrel, which comes, via French, from the ancient Germanic word *suraz*, meaning "sour." The taste probably discourages browsing insects and snails. The leaves were used in rural areas to curdle milk and to add a nice tartness to salads, soups, pies and apple sauce. The Ojibway, who called the plant *zeewunubugushk*, or "sour leaf," made a bittersweet dessert of the leaves cooked with maple sugar.

Still, eating too many wood sorrel leaves can cause kidney damage and internal bleeding. Cows and sheep have reportedly died from overgrazing the plant. Oxalic acid from wood sorrel is caustic enough to have been used in Europe as a stain remover, called "salts of lemon." A similar, synthesized chemical is used in industry to bleach clothes and wood and for cleaning automobile radiators.

Wood sorrel employs a few other strategies for success in the northern forests. Like many woodland herbs, it stays close to the ground, where carbon dioxide levels are 25 percent higher than in open areas. The extra supply of carbon – the primary building material of living cells – helps compensate for the poor supply of sunlight. The leaves also forecast bad weather, folding together before rain or cold temperatures, as well as at night. And, as a contingency in case of unsuccessful pollination, common when frosts encroach upon its early-summer blossoms, wood sorrel has both a backup flowering system and a colonial rooting network. After its regular flowers bloom in June and July, the plant produces low green buds, usually unseen beneath the leaf litter, containing self-fertilizing flowers that never actually open. Like the plants sprouting from spreading colonial roots, the abundant seeds yield genetic clones of the mother plant.

TREES AND SHRUBS

U P NORTH managed to cover most of central Ontario's most common trees, especially the conifers. This time around, we're featuring a number of deciduous trees, such as ironwood and mountain ash, that are not quite as abundant but are very important to wildlife. We've also included many smaller species, such as willows, chokecherry and dogwoods, that may grow as high as small trees but more often appear as tall shrubs. Though a shrub is technically any plant that grows with a woody stem, including some only centimetres high, we use the term here in the more popular sense of a large, bushy species. They occupy the middle ground between trees and wildflowers that often seems to be left out of guides on just one or the other.

Tree sizes listed in the sidebars are based on Ontario averages. Some species may get a little bigger farther south, where the growing season is longer.

BALSAM POPLAR
Spicy Fragrance by the River

Average mature height: 18–24 m (60–80 ft)
Average width of mature trunk: 30–60 cm (1–2 ft)
Maximum height: 25 m (82 ft)
Maximum width: More than 1.2 m (4 ft)
Alias: Rough-barked poplar, balm poplar, hackmatack, tacamahac, balm of Gilead, balm, *le peuplier baumier, Populus balsamifera*
Name origin: "Poplar" comes from the Latin *populus,* meaning "people," probably because poplars were planted in public squares
Preferred habitat: Moist, rich, alluvial flats, riverbanks, sandbars, swamp and bog fringes
Buds: Reddish brown, 2–2.5 cm (0.8–1 in) long, thin, very pointy, gummy and fragrant in spring and fall
Leaves: Thick, tough, 5–15 cm (2–6 in) long, spade-shaped or pointed at both ends, with finely toothed edges; dark,

DOWN BY THE river, before spring comes to the north woods, sticky, gummy balsam poplar buds fill the air with spicy fragrance. The scent, reminiscent of tropical medicinal balms, inspired the tree's name, and is especially strong when the long, pointy buds are squished. The Ojibway cooked them in fat to use as a greasy salve on cuts, bruises and sprained muscles or to put inside the nose to relieve congestion. Natives also used the clear bud resin to waterproof canoes, just as bees collect it to repair cracks in their nest walls. The resin is called bee glue by beekeepers, who often plant the trees near their apiaries.

With the first running of sap, balsam poplar would become a juicy, sweet-tasting spring treat for the Cree and Ojibway, who scraped long strips of the thick, white inner bark from the wood to eat. The inner bark, or phloem, was also sometimes eaten as an emergency food at other times of the year, when it's not as sweet or nutritious. Although balsam poplar is somewhat scattered in central Ontario, it was very important to the Cree farther north along riverbanks near Hudson Bay. Here it becomes the dominate broadleaf tree, providing better firewood and shelter than the dwarfed, spindly black spruce and tamarack of the surrounding muskeg. Though as lumber it doesn't stand up to the stronger, heavier wood of southern trees, its pulp yields fine paper used for magazine stock.

With the first running of sap, Cree and Ojibway scraped long strips of the thick, white inner bark from the wood to eat

After the tree's flower catkins open in spring, they develop seeds on silky tufts that cover the surrounding area in white fluff in late June. Carried by the wind, the seeds can only grow in open, shade-free areas. Germinating within a day of landing on a moist site, they grow very quickly, with long, straight trunks, narrow crowns and suckering roots that send up clones of the original tree all around it. Studies show that balsam poplar produces a substance that inhibits the growth of alder, allowing it to take over from such pioneer species on sites cleared by fire or heavy winds. Eventually, shade-tolerant spruce and fir come up from beneath the poplar and in turn take over the area.

shiny green on top, pale silver-green on bottom, with intricate bronze veining and splotches of resin; turn yellow and more resin-spotted in fall
Bark: Greenish brown, smooth and thin when young; dark grey and rough, with deep furrows and wide, flat ridges on older trees
Sex: Male and female flower catkins on separate trees; males are purple, 7–10 cm (3–4 in) long, females are green and purple, 10–13 cm (4–5 in) long; appearing before leaves open in spring; pollinated by bees
Seeds: Very tiny, attached to fine white fibres, spread by the wind in late June
Roots: Shallow and wide-spreading
Wood: Light grey-brown, sometimes reddish heartwood and thick layer of almost white sapwood; fragrant, soft, weak, and very light, 356.4 kg/m³ (22 lb/cu. ft), hard to split when wet
Companion trees and shrubs: Willow, alder, red osier, dogwood, white cedar, black ash, trembling aspen, white birch, fir and spruce
Common inhabitants: Barred owls
Lifespan: Largest trees around 70 years old
Range: All of Ontario to the tree line; also in all other provinces and territories
Number of poplar species native to Ontario: 4
Number of poplar species worldwide: 35
Also see: Largetooth Aspen. *Up North:* Trembling Aspen

BASSWOOD
Rope, Honey and
Porcupine Fodder

T HOUGH NEVER a dominant tree in the mixed and hardwood forest, basswood has been highly important to both beast and *Homo sapiens*. To the Ojibway, Algonquins, Ottawa, Hurons and Iroquois, it was the tree that binds. Basswood's inner bark holds some of the longest, strongest, toughest natural fibres on the continent. It was used for rope, thread, twine, thongs, nets and woven bags. In spring, natives easily stripped bark from the trees and either soaked it for several weeks – the softer material rotting away to leave only the strongest fibres – or boiled and pounded it until stringy and malleable. They then twisted the strands together to make flexible white rope and string esteemed by its native makers for being softer on the hands and less likely to kink and tangle than the white traders' hemp. Birch-bark containers, clothes, lodge poles, reed mats, even wounds were all held together by the wonder fibre.

The settlers also took to basswood in a big way, though not so much for its rope. They worked the wood, taking the lead of the Iroquois, who carved False Face masks right on the trunks of live trees, then cut them off and hollowed them out. Softest and lightest of all the hardwoods, with a fine, smooth, straight grain that is easily worked, basswood has long been highly valued by carvers. It was lathed to make bowls and platters, and carved into wooden spoons and toys. Today it is still crafted into duck decoys and models. Because the light wood could be worked thin and bent without cracking, it was also used for canoes and musical instruments, as well as picture frames, window sashes and yardsticks.

In the forest, basswood mixes sparingly with other broadleaf trees and never forms pure stands. In the dark understorey, shade-tolerant basswood saplings have the

Average mature height: 18–21 m (60–70 ft)
Average width: 60–75 cm (2–2.5 ft)
Maximum height: 40 m (132 ft)
Maximum width: 1.2 m (4 ft)
Alias: Linden, lime, American basswood, whitewood, bass, beetree, spoonwood, *le tilleul d'Amérique, Tilia americana*
Name origin: From "bast," the fibrous inner bark, or phloem, of trees, used to make rope
Lifespan: Large, mature trees commonly 200 years old
Preferred habitat: Deciduous forests with deep, rich soils, often on hillsides, less often in mixed forests
Leaves: 13–20 cm (5–8 in) long, about 7.5–15 cm (3–6 in) wide, slightly lopsided, with a pointed tip and large-toothed edges; long stems; turn crispy brown from edges toward centre in fall
Bark: Dark grey, with long, thin, flat ridges
Sex: Clusters of 10–20 small, fragrant, yellow flowers joined

virtue of patience. With huge, lopsided leaves, often bigger than a full-spread hand, they grow slowly. When a spot opens up in the canopy they shoot up and join the big trees. When an old tree dies, rather than give up a hard-won place in the sun, its still-living base sprouts new shoots, creating a clump of trunks where there had been just one. Standing dead basswood trunks are also very important for cavity-nesting or roosting woodpeckers, owls, mammals and bee colonies.

Even when basswood leaves are only high above on mature trees, porcupines make the effort to reach them. In many areas, basswoods are one of the most important foods of the moving pincushions. The mild-tasting, high-nitrogen leaves are about 13 percent protein. The trees' buds are also eaten by deer, chipmunks and ruffed grouse.

The strong, sweet scent of basswood flowers, sometimes noticeable for more than a kilometre (half a mile), attracts droves of bees that cross-pollinate the widely scattered trees. For the three weeks or so that basswood blooms in late June and July, its nectar is the focus for local hives, where it is made into a high-quality, strong-tasting white honey. Heavy cutting of basswoods around the start of the 20th century brought lean times for Ontario's beekeepers. Perhaps the flowers and honey are what prompted the ancient Greeks to associate the closely related European linden tree with sweetness, modesty, gentleness and conjugal love. The trees were said to be the husbands of the dryads, the wood nymphs.

Out of every five years among basswoods, two or three bring profuse bloomings and correspondingly large seed crops. After they mature, small bunches of seeds fall to the ground with attached leaflike blades acting as parachutes. When the real leaves drop, they replenish the earth with higher levels of concentrated calcium, nitrogen and potassium than most other decomposing leaves.

by a single stalk to the midpoint of a 7.5–12.5 cm (3–5 in) long, narrow leaflike blade; each flower has 5 petals and both male and female parts

Seeds: Bunches of several hard, pea-sized, green nutlets covered by soft, rust-brown hairs and holding 1–2 seeds; hang on branches into winter, take 2 years to germinate

Buds: Shiny, reddish, squat, slightly lopsided, about 6 mm (0.25 in) long

Roots: Deep, widespread, well anchored

Wood: Light brown, soft, fine-grained, even-textured and light, 421 kg/m^3 (27 lb/cu ft)

Associated trees: Sugar maple, yellow birch, beech, ironwood, black cherry

Common visitors: Porcupines, deer, chipmunks, squirrels, mice and ruffed grouse eat seeds, leaves or buds

False Face masks: Fierce images of the spirits that protect against disease and crop blights, worn during Iroquois False Face ceremonies before the start of each growing season; carved from living basswoods so that the mask would hold life, after rituals seeking the trees' permission

Range: Southern Ontario to around Lake Nipissing and Sault Ste. Marie; also in Manitoba, Quebec and New Brunswick

Also see: *Up North:* Porcupine, Bees

CHOKECHERRY
Harsh Fruits, Mellowing with Age

They are like small rubies
For a young queen who is small and graceful.

IRVING LAYTON, "Red Chokecherries"

S INCE TIME IMMEMORIAL, cherries have drawn hungry crowds seeking their sweet, juicy flesh. Cherry-eating creatures propagate the trees by swallowing the pits and spreading them in their droppings. Some, such as evening grosbeaks and chipmunks, cheat the trees by biting into the pits to eat the seeds inside. Bears can also be bad news, tearing whole branches off to get at the small red fruits, sometimes breaking or crushing most of the trees in a thicket during big crop years.

Chokecherries are not as dangerous as their name suggests, though they can taste harsh and astringent, causing the mouth to pucker and dry. The riper they become, especially when tempered by a frost, the sweeter and more palatable they are. But, as with all cherries, the seeds within the pits, the inner bark and the leaves are laced with prussic acid, or hydrogen cyanide, from which cyanide can be produced. Chokecherry leaves wilted by drought or frost are particularly poisonous to browsing cattle.

When cooked and dried, however, pit-bearing chokecherries are safe. The Ojibway mashed and dried them to mix into cakes. Farther west, they were one of the main wild berries added to flavour and sweeten pemmican, the dried-meat staple that fuelled the fur trade. Cherries were also dried or powdered for use in the winter, when they were added to soup. Today they're most often used in jams, pies, juice and wine. The Québécois, having long cultivated chokecherries, produce fairly sweet strains with fruits up to 2.5 centimetres (one inch) wide.

Pin cherry, with smooth, shiny, reddish-brown bark laced with hash marks, tends to grow in clumps and

Average mature height: 2–8 m (6.6–26.4 ft)
Average width: 5–15 cm (2–6 in)
Maximum height: Up to 10 m (33 ft) when in rich, moist soil
Maximum width: 20 cm (8 in)
Maximum black cherry height: 31 m (102 ft)
Alias: Common chokecherry, chuckley-plum, red chokecherry, wild cherry, *le cerisier à sauvage, Prunus virginiana*
Leaves: Dark green, 2–12 cm (0.8–4.8 in) long, 1–6 cm (0.4–2.4 in) wide, egg-shaped, broader than other cherry species, with finely serrated edges; turn dull yellow or reddish in fall
Bark: Smooth or finely scaled, dark grey; almost black on older trees
Sex: White blossoms, 8–10 mm (0.4 in) wide, clustered tightly around a 5–15 cm (2–6 in) long, arching central stalk at branch tips, with male and female parts found together in

patches, as does chokecherry. But it's more limited to drier, open areas, usually where there's been a fire or logging; hence its other common name, fire cherry. Pin cherry's blossoms and shiny, red, long-stemmed fruits appear a little earlier than those of chokecherry. Fast growing and spreading by root suckers, pin cherry quickly colonizes open spaces, often dominating them in the early years after a disturbance. During that time, pin cherry is a nurse tree for spruce and other slower-growing, shade-tolerant evergreen seedlings inching their way up beneath, providing them with shelter and building up a fertile layer of humus with its fallen, decomposing leaves and branches.

Pits are laced with prussic acid, from which cyanide can be produced

---

Black cherry, maturing deep in the forest into a tall tree with dark flaky bark, is considerably different from its shrubby relatives. It still needs open sunlight to get started, though, often getting its chance in the space opened up by an old, wind-felled tree. Less tolerant of extreme cold than the smaller cherries, black cherry doesn't grow much farther north than Parry Sound and the Algonquin highlands. In many areas, the axe and saw have made it much less plentiful than it once was. The tree's attractive, fine, smooth-grained wood was highly coveted for musket butts, carriages, cabinets, counters and bars, and is still considered by many to make the best canoe paddles. The characteristic mahogany-red colour is, in fact, the result of a stain applied to the naturally light-pink wood. Its black cherries were also widely used to flavour rum and whisky, giving the tree the alternative name "rum cherry."

each tiny, 5-petalled flower; blooming in late May and early June, cross-pollinated by mosquitoes, bees and other flying insects
Cherries: Bright red to purple-black, pea-sized, with a large stone; big crops every 2 years
Buds: Brown, 6 mm (0.2 in) long, sharply pointed
Wood: Light brown, hard, dense but weak and porous
Preferred habitat: Mixed with deciduous trees and shrubs along streams, forest and wetland fringes, open woods, rocky ridges and clearings
Associated trees and shrubs: Elderberry, raspberry, pin cherry, dogwood
Common visitors: Bears, foxes, moose, deer, chipmunks, red squirrels, flying squirrels, raccoons, hares, skunks, mice, ruffed grouse, crows, evening grosbeaks, robins and other thrushes, blue jays, grackles, cedar waxwings, white-throated sparrows, northern orioles, scarlet tanagers, rose-breasted grosbeaks, woodpeckers, flycatchers, bluebirds, cardinals, catbirds
Common nester: Chestnut-sided warbler
Homeland of the domestic cherry: Western Asia and southeastern Europe
Divine cherry tree: Buddha is said to have been born under a cherry tree called Sala
Chokecherry range: All of Ontario except the northern Hudson Bay lowlands; also in all other provinces and territories
Also see: Evening Grosbeak. *Up North:* Mosquitoes, Black Bear

DOGWOODS
Scrawny but Tough

Maximum height: Alternate-leaved dogwood up to 10 m (33 ft)
Alias: Cornels, *les cornouillers*, *Cornus*
Osier word origin: From Latin *osaria*, meaning "bed of willows," referring to long, flexible, willowlike stems of red osier dogwood
Scientific name meaning: *Cornus* comes from Latin *corneolus*, meaning "of horn," in reference to the hardness of the wood. *Stolonifera* (species name of the red osier dogwood) notes the ability of the branches and runners, "stolons," to take root
Leaves: Pointed tips, smooth edges, 5–8 prominent veins curve lengthwise up the leaf; appearing in opposite pairs, except on alternate-leaved dogwood

THOUGH MOST DOGWOODS are shrubs or scrawny trees, the wood of their thin branches and stems is the hardest in Ontario. The "dog" actually comes from the Old English word *dag*, meaning "stab." The smooth, fine, hornlike wood of European dogwoods was called "daggerwood," because it made ideal, long-lasting skewers and weapons. The sturdy spears of Roman soldiers are said to have been made from stems of the shrubby trees. Dogwood has also been used for implements that take a pounding, such as golf club and mallet heads, piano keys and bearings and shaker slides in old mills.

Early French settlers called dogwoods *bois de calumet*, meaning "pipe wood," because they, like the natives, pushed the soft pith from the centre of the steely shoots and used them for pipe stems. The dried inner bark of red osier dogwood (illustrated), called *kinnikinnick*, was mixed with tobacco and smoked in the pipes. Some authorities say it was mildly narcotic.

All dogwoods have distinctive leaves with prominent, arching veins running parallel to the leaf edge. In late summer and early fall, the leaves turn purple-red or bright crimson, alerting passing birds to the large-pitted, ripening berries. The birds, often migrants, spread the seeds with their sky bombs.

After its leaves fall, red osier dogwood becomes even more conspicuous, its deep-red bark contrasting sharply with the snow in low, damp thickets and along the edges of marshes, forests and shorelines. Usually under two metres (seven feet) high, it's also called red willow because of its many slender, flexible stems. Red osier bears clusters of little creamy-white flowers in June and white berries in late summer varying from tart to bitter. The Ojibway mixed the shrub's red bark with the inner bark of white birch and oak- and cedar-wood ashes to make a red dye. They also boiled the twigs for a drink to treat dysentery, and the Iroquois made a beverage from its bark to treat indigestion.

The leaves turn purple-red or bright crimson, alerting passing birds to the large-pitted, ripening berries

Alternate-leaved dogwood grows in the forest understorey and woodland borders as a small tree, usually two to four metres (6.6 to 13.2 feet) tall. It's also called the pagoda tree, because its tiers of wide-spread branches, with upward-bending tips, become smaller towards the top. As early as late July it bears many dark-blue to black berries on short, bright-red stalks. The fruit is extremely important to a wide variety of songbirds and other wildlife.

Round-leaved dogwood, a smaller shrub, grows in sandy or rocky open forests, thickets and ravines, and has purplish stems and light-blue or greenish-white berries.

Sex: Flat, dense clusters of small, white, greenish-white or yellow flowers in June, containing both male and female parts, pollinated by bees, butterflies and other insects
Berries: Size of small blueberries, containing a stone with 2 seeds, ripening in July to Sept.
Buds: Thin, pointed
Wood: Very hard, tough, dense, with smooth, hornlike texture
Roots: Strong, wide-spreading
Companion trees and shrubs: Willows, balsam poplars, speckled alders, chokecherries
Common visitors: Bears, raccoons, skunks, squirrels, chipmunks, wood ducks, ruffed grouse and dozens of songbirds, especially evening grosbeaks, robins and cedar waxwings, eat berries; beavers eat bark; moose, deer and hares browse winter twigs; gray treefrogs call from pondside branches in late spring
Common nesters: Least flycatchers
Official flower of British Columbia: Pacific dogwood
Range: Throughout Ontario; also in all other provinces and territories
Number of dogwood species native to Ontario: 8
Number of dogwood species worldwide: 40–100, depending on definition of species or subspecies
Also see: Willows, Staghorn Sumac. *Up North:* Bunchberry, Lowbrush Blueberry

RED-BERRIED ELDER
Of Pipe Stems and Peashooters

GROWING WITH TWO or more main stems where the sun penetrates the edges of the forest, elders have long been favourites of musicians, pipe-smokers and small children. Their popularity derives from the wide zone of soft pith at the centre of elder branches. The pith can be easily poked out, leaving a hollow stem that is ideal for flutes, pipes and peashooters. Early maple-sugar makers also used the tubes as spiles in tapped trees. The great Roman writer and naturalist Pliny noted 2,000 years ago that European elder was used for whistles and musical pipes. The scientific name for the genus, *Sambucus*, comes from an ancient Greek musical instrument, the *sambuke*, made from hollow elder stems. The similarly named, deadly sweet Italian liqueur sambuca is flavoured with elderberries.

Practitioners of the elder-stem arts, however, have to take extreme care to let their materials thoroughly dry out, or risk being poisoned – a mishap that has befallen more than a few pea-shooting children. Elder's bark, leaves, pith and roots all contain hydrocyanic acid, a protective toxic compound also found in cherry bark, pits and leaves (see page 202). In the case of red-berried elder, even the berries are off limits. A respect for elder's poisonous properties was probably the origin of many Old World superstitions about bringing evil into the house by cutting down and burning elder. On the other hand, in many areas planting elder in the garden was thought to keep away both lightning and evil spirits.

European and native North American healers also turned elder's dangerous qualities to their advantage, using a drink made from the inner bark to induce vomiting when a patient had ingested another type of poison. The Iroquois boiled the inner bark of Canada elderberry

Height: Usually under 3 m (10 ft), up to 4 m (13 ft)
Width: Up to 3 cm (1.2 in)
Alias: Red elderberry, eastern red elder, poison elder, mountain elder, boor tree, stinking elder, scarlet elder, boutry, *le sureau rouge, Sambucus pubens, Sambucus racemosa*
Preferred habitat: Edges of hardwood forests and swamps, shorelines, thickets, clearings, open woods, hillsides and ravines
Leaves: Compound, consisting of 5 and rarely 7 opposite leaflets, each 5–13 cm (2–5 in) long, 2.5–5.5 cm (1–2.2 in) wide, with a tapered, sharply pointed tip, sharp-toothed edges and pointy, often asymmetrical base, pale on bottom
Sex: Tiny yellow-white flowers in long, rounded or triangular

and then put it inside the cheek to ease toothaches. And studies have revealed the bark does contain a pain-killing compound. Elderberry flowers, berries and bark have been used to make ointments for wounds, burns, sores and cuts.

Deer, moose and hares can eat at least small amounts of red-berried elder buds and leaves without ill effect, and in July and August, bears and two dozen bird species snap up the berries. Once fully ripe, berries of the closely related Canada elderberry can be eaten by humans. They are used in jams and pies and were a popular source of homemade wine in the mid-1800s, while its flowers were dipped in batter to make fritters. Canada elderberry most often grows on wetter ground than does red-berried elder, and usually has seven leaflets per stem and contains white pith. Its flat-topped flower clusters don't bloom until July, yielding purple-black berries in late August and September.

Both elders are in the honeysuckle family, which includes six native "true honey-suckle" species in central Ontario, all with small, funnel-shaped flowers, diminutive red, orangish or blue berries and opposite pairs of leaves. One of the most common, fly honeysuckle, is a dense, finely branched shrub, up to 1.5 metres (five feet) tall, growing in hardwood and mixed forests and swamps. Mountain fly honeysuckle reaches less than half its height and tends to grow in coniferous forests and swamps. Both bloom with pale-yellow flowers in May and June. Hairy honeysuckle differs considerably, being a woody vine with shredding bark, climbing up to three metres (10 feet) and blooming from early to midsummer. Bush honeysuckle is another small shrub, with sharply serrated leaves. It is not a true honeysuckle and produces seed capsules instead of berries through the summer. It often grows in large colonies on rocky ridges and in open forests.

clusters, 5–13 cm (2–5 in) long, with strong scent, blooming as leaves open in late May and June; pollinated by bees
Berries: Bright red, about size of BB-gun pellets, pointed, holding 3–5 seeds, inedible
Bark: Yellow-brown and hairy when young; grey with little warty bumps with age
Root: Thick, gnarly
Buds: Large, thick and reddish, swelling as early as late Mar.
Wood: Very thin wood layer surrounds thick, soft, orange or reddish-brown pith core
Companion plants and shrubs: Raspberry, chokecherry, grasses
Common nesters: Goldfinches, yellow warblers, alder flycatchers
Common visitors: Hares, deer, moose, bears, raccoons, skunks, chipmunks, mice, ruffed grouse, yellow-bellied sapsuckers, phoebes, kingbirds, nuthatches, veeries, robins and other thrushes, waxwings, red-eyed vireos, rose-breasted grosbeaks, indigo buntings, white-throated and swamp sparrows
Range: Southern Ontario almost to James Bay; also in Manitoba, Quebec and Atlantic provinces
Number of elder species native to Ontario: 2
Number of elder species worldwide: About 30
Also see: Chokecherry, Hobblebush, Twinflower

BEAKED HAZEL
The Bristly-nutted Shrub

Average mature height: 1–3 m
(3.3–10 ft)
Maximum height: 4 m (13 ft)
Stems: Usually 2–3 cm
(0.8–1.2 in) wide
Alias: Hazel, filbert, *le noisetier
à long bec, Corylus cornuta*
Preferred habitat: Mixed forests,
woodland edges and clear-
ings, streambanks, often in
thickets
Leaves: Oval, 5–12 cm (2–5 in)
long, 2.5–7 cm (1–3 in)
wide, tapering to pointed tip,
with unevenly toothed edges,
bright green above, lighter
below; high in calcium and
manganese
Sex: Upright male flower
catkins 2–3 cm (0.2–1.2 in)
long after forming in
autumn, open out up to 5 cm
(2 in) long and dangle in
spring; tiny female flowers
have hairlike, bright-red

THE COMMONPLACE BEAKED hazel seems to blend undistinguished with the saplings and bushes that often crowd the hardwood and mixed forest understorey. It stands out, though, in April and early May, as one of the first shrubs to bloom. Winter's upright columns of closed male catkins suddenly unfurl and dangle from hazel branches as the year's last snow melts away on the ground below. Still more striking are the tiny, wind-pollinated female flowers, with their bold, bright-red stiles. Only after the shrub blooms do its leaves, and those of other understorey inhabitants, open to grab the sun and turn the forest interior green.

For the rest of spring and summer, hazelnuts slowly develop. Covered by a densely bristled, Velcro-like husk narrowing to a long, beak-shaped end, the nuts are both edible and nutritious, with high levels of thiamine, which builds muscle tissue, as well as compounds that lower blood cholesterol and remove liver fats. They're relished by a wide array of forest critters and often seem to disappear from the branch just as they ripen in late August. The Algonquins, Ojibway and Cree made a point of collecting the nuts, often peeling and then burying them for a few days to leach away any bitterness. They were eaten raw or boiled in soups. Many were also dried for winter. The Iroquois ground hazel nuts and mixed them into breads and puddings and boiled them to remove their oil for use with other foods.

Native peoples found a number of other uses for beaked hazel. The Ojibway used the shrub's thin, pliable twigs as the ribs for baskets, and the thicker branches were ideally suited for drumsticks, because they are often crooked and provide just the right enlarged base.

Hazel-twig charms protected sailors from shipwreck and riders from horse-spooking fairies

---

On the other side of the Atlantic, the European hazel, also known as the domestic filbert, was important to traditional cultures as well. Forked hazel branches were the choice of diviners in searching for water. The shrub was once said to be sacred to Thor, the Norse thunder god, both embodying lightning and preventing it from striking. Hazel-twig charms protected sailors from shipwreck and riders from horse-spooking fairies. The colour hazel is named after the yellow-brown shell of the filbert nut, as Shakespeare notes in *Romeo and Juliet*:

Thou wilt quarrel with a man for cracking nuts,
Having no other reason, but thou hast hazel eyes.

styles protruding from closed buds.
Nuts: Round, hard shells about 12 mm (0.5 in) long, within light-green, densely bristled sheath that forms a 3–4 cm (1.2–1.6 in) long, open-ended "beak," appearing in pairs, less often singly or in groups of 3–6; bristles quite irritating to skin
Bark: Smooth, grey
Roots: Extensive, shallow, mat-forming roots and rootlets with underground stems
Companion trees and shrubs: Sugar and red maples, aspens, yellow and white birch, hobblebush, white pine
Common visitors: Chipmunks, squirrels, bears, raccoons eat nuts in late summer; moose, deer, hares and ruffed grouse browse buds, catkins or leaves; beavers eat bark
Common nesters: Red-eyed vireos, chestnut-sided warblers
Range: Southern Ontario to the southern edge of the Hudson Bay lowlands; also in all other provinces
Number of hazel species native to Ontario: 2
Number of hazel species worldwide: 15

HOBBLEBUSH
Graceful Wild Viburnum

HOBBLEBUSH HAS a distinctive look that sets it apart from other woodland shrubs. Its large, rounded leaves grow in regimented pairs, on upright stalks, along the shrub's arching or horizontal branches. Sometimes the long, graceful limbs arch so low that they touch the ground and put down roots from their tips. The resulting snare formed by the grounded branch can trip up hikers cutting through the thick underbrush, which is how the shrub got its name.

From late summer through winter, hobblebush branch tips also sport large, pointed beige buds, which in late May and early June open up into a wide bouquet of white flowers. Most are tiny fertile blossoms, but they're surrounded by a fringe of snowy, large-petalled sterile flowers, which are extremely conspicuous in the spring understorey and attract insect pollinators. As the summer progresses, small green berries develop, gradually turning red, then purple, and finally blackish in September. In shadier woods, the shrubs produce no flowers or berries, reproducing only by suckering roots.

Hobblebush is actually a wild viburnum, as are several other native shrubs common in central Ontario. **Highbush cranberry** is a viburnum with maplelike leaves that presents its red berries along streamsides, swamp margins and in wet meadows in late summer. Another, **wild raisin**, bears oval leaves, frothy white flower clusters and dark berries on swamp and bog edges. **Maple leaved viburnum**, growing in dryer, rocky forest understorey as far north as Renfrew, is easily mistaken for a maple sapling, but has clusters of frothy white flowers in June followed by green berries that turn red and then dark blue in early autumn.

Height: Under 2 m (6.6 ft)
Width: Up to 5 cm (2 in)
Alias: Common hobblebush, wayfaring tree, witch-hobble, triptoe, moosewood, *le bois d'orignal, Viburnum alnifolium*
Leaves: Distinct, opposite pairs, each 10–20 cm (4–8 in) long, 7–18 cm (3–7 in) wide, finely toothed edges, dark green on top and lighter below
Sex: Rounded white clusters, up to 13 cm (5 in) wide, of small, 5-petalled fertile flowers surrounded by much larger, 2–3 cm (0.8–1.2 in) wide, sterile flowers
Berries: Purple-black; about 5–10 mm (0.2–0.4 in) long, with a large seed; edible
Buds: Very distinctive, large, wide, fairly flat, pointed, beige without scale coverings
Preferred habitat: Moist forests, especially in ravines, woodland edges and thickets
Range: Lake Ontario to just north of North Bay; also in Quebec and the Maritimes

IRONWOOD
Hard, Strong and Straight

Weight: 800 kg/m³
(50 lb/cu ft)
Red oak weight: 665 kg/m³
(42 lb/cu ft)
White cedar weight: 304 kg/m³
(19 lb/cu ft)
World's heaviest wood: South
African ironwood, up to
1,507 kg/m³ (95 lb/cu ft)
Average mature height: 8–12 m
(26–40 ft)
Average width: 15–25 cm
(6–10 in)
Maximum height: 22 m (73 ft)
Maximum width: 90 cm (3 ft)
Alias: Hop hornbeam, lever-
wood, Indian cedar, black
hazel, deer wood, hard hack,
eastern hop hornbeam,
American hop hornbeam,
rough-barked ironwood,
*l'ostryer de Virginie, Ostrya
virginiana*
Preferred habitat: Deciduous
and mixed forests, especially
on moist hillsides and ridges
Leaves: Like jagged-edged
spearheads, soft and thin,
6–13 cm (2.5–5 in) long,
2.5–5 cm (1–2 in) wide,
dark green on top, slightly
lighter below, turns pale
yellow in autumn
Bark: Grey-brown, fine, narrow,
vertical strips, often shredding, with loose ends
Sex: Male flower catkins green
with reddish tint, 1.5–5 cm
(0.6–2 in) long, dangle from
branch tips before leaves
open. Clusters, 3–5 cm
(1.2–2 in) long, of green,
sack-shaped, red-fringed

RISING LIKE a sturdy pole, ironwood grows straight up above the shrubs in the understorey, but not beyond the shade beneath the forest canopy. Its trunk usually stays on the straight and narrow until almost at the crown, which is formed by long, slender branches. With the densest and strongest wood in Canada, the tree is justly compared to an iron bar growing in the forest. Ironwood's other name, "hornbeam," means literally a horn-hard beam of wood. It's definitely not prime woodpecker real estate.

Though too thinly scattered to be commercially cut, and almost impossible to split, ironwood was long used by farmers and local tradespeople for levers needing a great deal of strength, axe and tool handles, mallets, oxen yokes, sleigh runners, cartwheel hubs and cogwheels for mills. Saplings were stripped down to their heartwood and used as fishing poles fit for the biggest of luggers.

The thin ironwood trunks are distinguishable at eye level by their narrow strips of fine, shredding grey bark, almost like white cedar in texture. In autumn, the trees litter the ground with distinctive bunches of overlapping seed sacs, resembling hop fruits. The air-filled sacs are

female flowers on tips of new shoots as leaves unfold
Seeds: 1 nutlet, 6–8 mm (0.3 in) long, inside each of about a dozen puffy, overlapping, yellowish-green sacs growing in bundles; each sheath 2 cm (0.8 in) long and covered by a light down irritating to skin
Buds: Greenish brown, 3–5 mm (0.1 in) long, quite pointy, sticking diagonally out from twig
Wood: Thick layer of almost white sapwood and pale-brown heartwood, very strong, hard, heavy and close-grained
Companion trees: Sugar maple, beech, basswood, white pine, white birch, red maple, red oak, largetooth aspen, white spruce, fir
Common visitors: Deer, hares, red squirrels, mice, ruffed grouse, purple finches, downy woodpeckers and rose-breasted grosbeaks
Range: Southern Ontario to about Lake Temiskaming, Sudbury and Sault Ste. Marie; also in Manitoba, Quebec, New Brunswick and Nova Scotia
Number of *Ostrya* species native to Ontario: 1
Number of *Ostrya* species worldwide: 8
Also see: Dogwoods, Beetles. *Up North:* Fungi

caught by the wind, spreading them farther. Their hairy coverings make them unpleasant to touch, discouraging birds and squirrels from eating their contents, though deer, hares and ruffed grouse don't seem to mind. The seeds take root wherever a little light makes it through to the ground, though once established, ironwoods are in general quite shade-tolerant.

Ironwood trunks are distinguishable by their narrow strips of fine, shredding grey bark

In wetter areas, along rivers and other bottomlands, young **white elms** might at first glance be mistaken for ironwood. Both trees have similar leaves, though elm leaves have even bigger teeth and a rough upper surface that feels like fine sandpaper. Mature elm bark also looks quite different, with deep, wide ridges. But older white elms are not common today; often the trees are killed by Dutch elm disease when still saplings, though many grow big enough to produce seeds before succumbing. A fungal scourge from central Asia, the disease, first identified by Dutch scientists, is spread by bark beetles. It first came to Canada in 1944 in a shipment of wooden crates, and within three decades wiped out a huge portion of the country's towering elms.

LARGETOOTH ASPEN
Donning Robes of Silver and Gold

LARGETOOTH ASPEN jumps into the limelight at least twice a year. First, in late May or early June, the downy surface of the tree's unfolding leaves looks like a dusting of frost amid the surrounding green. Though the silver lining is soon lost for the summer, the tree puts on another spectacular show around early October, when it dons a bright gold-orange mantle as the leaves change colour. While the largetooth has the prettier wardrobe, it is not as hardy as its sibling, the much-smaller-leaved trembling aspen. Less tolerant of cold temperatures, it leafs out two weeks after its trembling sister and changes colour about a week earlier in fall. Largetooths are less common above the southern portions of the Canadian Shield.

Like other poplars, largetooth aspen cannot grow in shade. In May or June, its tiny, fluffy seeds travel far and wide in the wind, the lucky few landing in open sites with lots of sunlight. Once a young tree is established, it spreads root suckers that send up identical sapling copies of itself. New shoots can even grow from old stumps. When 15 to 20 years old, they produce flower catkins and seeds. Though largetooth aspen's own seedlings cannot grow in the parent tree's shade, their falling leaves provide ready nutrients for the fir, spruce, oak and pine trees that grow beneath them and eventually take over.

The presence of salicin in the inner bark of largetooth aspen may explain the bark's use by the Ojibway as a poultice for wounds and as a splint lining. The medicinal compound, recreated in Aspirin, is common to most poplars and willows. During travel or times of food shortage, the inner bark was also sometimes boiled and eaten. The tree's soft wood is today used mainly for pulp, matches, veneer, plywood, boxes and crates.

Average mature height: 15–18 m (50–60 ft)

Average width: 30–60 cm (1–2 ft)

Alias: Bigtooth aspen, white poplar, big-toothed poplar, *le peuplier à grandes dents, Populus grandidentata*

Preferred habitat: Young forests, often on ridges

Lifespan: Most large trees around 60 years old, very rarely up to 200 years old

Leaves: 4–12 cm (1.6–4.8 in) long, 5–6 cm (2–2.4 in) wide

Bark: On young trees, smooth, light green to yellowish grey with an orange-yellow hue; o older trees, dark grey with deep furrows

Sex: Male flower catkins 5–10 cm (2–4 in) long, female catkins 7.5–12.5 cm (3–5 in) long when in seed, separate trees, opening befor leaves, pollinated by bees

Range: Southern Ontario to southern boreal forest; also in Quebec, the Maritimes and southeastern Manitoba

AMERICAN MOUNTAIN ASH
Feeding Winter's Hungry Mouths

I N THE WINTER, along moist shorelines and swamp fringes, dense bunches
of wild mountain ash berries are a
godsend for birds faced with a scarcity of
food. The clumps of tough-skinned,
orange-red berries cling so tenaciously to
the trees that, having fed overwintering
purple finches, evening grosbeaks and
cedar waxwings, they're often still around
for the first famished waves of spring migrants returning to their breeding grounds.

The feast begins when the bright, bitter berries ripen
in August. Bears have their fill before retiring for the
winter in mid-autumn. Ruffed grouse, downy woodpeckers, fishers and martens also visit the shrubby, narrow-
trunked trees, but many migrating birds of early fall give
them a miss in favour of more nutritious, sweet fruits, such
as cherries, which don't last as long. Mountain ash berries
are mellowed by autumn's first frosts, when, high in iron
and vitamin c, they are collected and used in sweetened
homemade jams. The trees are also visited during winter
by moose, deer and hares browsing on their twigs and fragrant inner bark. Beavers enjoy the bark as well.

Perhaps the winter bounty of berries is what inspired
the ancient Celts to name one of their cold-season
months after the European mountain ash, called the
rowan tree. It was popularly acclaimed for its magical
powers as well as its miraculous winter berries. The druids
summoned the spirits by stoking their fires with sacred
rowan wood. Witching wands cut from the tree were used
to search for metal ore deposits. The Vikings – who called
the rowan "Thor's tree," because its red berries were the
colour of the thunder god's hair – fastened a piece of
rowan to their boats for protection from the shipwrecking
wrath of Ran, wife of the sea god Ojir. Even into recent
centuries in the British Isles, rowan was planted outside
houses to keep away witches and in graveyards to keep the

Average mature height: Usually
3–7 m (10–23 ft)
Average width: 10–30 cm
(4–12 in)
Maximum height: 10 m (33 ft)
Alias: Rowan, mountain sumac,
rowan berry, winetree,
witchentree, dogberry, cat-
berry, pigberry, roundwood,
service-tree, *le sorbier
d'Amérique, Sorbus americana*
Word origin of *rowan*: From Old
Norse word for "red," referring to berries
Preferred habitat: Low-lying,
moist mixed and coniferous
forests and thickets,
lakeshores, bogs, rocky
outcrops, hillsides
Leaves: Compound, with 11–17
opposite, narrow, feather-
shaped, sharply pointed
leaflets, each 5–9 cm
(2–3.7 in) long and 6–25 mm
(0.2–1 in) wide, with serrated
edges, light green on top,
paler below, turning light
yellow in fall; poisonous
Sex: Tiny, fragrant, creamy-white
flowers in 5–15 cm (2–6 in)

dead from rising. Rowan twigs bound in loops by red ribbons, or made into crosses, were hung on horses and barns, and rowan wood rockers were often fastened to babies' cradles for protection from the unknown.

The Ojibway used the pliable limbs to make snowshoe frames, canoe ribs and lacrosse sticks

Though American and European mountain ashes are closely related, they are not true ashes at all. Rather, they're members of the rose family, like cherries, hawthorns and serviceberries. They were named for their ashlike composite leaves. **Showy mountain ash** also grows in central Ontario, especially along rocky shores, and becomes more common farther north. It's similar in most ways to American mountain ash, but has larger, bright-red berries and starts blooming about a week or so later in June. The Ojibway used the pliable limbs of both species to make snowshoe frames, canoe ribs and lacrosse sticks.

Many of the same animals that turn to mountain ash in the winter find sustenance in a handful of other low-fat, tart or bitter berries with mould-resistant properties that allow them to persist into winter. In alder swamps, they find bright-red **winterberries**, which don't even ripen until well into fall.

wide, flat clusters, appearing in June; each flower has both male and female parts

Berries: Bright orange-red, 4–6 mm (0.2–0.3 in) wide, each holding 2–10 seeds, ripe in Aug., bitter tasting

Bark: Smooth, light grey-green, thin; somewhat scaly on old trees

Buds: Reddish-brown, shiny, cone-shaped and gummy, about 1 cm (0.5 in) long

Wood: Light-brown heartwood, paler sapwood; soft, weak, close-grained, 550 kg/m³ (35 lb/cu ft)

Companion trees: Speckled alder, fir, white spruce, white cedar

Medicinal uses: Berries, high in iron and vitamin C, were eaten raw or brewed into a tea to treat scurvy; leaves, which have cyanide, ingested by natives to cause vomiting and rid the body of sickness

Other wild fruits persisting into winter: Winterberries, wintergreen berries, partridgeberries, hawthorn haws, staghorn sumac "berries"

Range: The Niagara Peninsula to the southern tip of James Bay; also in Quebec and Atlantic provinces

Number of mountain ash species native to Ontario: 2

Number of mountain ash species worldwide: About 75, mostly in East Asia

Also see: Chokecherry, Staghorn Sumac, Purple Finch. *Up North:* Hawthorns

SERVICEBERRY
Sweet Fruits with Big Draw

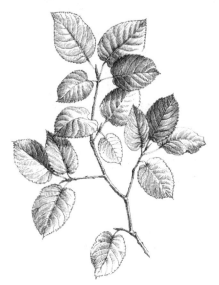

Average mature height: 2–10 m (7–33 ft)
Average mature width: 8–30 cm (3–12 in)
Maximum height: 18.3 m (60 ft)
Maximum width: 60 cm (2 ft)
Alias: June berry, shadbush, shadblow, service tree, sugar-plum, little pair, sugarpear, Indian pear, chuckley pear, sarvice tree, billberry, medlars, sarvi, Scotch apple, *les petites poires, Amelanchiers*
Berries: Red or purplish, blue-berry-sized, with dried remains of flower at one end; contain 4–10 large seeds; ripening in late July or early Aug.; sweet and tasty
Leaves: 2.5–10 cm (1–4 in) long, ranging from oval to nearly round, on thin stalks, with pointed tips and finely toothed edges; turn amber,

LOOKING LIKE MINIATURE apples, summer's small red or purple serviceberries are so sweet and tasty that birds and animals often gobble them up before they are fully ripe. With a sugar content of up to 20 percent or more, along with high levels of iron and copper, serviceberries are far sweeter than even blueberries and raspberries. The Algonquins and Ojibway ate them fresh or dried in cakes for the winter, while the Iroquois dried the berries and then mixed them with sugar and water to make an alcoholic beverage.

The variety known as Saskatoon berry, which grows west of Sault Ste. Marie, was the most important fruit for the native peoples of the Prairies and the interior of British Columbia. Large quantities were added to pemmican, a mixture of dried, pounded buffalo meat and fat, which in the west served as the stable of native, Métis and fur trader alike. They could subsist for long stretches in winter almost solely on the sweet, fatty mash, while getting their vitamin C from spruce tea and rose hips. A great abundance of Saskatoon berries once grew around the site of the city that now bears their name.

One of central Ontario's four common serviceberry species, round-leaved serviceberry is almost identical to Saskatoon berry, except its leaves have hairy undersides rather than smooth. Round-leaved serviceberry usually grows in clumps of branching stems, one to three metres (3.3 to 10 feet) high, on rocky lakeshores, ridges and cliffs, often rising from narrow crevices. It blooms in late May and June, around the same time as mountain June berry, a slightly smaller shrub of sandy shorelines, swamps and bogs.

Only two species, downy serviceberry and smooth serviceberry (illustrated), ever really reach tree size, growing up to 10 metres (33 feet) high. They usually appear in clumps of several thin trunks at the edges of clearings in mixed and coniferous forests, blooming in a snowy profusion. Another particularly showy species when in bloom, mountain June berry tends to inhabit wetland fringes and wet shorelines more than most other serviceberries. Because the various species commonly hybridize with each other, it's often hard to tell one from another.

Though their trunks seldom grow very wide, serviceberries are notable for having hard, heavy wood. It was used for arrow shafts, tool handles, fishing rods and cabinetry, appearing quite attractive when polished. The common name, serviceberry, was originally pronounced "sarvisberry," as it still is in parts of Appalachia, where hill folk stick to many old Elizabethan forms. Ultimately, it derives from the Latin *sorbus*, a name given by the Romans to a related fruit. The alternative name, shadbush, is often used in the Maritimes and the United States, where the shrubs are said to bloom around the time of the spawning run of the Atlantic coast shad.

rusty, bronze, red or purple in fall
Bark: Smooth, greyish, with darker, twisting vertical lines on shrubs and young trees; rougher and scaly on old trees
Sex: Drooping clusters of flowers with 5 long white petals, open with unfolding leaves, pollinated by bees and other insects
Buds: Reddish, 1 cm (0.5 in) long, thin, very pointy and often curved, clinging lengthwise to the twig
Wood: Reddish-brown heartwood and pale sapwood, hard, strong, close-grained, heavy, 842 kg/m^3 (53 lb/cu ft)
Common nesters: Robins, cardinals
Common visitors: Squirrels, chipmunks, bears, foxes, skunks, raccoons, martens, mice, cedar waxwings, veeries, orioles, blue jays and more than a dozen other birds eat berries; moose, deer and snowshoe hares browse leaves and twigs; beavers eat bark
Word origin of pemmican: From the Cree *peme*, meaning "fat"
Range: All of Ontario except the far northwest; also in all other provinces and territories
Number of serviceberry species native to Ontario: 7
Number of serviceberry species worldwide: About 28, mostly in eastern North America
Also see: American Mountain Ash, Wild Red Raspberry. *Up North:* Cedar Waxwing

STRIPED MAPLE
Understorey's Resilient Moosewood

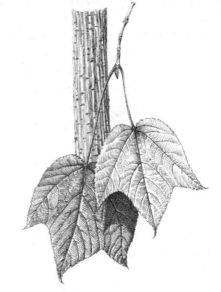

Average height: 1.5–4.6 m
(5–15 ft)
Average width: 2.5–5 cm
(1–2 in)
Maximum height: 12 m (40 ft)
Maximum width: 25 cm (10 in)
Alias: Moosewood, goosefoot maple, whistlewood, northern maple, striped dogwood, moose maple, *l'érable de Pennsylvanie, Acer pensylvanicum*
Preferred habitat: Deciduous forests, especially in moist valleys and south-facing hillsides
Lifespan: Up to 100 years
Bark: Vertical white stripes on a smooth, greenish-brown background; on older trees becoming grey with darker stripes
Leaves: 3 sharply pointed lobes joined by a widely rounded bottom, finely toothed, length and width both 10–18 cm (4–7 in), light, bright green on both sides, turning clear, pale yellow in autumn
Sex: Pretty, hanging strands, 7–15 cm (3–6 in) long, of small, 5-petalled, bright yellowish-green flowers, each 3–6 mm (0.2 in) wide, on slender stalks, appear on branch tips as leaves become full grown; pollinated by bees
Seeds: Winged pairs, each side 1.5–3 cm (0.6–1.2 in) long, joined to form a 90° angle, with a small indentation on one side of each seed,

WITH ITS GIANT, three-pointed leaves and pinstriped stems, one of the smallest of the maples presents a sharp appearance beneath the shade of its loftier relations. Seldom growing bigger than a thin-stemmed sapling with long, flimsy branches, striped maples reach out with their huge, open-palmed leaves to grab every drop of sunlight that manages to penetrate the forest canopy. Moose and deer love the lush foliage. Along with hobblebush and beaked hazel, it's an important part of their all-you-can-eat summer salad, hence the shrubby maple's other common name, moosewood. In winter, the tree's large reddish buds and seeds also provide sustenance for the hooved vegetarians, as well as for evening grosbeaks and ruffed grouse.

Heavily browsed striped maples have evolved to take the pressure of constant grazing in the understorey, and resprout with redoubled vigour each spring. Whatever buds survive swell up to five centimetres (two inches) long and turn rose or yellow before opening in May. By the end of the month, and in early June, long strands of pretty yellow-green flowers droop from the tips of freshly leaved branches. For most of their lives, striped maples only expend enough energy to produce male flowers, which release their pollen to the wind. A few trees, growing strong enough to pour their resources into seed production, switch to making female flowers.

However, openings in the canopy that allow enough sun through for striped maples to get started often later close up. This cuts off even the minimum light needed by the thrifty, diminutive trees. Under such stress, even smaller striped maples switch sexes, putting everything they have into nourishing seeds before the final curtain.

Clusters of paired, thin-winged keys develop on striped maples through summer and begin falling in September. Like the seeds of other maples, they're spread by deer mice, chipmunks and squirrels, who collect them in winter caches, but inevitably drop or forget some, or die before they've eaten everything they've stashed away.

A few trees, growing strong enough to pour their resources into seed production, switch to making female flowers

---

Mountain maple feeds many of the same animals, often growing alongside its striped relation. Though the smallest of the maples, never taller than six metres (20 feet), it is also the hardiest, reaching as far north as Moosonee. Its leaves look a lot like those of red maple, but are even more jagged and more rounded along the bottom, with deep-set veins that give them a wrinkled texture. Upright spikes of light, greenish-yellow mountain maple flowers appear in late May and early June, with female blossoms near the base of the spike and males above them. Their bright-red pairs of winged seeds follow later in July and August, gradually fading to yellow and brown before falling in autumn and early winter.

hanging in clusters from July to Sept.
Roots: Shallow, widespread
Buds: Bright reddish-brown, pointed, 13 mm (0.5 in) long
Wood: Soft, light, weak, pale- or pinkish-brown heartwood, almost white sapwood
Companion trees and shrubs: Sugar maple, beech, hemlock, yellow and white birch, mountain maple, hobblebush, beaked hazel
Common visitors: Moose, deer, porcupine browse leaves and twigs; beavers and hares gnaw bark; chipmunks, squirrels, mice, evening grosbeaks, nuthatches, purple finches, goldfinches, ruffed grouse eat seeds or buds
Range: North central shore of Lake Ontario to southern Lake Timiskaming and a little north of Sault Ste. Marie; also in Quebec and the Maritimes
Number of maple species native to Ontario: 7
Number of maple species worldwide: About 150
Also see: Hobblebush, Beaked Hazel. *Up North:* Sugar Maple, Red Maple, Deer Mouse

STAGHORN SUMAC
Fuzzy Shrub of Dry Places

Average mature height: 2–5 m (7–16.5 ft)
Average width: 5–10 cm (2–4 in)
Maximum height: 9 m (30 ft)
Maximum width: 36 cm (14 in)
Alias: Velvet sumac, vinegar-tree, American sumac, Virginia sumac, *le sumac vinaigrier, Rhus typhina*
Preferred habitat: Sandy meadows, fields, grassy hillsides, rocky outcrops and ridges, thickets, riverbanks and forest edges
Lifespan: Up to 50 years
Leaves: 30–60 cm (1–2 ft long) composites of 11–31 narrow, pointed leaflets, each 5–13 cm (2–5 in) long, with serrated edges, dark-green tops and lighter, hairy undersides
Bark: Dark grey-brown, thin, smooth, with many small marks; scaly on old trees

STAGHORN SUMAC is best known for the purple-red plumes that persist on its sparse and crooked limbs through winter. The plumes, composed of fuzzy-coated seeds, don't draw many birds when they first ripen in summer. But like the least-favoured bits of a party mix left at the bottom of the bowl, eventually some are eaten by hungry mouths. Sumac seeds are most often sought as an emergency food by ruffed grouse and other overwintering birds, as well as by early-spring migrants such as robins and bluebirds.

The Algonquins, Ojibway and other native peoples mixed sumac's acidic seeds – hence the name "vinegar tree" – with maple syrup and water to make a refreshing, lemonadelike drink. They also made use of other parts of the tree. Sumac leaves were the most common pipe-blend ingredient added to tobacco, which was usually too strong and valuable to be smoked alone. The root bark was brewed into a tea to help stop bleeding, a use that prompted botanists to name the sumac genus *Rhus*, a Greek word meaning "to flow." Various parts of the shrub have been used by natives and settlers for centuries for other ailments, ranging from sore throats to diabetes.

The scientific species name for staghorn sumac, *typhina*, comes from its 19th-century application as a folk medicine for typhoid fever.

The "staghorn" name comes from the soft, dense fuzz that covers the sumac's blunt-tipped branches, reminiscent of the velvet coating on a stag's antlers. A thick, orange, pithy core inside the branches requires less energy and material to produce than solid wood, allowing sumacs to grow very quickly. At the same time, they spread beneath the soil with suckering roots that send up new shoots and rapidly form thickets on dry, previously open ground. The twigs are eaten by moose and deer, and ooze a sticky, milky sap when broken.

In early autumn, sumac is noted for the brilliant colour of its leaves, which turn from deep green to crimson or purple-red. The colour change occurs when chlorophyll production shuts down and a surplus of sugars left in the leaf causes red anthocyanin pigments to form, the same process that turns maple and other leaves red. Sumac leaves and bark also have high levels of tannin (protective compounds that discourage browsers), which was once used by natives to cure deer hides and by settlers for tanning leather.

Staghorn sumac is sometimes mistaken for **poison sumac**, a related species that actually looks quite different, with shorter, more rounded leaves and round white berries instead of hairy plumes. A trick for avoiding it, as well as the related poison ivy, is to remember, "Berries white, a poisonous site." It's mostly restricted to swampy forests in far southern Ontario, though a few reach the southern edge of the Canadian Shield. Poison ivy is a member of the same genus, and all belong to the mostly tropical plant family that includes cashews, pistachios and mangos.

Sex: Tiny, light yellowish-green male flowers at branch tips in 13–30-cm-long (5–12-in-long) Christmas-tree-shaped clusters; similarly coloured female flower clusters are smaller and denser, on the branch ends of separate trees; blooming in late June and July; pollinated by bees

Seeds: Dense red plumes, about 18 cm (7 in) long, of hair-covered seeds, each 3–5 mm (0.1–0.2 in) long

Buds: Tiny, rounded, light brown and densely haired

Roots: Shallow and widespread, sending up shoots of new trees

Wood: Soft, brittle, light, green with orange-brown pith

Fake fruits: Almost hollow, chestnut-sized red and yellow growths, common on sumacs, are actually thin-walled galls containing scores of tiny flies, each about a millimetre (0.04 in) long

Leaf tannin content: Up to 35% of dry weight

Range: Southern Ontario to Lake Temiskaming and Sault Ste. Marie; also in Quebec and the Maritimes

Number of *Rhus* genus species native to Ontario: 5

Number of *Rhus* genus species worldwide: More than 100, mostly in tropics

Also see: Mountain Ash. *Up North:* Poison Ivy, Sugar Maple

WILLOWS
Ever Content with Wet Feet

S OMEHOW, WITH SNOW still covering the ground and the ice on silent lakes still weeks from breakup, velvety grey fur sprouts from the dark buds of scrubby streamside trees and meadow shrubs. Pussy willows are to many the first real sign that spring is finally on the way. In fact, all willows, and poplars, produce furry buds in late winter or early spring, warming the hearts of millions. Furry-budded willow switches were once collected as an early-spring rite, by Christians on Palm Sunday and by the Chinese for the Ching Ming festival.

Throughout the Northern Hemisphere, willow proliferates on low, open ground wherever it can get its feet wet in damp earth, often forming dense thickets of multiple stems and slender branches. It is the biggest group of woody plants in North America, with more than 90 species, most only shrub-sized. Some cling to the wind-swept Arctic tundra and never grow more than three centimetres (1.2 inches) high. Others, in the south, may shoot up to 24 metres (80 feet) in 15 years. Willows are often planted on streambanks and slopes to prevent erosion, spreading rapidly from mere twig cuttings.

A willow is either female or male. In the weeks after the grey-furred buds first appear, they expand into fuzzy, flowering catkins, before leaves open on the branches. Though not resembling conventional flowers, the catkins do produce nectar, enticing bumblebees and other insects to rise from winter dormancy and spread pollen from male to female trees. Willows are probably the most important source of sustenance for early-spring pollinators, allowing them to reproduce early enough for large numbers of off-spring to be around to pollinate great blooms of wild-flowers later in the season.

Tallest native Ontario willow: Peach-leaved willow, up to 20 m (66 ft)

Alias: *Les saules, Salix*

Meaning of *Salix*: From the Celtic words for "near," *sal,* and "water," *lis*

Leaves: Long, narrow, pointed at both ends on most species, often red-tinted when young, yellow in autumn; falling later than those of most trees and shrubs

Sex: Male flower catkins, several cm long, look like fuzzy yellow caterpillars on most species, female catkins are denser and greenish, expanding up to 9 cm (3.6 in); insect- and prob-ably wind-pollinated

Catkin word origin: From the Dutch *katteken,* meaning "little cat"

Seeds: Very tiny, attached to long fluffs of silk contained in tiny

222

Willows are vitally important to many other creatures throughout the year. All the bug activity around catkins in early spring attracts newly arrived tree swallows, who can often be seen courting on willow limbs. Many later migrants build their nests in the same dense tangles. The bark, buds and high-protein leaves are staples of browsing and gnawing moose, deer, hares, beavers and ruffed grouse. When too heavily browsed, though, willows, like birch, protect themselves by cranking up levels of resin and other defence chemicals in new shoots that may make nibblers ill. Hares lose weight faster by eating such fortified twigs than if they ate nothing at all, a reaction that could in part cause their cyclical population crashes.

Sugar-based chemicals possibly used by willows to rid themselves of impurities have been among humankind's most important medicines for thousands of years. Both the ancient Greeks and native healers in Ontario used the tree's bitter inner bark, often brewed as a tea, to ease pain and break fevers. The Ojibway applied the bark to sores and wounds as well, and smoked it mixed with tobacco. Europeans used it specifically for headaches at least as far back as the 1400s. In the early 19th century, chemists discovered the compound salicin to be the active ingredient. By the end of the century, salicylic acid was synthesized and packed into a new German wonder pill called Aspirin.

Prehistoric cultures around the world found willow ideally suited for a wide variety of other uses. Its thin, whiplike branches and twigs were perfect for basketry, one of the oldest crafts. Pieces of baskets 10,000 years old have been found in caves in Utah, and in the Middle East impressions made by baskets in mud are 6,000 to 7,000 years old. Houses in Europe's first farming communities had wattle walls of willow stems woven between upright posts. Branches were also bent or woven to construct fishing weirs, bows, grain sieves, snowshoes, kayak ribs, coffins and many other items. The bark of some species, such as Ontario's sandbar willow, was used to make rope, string, clothes, bags and blankets.

pods that split open when seeds mature in late spring or early summer; germinate or die within two days of landing

Deceiving cones: Apparent seed cones are actually abnormal growths, called galls, which willows commonly produce in response to the willow pinecone gall midge laying eggs in their buds. Larvae feast inside the cones and eventually emerge as adults

Buds: Dark, slender, curved, clinging close to twigs

Roots: Close to surface, spreading extensively

Wood: Light, soft, weak but tough, shock absorbent

Lifespan: 20 years is old for most species; large black willows are commonly about 70 years old

Pussy willow: Usually 2–3 m (7–10 ft) high, rarely up to 9 m (30 ft) tall, growing in clumps in both wet, swampy sites and dry, sandy places; leaves vary from bluntly pointed to gradually tapered

Beaked willow: Commonly 6–8 m (20–26 ft) high when mature, with 1 or more stems, in moist thickets, swamps, open forests and banks of rivers, lakes, beaver ponds and in clearings; furry catkin buds smaller than those of pussy willow and appear later; spiky seed capsules shaped like long beaks; leaves wider, more oval than those of other willows

Upland willow: 1–3 m (3.3–10 ft) high, growing in dry, open forests of scattered aspens, jack pines and red oaks, or along lakeshores, alder swamps and boggy sites

Shining willow: Very pointy leaves with shiny lustre on both sides; found in swamps, marshes, lakeshores and bogs
Companion trees and shrubs: Speckled alder, dogwood, high-bush cranberry, black ash, silver maple, balsam poplar, white cedar, white elm
Common nesters: Alder and least flycatchers, yellow warblers, common yellowthroats, song sparrows, grackles, snipes
Common visitors: Moose, beavers, hares, muskrats, deer, porcu-pines, voles, red squirrels, ruffed grouse, tree swallows, veeries, white-throated spar-rows, gray treefrogs
Willow wood specialties: Wicker, folksy furniture, cricket bats, artificial limbs
Polo connection: Polo comes from the Persian word for willow root, *pulu*, from which the sport's balls are made
Willow warfare: Once used for bows; in the manufacture of gunpowder, very fine-pow-dered willow charcoal was pre-ferred for use in muzzle-loading cannons
Charcoal production: Created when wood smoulders slowly under low-oxygen conditions, originally achieved by partly covering piles of wood with earth and setting them on fire
Range: Throughout Ontario; also in all other provinces and terri-tories
Number of willow species native to Ontario: About 30
Number of species worldwide: More than 400, with hybrids very common
Also see: Largetooth Aspen

Archaeological evidence shows that at least in some areas, basketry led to pottery when the clay covering baskets used for cooking became fired and took a hard-ened, permanent form. Willow may well have figured prominently in the genesis of metal-working and smelting as well, which was best accomplished with the intense heat reached by burning charcoal. Though not good firewood, willow is slow burning (as it lacks oils) and is therefore perfect for making charcoal.

Willow, it seems, was also preferred for making magic. Wands brandished by pagan priests and priestesses were most commonly willow switches. Both "wand" and "willow" come from ancient Germanic and Indo-European words meaning "bend," describing their flexibility. In China – which gave the world the weeping willow – the Taoist goddess of mercy, Kuan Yin, used a willow wand to sprinkle her followers with the divine nectar of life.

Perhaps because willows usually grew around sacred springs, considered portals to the underworld, they were linked with Persephone, Hecate and other Greek god-desses of death. Even into modern times, willow boughs are often depicted on tombstones. In the Middle Ages, when the meaning of "witch" changed from priestess to evil sorceress, the queen of black magic was said to be Hecate, who was also known as Helice, meaning "willow." Along with its connotations of death and sorrow, the tree in Europe came to stand for forsaken love, perhaps in part because it is short-lived. Many a cautionary traditional song concludes with these sentiments:

So come all you pretty fair maids, a warning take by me
Don't ever put your trust in the green willow tree
For the leaves they will wither and the root it will die
Make you think of all the times when you said "oh no, not I."

"Oh No, Not I" (traditional Newfoundland ballad)

YELLOW BIRCH
Big, Tough and Animated

B RONZED, SHAGGY YELLOW birch trunks add colour and animate beauty to the dark reaches of the forest interior. The trees' thick, flexing roots clutch the ground, stumps and boulders like giant birds' claws, making the birches look as if they're picking up and moving through the woods. Whole trunks may also bend and contort around rock outcrops or similarly snaking cedars. When toppled, yellow birches refuse to die, with upturned branches growing to become new trunks.

A great many yellow birches, though, go completely unrecognized by passersby at their feet. Unlike white birch, they can live a very long time, with the smooth, papery bark of their youth greying and cracking into deep fissures separating large, rough plates. They become thick-bodied monarchs, towering above with mature maples, beech and hemlocks.

Yellow birch has to be long-lived to keep its place in the mixed and hardwood forest. Opportunities for its seeds to get a start are few, so for year after year the tree must keep producing them. Although the tree is much more shade-tolerant than white birch, it still needs small openings in the forest to grow. And when they germinate

Average mature height:
18–23 m (60–75 ft)
Average width: 60–90 cm
(2–3 ft)
Maximum height: 31 m (102 ft)
Maximum width: 120 cm (4 ft)
Alias: Sweet birch, gold birch, red birch, curly birch, hard birch, tall birch, Newfoundland oak, *le bouleau jaune, Betula alleghaniensis*
Maximum lifespan: More than 300 years
Bark: Shiny bronze or yellowish silver with numerous horizontal lines, smooth, soft and paperlike, usually shredding, curling and hanging in fringes; trunks of old trees develop rough, grey irregular plates; shiny, dark purple-red on saplings
Leaves: Oval with a pointed tip and serrated edges, 7–13 cm (3–5 in) long, dark green on

top, lighter on bottom, turning yellow in fall

Sex: Dark, initially upright male catkins, 2 cm (0.8 in) long in fall and winter, open in early spring and hang from twig tips like yellow caterpillars, 7–9 cm (3–3.5 in) long, before leaves unfold; green female catkins, 1.5–2 cm (0.6–0.8 in) long, stand erect at the ends of new roots

Seeds: Tiny, with flakelike wings, released from upright, oval cones, 2.5–4 cm (1–1.5 in) long, from Sept. well into winter. Large seed crops, about every 3 years, may drop more than 2.5 million seeds per ha (2.5 acres)

Buds: Chestnut-brown, 6 mm (0.2 in) long, pointed, slightly sticky

Wood: Reddish-tinted, golden-brown heartwood and light-yellow or white sapwood, fairly hard, strong, with fine and often wavy grain, heavy, 697 kg/m³ (44 lb/cu ft)

Preferred habitat: Deciduous and mixed forests on moist, rich soil, especially on the lower slopes of hills

Companion trees: Sugar maple, beech, hemlock, basswood, white pine, white cedar, fir and white spruce

Honours: Official tree of Quebec

Range: Southern Ontario to Lake Temiskaming and Wawa; also in all other eastern provinces

Number of birch species native to Ontario: 6

Number of birch species world-wide: About 50

Also see: Wintergreen. *Up North:* White Birch, Sugar Maple

in spring, its tiny, thin seeds – which may be carried for kilometres in the wind – cannot produce root sprouts strong enough to break through the leaf litter to reach down to the mineral soil. Light autumn brush fires that burn away the leafy duff layer, or slope erosion, create good conditions for yellow birch seeds over a wide area. The seeds also survive where the wind has taken down one or more trees, settling either in soil exposed by an uprooted trunk or in the decaying wood of an old stump or log. In later years, those that have grown out of stumps are often on stiltlike roots as the rotted wood has disintegrated beneath them.

Once established, yellow birch seedlings can usually outrace maple seedlings to fill the gap in the canopy, growing up to three metres (10 feet) in their first six years. Many saplings, however, meet an early end in areas with lots of deer, who love the sweet wintergreen flavour of the trees' buds and twigs. Broken twigs give off the aromatic bubblegum scent. Moose, ruffed grouse and red squirrels are also common nibblers.

The shiny bark of younger trees burns almost as well as white birch bark, but tends to curl in only small shreds on the trunk, rather than in large, loose sheets. It's extremely durable, sometimes holding together the rotted wood of dead trees for many years. When dried, such soft, crumbly "punkwood" was ideal lighting material for the friction-started fires of native camps.

In pioneer Ontario, yellow birch wood was popular for sled frames, ox yokes and, especially, wheel hubs, because it never released its grip on wooden spokes. But because the dense wood, when green, doesn't float, it wasn't widely cut in the days of the big river log-drives. Demand zoomed during the Second World War, when yellow birch plywood was added to British Columbia sitka spruce and balsa wood in Canadian-built Mosquito fighter-bombers, the fastest and most versatile Allied aircraft of the war. Today, yellow birch, used for floors, furniture, veneer, doors and trimmings, is second only to sugar maple in Ontario's hardwood lumber industry.

THE HEAVENS

OR THE ANCIENTS, *the ever-changing night sky was not only a source of wonderment, it was their calendar. The setting of the Pleiades star cluster in spring was a sign for native North Americans that the time to plant crops had come. Similarly, the first appearance of the brilliant star Sirius in the dawn sky was among the most important events of the year for ancient Egyptians. It foretold the flooding of the Nile, which irrigated and enriched the croplands and made possible the flowering of Egyptian civilization.*

Learning to identify a handful of constellations and bright stars – and knowing the stories connected with them – is a good start to one's own lifetime relationship with the heavens. Up North dealt with major summer constellations – the Big Dipper and the like – and oft-seen phenomena including meteors and the northern lights. This book expands the scope by taking a look at some of the major winter, spring and autumn constellations, a few summer constellations not covered in Up North and the phenomenon of eclipses. The seasonal star charts published in Up North are reprinted here.

Two measurement systems used by astronomers to help classify and identify stars, magnitude and distance in light-years, are explained in the entry for the constellation Auriga, the first in this section.

AURIGA & CAPELLA
The Charioteer and the She-goat

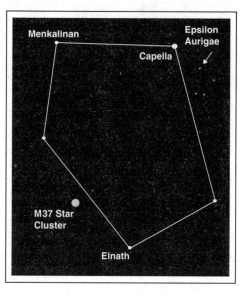

Menkalinan

Epsilon
Aurigae

Capella

M37 Star
Cluster

Elnath

Best viewing time: Winter constellation. A bright alpha star, Capella rises in the northeast at dusk in mid-Oct. Capella is high overhead, almost at zenith, around 9:00 P.M. by late Jan. Auriga constellation fades away in the northwest horizon by late Apr.'s dusk Location: Look for Auriga between Orion and the North Star (Polaris). A line drawn north (up) from the middle star in Orion's belt and bisecting a line between the two bright "shoulder" stars of Orion points roughly to Capella. (See the star map on page 269) Capella: Magnitude 0.1, distance 43 light-years. (All star magnitudes and distances in this book are from the *Observer's Handbook*, 1996, published by the Royal Astronomical Society

AURIGA IS ONE of those constellations, like Canis Major, known mostly for one brilliant star. In this case it's Capella, the sixth-brightest star to earthbound observers, second only to famed Sirius (of Canis Major) in the winter night sky. *Capella* is Latin for "she-goat," and is usually identified classically with Amalthea, the goat that nursed the infant Zeus. The Greek god later snapped off one of the goat's horns and transformed it into a magical device for dispensing vast amounts of food and drink. This is the legendary horn of plenty, and the origin of the word "cornucopia." (A Roman version of the story says the horn came from the bull Achelous.) Capella is thus a fitting stellar mascot for many of the pleasures associated with up north.

Capella's home constellation is typically depicted on modern star charts as a skewed pentagon. But the ancient Greeks imagined in Auriga a charioteer wheeling across the sky. One account says this is Hephaestus, the Greek god of fire, or his son Erechtheus; the Roman equivalent is Vulcan. Hephaestus required a chariot for transportation because he was born lame. As the god of fire, Hephaestus ran the forge that made the weapons, armour and furniture for the immortals. Some classical poets said his forge was located under one of several volcanoes and caused eruptions. Perhaps it's easier to imagine the stars in Auriga as a volcano rather than a charioteer. Along with the goddess Athena, Hephaestus was revered as a patron of crafts.

Auriga is also popularly depicted as a herder. Many ancient star maps show him carrying a goat (Capella) in one hand or on his shoulder, while his other hand grasps a staff. Some show him with kids on his arm, which could be linked to the three dimmer stars forming a neat triangle just south of Capella.

The Salish Indians of Oregon, Washington and Idaho tell a tale that links the stars of Auriga to those of the constellation Perseus, which lies just to the west. The story goes that a hungry skunk picked up the scent of a fabulous dinner being cooked by a group of sky-women. When the skunk approached their camp, the startled women prudently backed off. But stiffened by the possible loss of the meal they had so lovingly prepared, the women took up a defensive position around their fire pit. The skunk figured he would stand his ground, too, and simply wait until the women grew tired. They never did, and to this day the standoff is apparent every winter's night in the heavens, the women represented by Auriga's pentagon and the skunk by the loose K-shaped Perseus (see page 248).

Auriga straddles the Milky Way, so this is a prime constellation to scan with binoculars. It contains several star clusters, each grouped together by gravity. The best to find with binoculars or a small telescope is dubbed M37, the 37th object in French astronomer Charles Messier's catalogue of deep-sky objects compiled in the late 18th century. The cluster of perhaps 150 stars is about 4,200 light-years away, or 100 times more distant than Capella.

Capella is also an intriguing astronomical object. Like many stars, it is actually a double-star system. Two stars, each brighter than our sun, orbit each other every 104 days around a common centre of gravity. These stars are unusually close to each other for a double-star system, less than the distance between Earth and the sun. Only the most powerful telescopes can distinguish the two astral companions.

of Canada. See the Resource Guide on page 303 for information)

Menkalinan: The second-brightest star in Auriga, magnitude 1.9, distance 55 light-years; name means "shoulder of the charioteer," derived from Arabic

Magnitude: A brightness scale devised by the Greek astronomer Hipparchus in the 2nd century B.C. On his scale, the brightest stars were ranked 1, while those at the limit of naked-eye visibility were ranked 6. The system has been refined to include stars below naked-eye visibility, while some brighter stars have magnitudes of 0 or even negative (brighter) values. Each increment in magnitude is 2.5 times brighter or dimmer

Light-year: The distance light travels in one year, approximately 9.46 trillion km (5.88 trillion mi); a 43-year-old observer of Capella sees light that left the star when he or she was born

Kidnapped star: The southernmost star in the traditional pentagonal depiction of Auriga – named Elnath (also spelled Alnath or Al Nath), which in Arabic means "the butting horn" – is officially part of the neighbouring constellation Taurus, the bull. The International Astronomical Union set the official constellation boundaries in 1930

Also see: Perseus, Sirius & Procyon, Taurus. *Up North: Stars*

CEPHEUS
A King, a Cabbie and the Big Bang

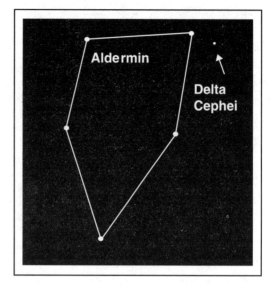

Aldermin

Delta
Cephei

Best viewing time: Cepheus is a circumpolar constellation, located close enough to the North Star (Polaris) that from Ontario latitudes it never sets below the horizon. In mid-summer, it arcs from the northeast towards the north-west over the course of the evening. Reaches highest point roughly midway between the horizon and the zenith around midnight in early Sept.

Location: Roughly between the familiar W- or M-shaped con-stellation Cassiopeia (King Cepheus's wife in classical mythology) and Polaris; on the opposite side of Polaris from the Big Dipper

Future role: In about 4,000 years, the north celestial pole, now marked by Polaris, will

KING CEPHEUS, the mythological ruler of ancient Ethiopia, faced a father's worst nightmare. The sea god Poseidon was in an Olympian rage because Cepheus's queen, the arrogant Cassiopeia, had boasted she was more beautiful than Poseidon's fair sea nymphs. Poseidon ordered the sea monster Cetus to attack Ethiopia and its innocent citizens (the Greek gods were rarely motivated by honourable impulses) but kindly offered to call off the assault if Cepheus would sacrifice his daughter Andromeda to the beast. Confronted with saving his entire kingdom at the horrendous cost of his daughter, Cepheus reluctantly had Andromeda chained to a rock in the sea to await her doom. By a stroke of luck, she was rescued by the hero Perseus, who happened by after slaying the hideous, snake-haired Medusa. Perseus and Andromeda were married and lived happily ever after, except for an unfortunate incident regarding Perseus's grandfather, but that's another story (see page 248).

All the major characters in this famous Greco-Roman myth (of which there are several versions) are constella-tions in the same general area of the heavens. In modern star charts, the diagram outlining Cepheus looks more like his house or palace than Rex himself. The peaked-roof home appears to us upside-down.

Other ancient cultures did not group the same stars into the constellations we know today from Western classical roots. Chinese constellations, for example, were generally much smaller star formations. Yet there is an old Chinese story for the stars of Cepheus. They represented a charioteer called Tsao Fu, said to have lived around 950 B.C. Like a cab driver who performs miracles for his fares, Tsao Fu was hired by emperor Mu Wang to deliver him to an enchanted place called the Western Paradise, where precious gems supposedly grew on trees and a magical garden of peach trees bore fruit only once every 3,000 years. The upside to the slow-blooming fruit, however, was that anyone who ate it got to live 3,000 years. Peachy. Mu Wang and Tsao Fu never appeared again, so it was assumed they reached the Western Paradise. The charioteer was honoured in the celestial dome as his reward.

In ancient times it was thought all the stars were, in fact, fixed on the inside of a sphere known as the celestial dome. After all, that's what your eyes tell you. But through precise observations, astronomers gradually came to understand that the stars were at hugely varying distances from Earth, and that constellations are simply a line-of-sight effect. Until the beginning of the 20th century, however, it was still thought that our Milky Way galaxy *was* the universe. The fourth-brightest star in Cepheus, called Delta Cephei (after the astronomical practice of designating stars in order of magnitude with the corresponding Greek letter), played a crucial role in changing that perception forever.

Delta Cephei is the archetype of a class of "variable" stars known as cepheids. Like all variable stars, cepheids pulsate in brightness. They do so because an outer layer of their helium atmosphere is in an elastic state. Pressure from the star's hot core forces this layer outward until it reaches a point where it "loses steam." Then gravity takes over and pulls the layer back in. The pressure builds up

move inside Cepheus, due to the effects of precession, a wobbling in Earth's rotation

Aldermin: The brightest star in Cepheus, magnitude 2.4, distance 48 light-years; name means "forearm" or "shoulder," and refers to old celestial maps depicting King Cepheus in the night sky

Delta Cephei: Variable star, magnitude 3.6 to 4.4, period 5.4 days

Variable star types: Pulsating variables (includes cepheids); eruptive variables (includes novas and supernovas); eclipsing binaries (see Perseus, page 248); rotating variables (stars with large "sunspots")

Henrietta Leavitt: U.S. astronomer, 1868–1921; deaf daughter of Congregationalist minister, worked at Harvard College Observatory and painstakingly observed 2,400 cepheid variables to discover period-luminosity relation

Harlow Shapley: U.S. astronomer, 1885–1972; used Leavitt's discovery to measure the Milky Way and our position in it (about $2/3$ out from centre of galaxy)

Edwin Hubble: U.S. astronomer, 1889–1953; used cepheids to prove that galaxies exist outside our own, leading to modern view of the universe and development of Big Bang theory; namesake of Hubble Space Telescope, one of the most advanced scientific instruments ever built,

launched in orbit April 1990 by space shuttle *Discovery*
Also see: Auriga & Capella, Ophiuchus & Serpens, Perseus. *Up North:* Cassiopeia, Milky Way, Pegasus & Andromeda, North Star & Little Dipper, Stars

again and the cycle repeats. These cycles have extremely regular periods; in Delta Cephei's case, every 5.4 days which can be observed with the naked eye in dark cottage-country skies. In 1912, the American astronomer Henrietta Leavitt made a stunning breakthrough when she concluded that a cepheid's *absolute* brightness (rather than its *apparent* brightness to us far-away earthlings) was directly related to the pulse rate. The slower the pulse, the brighter the star. Then, by comparing the star's absolute brightness to its apparent brightness from Earth, astronomers could measure the star's distance from Earth. Cepheids thus became mileposts scattered throughout the heavens. Soon the breadth and depth of the Milky Way was calculated (approximately 100,000 light-years X 30,000 light-years), as was our solar system's position in it.

American astronomer Edwin Hubble found that some cepheids inside "spiral nebulae" were clearly positioned well *outside* our galaxy. Other discoveries around the same time showed that virtually all these "spiral nebulae" were moving away from each other, and us, at high speeds. It quickly became clear that the Milky Way was just one galaxy in a vast, expanding universe stocked with billions of galaxies, each with billions or trillions of stars. Because almost all the galaxies were moving away from each other, astronomers worked backwards to conclude that all matter in the universe originated from one point. The stars and galaxies formed only after a stupendous explosion at this fantastical point, about 15 to 20 billion years ago: the Big Bang.

Though widely accepted, the Big Bang theory has many unanswered questions, preoccupying legions of scientists. Woody Allen has also wondered, "If the universe is expanding, why can't I still find a parking spot?"

ECLIPSES: LUNAR & SOLAR
A Conqueror's Tool

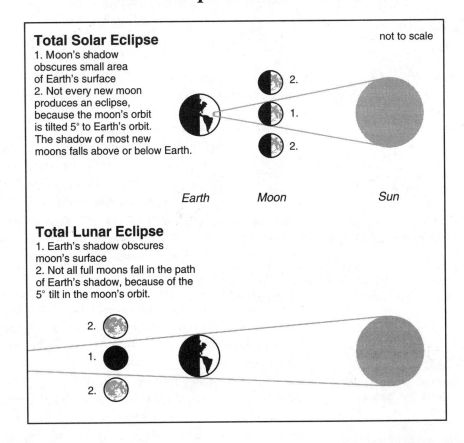

Total Solar Eclipse

not to scale

1. Moon's shadow obscures small area of Earth's surface
2. Not every new moon produces an eclipse, because the moon's orbit is tilted 5° to Earth's orbit. The shadow of most new moons falls above or below Earth.

2.

1.

2.

Earth　　　　Moon　　　　　　　Sun

Total Lunar Eclipse

1. Earth's shadow obscures moon's surface
2. Not all full moons fall in the path of Earth's shadow, because of the 5° tilt in the moon's orbit.

2.

1.

2.

THE SUBLIME SIGHT of a lunar eclipse under dark northern skies is rare. Total lunar eclipses happen up to three times a year, but many aren't visible because the event takes place during our day, when the eclipsed moon can be seen only from the other side of Earth. The accompanying chart shows total and partial lunar eclipses for Ontario viewers until the year 2010. Not only are they infrequent, but most are during chilly months. The best bet for outdoor viewing might be May 15, 2003, when the snow is gone (or should be), the bugs aren't too bad yet (let's hope) and the cottage and camping season is just getting underway.

A total solar eclipse is even more rare. Often described as the most awesome heavenly event visible from Earth,

Danger: It is safe to look at a total solar eclipse only when the sun is completely covered, *not before or after*. Even the smallest amount of sunlight striking the eyes can cause permanent damage. All lunar eclipses are perfectly safe to watch, because there is no direct sunlight

Eclipse: From the Greek, meaning "to leave out"

Umbra: Area of totality or deepest shadow in an eclipse; from the Latin word for

Solar Eclipses Visible from Ontario Until 2010 [*]

Partial	Feb. 26, 1998	1:08 P.M.	Part of a total eclipse that crosses the Galapagos, northern South America, Caribbean
Partial	Aug. 11, 1999	dawn	Early risers in Ontario may catch a partial eclipse that's part of a total eclipse crossing southern England, northern France, southern Germany, Austria, Hungary, Romania, Turkey, Iran
Partial	Dec. 25, 2000	12:36 P.M.	A good partial eclipse
Partial	Dec. 14, 2001	sunset	A brief partial eclipse may be visible
Partial	June 10, 2002	sunset	A brief partial eclipse may be visible

No other partial or total solar eclipses visible from Ontario until a partial eclipse on Aug. 21, 2017. This eclipse will be total in some parts of the United States.

[*] Eclipse data calculated from *Voyager II* astronomy software, published by Carina Software, California, 1993. Times, indicating the peak of each eclipse, are based on an observing position in Algonquin Park, and are applicable to south-central Ontario.

shadow or shade, as in "umbrella"
Penumbra: The area of partial shadow; from the Latin, *paene*, meaning "almost"; *umbra*, meaning "shadow"
Awesome Scrabble word: Syzygy, denoting the two points (the nodes) in the moon's orbit when it aligns with the sun and Earth; in other words, when eclipses occur. From the Greek, meaning "to yoke together." Worth 21 points, not including bonuses, but both Ys and a blank are needed to bag it
Danjon scale: French astronomer André-Louis Danjon devised a 5-point scale (0–4) for recording the moon's appearance during a total lunar

total solar eclipses may occur up to five times during the year, and no less than twice. But the chances of seeing the sun blotted out from any particular spot on Earth are as slim as a canoe paddle. On average, the same location on Earth witnesses a total solar eclipse only once every 360 years. There have been just eight total solar eclipses in Canada in the 20th century. The next one to darken the country won't occur until August 2008, and the eclipse path lies over Canada's sparsely populated Arctic islands. A total solar eclipse will cut a swath through the middle of the United States on August 21, 2017, showing as a superb partial eclipse in Ontario.

The precise orbital geometry required for an eclipse explains their rarity. In the case of a lunar eclipse, Earth must be positioned exactly between the sun and the moon for our planet to block sunlight from illuminating the moon's surface. For a solar eclipse, the moon must be aligned directly between the sun and Earth.

One might expect a lunar eclipse to happen every full moon, since that's when the moon swings behind Earth from the sun. Similarly, it's reasonable to think that every new moon would cause a solar eclipse. But the moon's orbit around Earth is tilted five degrees to Earth's orbit around the sun. So most full moons fall slightly above or below Earth's shadow. Likewise, at most new moons, Earth is above or below the moon's shadow.

At two points along the moon's orbit, however, our cratered companion crosses Earth's orbital plane. These points are called nodes. Whenever a node lines up with a full moon, a lunar eclipse occurs. When a node aligns with a new moon, we get a solar eclipse.

Shadows from both the moon and Earth have a dark, cone-shaped area called the umbra, and a brighter area called the penumbra. A total lunar eclipse occurs when Earth's umbra completely covers the lunar surface. A total solar eclipse happens when the moon's umbra completely covers a particular spot on Earth. When the alignment isn't quite exact, a partial eclipse may occur.

Many more people see lunar than solar eclipses, because Earth's shadow is much bigger than the moon's. A total lunar eclipse can last up to one hour and 45 minutes, and is visible to anyone on the same side of Earth facing the moon. The moon's umbra, on the other hand, is typically about 160 kilometres (100 miles) wide when it reaches Earth's surface during a total solar eclipse. The small area moves at incredible speeds, which vary during the eclipse because of the combined effect of the moon's velocity through space and Earth's rotation. The shadow races at between 2,200 kilometres per hour and 29,000 kilometres per hour. At any one spot on Earth, total solar eclipses last no more than seven and a half minutes, and most are over in about two to four minutes. Sometimes, when the moon moves in front of the sun but happens to be near its farthest point (apogee) from Earth in its elliptical orbit, the lunar orb isn't quite big enough to cover the solar disk completely, and the umbra doesn't touch Earth at all. We then see a ring eclipse, also called an annular eclipse, after the Latin word *annulus*, for "ring." Millions of Ontarians witnessed an annular eclipse on May 10, 1994.

Solar eclipses are so elusive that a subsector of the travel industry has evolved devoted entirely to obsessed eclipse chasers. Luxury cruise ships are chartered to patrol the seas in search of cloudless skies along the eclipse path; meteorologists are employed to find the terrestrial

---

Lunar Eclipses Visible from Ontario Until 2010[*]

Partial	Mar. 23, 1997	11:40 P.M.
Total	Jan. 20, 2000	11:48 P.M.
Total	May 15, 2003	11:44 P.M.
Total	Nov. 8, 2003	8:20 P.M.
Total	Oct. 27, 2004	10:04 P.M.
Partial	Mar. 14, 2006	6:44 P.M. (in twilight)
Total	Mar. 3, 2007	6:20 P.M. (in twilight, rises eclipsed)
Total	Feb. 21, 2008	10:20 P.M.
Total	Dec. 21, 2010	3:16 A.M.

[*]Eclipse data calculated from *Voyager II* astronomy software, published by Carina Software, California, 1993. Times, indicating the peak of each eclipse, are based on an observing position in Algonquin Park, and are applicable to south-central Ontario.

---

eclipse. 0 indicates darkest eclipse; 4 means brightest, copper-red or orange eclipse

Amazing coincidence: Total solar eclipses occur because of a fortuitous relationship between the sun and moon. The sun is about 400 times the moon's diameter, but the sun happens to be 400 times farther away. The disks therefore appear the same size in the sky

Baily's beads: Named after English astronomer Francis Baily, who in 1836 observed in detail the effect of sunlight shining through lunar valleys during a solar eclipse

Chromosphere: A thin layer of the sun's outer atmosphere, visible only during solar eclipses and with special scientific instruments

Corona: The spectacular, feathery halo of ionized gas

around the sun, visible only during solar eclipses. It extends well beyond the sun, and can appear in many colours, like an iris around a jet-black pupil. Observations of the corona over the centuries have led to the popular "sunburst" depiction of the sun as a disk with rays emerging directly from it, a view favoured by children

Prominences: Gargantuan flamelike eruptions from the solar surface, related to fluctuations in the sun's magnetic field. May extend for tens of thousands of kilometres, more than Earth's diameter

Einstein's friend: Observations taken during solar eclipses, including those by University of Toronto astronomer Clarence A. Chant in 1922, helped prove Einstein's theory of general relativity. Chant and others showed that the sun's gravity "bent" light from other stars, just as Einstein had predicted. Photos of stars near the sun during the eclipse were compared to photos of the same stars at other times. The starlight was displaced

Helium: Discovered by English astronomer Sir Joseph Norman Lockyer in 1868 through spectral analysis of the chromosphere during a solar eclipse. This new, unknown element was named after the Greek sun god Helios. Four hydrogen atoms fuse into one helium atom during thermonuclear fusion

location with the best chance of clear skies. All chasers want to avoid the fate of Simon Newcomb, an astronomer from Boston, who in 1860 travelled five weeks by steamer, covered wagon and canoe to see a total solar eclipse from northern Manitoba, only to be clouded out. Or that of the early 20th-century astronomer J. W. Campbell, from the University of Alberta, who was clouded out on his eclipse chases – 12 times!

A total solar eclipse is a truly spectacular sight. "Just before the onset of totality," writes the popular British astronomer Patrick Moore, "there is a sudden drop in temperature; the Moon's shadow comes racing towards you at a fantastic speed. . . . Then, as the last sliver of the Sun disappears, there is a wonderful 'diamond ring' effect, together with bright spots around the Moon's edge known as Baily's beads; they are caused by the sunlight shining through lunar valleys. Then, suddenly, the sky darkens, and the chromosphere, corona and prominences flash into view. It seems as though Nature comes to a halt; the wind drops, and there is an abrupt silence."

A lunar eclipse isn't quite so startling, but still ranks high among the many marvels in the sky. Though Earth's umbra may completely mask the moon's surface, the moon never fully disappears from view. A small amount of sunlight refracted through Earth's atmosphere illuminates the lunar disk to perhaps $1/10,000$ the brightness of a full moon. Eclipse watchers are particularly keen to observe the eclipsed moon's colour; it can range from dark-grey or brown to a rich coppery red. The colour depends on Earth's atmosphere. Dust, pollution, volcanic ash, forest-fire smoke and water vapour all affect the colour of the light "bending" through Earth's atmosphere and projecting onto the moon.

Eclipse science and lore date back thousands of years. The Chinese are usually credited with making the first record of a solar eclipse, in 2136 or 2137 B.C. Some nod to the Greek astronomer Thales as the first to predict a solar eclipse, in 585 B.C.; others note that the Babylonians could predict eclipses by about 700 B.C. Early eclipse predictions were based on the knowledge of the saros. A saros series is a set of eclipses that, due to a particular alignment of the nodes, occur approximately every 18 years and 11 days. Careful eclipse observations by ancient astronomer-priests working over decades led to the discovery of the saros. Once a saros was described, future eclipses could be predicted with reasonable accuracy. Several saros series are in progress at any one time, each lasting more than 1,000 years.

Europeans used their knowledge of eclipses as a powerful tool to gain influence over the first peoples of the New World during the early days of exploration and conquest. One well-known tale relates how Christopher Columbus, stranded in Jamaica in 1504, told the Arawak people that unless he and his crew were provided with fresh food, God would erase the moon. Sure enough, as Earth's umbra began to shade the moon, the Arawaks began to see Columbus in a new light. Jesuit priests in New France employed a similar technique. The Jesuit *Relation* of 1673–74 tells of a missionary challenging a local native diviner to predict an eclipse. It was, of course, an unfair contest: the missionary simply had to check his almanac. "You are Manitous, you Frenchmen, you know the sky and the earth," a native is reported as saying.

The Jesuits, great students of astronomy, used eclipses for scientific purposes as well, chiefly as a way to measure longitude. If the same eclipse was observed in France, a comparison of the different starting and finishing times could be used to compute the longitude of the observer in New France. English explorers in the Hudson Bay area used the same method. Captain Thomas James recorded the lunar eclipse of October 29, 1631, that led to a surprisingly accurate (for the time) reading for his position on Charlton Island in James Bay. Such eclipse-based surveying helped pave the way for the fur trade and the opening of the Canadian interior to Europeans.

in a star's core. Helium was later found on Earth

Hsi and Ho: The ancient Chinese, like people in many cultures, banged drums and pots, shouted and shot arrows into the sky to scare off dragons that ate the sun. And who can say it doesn't work? Court astronomers were hired to warn emperor and country of impending attacks on the sun. About 4,000 years ago, two Chinese astronomers, Hsi and Ho, were reportedly drunk at the time of an eclipse and failed to warn their superiors. They were hanged for falling down on the job

Rahu: This Hindu sun-eating demon is offered joss sticks and jelly in appeasement during a solar eclipse

Inti: Ancient Inca sun god, said to be eaten by a supernatural puma during an eclipse. To scare away the puma, men bit dogs and in extreme cases flayed children and women to make them howl. Fires were also lit to give life back to the sun

GEMINI
The Stars of Brotherly Love

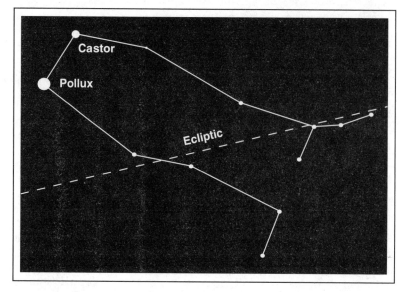

WERE CASTOR and Pollux, the two brothers represented in the famous zodiacal constellation Gemini, twins after all? The evidence is surprisingly inconclusive. While stories from classical mythology agree that their mother was Leda, a mortal and also the mother of Helen of Troy, their paternity remains in question. Some say the god Zeus fathered both boys, but other tales claim the skirt-chasing Zeus was the father of Pollux only. Castor's father in this version was Leda's husband, Tyndareus, the king of Sparta. If this were the case, Castor and Pollux were half-brothers: one mortal, fathered by a king; the other immortal, fathered by a god.

No matter. The two boys stand for brotherly love, their stories entwined in life and in death. Raised by the learned centaur Chiron, Castor and Pollux later became valued crewmen on Jason's *Argonaut*, searching for the Golden Fleece. The two are credited with helping the ship survive a terrible storm by calming the roaring winds, and mariners since have looked upon Castor and Pollux as patrons. The brothers are said to appear in the phenomenon called St. Elmo's fire, a lightning-like discharge that sometimes occurs around a ship's mast during electrical storms. (St. Elmo was another patron saint of sailors, from the 4th century A.D.) Castor was also known as an ace horseman, and Pollux as a crack boxer. For all these reasons they were a popular pair, and had a large following in Sparta and ancient Rome, where they were sometimes misidentified with Romulus and Remus, the legendary founders of that city. (Pollux is actually the Roman name; the Greeks called him Polydeuces.)

Castor was killed in a dispute over cattle or women, depending on who tells the story. The grief-stricken Pollux couldn't bear to live without his brother, so Zeus let him share his immortality with Castor. Now they spend eternity together, one day in heaven, the next in Hades. And their stars are near each other in the constellation Gemini.

It's easy to imagine the two brothers in their heavenly perch. The bright stars named Castor and Pollux mark the two heads, while the stars below make up the bodies. In old celestial maps, Castor is usually shown sitting in Pollux's lap. Pollux is the slightly brighter of the two stars – a reflection of his immortality, perhaps.

Many other cultures also paired Castor and Pollux in their star stories, which is not surprising given the prominence and proximity of these two celestial beacons in a relatively dark area of the night sky. The Klamath first peoples of Oregon saw in Castor and Pollux a boy and a girl whose gaze froze Crater Lake in the Cascade Mountains when they appeared above the horizon each winter. To the Blackfoot plains natives, the stars were two brothers named Rock and Beaver, sons of a hunter. Medieval Arabs saw two peacocks, and the ancient Egyptians regarded the stars as a pair of flowering plants. In ancient China, the stars were considered manifestations of the yin and yang principles, the dual but complementary forces of nature which originally represented shade and sun but were later developed into a complete cosmological system in the 3rd century B.C.

a constellation's brightest star "alpha," the second-brightest "beta" and so on down the Greek alphabet

Castor: Magnitude 1.6, distance 49 light-years. Actually a sextuple star system composed of 3 double stars

Uranus: The first planet discovered with a telescope was found in Gemini by the English amateur astronomer Sir William Herschel, from his garden at 19 New King St., Bath, in 1781. Herschel, an organist, was named court astronomer by "mad" King George III in honour of the discovery. Uranus was the earliest supreme being in Greek mythology, representing the sky, who with Gaea (the Earth) brought forth the Titans

Pluto: The last and most distant planet discovered in our solar system was also found in Gemini, by the American astronomer Clyde Tombaugh in 1930. Pluto was the Roman god of the underworld

Astrological period: May 21–June 20. Fittingly, Gemini, with its two bright stars, is said to rule the breast

Gemini space program: NASA used the *Gemini* spacecraft in the mid-1960s as an intermediate step between the early *Mercury* program and the *Apollo* program that went to the moon. Gemini orbiters carried two astronauts (hence the name) and performed the first rendezvous and docking in space

Also see: Leo, Orion. *Up North:* Stars, Zodiac & Ecliptic

LEO
The Pouncing Spring Lion

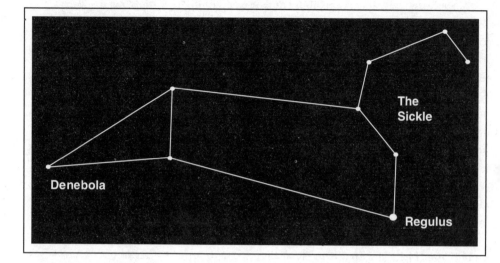

The Sickle

Denebola

Regulus

Best viewing time: Leaps head-first across the southern night sky from about mid-Jan. to late June. Most prominent in the evening sky by mid-Apr. Location: Find the Big Dipper, then draw a line extending south from the two "bowl" stars closest to the handle. This line points to Regulus. From Regulus, try to define the sickle and the rest of the constellation. (See the star map on page 266) Regulus: Magnitude 1.3, distance 69 light-years; located almost exactly on the ecliptic, the line in space defined by Earth's orbit, along which all the planets travel and all the zodiacal constellations lie Denebola: Magnitude 2.1, distance 40 light-years

NOVICE STARGAZERS often remark on how little the constellations resemble the mythological figures they're named after; the ancients stretched the limits of poetic licence when they imagined a charioteer in the winter constellation Auriga, for example, or a herdsman in the great summer constellation Boötes. Of the exceptions to this rule, Leo is one of the most striking. The stars in this zodiacal constellation clearly resemble the king of the beasts, pouncing across the dark spring skies.

Leo has three chief features. The famous "sickle," which also resembles a backwards question mark, defines the lion's head, mane and chest. The constellation's brightest star, the brilliant Regulus, lies at the bottom of the sickle and is Leo's heart. A triangle of stars with its apex at the bright star Denebola outlines the lion's hindquarters and tail. *Denebola* is Arabic for "lion's tail," while *Regulus* is Latin for "little king."

This stellar suite has been described as a lion since at least 3500 B.C. All the major Western cultures, from the Sumerians to the Romans, saw a lion. One ancient tale says

Leo is the soul of the Nemean Lion, strangled by Hercules as the first of his 12 labours to atone for killing his own wife and children. (He didn't mean to, but Zeus's vindictive wife, Hera, had cast a spell of madness over Hercules because he was the son of Zeus by one of his many mistresses.) Several Mediterranean cultures associated Leo with the sun, because from approximately 2500 B.C. to the time of Christ, the sun was in Leo during the hottest days of summer. Nowadays the July sun is one zodiacal constellation over, in Gemini, a shift due to a wobble in Earth's rotation called precession. If precession didn't exist, perhaps we'd call the scorching summer season "the lion days of summer," rather than "the dog days." (For that story, turn to Sirius & Procyon on page 258.)

Astrological period: July 23–Aug. 22. Leo is said to rule the heart
Also see: Sirius & Procyon. *Up North:* Hercules, Stars, Zodiac & Ecliptic

This stellar suite has been described as a lion since at least 3500 B.C.

Within the official boundaries of Leo are several galaxies visible through a backyard telescope but not to the naked eye. Also invisible to the naked eye is a star called Wolf 359. It is notable as the closest star to Earth in northern skies, and the third-closest neighbour overall, at 7.7 light-years. It is a dim "red dwarf," only 10 percent the mass of the sun, and about 0.00002 times as bright. Modern spacecraft could reach Wolf 359 in about 262,000 years, making dreams of interstellar travel seem impossibly quaint.

OPHIUCHUS & SERPENS
The Humble Physician and His Snakes

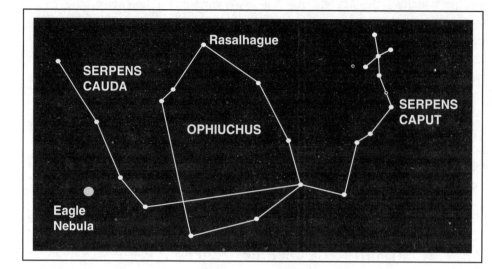

Rasalhague

SERPENS
CAUDA

SERPENS
CAPUT

OPHIUCHUS

Eagle
Nebula

Best viewing time: Summer constellations requiring dark skies for viewing, in July and Aug., in the southern sky before midnight, just above Scorpius

Bright star: Rasalhague, the alpha star in Ophiuchus, is the apex of the roughly house-shaped constellation depicted on modern star charts. It is halfway between the bright star Vega, high overhead, and shimmering Antares in Scorpius. (See the star map on page 267)

Caput: Latin for "head," from which we get "cap," "capital," "decapitate"

Unlucky 13: The ancient zodiac comprises the 12 constellations found along the ecliptic, the line in space defined by Earth's orbital plane. But

SHY OPHIUCHUS is a good example of the many dim, often overlooked, constellations sandwiched between the night sky's flamboyant aristocrats and fearsome beasts. But we often forget that the urban light pollution of today has been with us only one hundred years or so. In centuries past, every clear night glittered with thousands of stars, and the less-ostentatious constellations were better known. Some evidence suggests Ophiuchus has been identified as a constellation for about 4,000 years, though today it's invisible to anyone living in a built-up area.

Ophiuchus is the sky's only doctor. In Greek mythology, it's said he watched in amazement one day as one dead snake was brought to life by another using herbs. Ophiuchus learned the skill and became a healer. His name means "serpent-bearer," and in early celestial maps he is shown naked, in a rather suggestive pose, grasping a large snake between his legs. The constellation Serpens represents this snake, and is the only constellation found in two parts. Serpens Cauda, the tail, is just east of Ophiuchus, while Serpens Caput, the head, is to the west.

Ophiuchus is generally thought to be another name for Asclepius (also spelled Aesculapius). He was the son of Apollo and Coronis, though he was raised by the centaur Chiron, who ran a busy daycare for the philandering Greek gods (see Gemini, page 238). Chiron taught Asclepius the ways of a healer, and the boy went on to become the greatest physician of all time. Too great for his own good, unfortunately. His ability to revive the dead deeply concerned Hades, god of the underworld, who feared losing business. It also dismayed Zeus, who couldn't countenance a mere mortal having the power of life over death. A thunderbolt finished off Asclepius; apparently his ability to pluck life from death didn't apply to himself. Zeus placed Asclepius and his snakes in the heavens as a back-handed honour. To this day, snakes are portrayed wrapped around Asclepius's staff in the symbol of medicine, the caduceus. Perhaps the ability of snakes to shed their dead skin and thus "revive" or "heal" themselves is a clue to the origins of this relationship.

Galileo and others used a spectacular cosmic event occurring in Ophiuchus in 1604 to undermine a cornerstone of Aristotelian orthodoxy. The ancient Greek scholar Aristotle believed the universe was essentially "ageless, unalterable and impassive." But the massive explosion of a star – a supernova – observed on October 10, 1604, seemed to confirm theories that stars were born, lived and died, and that the universe was, in fact, a cauldron of change. Only a handful of supernovas have been recorded over the millennia, and the only one to be observed with the naked eye since 1604 was in 1987, when University of Toronto astronomer Ian Shelton spotted a supernova occurring in the Large Magellanic Cloud, a small companion galaxy to the Milky Way visible only from the Southern Hemisphere. (Shelton was at U of T's observatory in Chile at the time.)

there are actually 13 constellations along the ecliptic; the line cuts across the bottom portion of Ophiuchus, according to the official constellation boundaries set down by the International Astronomical Union in 1930 Also see: Cepheus, Gemini, Orion, Scorpius. *Up North:* Draco, Stars

ORION
The Spoke-too-soon Hunter

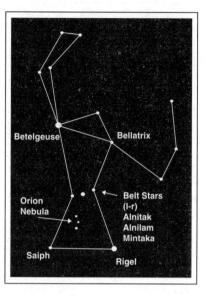

Betelgeuse | Bellatrix

Orion Nebula | Belt Stars (l-r) Alnitak Alnilam Mintaka

Saiph | Rigel

Best viewing time: Stands indelibly in the southern sky throughout most winter evenings, moving from east to west as the night progresses. At due south around 9:00 P.M. by late Jan. and early Feb. Early risers can catch a glimpse by mid-Aug. about two hours before sunrise

Location: Virtually impossible to miss in the southern winter sky; look for three belt stars close together in a straight line. Like the Big Dipper, Orion serves as a "pointer" constellation to other stars. The belt stars point northwestward to the bright star Aldebaran and, beyond that, to the Pleiades star cluster. The belt stars point the other way to Sirius, the brightest star in the sky. (See the star map on page 269)

MINTAKA, ALNILAM, ALNITAK: the names aren't terribly familiar, but they are perhaps the three most famous stars after Polaris. These are the "belt stars" of mighty Orion, aligned in such a tight, unmistakable formation that they have probably captured the gaze of every human who's peered into the night sky.

Orion is such a celebrated constellation because not only is it composed of this stellar trio and other brilliant astral beacons – Betelgeuse and Rigel in particular – it can also be seen around the world. Orion bridges the celestial equator, the projection of Earth's equator into space, and so is visible to inhabitants of both the Southern and Northern hemispheres. During our winter, Orion commands the southern night sky. Meanwhile, it is summer in the Southern Hemisphere, where Orion struts across the northern night sky. Constellations closer to the North Star, such as Ursa Major (the Big Dipper), aren't visible to southerners – just as bright southern constellations like the Southern Cross are beyond our range.

With such a prominent perch, it's no wonder that cultures spanning the globe have told stories about Orion. Many focus on the belt stars. The Chumash and Shoshoni first nations of western North America, among others, called the stars "Three in a Row." The Tachi Yokut natives of California told a parable of how a selfish wolf, married to a crane, never brought food home for his wife and two sons. A terrible domestic fight ensued, during which the crane killed the wolf and escaped with her children to become the belt stars. People on the Indian subcontinent saw a stag shot with an arrow; a more elaborate story recounts how the incestuous lord of creatures chased one of his daughters (represented by the star Aldebaran in Taurus) and was shot with an arrow by a character represented by the star Sirius. (Aldebaran, the belt stars and Sirius form an almost straight line.) In Brazil, the three stars were a caiman, an alligatorlike reptile. The Maoris of New Zealand saw a canoe. The Inuit looked upon three hunters.

Orion is famous in Egypt for representing the soul of the god Osiris, ruler of the afterworld and brother of Isis. Some modern Egyptologists have determined that tunnels in the renowned pyramids at Giza aligned with the stars in Orion and with Thuban, the north star at the time, when they were built about 4,500 years ago. They apparently served as conduits to the heavens for the pharoah's spirit. Robert Bauval, in his book *The Orion Mystery*, has observed that the arrangement of the three main pyramids at Giza matches almost precisely the three belt stars in alignment and relative size. Aerial photos of the pyramids compared with astrophotos of the stars reveal astonishingly similar patterns. (Some astronomers take issue with this conclusion, however.) The pyramids were built west of the Nile to reflect the fact that the afterworld was associated with the west, where the sun sets. Osiris-Orion is also located west of that great river in the sky, the Milky Way.

The idea of these stars as a "belt" comes to us, of course, from Greek mythology. Orion was the great Boeotian hunter, and it's easy to discern his form in the stars. The belt stars define his waist. Below them, another string of dimmer stars make up his sword or scabbard. To the upper left of the belt stars shines the unmistakable Betelgeuse, a red giant about 50 times the size of the sun and perhaps 15,000 times brighter. Betelgeuse is usually

Orion's origins: Some say he was the son of the sea god Poseidon, but others say he emerged from the hide of an ox upon which Poseidon, Hermes and Zeus had peed (leading to his original name, Urion, meaning "urine"). Which goes to show that even the gods had to go to the bathroom

Mintaka: Westernmost belt star, magnitude 2.2, distance about 1,400 light-years, though distances hard to pin down this far away. Name is from the Arabic for "belt." A double-double star

Alnilam: The middle belt star; magnitude 1.7, also about 1,400 light-years away. From the Arabic name for the entire belt, which translates as "string of pearls"

Alnitak: Easternmost belt star; magnitude 2.0, distance 1,400 light years. Also derived from the Arabic for "belt"

Betelgeuse: Pronounced *bet*-el-jooz, this star is a red super-giant that may be in its final stages of life; magnitude 0.5 (varies), distance 1,400 light-years. Astronomers believe it has used up its main hydro-gen fuel, and is now "burning" other elements, causing it to expand and con-tract, a phenomenon visible in the star's varying brightness. The variability is usually not detectable with the naked eye. Two companion stars too faint to see

Rigel: Brightest star in Orion; magnitude 0.1, distance

1,400 light-years. Two companion stars too faint to see

Nebula: From the Latin *nebula*, meaning "cloud" or "mist." An interstellar nebula is vastly less dense than an Earth cloud, but does mark an area more gaseous than "empty" interstellar space

Fire of creation: The ancient Maya of Mexico believed the Orion Nebula was the smoke from the fire of creation at the heart of the universe. The fire's hearth was defined by the triangle created by the stars Alnitak, Rigel and Saiph

M and NGC: Celestial sights denoted with an M are those plotted by Charles Messier of France in the late 18th century. A comet hunter, Messier wanted to mark all the fuzzy nebulae and star clusters that could be mistaken for comets. NGC stands for New General Catalogue, a much more extensive record of thousands of deep-sky objects, first established at the turn of the 20th century

Also see: Auriga, Ophiuchus & Serpens, The Pleiades, Scorpius, Sirius & Procyon, Taurus & the Hyades. *Up North:* Stars

translated from the original Arabic as "armpit of the great one," and, indeed, marks the right armpit or shoulder of the hunter in many ancient sky maps. His other shoulder is marked by Bellatrix, somewhat dimmer but still easily visible to the naked eye, even in light-polluted urban areas. Kitty-corner from Betelgeuse, on the other side of the belt stars, is Rigel – from the Arabic for "foot" – one of the earliest-named stars. Rigel is the seventh-brightest star from Earth and one of the true powerhouses of the galaxy, with a luminosity estimated at 60,000 times our sun. Orion's right foot is pinpointed by Saiph, though in some old maps Saiph and Rigel mark the hunter's knees. Other stars in the constellation show Orion holding his shield towards next-door Taurus, the bull, whom he hunts, while his right hand wields a club.

Most of the Greco-Roman myths focus on Orion's death, and there are at least seven versions of his demise, falling under two broad types: he was either killed by the goddess Artemis or her brother Apollo, or was stung to death by a scorpion. The scorpion tales are the most intriguing, because they involve another constellation, Scorpius. Orion was a hunter, who boasted that no animal could get the better of him. As usual with the Greeks, this hubris proved fatal. The spiteful goddess Hera sent a tiny scorpion to deliver a mortal, mocking sting. Orion was placed in the heavens as a lasting warning to all, and opposite Scorpius so that the two constellations would never appear together in the night sky. His two hunting dogs – the constellations Canis Major and Canis Minor, notable for their stars Sirius and Procyon – were placed near their master. Orion was said to have coveted the Pleiades, the daughters of Atlas, and they became the famous star cluster near Orion – but always out of reach.

An Iroquois story also features a great hunter, and relates to his position in the sky. A noble hunter, the story goes, climbed a mountain to prepare for death. When the end came, he ascended the heavens where, remarkably, he recovered his powers. He was assigned a new job, to carry the sun high in the sky during summer. (Orion is, indeed, located in the day sky during the warm months, his presence blotted out by the glare of the sun.) But as winter approached, the hunter grew tired again, and had to pass the job to his son. The layabout son shouldered his responsibilities poorly, and barely managed to carry the sun above the horizon, bringing cold, wintry days. His father, meanwhile, rested in the winter night sky, gaining strength to resume his role in the summer.

Like many stars and constellations, Orion is a harbinger of the changing seasons. It is first visible to early risers by mid-to late August, clambering over the dark eastern horizon about an hour before the sun. It rises earlier every night as autumn progresses. "Its arrival is an announcement that the outdoor season is past, that the nights are becoming more and more frosty, and that the gorgeous tapestry with which the autumn hills seem covered will soon fall away and give place to the lovely low tones of winter," wrote the late Martha Evans in her popular book *The Friendly Stars*. By mid-December, the hunter is rising over the eastern horizon shortly after sunset.

On a clear winter night, take a close look at Orion's "sword." It contains one of the most studied celestial bodies: the Orion Nebula, known officially as M42 or NGC1976. The middle star in a band of three small stars defining the sword roughly marks the centre of the nebula, and a faint-but-distinct hazy patch can be seen with the unaided eye and through binoculars. The bright star here is, in fact, a quadruple star system known as the Trapezium. The four separate stars are just visible with a small backyard telescope. They are among the youngest stellar furnaces in the galaxy, perhaps 100,000 to one million years old, much younger than the one-billion-year-old rocks of the Canadian Shield in cottage country. The Trapezium's blazing thermonuclear starlight illuminates the surrounding nebula, a wispy cloud of mostly hydrogen gas estimated to be 56 trillion kilometres wide. Throughout the cloud, new stars and perhaps entire solar systems are being born. The Hubble Space Telescope has returned stunning astrophotographs of this marvellous Milky Way region. Perhaps one day, intelligent creatures on a planet in M42 will take pictures of us. Say cheese.

PERSEUS
The Hero . . . Except to Granddad

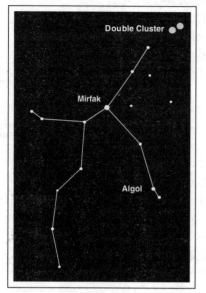

Double Cluster

Mirfak

Algol

Best viewing time: Summertime viewing hours are after midnight, when Perseus rises far in the northeastern sky. By early Jan. it is almost directly overhead around 9:00 P.M.; by mid-Apr. it is low in the northwest at this hour

Location: The stick-figure or straggly K-shaped Perseus is found between Cassiopeia (his mother-in-law) and Taurus, the bull. (See star map on page 269)

Mirfak: The brightest star in Perseus, magnitude 1.8, distance 630 light-years; also spelled Mirphak, from the Arabic for "elbow"

Atlas shrugged, and paid: King Atlas refused to help Perseus with his journey, and paid for it by glancing at Medusa's head and turning into a mountain of stone. He was

THE CONSTELLATION Perseus is home to fascinating celestial sights best viewed under dark wilderness skies. One of these is Algol, the brightest eclipsing binary star. An eclipsing binary is a double-star system in which two stars orbit each other around a common centre of gravity. From our point of view on Earth, one of the stars eclipses the other as it completes its orbit. Though the unaided eye can't discern the two stars – they are about 92 light-years away, or 870 trillion kilometres – the "wink" with each eclipse is plain to see.

Algol is a nightwatcher's favourite, because its period – the time it takes for one eclipse to occur – is relatively short, only 69 hours, or 2.87 days. The star's brightness varies by a factor of more than three times, dimming from magnitude 2.1 to 3.4 in about four hours, staying at minimum for almost half an hour, then brightening again over the next four hours, for a roughly nine-hour eclipse. (For an explanation of magnitude, see Auriga, page 228.) The invaluable *Observer's Handbook*, published annually by the Royal Astronomical Society of Canada, plots Algol's each eclipse in a month-by-month viewing almanac. (See the Resource Guide on page 303 for the RASC's address.)

Another attraction is the Perseus Double Cluster. Though these two star clusters, at about 7,000 light-years away, are immensely more distant than Algol, they, too, are visible to the naked eye as distinctly fuzzy patches against the backdrop of the Milky Way, which cuts through Perseus. Binoculars provide a lovely view. Such "open" clusters are essentially families of stars, each of which was born from the same ancient nebula of gas and dust, long since dissipated or absorbed in the star-making process. The stars in a cluster are linked by gravity, but they drift away from each other over the eons. Our sun was once part of a cluster that disbanded long ago.

Family stories revolve around Perseus in Greek mythology. Perseus was the son of Danae, a mortal, and Zeus. An oracle had told Danae's father, King Acrisius, that his grandson would one day kill him, so the king took out an insurance policy: He packed his daughter and grandson in a trunk and tossed them in the sea. The trunk beached on an island ruled by Polydectes, and he fell in love with Danae. As a ruse to get rid of the prying Perseus, Polydectes tricked the lad into pursuing the hideous Gorgons, three sisters with snake-hair, scales and wings, who turned to stone anyone who looked upon them. Perseus took up the challenge and with the help of some gadgets that would have impressed James Bond's colleague Q – a cap that made the wearer invisible, a magic wallet that adjusted its size to whatever was placed within, a shiny shield and winged sandals – was able to slay Medusa, the only mortal Gorgon. On his return, he rescued the maiden Andromeda from the sea-monster Cetus, and wed her. Andromeda, her mother Cassiopeia and her father Cepheus are all nearby constellations. And Algol in Perseus is said to be the blinking eye of Medusa; hence the Arabic root for its name, the Demon or Ghoul Star.

When Perseus arrived home unexpectedly, Polydectes met his fate by looking at the head of Medusa and turning to stone. Danae wasn't upset – she didn't like the guy. Many years later, at an athletic competition, the oracle's prediction was fulfilled when Perseus misthrew a discus and it killed his grandfather, a spectator in the stands. Perseus and Andromeda's son Perses became the legendary ruler of Persia.

thus forever burdened with shouldering the heavens

Perseid meteor shower: The best meteor shower of the year, usually peaking the night of Aug. 11, is called the Perseids, because the meteors appear to emanate from a spot in Perseus. This point is called a radiant. It is the location in space where Earth's orbit crosses the old trail of a comet. Dust and particles left behind in the comet's path cause the meteors

Also see: Auriga, Cepheus, The Pleiades. *Up North:* Pegasus & Andromeda, Stars

THE PLEIADES
Merry Siblings of the Night Sky

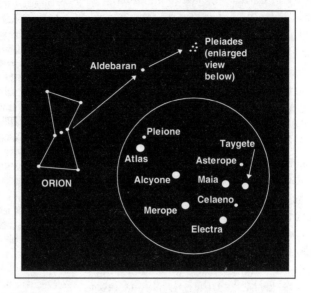

THE GLITTERING PLEIADES star cluster lies within the boundaries of the zodiacal constellation Taurus. Yet, like a brilliant child who has soared higher than her parents or siblings, the cluster's fame outshines that of its home constellation. "Minstrels and poets of the early days sang of their bewitchment and beauty," wrote the popular astronomy writer Roy Gallant in 1986, "and many of the great poets, from Homer and the author of Job down to Tennyson and the men of our own day, have had their fancy enlivened by them, and in one form or another have celebrated their sweetness and mystery and charm."

The Pleiades are also called the Seven Sisters, after the seven daughters of Atlas and Pleione in Greek mythology. Casual stargazers sometimes mistake them for the Little Dipper, for the shape is similar. But the Little Dipper, or Ursa Minor, is much larger and dimmer and is located in a different part of the night sky. The North Star, Polaris, marks the end of the Little Dipper's handle, and is therefore visible all year long from northern latitudes. The compact, sparkling Pleiades, on the other hand, are best viewed on a clear winter's evening. They rise in the evening in mid-October, reach their highest point in the southern sky by chilly early January and set close to the western horizon by late March.

There is nothing in the sky quite like this tight formation of bright stars. A pair of binoculars will startlingly reveal dozens of jewels in the cluster, which, for most people, appears as only six stars to the naked eye. This has given rise to the mystery of the lost Pleiad: Where is the seventh sister? Curiously, several ancient cultures, including some in North America, refer to seven stars in the group, but by the time of the classical Greeks, one seems to have vanished. The storytellers of the day suggested that one of the daughters, Merope, may have hidden in shame because she married a mortal, the unfortunate Sisyphus, who was condemned by Zeus to spend eternity pushing a boulder uphill, only to have it forever roll down again. Or perhaps it was Electra, who retreated in mourning over the devastation of Troy, which had been founded by her son Dardanus. Some astronomers suggest one formerly bright cluster star may have dimmed at some point, but there is no conclusive answer to the puzzle. It is still common for stargazers to compare how many stars they can see unaided; some have claimed they can discern as many as 11.

It is no doubt because the Pleiades are so compact that virtually all myths about them involve a group of siblings, often children. An Iroquois star parable, for example, recounts how a group of braves ignored their chores and danced instead. Elders warned that bad things might happen if they continued their merriment; the braves paid no heed and danced away. Soon they grew light-headed and, frightened, began to rise into the sky. In one version of the story (these tales, remember, were all passed on orally and elaborated upon constantly), one of the eight braves recognized his father below, and became a falling star to reach him. That left the seven Pleiades, called *Oot-kwa-tah* by the Onondaga Iroquois.

The Kiowa first peoples of Wyoming tell one of the most memorable Pleiades myths. Seven young sisters were playing in the woods when a bear found and chased them.

is that Electra was mother of Dardanus, founder of Troy
Job 38: God, demonstrating to the self-righteous Job that he knows nothing of the Lord's way, rhetorically asks the unfortunate farmer, "Can you bind the cluster of the Pleiades / or loose Orion's belts? / Can you bring out the signs of the zodiac in their season / or guide Aldebaran and its satellite stars?" The satellite stars are the Hyades star cluster
Alfred, Lord Tennyson's two bits: "Many a night I saw the Pleiads, rising thro' the mellow shade / Glitter like a swarm of fireflies, tangled in a silver braid"
Australian aboriginal view: The earliest Aussies saw a cluster of young girls serenading the Three Young Men (the belt stars of Orion)
Star fragments? A Polynesian myth says the Pleiades were once one bright star that boasted of its beauty. But gods disapprove of boasting. The god Tane fixed things by throwing the nearby star Aldebaran at its neighbour, smashing it into smaller, dimmer pieces
Brightest Pleiad: Alcyone, magnitude 2.9
Dimmest named Pleiad: Asterope, magnitude 5.8
Also see: Auriga, Orion, Perseus, Taurus & Hyades. *Up North: Stars*

They leapt onto a large rock and prayed to it to protect them. The rock responded, and grew to such a height that it was able to place the girls safely in the heavens as a star cluster. The bruin clawed madly but impotently against the rock, leaving deep grooves. The rock stands today as Devil's Tower in northeast Wyoming.

The Greek myth also involves pursuit and escape. Orion desired the seven nymphs borne of Atlas and Pleione, but Zeus denied the hunter his quarry by turning the nymphs into doves and placing them among the stars. They remain in the celestial realm just out of his reach.

There is no conclusive answer to the mystery of the lost Pleiad

The Greeks called the Pleiades the "sailing stars," and seamen were said to set sail when the Pleiades were in the night sky. This calendric use of the Pleiades was common to many cultures. North American native groups, including the Iroquois, timed their plantings with the setting of the Pleiades in the western sky in spring twilight. The star group even resembles a small packet of seeds, following the fertilizing sun into the ground. Earlier in the year, when the Pleiades reach their highest point in the night sky in January, the dancing braves are situated appropriately over the Iroquois Long House, where the new year's celebration called *Ganahaowi* takes place.

The Pleiades assume a notable role in astronomy as well as mythology. Officially known as M45, the Pleiades are young stars born from the same interstellar nebula of gas and dust. Sometimes a faint blur is visible in the region on a dark, clear night. Astronomers count about 400 stars in the family. The youngest stars are estimated to be about 20 million years old. By comparison, our sun is a 4.5-*billion*-year-old fogey.

SAGITTARIUS
The Teapot Pointing the Way Home

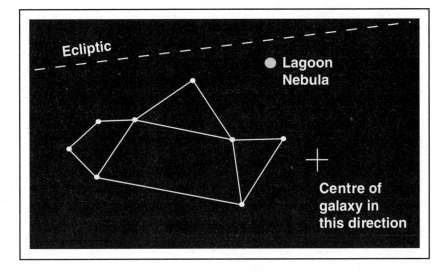

WHEN IS a constellation not a constellation? When it's an asterism. Asterisms are groups of stars connected to form what are popularly called constellations, but aren't officially recognized as such by the pooh-bahs at the International Astronomical Union. The Big Dipper is the most famous asterism; it's part of the official constellation Ursa Major, the Big Bear. Another asterism – also from the kitchen, curiously enough – is the Teapot, found in the constellation Sagittarius.

The Teapot is one of those constellations – sorry, asterisms – that shines brilliantly in the inky-black skies of the wilderness, but is difficult if not impossible to see in light-polluted areas. It's a summer treat, positioned just over the southern horizon on mid-August evenings, as if it were pouring its steaming contents onto the ground below. The star that serves as the tip of the spout is astronomically notable: think of it as a gunsight, targeting the centre of the Milky Way. On dark nights the ghostly swath of the Milky Way clearly bulges in this area. The galactic core lies about 30,000 light-years away in this direction, teeming with billions of stars. Some astronomers

Best viewing time: Summer constellation. Prominent before midnight

Location: Low in the southern sky, to the east (left) of Scorpius

Planet zone: The ecliptic, the path of the planets, cuts across the sky just above the top of the Teapot. Look for planets in this zone; they make a fine sight with the Milky Way as a backdrop

Lagoon Nebula: About 4,500 light-years away; second only to the Orion Nebula in brightness

Milky Way: About 100,000 light-years across, with up to a trillion stars

Black hole: The collapsed corpse of a mammoth star. Its gravity is so powerful even light can't escape, hence its name

253

The Muses: Nine daughters of Zeus and Mnemosyne (memory), patron goddesses of the arts. They were Calliope (muse of epic poetry and eloquence), Euterpe (music and lyric poetry), Erato (love poetry), Polyhymnia (oratory or sacred poetry), Clio (history), Melpomene (tragedy), Thalia (comedy), Terpsichore (choral song and dance) and Urania (astronomy)

Astrological period: Nov. 22–Dec. 21. Sagittarius was said to rule the thighs

Also see: Gemini, Orion, Scorpius. *Up North:* Milky Way, Stars, Zodiac & Ecliptic

now think a black hole is the central gravitational spike holding the galaxy together.

This prime patch of celestial real estate is excellent for binocular-assisted viewing. Through the glass, thousands of stars are seen to share the neighbourhood with dozens of deep-sky objects: open star clusters, globular star clusters and interstellar nebulae. The Lagoon Nebula, located above the Teapot's spout, is visible to the unaided eye on a dark night as a fuzzy patch distinct from the background Milky Way. But it's a better sight with binoculars.

Sagittarius is the mythological archer, half-man, half-horse, but his origins are murky. Sometimes he is identified with Chiron, ancient Greece's best-known mythological centaur. But another constellation, Centaurus, is usually said to be Chiron. (Centaurus is in the southern sky and hidden from our view.) Other theories suggest he represents Nergal, a Sumerian archer deity, or Crotus, the mythological founder of archery who lived with the nine Greek Muses. Old star maps depict Sagittarius firing his arrow at Scorpius to the west, but the reason for his enmity – other than the fear of getting stung – is not known.

SCORPIUS
The Celestial Stinger

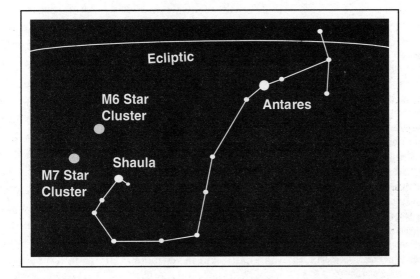

Ecliptic

M6 Star Cluster

Antares

M7 Star Cluster

Shaula

S CORPIUS HAS an evil reputation in some quarters, but the scorpion's appearance in the night sky is really a welcome sight. He moves to the beat of ur brief summers. Come late May, he pokes his head bove the southeastern horizon after sunset, as if sniffing he evening air for signs of Orion, his legendary quarry. By mid-July the astral arthropod is due south at 10:00 P.M., ust over the horizon, as high in the sky as he'll get. Then, s summer turns to autumn, Scorpius scrambles below the vestern horizon in the evening twilight. He holes up for vinter just as the leaves turn colour.

In classical mythology, Scorpius's notoriety derives, no loubt, from that of his earthbound relatives. Most of the pproximately 1,000 species of scorpions worldwide are, n fact, harmless, but some deliver a painful toxic wallop vith their sting, which in a few cases can be fatal. In Greek myth, scorpions were the instruments of evil (if not nherently evil themselves) in the deaths of Helios's son Phaeton and the great hunter Orion. Phaeton lost control of Helios's sun chariot, one version of the myth goes, ecause a scorpion stung one of the horses. (The careening chariot scorched the night sky, creating the Milky

Best viewing time: Any dark summer night
Location: Skitters above the treetops along the southern horizon from east to west during the course of a night; just west (right) of Sagittarius
Antares: The 15th-brightest star, magnitude 0.9, distance 522 light-years; slightly variable because it's a double star with a dim companion
Shaula: Magnitude 1.6, distance 330 light-years
Navajo Coyote star: A Navajo myth says the trickster Coyote spoiled the Black God's careful creation of all the major constellations by stealing magic crystals and scattering them in the sky. They became all the other dimmer stars that clutter up the heavens. The Coyote then placed his own wandering red

star (Antares) in the sky as a counterpoint to the fixed North Star
Astrological period: Oct. 23–Nov. 21. Said to rule the "secrets" (genitals)
Chinese zodiac: Scorpius was a hare in the ancient Chinese zodiac. Later it became known as the Azure Dragon, a sign of spring. Because of the effects of precession (a slow wobbling in Earth's rotation), Scorpius is now a summer rather than spring constellation. In 4,000 years it will become a fall constellation
Arthropod: The huge phylum that includes insects, arachnids, centipedes, millepedes, crustaceans and other exoskeletal creatures. Scorpions are arachnids, a class that also includes spiders. Only one scorpion species is found in Canada, in southern Saskatchewan, Alberta and British Columbia. Scorpions are among the oldest land creatures, dating back 400 million years
Other celestial invertebrates: Cancer the crab, a dim zodiacal constellation between Leo and Gemini, and Musca the fly, visible only from the Southern Hemisphere
Also see: Auriga, Orion, Sagittarius. Up North: Stars, Zodiac & Ecliptic

Way, then burned all the vegetation off the Sahara.) And the gods proved Orion's mortality by sending a tiny scorpion to kill the hunter, who had foolishly claimed he was invincible. In the afterlife, the Olympians placed the scorpion and Orion in opposite parts of the sky, one pursuing and one fleeing the other.

The constellation's famous bright star Antares also has sinister overtones. Some myths say the Greek god of war, Ares (Mars to the Romans), was forged from the flames of Antares, which translates as "rival of Mars." The connection is visual; the brilliant red star looks a lot like the planet Mars from our point of view on Earth. The pair sometimes appears together in the night sky, because Antares lies just below the ecliptic, the path of the planets across the celestial dome. Astronomically, of course, they couldn't be more different. Rocky, dusty Mars is smaller than Earth and never more than 378 million kilometres away. Antares, on the other hand, is a red supergiant, one of the biggest stars in the galaxy, about 500 times the diameter of the sun, and 522 light-years, or 4,938 *trillion* kilometres, distant. Appropriately, the red star marks the scorpion's heart. The Chinese worshipped Antares as the "fire star."

Scorpius is among the original zodiacal constellations described by the Sumerians about 5,000 years ago. Its shape easily suggests a scorpion with its curled tail, and the names for some of its stars are in keeping. The tip of the tail, for instance, is called Shaula, Arabic for "stinger." For reasons that aren't entirely clear, however, the scorpion's claws were long ago separated from the constellation to form another, dimmer zodiacal constellation, Libra. The two brightest stars in Libra, Zubeneschamali and Zubenelgenubi, mean "northern claw" and "southern claw" respectively in Arabic. But now they represent the two pans of Libra's scales.

Another common description for the stars of Scorpius has more resonance for Ontario's cottagers and campers. Pacific cultures thought of Scorpius as a giant celestial fishhook. A Maori story from New Zealand recounts how a young man named Maui was given a magical fishhook by the goddess of the underworld. Maui used it to hook an enormous fish, which when brought to the surface turned out to be the islands of New Zealand. Pleased with this tremendous catch, Maui hurled the fishhook into the heavens, where it became the constellation we call Scorpius. The Hawaiian island chain was similarly formed, according to a myth from that enchanted part of the Pacific.

Pacific cultures thought of Scorpius as a giant celestial fishhook

Scorpius, like its next-door-neighbour Sagittarius, lies partly across the Milky Way. On pleasant July nights, after the mosquitoes have gone to bed, Scorpius makes a good target for binocular-equipped stargazers. It's home to dozens of deep-sky objects, the brightest being M7, a cluster of 50 to 80 stars that looks like one out-of-focus star to the naked eye. A good set of binoculars reveals about 15 brighter stars arranged in a pinwheel-shape. The so-called Butterfly Cluster, M6, is also located in Scorpius. Good binoculars and small telescopes indeed reveal a delicate sidereal butterfly. It's hard to believe Scorpius bespeaks evil when it offers such lovely sights.

SIRIUS & PROCYON
The Dog Stars of Orion

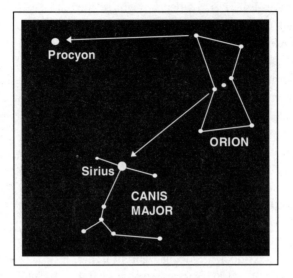

OF ALL THE HOUNDS in heaven, Sirius barks
loudest. The famous Dog Star is the brightest star
in the night sky, a brilliant white point piercing
the black velvet of a winter's evening. His companion,
Procyon, less bright but still ranked eighth in the astronomical Top 20, shines to the northeast. Sirius is the
alpha star of the constellation Canis Major, the Great
Dog, and Procyon is the alpha of Canis Minor, the Little
Dog. The two canines are the hunting dogs of Orion,
winter's mightiest constellation, who lies just to the west.
When the Greek gods placed Orion among the stars after
he was fatally stung by the scorpion, they thoughtfully
elevated his best friends along with him.

Sirius, Procyon and Orion command the southern
night sky in winter. Six months later, these stars occupy the
same area of the day sky. The ancient Egyptians believed
the heat from Sirius was added to that of the sun, thus producing the "dog days of summer." Sirius is derived from the
Greek word *seirios*, meaning "hot" or "scorching." (Procyon
means "before the dog," because it rises before Sirius.)
During the Mediterranean dog days, hounds were said to go
mad, food and drink spoiled, lethargy reigned and everyone

became just a little bonkers in the oppressive heat. The modern dog days are roughly July 3 to August 15.

To the ancient peoples of the Nile, Sirius was the most important star. About 4,500 years ago, Sirius appeared briefly in the dawn sky before the sun in mid-July, just as intense summer rains in the Nile's headwaters brought the floods that lasted until October. The overflowing Nile irrigated and fertilized the croplands along its banks, sustaining the entire Egyptian civilization. So important was this event that Sirius's sighting marked the beginning of the year in the Egyptian calendar. This led the Egyptians to devise a 365-day calendar as early as 3000 B.C., while other cultures used a lunar calendar. The Egyptians still had 12 months, of 30 days each, but tacked on five days at the end to equal 365. Later observations of Sirius revealed the year actually comprised 365 ¼ days.

Sirius is bright because it's a big brute and is nearby – indeed, the closest star to our own sun visible from the Northern Hemisphere, and the fifth closest overall. Astronomers reckon it's about twice the diameter of the sun, and 23 times as luminous. It is 8.7 light-years away; a hop and a skip in cosmic terms, but still distant enough that it would take our fastest spacecraft about 300,000 years to get there.

Once the spaceship arrived, its occupants would see that Sirius is a double star. The companion star, dubbed the Pup by some wag after its discovery in 1862, is a so-called white dwarf, a burned-out star radiating its remnant heat like an ember. It was the first white dwarf discovered, and astronomers now know the universe is full of them. They are small, having collapsed after the main hydrogen fuel ran out, but are super-dense. The Pup is perhaps only twice the size of Earth, but is as dense as the sun. Some astronomers, noting irregularities in the 50-year orbit of Sirius and the Pup around each other, believe there is a third, even-smaller star in the Sirius system. The Pup and this third star, if it exists, are too small to be seen with the naked eye or binoculars.

A mystery surrounds Sirius. Virtually all the ancient writings about the star, including those by Virgil, Seneca

dim constellation between Boötes and Ursa Major (Big Dipper). Lupus the wolf is another dim constellation, not visible from mid-northern latitudes. Vulpecula the fox comprises faint stars near Cygnus, the great swan of summer Feline rivals: The heavenly cats are: Leo the lion; a dim companion to Leo named Leo Minor; and Lynx, a large but faint constellation between Ursa Major and Gemini. A French astronomer once proposed a domesticated cat, Felis, as a constellation, but kitty was never officially adopted

Winter views: It's popularly thought that clear, winter air makes it possible to see more stars. The air is, in fact, no clearer in winter than in summer. It just so happens there are more bright stars in winter than in summer skies Twinkle, twinkle: Stars located close to the horizon often seem to twinkle. The effect is caused by air turbulence, and is more apparent with stars near the horizon because our oblique view cuts through more of Earth's atmosphere Archibald Lampman: Poet, columnist, wilderness canoeist, post-office clerk, born 1861 in Morpeth, Ontario (then Canada West), died 1899 in Ottawa. Influenced by Keats and Tennyson, preoccupied with nature and its healing powers Also see: Auriga, Orion, The Pleiades. *Up North:* Stars

and the renowned Alexandrian astronomer Ptolemy, refer to Sirius as a fiery red star, when today it is clearly white or blue-white. Theories explaining this anomaly range from atmospheric phenomena turning the light red to a suggestion that the Pup was once a red supergiant star before it became a white dwarf. According to current astronomic theory, the Pup was, indeed, once a red supergiant – dying stars of a certain size all experience this phase of stellar life. But it would have passed this stage long before the ancient scribblers made their observations. The atmosphere *can* affect a star's colour, particularly those stars close to the horizon, and Sirius does appear to twinkle when the air is turbulent. But that's not enough to explain the consistent descriptions of a red star.

Sirius's mystic allure (if not its astronomical mystery) has captured the imagination of poets and writers around the world. Ontario's great poet of the late 19th century, Archibald Lampman, wrote often about the stars, and in his sonnet entitled "Sirius," he dreams about Hathor, the Egyptian sky, joy and fertility goddess, whose temple at Dandarah still stands:

The old night waned, and all the purple dawn
Grew pale with green and opal. The wide earth
Lay darkling and strange and silent as at birth,
Save for a single far-off brightness drawn
Of water gray as steel. The silver bow
Of broad Orion still pursued the night,
And farther down, amid the gathering light,
A great star leaped and smouldered. Standing so,
I dreamed myself in Denderah by the Nile;
Beyond the hall of columns and the crowd
And the vast pylons, I beheld afar
The goddess gleam, and saw the morning smile,
And lifting both my hands, I cried aloud
In joy to Hathor, smitten by her star!

TAURUS & THE HYADES
The Bull and the Rainy Stars

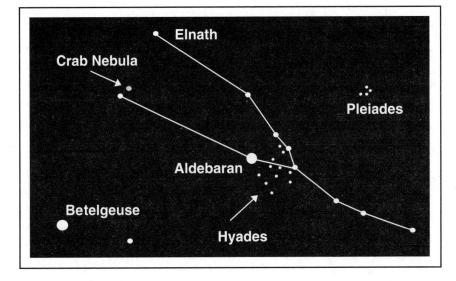

Elnath

Crab Nebula

Pleiades

Aldebaran

Betelgeuse

Hyades

"RICH IN MAIDENS," the ancient poets said of the constellation Taurus. The ladies in question are two groups of half-sisters, the Hyades and the Pleiades, both sparkling star clusters within the constellation's boundaries. Their lovely presence in the heavens has led to grand histories rivalling that of their home constellation. This is especially true of the unique Pleiades (see page 250).

Which is not to overlook Taurus himself, the great zodiacal bull, a symbol of virility and brute strength. He's one of the oldest constellations in history, with mentions dating back to at least 3500 B.C. In early Western star maps, the bull is usually depicted in a standoff with Orion; Taurus's horns point east to Orion, while the legendary hunter swings his shield against the charging bull.

Only the bull's forequarters appear in these drawings, as if he were swimming. This hints at just one of several myths involving Taurus. In one Greek tale, Taurus was the disguised Zeus, who lured Poseidon's beautiful grand-daughter Europa onto his back and swam off with her to Crete. The scene was immortalized by the Venetian

Best viewing time: Winter constellation, visible in the evening sky from mid-Oct. to mid-Apr. Bright star Aldebaran visible from urban and wilderness areas

Location: Follow Orion's three "belt stars" northwest to a bright orange-red star; that's Aldebaran. The loose agglomeration of stars around Aldebaran is the Hyades star cluster

Aldebaran: The 14th-brightest star, magnitude 0.9, distance 60 light-years. A double-star system; the dim companion is invisible to the naked eye

Elnath: Second-brightest star in Taurus, marks the tip of the northern horn. Magnitude 1.7, distance 140 light-years. Name means "the butting one" in Arabic

Astrological period: Apr. 20–May 20. Taurus was said to rule the neck
Also see: Auriga, Orion, The Pleiades. *Up North:* Stars, Zodiac & Ecliptic

painter Titian in his famous 1562 painting the *Rape of Europa*. The coupling produced King Minos of Crete. Poseidon later gave Minos a bull to sacrifice as a demonstration of the king's divine right to govern, but for some reason Minos wouldn't perform the deed. Poseidon wasn't pleased. The sea god cast a spell on Minos's wife, Pasiphae, and she fell in love with the bull. This match produced the dreaded Minotaur, a man with the head of a bull.

In the Minoan civilization on Crete, a sacred bull was considered the animal form of the priest-monarch Minos and the consort of his goddess wife, Pasiphae. Similarly, the ancient Egyptians associated Taurus with Apis, a real bull chosen to carry the spirit of Osiris, god of the afterworld. (Orion represented Osiris in the heavens.) As each Apis died, another was chosen as successor.

The bright star Aldebaran marks the bull's eye

Taurus was important in another way to many ancient civilizations. Early stargazers, the astronomer-priests, observed that the sun was in Taurus at springtime, the start of many calendars. Due to precession, a 26,000-year wobble in Earth's rotation that alters the apparent position of the stars in our sky, the sun today doesn't enter Taurus until mid-May. But it can still play a role in modern New Year's celebrations; the bull is high overhead in the night sky at midnight on December 31.

The bright orange-red star Aldebaran marks the bull's eye. Aldebaran, just east of the Pleiades, appears to follow the star cluster as the constellations move westward across the sky. Its name means "the follower" in Arabic. The Hyades and the Pleiades were the daughters of Atlas in classical mythology, but astronomically, they are so-called "open clusters" of stars, each star born from a vast nebula of gas and dust. The Hyades is a much looser cluster than the Pleiades, but is still an impressive sight on a dark night, with the naked eye or with binoculars. More than 200 stars make up the cluster, about 150 light-years away. The Hyades are known as the "rainy stars," because their evening setting in May and morning setting in November marks the rainy seasons in many regions. "Through scudding drifts the rainy Hyades / Vext the dim sea," wrote Tennyson in his poem "Ulysses" (the Greek Odysseus).

On July 4, 1054 A.D., a spectacular sight astounded people around the world. It was a supernova, the explosion of a massive star, so bright that it reportedly could be seen in daytime. Records from Asia to pre-Columbian North America document the event, which took place within Taurus. Today the "shrapnel" from that explosion can be seen as the Crab Nebula, a thin cloud of gas and dust faintly visible through a small telescope. Very large telescopes reveal something even more intriguing: the star's surviving core. It has been transformed into a pulsar, one of the universe's most bizarre characters. The Crab Nebula pulsar is estimated to be about the diameter of Lake Simcoe but with the same mass as the sun and spinning at 30 revolutions per *second*. It is a source of intense radio waves. The Crab Nebula is also called M1, the first object in Charles Messier's list of nebulae, star clusters and galaxies composed in the late 1700s to help comet hunters avoid confusing comets with other objects. M1 is about 4,000 light-years away, which means the explosion witnessed in 1054 actually happened 4,000 years earlier. The light took four millennia to reach Earth.

VIRGO
A Maiden for All Maidens

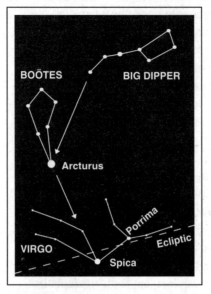

BOÖTES

BIG DIPPER

Arcturus

Porrima

Ecliptic

VIRGO

Spica

Best viewing time: The evening sky from mid-Mar. to mid-Aug. Climbs highest in the southern sky in late May

Location: South of (below) the bright star Arcturus and east (left) of Leo in the southern sky

Lucida: The brightest star in a constellation; is usually designated "alpha"

Spica: Magnitude 1.0, distance 220 light-years; the 16th-brightest star

Porrima: A dimmer star in Virgo, magnitude 2.7, distance 31 light-years. Name is Latin for "goddess of childbirth." Located at the crotch of the Y usually drawn on modern star maps to show Virgo

Zodiacal taxonomy: 3 men (including the twin boys), 1 woman, 1 mythological creature, 1 inanimate object,

NEW STARGAZERS LEARN to identify stars and constellations by using the easy-to-find Big Dipper and Orion as signposts. The zodiacal constellation Virgo and its bright star Spica are often the second stop on this course. Find the bent handle of the Big Dipper, then, extending that curve, "arc to Arcturus," the teacher will say. Arcturus is the bright star of the constellation Boötes – the brightest star, in fact, in the summer night sky. Then continue to follow the arc southward to the next bright star, or "spike to Spica." Spica is the lucida of Virgo the Maiden. Other stars in the Big Dipper point to other celestial highlights in a similar manner, and Orion serves the same purpose in winter.

"Spike to Spica" is an appropriate memory trick, because Spica represents a spike, or ear, of wheat held by Virgo, the only female zodiacal constellation. Virgo is one of those constellations that doesn't represent a single character or creature from classical mythology. Instead, she stands for just about every female deity, particularly those representing agriculture, the arts (including war and hunting), justice and fertility. They are not necessarily all virgins, one of the meanings for "maiden." Of the Greek goddesses just three were virgins: Athena, Artemis and Vesta. (The Roman equivalents are Minerva, Diana and Hestia.) Athena, Zeus's favourite child, was famed as the goddess of war, but she also represented civilization; that is, arts, crafts, agriculture and wisdom. She had no mother, springing fully grown from her father's head. Artemis was the goddess of the moon and of hunting. Vesta was the goddess of the hearth. In ancient Rome, the public hearth was cared for by six maidens – the vestal virgins.

7 animals. *Zodiac* is Greek for "circle of animals"
Also see: Asters, Leo, Scorpius.
Up North: Stars, Zodiac & Ecliptic

Other deities associated with the constellation include the fertility goddesses Isis and Ishtar, of ancient Egypt and Babylonia respectively, Demeter, the Greek goddess of agriculture, and Demeter's daughter Persephone, the spring maiden. One of the great Greek myths describes how Hades kidnapped Persephone and brought her to his underworld. Grief-stricken Demeter went searching for her daughter, and in her absence Earth fell barren. Not wishing mortals to die of starvation, the Olympians struck a deal: Demeter could have her daughter back every spring, but later in the year she would return to the underworld. Thus was established the cycle of the seasons, and Virgo represents this as a spring constellation.

The Greek goddess of justice, Astraea (sometimes called Dike), is also often identified with Virgo. Her name translates as "star-maiden." The scales of justice lie at Virgo's feet in many old star maps, because the dim constellation Libra lies just to the east of Virgo.

Astronomers take great interest in Virgo, home to the Virgo supercluster of galaxies. A small backyard telescope may reveal a handful of these galaxies as dim, hazy patches. But there are thousands in the cluster, each containing billions of stars. Our own "Local Group" of galaxies, which includes the Milky Way, is at the edge of this supercluster. Recent observations suggest that an even larger grouping of tens of thousands of galaxies, dubbed "The Great Attractor," encompasses the Virgo superclusters. Astronomers are studying these unbelievably massive galactic structures in their never-ending quest to figure out the grand architecture of the universe.

STAR CHARTS
Navigating the Night Sky

FOR THOUSANDS OF YEARS, different cultures around the world had their own ways of organizing the heavens. It wasn't until 1930 that the International Astronomical Union agreed on a common set of names and boundaries for the 88 modern constellations. Of those, 48 were descended from the *Almagest*, a star catalogue hand-produced by the Alexandrian astronomer Claudius Ptolemy around 150 A.D. His constellations were derived from traditions dating back to at least 2000 B.C.

The names of many bright stars have also been handed down over the centuries. Most are Arabic, because the Arabs preserved and translated the classic works of Greco-Roman civilization while the

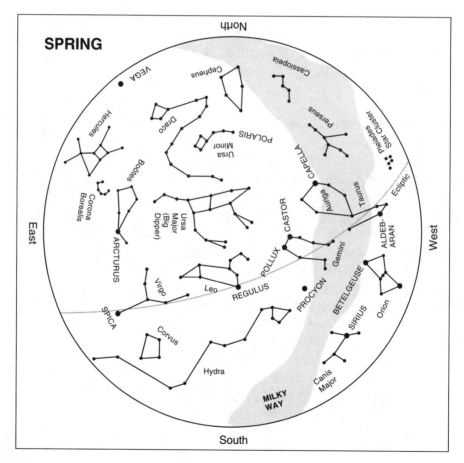

barbarians cast Europe into the Dark Ages. In 1603, the German astronomer Johan Bayer took a scientific approach to naming stars. He named the brightest star of each constellation *alpha*, after the first letter of the Greek alphabet. The second-brightest star was named *beta*, and so on. (There are a few exceptions to this scheme.) Thus, astronomers refer to the brightest star in Lyra as Alpha Lyrae, although it also has an ancient Arabic name, Vega.

The rotation of Earth makes it appear as if all the stars are circling Polaris, the North Star, in a counterclockwise direction. Because of this motion, the star charts reproduced here (they are also found in our first book, *Up North*) are not exact for every time of night, every night of the year, or every location in the Northern Hemisphere. But they are good guides to the heavens shortly after nightfall in the middle of each season in central Ontario.

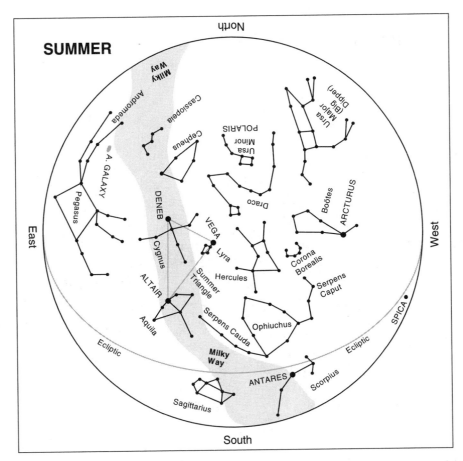

To use a chart, hold this book upside-down, place it over your head and face north. The side of the chart marked "north" should point towards the north, the side marked "east" should face the east, and so on. The position of the constellations in the night sky will roughly match those in the chart. Find the most prominent features first – the Big Dipper, Summer Triangle or Orion in winter – and use them as guideposts to the other constellations. Star names are printed in UPPER CASE, while constellations are printed in Upper and Lower case. If you're under clear, dark skies in a wilderness area, you'll see many more stars than are indicated here. If you're in a light-polluted urban area, you'll see fewer.

To find planets, look for what appear to be bright stars along the ecliptic. Planets travel along this imaginary line in space. The ecliptic roughly defines the plane of the solar system – technically, it's the

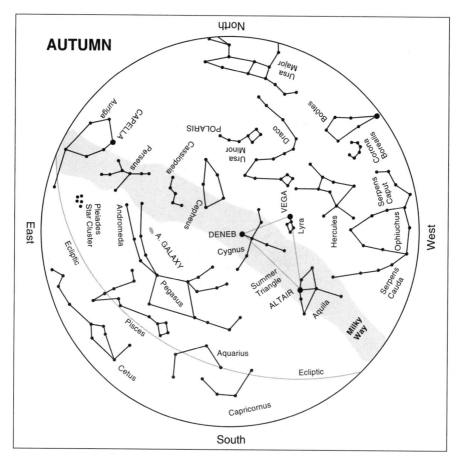

plane defined by Earth's orbit around the sun. Most of the constellations have their own entries and star maps in this book or in *Up North*. Many have interesting astronomical features, such as double-stars and star clusters. A good pair of binoculars is an excellent viewing aid.

To help your eyes adjust to the dark, use a flashlight with red cloth or red paper wrapped around the light.

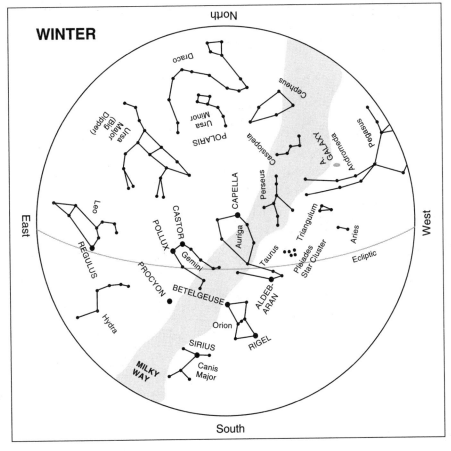

NATURE ALMANAC:

THE YEAR OUTDOORS

A YEAR IN NATURE *is a constantly changing combination of sproutings and migrations, bloomings and matings, fruitings and births. The sky, the sun and moon, stars and planets, are always moving in grand circuits. Every day is different; that is one of the wonders of living in a temperate, continental climate, experiencing profound effects with each degree shift of the Earth's angle to the sun. The more time we spend outdoors, the more we become aware of the cycles of life and of the Earth, known intimately by generations before us.*

This almanac attempts to tie together the material covered both in Up North *and* Up North Again *by chronicling those changes, month by month, through the year. Though the timing of each event in nature often varies from year to year, subject to the weather, we've used the recorded averages for the area covered by this book. Events may also begin before and last longer than the particular part of the month in which they are listed. We've tried to give a good approximation and show how the various comings and goings and transformations are intricately connected to each other.*

In order to group the seasons more naturally, this almanac begins with December, the start of winter.

DECEMBER

Early December

- Herring gulls are among the last laggards to drift south out of central Ontario, leaving behind a winter skeleton crew of about two dozen of the hardiest birds.

- Resourceful chickadees, nuthatches, downy woodpeckers and brown creepers find much of their winter sustenance in the egg cases or hibernating pupae of spiders and insects secreted in the nooks and crannies of tree trunks and branches. Pileated woodpeckers chisel deep into tree trunks to raid dormant colonies of carpenter ants.

- Winged black ash seeds whirling to the ground in December are eaten by purple finches, evening grosbeaks, cedar waxwings and deer mice. Conifer, alder and birch seeds also keep these and other species alive through the winter.

- Once every few years, bumper crops of cones attract large numbers of winter nomads. Common redpolls from the tundra feast on tamarack, alder, cedar and yellow birch cones. Pine siskins pick seeds from yellow birch, alder and spruce. White-winged crossbills pry nutlets from unopened spruce and tamarack cones. Red crossbills do the same with pine cones. Crossbills sometimes fill the forest with song in the dead of winter as they nest in response to bountiful crops.

- Most lakes in central Ontario freeze over in early December, a little later in the Georgian Bay hinterland. Muskrats chew holes in the ice and pile mud and debris around the openings, creating "push ups" to serve as breathing holes. Otters break the ice at weak points around rocks and stumps, or slip through beaver dam spillways. Mink and raccoons use ice holes to probe for crayfish or hibernating frogs.

Mid-December

- The Geminid meteor shower, one of the year's best, peaks around Dec. 13, with more than 90 meteors an hour visible under ideal conditions.

- Skunks retreat into winter dens in December, though mild spells stir them to go out in search of middle-of-the-winter-night snacks.

Late December

- The chances of a white Christmas are 80 percent or better throughout central Ontario, according to Environment Canada records.

- Unable to cope in snow deeper than 50 cm (20 in), deer migrate to hemlock, spruce or cedar "yards" for shelter. Yards in the Loring Valley, south of Lake Nipissing, draw up to 15,000 deer in winter. Others congregate at Kennisis Lake and Round Lake, near Algonquin Park, and at the northern tip of the Bruce Peninsula. Porcupines, taking up winter residence in hemlock stands, help feed the deer by dropping lots of twigs to the ground below.

- Wolf packs make many winter kills by forcing weak, old or young deer into deep snow on rivers and lakes. Ravens earn their winter livelihood by cleaning up the carcasses. Wolf leftovers around the Peterborough Crown Game Reserve and Algonquin Park also regularly attract a smattering of scavenging bald or golden eagles. Fishers, martens and foxes vie for deer or moose remains as well.

JANUARY

Early January

- Moose ring in the new year by dropping their antlers in late December or early January. Deer may keep their horns till February. Discarded antlers are gnawed by mice, hares, porcupines and other vegetarians to obtain calcium and salt, in short supply during winter.

- The Quadrantid meteor shower peaks around January 4, with up to 40 shooting stars visible an hour.

- Clear, sparkling winter nights also feature Orion and the other constellations of the Winter Six, the year's most dazzling collection of bright stars.

Mid-January

- In the dead of winter, great horned owls begin hooting it up with the year's first avian mating calls. Hairy woodpeckers soon join in, drumming the opening beats of another season's symphony of bird song.

- Mammalian romance stirs as well, with beavers breeding beneath the ice in January or February.

Late January

- A balmy break often occurring late in the month is known as the January thaw. On such mild, sunny, midwinter days, tiny snowfleas often cover the surface of the snow like soot. Stoneflies crawl out from under sun-warmed riverside rocks to mate and lay eggs.

- Many lichens on south-facing trees and rocks also stir to photosynthesize in the sun on mild days. If temperatures rise above freezing, fungi such as winter polypor and orange witches' butter may swell up on tree bark.

- Mild weather followed by a freeze can leave a crust on the snow thick enough to support deer, who take the opportunity to browse on previously unreachable vegetation. A thinner crust may make progress difficult for them but support the wolves at their heels.

- When snowstorms are on their way and the air pressure drops, spruce and fir trees act as weather barometers, their branches closing together in anticipation of heavy loads.

- Fox and coyote breeding season comes in late January and early February. Mates remain together to raise their young in the spring.

- Bear cubs are born in late January or early February, while their mothers hibernate. Deaf and blind, they find their mothers' nipples by zeroing in on the heat escaping from them.

FEBRUARY

Early February

- Though they don't mate till April, chickadees begin whistling their high, clear songs – often rendered as "fee-bee" or "fee-bee-ee" – in midwinter to establish territorial dominance within the winter flock.

- While it may seem frozen and silent on land, much life goes on below the ice, with many fishes and the larvae of dragonflies, midges, blackflies, deer flies and craneflies swimming or wriggling about, albeit sluggishly in some cases.

- Winter offers the best opportunity to detect signs of the lynx, with its great furry feet leaving up to 11-cm-wide (4.5-in-wide) tracks in the snow. Perhaps the most retiring of all Ontario's mammals, the nocturnal mystery cat prowls the runs of snowshoe hares in thick evergreen brush, ambushing the bunnies as they go about their business.

- After eating all the easy-to-reach buds, hares resort to less-nutritious bark in winter. To gain as much nourishment from their food as possible, they recycle their own droppings, which come in both edible and already-recycled varieties.

Mid-February

- Ravens write their valentines in the skies of February with breathtaking courtship flights, soaring and diving with wild abandon.

- The call of the wild also beckons the furry crowd between mid-February and March. Skunks rouse from hibernation to look for mates, though the luckiest males may overwinter with a harem. Minks use their own stinky musk glands to send out odoriferous overtures to potential partners. Raccoons, too, after hibernating intermittently through winter's cold spells, wander the woods in search of the opposite sex.

- Continually released throughout the season, cattail seed fluff is often used by resourceful mice to insulate their nests beneath the snow. Some mice also take up quarters in cosy high-rise apartments of old-but-well-made goldfinch nests.

- For their part, red squirrels come down from the trees and do much of their winter scurrying in warm tunnels beneath the snow.

- Ruffed grouse also seek cover beneath the snow during extreme cold snaps, burying themselves until things warm up a little.

Late February

- After months of rising sexual tension, wolves mate between late February and mid-March, with the dominant female choosing her partner. For the rest of the pack, it's enforced celibacy.

- Before laying their eggs in late winter, great horned owls can choose from the finest in still-vacant crow and hawk nest accommodations.

- Late winter is the bleakest time of the year in the natural world, when food supplies of all kinds run low, bringing wildlife populations to their lowest.

MARCH

Early March

- Central Ontario's first returning migrants are usually crows and saw-whet owls, which begin arriving in early or mid-March, some coming from wintering grounds just south of the Canadian Shield.

- Gray jays, still living well on last year's hidden seeds, start nesting this month, sometimes even earlier. Studies suggest they easily outdo humans in remembering where things are stashed.

- Red-breasted nuthatches also begin building nests in coniferous tree cavities in late winter, smearing sticky sap around the edges of the entrance to help keep unwelcome visitors out.

- Lake trout eggs hatch in frigid waters in late winter.

Mid-March

- Mild breaks of above-freezing daytime temperatures bring the first stirrings of spring in the forest. Tree sap starts running, roots awaken in the ground, and buds, imperceptibly at first, begin to swell.

- The scent of such proto-spring days sometimes rouses chipmunks from their subterranean winter naps, enticing them to step out gingerly onto the snow to gauge the season.

- Among red squirrels in the trees above, formerly hostile male and female neighbours react to the mid-March glow by suddenly, but briefly, becoming the objects of each other's desire. Flying squirrels mate around the same time.

- In remote areas of thick brush, lynx eager to meet and mate beckon with chilling caterwauls in late winter.

- Beneath a thick layer of slowly melting snow, sugar maple keys start to germinate, giving them a one- to two-month head start over other seeds. When the snow cover is down to only 5 cm (2 in), enough light can filter through on mild, sunny days to reactivate ground mosses and lichens.

- Herring gulls, which may return to areas with dumps or other scavenging grounds earlier in March, move to the water as the ice breaks up on rivers and streams.

- Over-wintering male goldfinches start putting on their familiar yellow jackets around mid-month and are fully dressed in April.

- The barred owl's "Who cooks for you, who cooks for you all?" can be heard throughout much of the year. But on March and April nights, the hooting is augmented by screams, barks, hisses and cackles, as owls get down to the serious business of courtship.

- Downy woodpeckers also drum out solicitations to each other in March.

- The very first robins usually begin trickling in to central Ontario in mid- to late March.

Late March

- Fishers give birth in late March or early April, going out within a week or so afterwards to mate again for next year's litter. Foxes and coyotes are born in ground burrows around the same time.

- Changing to spring fashions also seems to put snowshoe hares in the mood for procreation, with their coats turning from white to brown through to April. Weasels change from white winter ermine during the same period.

- Flocks of male red-winged blackbirds begin returning to marshes and riversides in late March to set up territories. A few weeks later, females arrive to pick and choose from whoever's ended up with the best nesting real estate.

- Killdeer, song sparrows, grackles and woodcocks soon follow, while winter residents, such as pine grosbeaks, northern shrikes and redpolls, leave for breeding grounds in the boreal forest and points north.

- Other northerners, snow buntings and tree sparrows, pass through central Ontario from the south for about a month.

- Uncrating colonies of hibernating carpenter ants at home in Ontario through the winter, pairs of pileated woodpeckers chisel out nesting chambers in late March or April.

- Pine siskins also nest in mixed and evergreen forests around the end of the month.

APRIL

Early April

- Willow and aspen flower buds sprout soft fuzz in late winter and early spring, while the leaf buds of balsam poplar grow large and fill the air with a spicy fragrance.

- Porcupines switch to nutritious, sap-swollen sugar maple buds in April after subsisting on a bark-and-twig diet that slowly starves them through winter.

- Sap dripping from broken maple twigs is slurped by squirrels and mourning cloak butterflies, which rouse from hibernation on mild days with snow still on the ground. Pale geometrid moths may also rise from their cocoons.

- Pickerel make nightly spawning runs at stretches of rapids, rocky riffles or the bases of waterfalls and dams for about three weeks in April after the ice breaks apart on rivers.

- Great blue herons, mergansers, goldeneyes, black and ring-necked ducks press inland from the Great Lakes wherever they find shallow, open water.

- Sharp-shinned hawks arrive to cruise the forests for growing numbers of songbirds. In less-treed areas and at forest edges, early April usually sees the return of turkey vultures, kestrels, northern harriers, meadowlarks and cowbirds.

- Rising from their holes in April, male groundhogs forsake breakfast to look for sex.

Mid-April

- The ice usually starts breaking up on most Shield lakes south of Lake Nipissing. Pairs of loons reoccupy baywater nurseries soon afterwards.

- Stretches of open water draw Canada geese northward over central Ontario, along with pintails, buffleheads, teal and scaup, most touching down only to sleep and refuel.

- Wood ducks and mallards start flying in to stay around quiet, backwater areas. Bitterns and diminutive pied-billed grebes arrive to call out over marshy sites.

- Young muskrats disperse from their maternal lodges in slow, weedy waters after the ice disappears and shortly before a new mating season begins.

- For about a week, pike spawn by day on flooded, grassy riverbanks and marshy lake edges. Perch spawn nightly in lake shallows and tributaries into early May.

280

- Trout lily leaves begin pushing up through the leaf litter, with patches of snow still nearby. Red maples above glow red with tiny blossoms. Hazel and alder unfurl flowering catkins.

- Kingfishers, ruby- and golden-crowned kinglets, flickers, winter wrens, phoebes, yellow-bellied sapsuckers, hermit thrushes and snipes start touching down in the region around mid-month. Meanwhile, blue jays, ravens and chickadees are usually already nesting.

- Ospreys and broad-winged, red-shouldered, red-tailed and Cooper's hawks also arrive in the second half of the month. Natives said the year's first thunder came with the return of raptorlike, supernatural thunderbirds.

- Showers draw hordes of salamanders, spring peepers and wood frogs at night from their torpor on the forest floor to sometimes-still-icy ponds. In a week or so, the peepers will be singing and mating.

- Ruffed grouse "drumming" goes on through most of the spring. Male spruce grouse also perform mating-season flutter flights up to tree branches.

- Around dense, wet thickets of alder at dusk, woodcocks make their own spiral, beeping courtship flights. In the thick woods this month and next, the short, whistled mating call of the saw-whet owl sounds like a saw being sharpened.

- This is baby-boom month for the weasel family. Mink, martens, otters, fishers, long- and short-tailed weasels all bear litters in their respective dens. Raccoons are born as well.

- Bats come out of hibernation when temperatures begin to rise consistently above 10°C (50°F), generally in mid- to late April. Females fly to nursery colonies to give birth.

Late April

- Towards the edge of the Shield, forests usually start blooming with bright-yellow trout lilies, pink hepaticas, white and woolly blue violets by the end of the month. Horsetail and many mosses also send up shoots with spore-bearing heads. Among the trees, aspen, birch and willow catkins unfurl and droop like fuzzy yellow-green caterpillars.

- Hardy bumblebees may be out on warm days collecting pollen from willow and alder catkins. Carrion beetles also start emerging to feed on the remains of winter carcasses.

- As recently melted lake tops warm, midges begin emerging from the water. They are quickly swooped down upon by returning tree and barn swallows. Water striders also appear.

- Returning pine and yellow-rumped warblers, and white-throated, chipping, savannah, vesper and swamp sparrows fan out over the region.

- Ice-out is usually in late April north of Lake Nipissing and in the Algonquin highlands.

MAY

Early May

- Spring beauties and trout lilies come into full bloom in early May hardwood forests. Southern areas also see marsh marigolds, bloodroot and blue cohosh flowers.

- Out in the bogs, leather leaf is usually the first plant to blossom, with tiny white urns hanging from its evergreen branches. Clusters of pink bog laurel and white bog rosemary flowers soon follow. Serviceberry and hawthorns bloom at forest edges.

- The tips of blooming sweet gale catkins trace shrubby shorelines with a reddish hue.

- Ovenbirds, northern waterthrushes, and Nashville, pine, black-throated green, and black-and-white warblers all usually swell the ranks of returning songbirds early this month. Their numbers are bolstered by whip-poor-wills, bluebirds, brown thrashers and spotted sandpipers.

- Moose and porcupines become common roadside attractions at this time of year as they lap from puddles of road-salt-enriched snowmelt.

- May is the month of mammalian motherhood in the northwoods. White-tailed deer, beavers, groundhogs, red and flying squirrels, wolves, porcupines and skunks all give birth, while she-bears usher their cubs out of the den.

- Sun-warmed rocks awaken groups of hibernating garter snakes, while turtles and frogs stir and rise from the muddy depths of lakes and streams.

- After rising from sleep below the frost line, toads migrate to the ponds of their youth to sing and procreate before returning to their land-roving ways.

Mid-May

- Trilliums, like most other spring ephemerals, bloom only until the forest canopy closes overhead and shades out the sun later this month. White dominates, with trailing arbutus, mayflowers, foam flowers, false Solomon's seal and the hanging bells of true Solomon's seal all blooming in the woodlands. Fern fiddleheads roll open and rise.

- Trembling aspens start to leaf out. Flower cones appear on pine, fir and spruce.

- Blackflies begin transforming from aquatic larvae in fast-running Shield streams, becoming steadily worse through the month and into June, with up to billions per hectare (or acre).

- The peak of warbler migration is timed to take full advantage of the insect hordes. Common yellowthroats, redstarts, blackburnian, magnolia, yellow, Wilson's, chestnut-sided, Canada, bay-breasted and black-throated blue warblers join the throngs filling the forests with song.

- Also coming back are scarlet tanagers, hummingbirds, red-eyed, warbling and solitary vireos, rose-breasted grosbeaks, Baltimore orioles, kingbirds, veeries, wood thrushes, catbirds, swifts, wood-pewees and least and great-crested flycatchers.

- Wood ducks and common and hooded mergansers all nest inside tree cavities in May.

- Suckers spawn in such profusion along gravelly rivers and lake margins at this time that the Ojibway named May the month of the Sucker Moon.

- Male leopard frogs begin their odd mating song – a deep staccato snore followed by grunts.

Late May

- Most trees usually leaf out late in the month. Largetooth aspens appear silvery white, with down on their unfolding leaves. Striped and mountain maples also sprout large, yellow-green flower clusters in the forest understorey.

- Legions of caterpillars hatch with the sprouting leaves. Many butterflies and moths also emerge from their cocoons to mate and lay eggs on the leaves. Canadian tiger swallowtails, among the most common till the end of June, frequent roadside puddles to obtain salt.

- The forest floor is now rich with growth and colour. Hooded jack-in-the-pulpits, red columbines, rose twisted-stalk and batches of purple, white and yellow violets bloom in profusion well into June or later. Large white hobblebush and pale-yellow honeysuckle blossoms also appear in the understorey.

- Nighthawks, cedar waxwings, olive-sided, yellow-bellied and alder flycatchers, indigo buntings, Swainson's thrushes, Philadelphia vireos and blackpoll and mourning warblers are among the last migrants in late May and early June.

- In addition to feeding the birds, blackflies pollinate blueberries, blooming now and into June. Rising numbers of emerging mosquitoes pollinate wild cherry blossoms.

- The first welcome dragonflies transform from aquatic nymphs to prey on biting insects.

- Water snakes crawl out of the water onto branches to mate in May or early June.

- Last frost usually comes around the end of the month in much of the southern Shield.

JUNE

Early June

- Lustful male bullfrogs drone loudly from lakes and bays through June and into July. Those with the best tadpole-raising real estate may mate with up to six egg-swelled females.

- Though this month is prime listening time for the whip-poor-will's sharp, echoing call in the night, perfect camouflage means the vociferous insectivore is almost never seen.

- Pink moccasin flowers, called the whip-poor-will's slippers by the Iroquois, are among the most beautiful and common orchids now blooming on the Shield.

- Yellow lady's slippers, rose pogonia, dragon's mouth, coral-root and many other orchids are also most abundant in June. The Bruce Peninsula's woods and wetlands put on Ontario's best display. A single orchid may produce millions of minute seeds, which sprout and join with strands of fungi to get nutrients.

- White bunchberry and snowberry flowers. Wild sarsaparilla, goldthread, dogwood, blue bead lilies, twinflower, starflower, doll's-eyes, red-berried elder and mountain ash also bloom this month. Around bogs and moist shorelines, Labrador tea opens its white blossoms, and in meadows and other open spots, daisies, hawkweed, yarrow and heal-all come into flower. Clusters of tiny flowers also appear on oaks and beech.

- Baby groundhogs begin emerging from burrows.

- In June, just before gray jays begin collecting food to store for the winter, sibling rivalry among fledglings leads to one bird kicking the others out of their parents' territory, while the victor remains till the following spring.

- Late May and June usually see the biggest swarms of mayflies emerging from the water for their fleeting mating flights.

Mid-June

- Turtles crawl onto land to lay and bury their eggs in June. Though few survive to hatch and make it to adulthood, snappers that do may live up to 90 years.

- Gray treefrogs sound birdlike mating trills into July.

- Ringneck, milk, black rat and fox snakes lay eggs through June and July.

- Bears take a break in their relentless summer feasting for a brief fling with the opposite sex in June. Next month, when berries ripen, they start gaining a kilogram (2.2 lb) a day.

- Among the smallest of carnivores, short-tailed weasels also mate this month.

- Chipmunks raise a racket as young leave home and scatter to establish their own territories in June, making easy pickings for predators.

- After a 10-month sleep in its cocoon, Ontario's largest moth, the cecropia, spreads its tawny, 17-cm-wide (7-in-wide) wings for its maiden voyage. One of many silk moths now common, the big flutterer lays its eggs on birch and cherry trees by the end of the month.

- Migrant monarch butterflies return. Often, painted lady butterflies also arrive from the southwest United States to breed in Ontario in June. But unlike monarchs, whose descendants return to Mexico every fall, painted lady offspring are wiped out by autumn frosts. They neither return home nor produce eggs that can survive the winter.

Late June

- Fireflies light up early summer nights with sexual solicitations.

- Male smallmouth bass create saucer-shaped impressions in gravelly shallows in late June and July and then guard eggs left there by females after they spawn. Catfish are also protecting their eggs and young around the same time.

- As water temperatures rise, aquatic plants such as purple iris and water arum come into bloom.

- Wood sorrel and sheep laurel flower by late June.

- Balsam poplars cover parts of the forest with the white fluff of their airborne seeds, while red maple seeds propeller to the ground.

- Crows and red-winged blackbirds finish nesting and begin reforming in flocks.

- Gulping green frog mating calls continue well into the summer. Meanwhile, bee-sized spring peepers, newly transformed from tadpoles, spread out over the land from small pools. Young wood frogs also emerge around the same time.

- Seldom-seen, though extremely numerous, redback salamanders lay eggs in cavities of rotted logs and guard them through the summer.

JULY

Early July

- Water lilies are in full bloom through much of summer, as is meadowsweet along lakeshores. In meadows and roadsides, dogbane, St. John's wort and blueweed also bloom through much of the season.

- With their first batch of young barely fledged, some songbirds, such as robins, swallows, kinglets, song sparrows and phoebes, nest again this month. Hares often mate again as well, and may even go in for thirds.

- While many other birds fall silent in the summer, red-eyed vireos continue to sing their seesaw solos ceaselessly from the treetops – even with their mouths full of food.

- Sunfish spawn near shorelines in early July. Like their better-respected bass cousins, fathers dutifully guard their nests (with no help from their long-gone mates) until the hatchlings are about a week old.

- Summer is the best time for viewing the Milky Way, when Earth looks towards the centre of the galaxy.

- Grasshoppers reach full adult size and become conspicuous in open areas.

Mid-July

- Raspberries, blueberries, serviceberries, red currents, red elderberries, gooseberries and snowberries all ripen this month, though a little later in more northern areas such as Temagami.

- Cedar waxwings nest as berry crops – their mainstay – mature. Goldfinches also wait till now, or even later, to build their nests, which are woven with the down of seeding thistles.

- Blooming alongside thistles in open areas through most of summer are fireweed, tall meadowrue, buttercup, chicory, yarrow and Queen Anne's lace. Jewelweed and Canada elderberry begin blooming on wetter ground.

- Yellow-rumped warblers start foraging in small bands with their newly fledged young.

- Adult least flycatchers begin heading south for Mexico, leaving their newly fledged offspring behind to make their own way south four or five weeks later. Southbound adult shorebirds also begin passing over from Arctic nesting grounds. Their young follow them weeks later, some not coming through until late into September.

- Young groundhogs disperse to dig their own burrows.

- Stark, white Indian pipe sprouts in the darkest reaches of the forest at midsummer.

- Butterfly numbers and variety peak in July, with some species emerging from cocoons, mating, laying eggs and dying all within a week, without having so much as a meal. White admirals, clouded sulphurs, mustard whites, great spangled fritillaries and ringlet butterflies are among the many.

- Seven or eight weeks after leafing out to capture the sunlight of the longest days, most trees start withdrawing nutrients from their leaves and storing them in the latter half of July. But basswood trees, summer favourites with porcupines, actually flower this month, attracting great numbers of bees.

- Armies of newly transformed, bug-sized toads hit the beaches and fan out overland on rainy, midsummer nights. Bullfrogs and green frogs metamorphose through the summer.

- Mink frogs are the last amphibians of the year to sound off, their night-time mating call reminiscent of two large sticks being struck together.

- Though the heat seems to burn off the worst of the blackfly scourge, deer flies relish languid summer days.

- Unique among Ontario's domed inhabitants, wood turtles leave the water in summer to roam the forest, scaring up worms by stomping on the ground.

Late July

- Bumblebees throng in riverside tangles of purple pickerelweed, while hummingbirds dip into red cardinal flowers. Later, the night-blooming yellow flowers of evening primrose attract large, hovering sphinx moths.

- Having arrived, mated and raised their young, all in little more than 2 months, northern waterthrushes are another of the first birds to begin leaving Ontario, flying all the way back to South America.

- Martens mate in July and August.

AUGUST

Early August

- Otters become a more common sight in August after mothers bring their young out of dens and they start swimming in family groups.

- More blue herons grace the shallows as young birds venture out on their first fishing trips.

- The first yellow-bellied flycatchers, Swainson's thrushes and yellow, Canada, Tennessee and black-and-white warblers usually start migrating south, as do sandpipers, killdeer and other local shorebirds.

- Little brown bats form swarms at caves and old mine shafts this month before mating and going into hibernation in September.

- Wolf howling becomes most common in August and September as cubs become more active and travel with the pack.

- Pink Joe-Pye weed, white wintergreen and wild mint flowers bloom through the month.

Mid-August

- The Perseid meteor shower, one of the year's two best, builds to a peak around the 11th, with up to 100 shooting stars visible an hour in clear, dark skies.

- Goldenrod, blooming in profusion in late-summer meadows, yields some of the richest honey bees can make. Butterflies, moths and many others are also attracted to the flowers. Blue bead lily berries, bunchberries and white doll's-eyes ripen around the same time, often lasting into September.

- Male crickets begin "chirping," hoping to attract mates with the sound made by rubbing their stiff wings together.

- Tiny yellow-spotted salamanders and leopard frogs emerge from their birth ponds and lakes.

- White River, reputedly Ontario's coldest town, usually gets its first frost in mid-August.

- Portents of cooler weather send the first restless blackburnian, bay-breasted and magnolia warblers barrelling south at mid-month, along with veeries, indigo buntings, alder and olive-sided flycatchers and Philadelphia vireos.

• As midge meals begin to thin out, swallows flock by the tens of thousands at Pembroke, at Kingston's Cataraqui marshes and at other communal roosting sites in mid-August shortly before flying south.

• With their unfledged young able to feed themselves, adult loons begin making daily flights to larger lakes to congregate, getting used to each other again before flocking south in fall.

• Chickadees reform in small flocks to forage together until spring.

Late August

• Ripening acorns and beech and hazel nuts provide a late-summer feast for bears, porcupines, chipmunks, squirrels, deer, raccoons, ruffed grouse, blue jays, wood ducks and nuthatches. Only in intermittent big-crop years do many acorns or beech nuts survive to germinate.

• Wild cherries ripening now and in early September attract an even greater variety of visitors, including flocks of evening grosbeaks and cedar waxwings. Dogwood, Canada elder and hobblebush berries also mature around the same time.

• Silhouetted swarms flying past the face of the moon suggest the vast numbers of songbirds now migrating south on cool, clear nights. Wood thrushes, Baltimore orioles, kingbirds, scarlet tanagers, whip-poor-wills, wood-pewees, great-crested flycatchers, catbirds, brown thrashers, black-billed cuckoos, cowbirds and chestnut-sided, blackpole, mourning, Wilson's, black-throated blue and black-throated green warblers share the spotlight.

• During the day, swifts and large flocks of nighthawks also head out, fishing insects from high in the sky as they migrate. Hummingbirds zip south by day much closer to the ground.

• Monarch butterflies and squadrons of green darner dragonflies wing south in late summer along with the birds.

• Most snakes hatch or are born live in late summer. Garter snake mothers stay close to their newborns for several days. Siblings, about 12 cm (5 in) long, stick together in groups of 20 to 40 for a few weeks.

• Red efts, metamorphosing from aquatic juvenile newts, take to the forest floor in August and September.

• Yellow jackets fan out and become bothersome around open food as their colonies break apart in late summer.

• The young of many animals, including fishers, foxes, skunks, weasels, flying squirrels and ravens, scatter from their parents' territories in late summer.

SEPTEMBER

Early September

- White and purple asters bloom amid the goldenrod, gradually succeeding it to dominate autumn meadows. Other late bloomers include fringed gentian and lady's tresses.

- With about 50 percent of their nutrients withdrawn by early September, sugar maple leaves can no longer produce chlorophyll and start to change colour.

- After a summer of relative ease, beavers note the days growing shorter and start felling more trees for winter food stores beneath the ice. Red squirrels also quicken the pace of stockpiling clipped pine cones.

- Cold, late-summer nights send most bats into hibernation. Hoary and red bats, however, fly south in September.

- Fall migration usually peaks on early-September cold fronts, with flickers, ovenbirds, redstarts, pine, palm and Nashville warblers swelling the numbers of other late-summer migrants. Waves of up to 2 million songbirds have been detected by radar at night.

- Migrating by day, sharp-shinned, broad-winged and Cooper's hawks, ospreys, harriers and kestrels stream south throughout September.

- Gray jays come out of their spruce tree haunts in September to top up winter food caches, tamely entering human company and accepting anything edible on offer.

- Like other winter hoarders, nuthatches spend fall building up their supplies, hiding seeds and nuts in bark furrows and covering them with lichens.

- Spider romance, budding around this time of year, is perhaps the most bittersweet of all. With bug food getting scarce, a female has few qualms about killing her mate to gain his protein for nourishing her eggs, which will hatch in spring.

Mid-September

- Common yellowthroats become less common, as do rose-breasted grosbeaks, hermit thrushes, yellow-bellied sapsuckers, winter wrens, grackles and red-eyed, solitary and warbling vireos as they leave for warmer climes in mid-September. Robins forage in large flocks before flying south as well.

- Turkey vultures, red-tailed and red-shouldered hawks circle upwards on rising thermals as they join the raptor migration on fresh, clear days. Small numbers of scattered bald eagles pass over from points north as well.

• At the base of beech trees, spindly, reddish-brown beechdrops bloom in September. The plant is a parasite on the roots of the trees and needs no chlorophyll to survive.

• Late-summer and early-autumn rains can transform a forest overnight into a magic kingdom of suddenly fully sprouted mushrooms.

• On rainy nights in September or early October, redback salamanders seek each other out on the forest floor to mate, while pencil-thin red-belly snakes leave their meadow hunting grounds and slither into the woods to find rocks or logs to bed down beneath for the winter.

• The year's first killing frost usually comes in mid- or late September in many locations, withering bracken ferns, jewelweed and many other tender plants and turning them brown. Jack Frost, however, is not responsible for the changing colours of the trees.

Late September

• Fall colours peak on the Shield in late September and early October, with red and sugar maples providing the most brilliant reds, yellows and oranges.

• Waves of Canada geese V-formations are heaviest in early autumn. Pintails and blue-winged and green-winged teal pass through with them from northern nesting grounds. The waterfowl migrations also suck up local wood ducks and mallards.

• White-throated, chipping, swamp, savannah and vesper sparrows figure prominently amongst night migrants into early October. They're accompanied by yellow-rumped warblers, ruby- and golden-crowned kinglets, migrant blue jays, phoebes, juncos, wood-cocks, snipes, meadowlarks and the last of many early-migrating warblers.

• Adult goldfinches lie low in groups while moulting in fall. Juveniles form their own flocks.

• The height of the moose rut comes in late September or early October, with sex-crazed bulls eating little and losing up to 70 kg (150 lb) during their single-minded three-week prowl for as many females as will have them.

• When September's sun can no longer warm their blood enough to power efficient digestion, turtles plunge into the mud of lake and marsh bottoms for a long winter sleep. Snapping turtle hatchlings also dig out from sandy nest sites and scurry to the water. Late-hatching painted turtles stay put in subterranean nests, living off yolk sacs and hibernating till spring.

• Sugar, striped and mountain maple keys, as well as little white birch seeds, rain down through the fall, many being eaten by evening grosbeaks, chickadees, ruffed grouse and goldfinches, or stockpiled by deer mice and chipmunks for winter.

OCTOBER

Early October

- Song sparrows, migrant brown creepers, bluebirds and Lincoln's sparrows accompany the last common yellowthroats, Nashville warblers, solitary vireos and Swainson's thrushes out of central Ontario. Rough-legged hawks, horned larks, dunlins, white-crowned, tree and fox sparrows also pass through from nesting grounds near the timber line and beyond.

- Thousands of migrating loons and cormorants gather on Lake Couchiching and Lake Simcoe. Many kinds of migrating ducks also throng there through November.

- Ruffed grouse young leave their mothers and disperse to new territories in the "fall shuffle."

- Some butterflies, such as mourning cloaks, clouded sulphurs and commas, continue to feed on asters and other late flowers in October before going into hibernation.

- Groundhogs begin hibernating in early autumn, as do woodland jumping mice, which sleep for eight months in their burrows.

- Low in sugars, but mould-resistant, wintergreen berries, partridgeberries and winterberries persist into or even past winter, providing food for mice and birds.

- Balsam fir cones fall apart in autumn, dropping seeds to the ground. Seeds also fall from tiny hemlock and tamarack cones throughout fall and winter.

- Lakes begin to "turn over" in early autumn as the temperature of the top layer drops to that of the bottom layer and they circulate together again as one body, making for bigger waves on windy days than in the summer.

- Cooling waters bring lake trout and whitefish from their cold summer retreats in the deep to spawn in rocky shallows on October nights. Brook trout also spawn in gravel or sandy stream headwaters from late September to November.

Mid-October

- Though maple colours peak earlier, the more muted ambers of birch and trembling aspen, and oak's rusty reds, are prominent through mid- to late October. Tamaracks, around the edges of bogs and swamps, also turn bright gold before discarding all of their needles – Ontario's only coniferous tree to do so.

- Most evergreens keep their needles or leaves from freezing through "winter hardening"; heavy flows of resin increase the sugar content of plant cells, lowering their freezing point.

Individual pine needles tend to last three to five years before falling from the branch, usually in autumn. Spruce needles last even longer.

Bumblebee queens, protected by woolly coats, are among the last insects left buzzing about, tapping dregs of nectar from late asters before hibernating underground for winter. Like hornet and paper wasp queens, they go to sleep pregnant and start new colonies in spring.

By mid-October most frogs are sleeping in the watery depths and toads have buried themselves in the earth. Red-spotted newts crawl out of ponds and marshy lakes to hibernate on land as well. Garter snakes go into hibernation in rock piles and crevices around the same time, often in groups.

Bears den up under fallen trees, roots or rock ledges between late September and early November.

Porcupine mating season comes in October. Male porkies sometimes thrash it out in courtship duels, leaving hundreds of quills in their wake.

Red-winged blackbirds join with the last yellow-rumped warblers, ruby-crowned kinglets and juncos heading out of the Shield. The remaining sharp-shinned and red-shouldered hawks usually leave around now.

Some saw-whet owls migrate south, while others tough winter out on the Shield.

Snow buntings from the north begin passing through.

Late October

• The Orionid meteor shower peaks around the 21st, with up to 24 meteors visible an hour.

• Most of the last white-throated sparrows, hermit thrushes, winter wrens and turkey vultures leave central Ontario. Meanwhile, bufflehead and ring-necked ducks from the north start passing through. Some northern shrikes also fly in from the Hudson Bay hinterlands to spend the winter hunting small birds and mice on the southern Shield.

• Kingfishers become scarce, but where the fishing is good some stay until freeze-over.

• Winter's white veil spreads south over the boreal forest, usually reaching Wawa and Kapuskasing with at least 2.5 cm (1 in) of snow cover by the end of the month.

• Hares and weasels don their white winter coats between mid-October and mid-November. Hares and lynx also grow very thick fur beneath their paws, which keeps them aloft on the snow. Ruffed grouse, too, put on snowshoes for winter, growing comblike appendages on the sides of their toes that double the surface area of their feet.

NOVEMBER

Early November

- Though many leave much earlier, the last die-hard great blue herons finally retreat from the leading edge of winter. Around the same time, grackles, crows, robins and golden-crowned kinglets are normally among the last migrant songbirds to flitter out of the Shield.

- During the white-tailed deer rut, bucks become aggressive, sometimes going antler-to-antler with their rivals in the quest to mate this month.

Mid-November

- By around the 10th, a blanket of at least 2.5 cm (1 in) of snow usually covers the Algonquin and Haliburton highlands, as well as most areas north of Sault Ste. Marie and North Bay.

- A solid week of freezing temperatures prompts porcupines to find daytime winter dens, usually in rock-outcrop crevices at least 3 m (10 ft) deep. They still spend nights eating in the trees above.

- Hawthorn fruits, fuzzy sumac seed clusters and reddish-orange mountain ash berries remain on shrubby trees through much of the winter, helping to feed the season's birds, especially cedar waxwings, purple finches and evening grosbeaks. Flocks of wandering Bohemian waxwings from the west often appear in late fall and winter when there's a bumper crop of mountain ash berries.

- Having only recently learned to fly, young loons abandon frigid Shield lakes, considerably later than their parents, now fishing on the Atlantic seaboard. The last goldeneye ducks also leave.

Late November

• Most of central Ontario is by now usually covered with at least 2.5 cm (1 in) of snow.

• Mice and voles welcome the snow, which provides an insulating layer over frozen ground; if temperatures drop below −20°C (−4°F) without snow, many freeze to death. But when deep snow forms a crusty top, the rodents are forced to clear ventilation shafts up from their tunnels, giving owls and other predators a better chance of finding them.

• Cyclical population crashes of voles and lemmings in the Arctic send snowy owls and other northern raptors south into central Ontario in late fall or winter. Unlike most other owls, snowies will hunt by day, being accustomed to the midnight sun of the Arctic summer.

• Black ducks and common and hooded mergansers stick it out on Shield lakes the longest, the last usually flying out now or in early December.

• Most lakes north of Wawa and Haileybury have usually frozen over by the end of the month.

• Though the natural world may now be silent and still, the forces of life are packed into every bud and seed, egg and dormant creature, ready to burst out and reproduce again when this end of the Earth tilts just a few degrees back towards the sun.

Federation of Ontario Naturalists
and Ontario Field Ornithologists

Field Checklist
of Ontario Birds
1997

Black-and-white Warbler / Michael King

This list comprises all of the bird species (467) that have been recorded in the Province of Ontario, on the basis of specimens, photographs, recordings or documented sight records accepted by the Ontario Bird Records Committee (OBRC) to March 1997. Classification and nomenclature follow the American Ornithologists' Union *Check-list of North American Birds* (6th ed.1983), and its supplements.

LEGEND

Ontario is divided into north and south regions at the 47°N.

* Breeding species.

N Species recorded in North.

(N) Indicates the OBRC requests documentation when the species is recorded in the region.

S Species recorded in South.

(S) Indicates the OBRC requests documentation when the species is recorded in the region.

FEDERATION OF
Ontario Naturalists   **OFO**

LOONS AND GREBES
* Red-throated Loon N/S
* Pacific Loon N/(S)
* Common Loon N/S
Yellow-billed Loon (S)
* Pied-billed Grebe N/S
* Horned Grebe N/S
* Red-necked Grebe N/S
* Eared Grebe (N)/S
Western Grebe (N)/(S)

TUBENOSES
Northern Fulmar (N)/(S)
Black-capped Petrel (S)
Audubon's Shearwater (S)
Wilson's Storm-Petrel (S)
Leach's Storm-Petrel (N)/(S)
Band-rumped Storm-Petrel (S)

GANNETS, PELICANS & CORMORANTS
Northern Gannet (N)/(S)
* American White Pelican N/S
Brown Pelican (N)/(S)
Great Cormorant (S)
* Double-crested Cormorant N/S
Anhinga (S)
Magnificent Frigatebird (S)

HERONS, STORKS & IBISES
* American Bittern N/S
* Least Bittern (N)/S

* Great Blue Heron N/S
* Great Egret (N)/S
* Snowy Egret (N)/(S)
Little Blue Heron (N)/(S)
Tricolored Heron (N)/(S)
* Cattle Egret (N)/S
* Green Heron (N)/S
* Black-crowned Night-Heron (N)/S
Yellow-crowned Night-Heron (S)
White Ibis (S)
Glossy Ibis (S)
White-faced Ibis (S)
Wood Stork (S)

SWANS, GEESE & DUCKS
Fulvous Whistling-Duck (S)
Black-bellied Whistling-Duck (S)
* Tundra Swan N/S
Trumpeter Swan (S)
* Mute Swan (N)/S
Greater White-fronted Goose N/(S)
* Snow Goose N/S
* Ross's Goose N/(S)
Brant N/S
* Canada Goose N/S
* Wood Duck N/S
* Green-winged Teal N/S
* American Black Duck N/S
* Mallard N/S
* Northern Pintail N/S
Garganey (N)/(S)
* Blue-winged Teal N/S
* Cinnamon Teal (N)/(S)
* Northern Shoveler N/S
* Gadwall N/S
Eurasian Wigeon (N)/(S)
* American Wigeon N/S
* Canvasback N/S
* Redhead N/S
* Ring-necked Duck N/S
Tufted Duck (N)/(S)
* Greater Scaup N/S
* Lesser Scaup N/S
* Common Eider N/(S)
* King Eider N/S
Harlequin Duck (N)/S
* Oldsquaw N/S
Black Scoter N/S
* Surf Scoter N/S
* White-winged Scoter N/S
* Common Goldeneye N/S
Barrow's Goldeneye (N)/S
* Bufflehead N/S
Smew (S)
* Hooded Merganser N/S
* Common Merganser N/S
* Red-breasted Merganser N/S
* Ruddy Duck N/S

VULTURES, HAWKS, EAGLES & FALCONS
Black Vulture (N)/(S)
* Turkey Vulture N/S
* Osprey N/S
Swallow-tailed Kite (N)/(S)
Mississippi Kite (S)
* Bald Eagle N/S
* Northern Harrier N/S
* Sharp-shinned Hawk N/S
* Cooper's Hawk N/S

* Northern Goshawk N/S
* Red-shouldered Hawk N/S
* Broad-winged Hawk N/S
  Swainson's Hawk (N)/(S)
* Red-tailed Hawk N/S
  Ferruginous Hawk (S)
* Rough-legged Hawk N/S
* Golden Eagle N/S
  Crested Caracara (N)/(S)
* American Kestrel N/S
* Merlin N/S
* Peregrine Falcon N/S
  Gyrfalcon N/S
  Prairie Falcon (S)

GROUSE & TURKEYS
* Gray Partridge N/S
* Ring-necked Pheasant N/S
* Spruce Grouse N/S
* Willow Ptarmigan N/(S)
  Rock Ptarmigan N
* Ruffed Grouse N/S
* Greater Prairie-Chicken (N)/(S)
* Sharp-tailed Grouse N/S
* Wild Turkey S
* Northern Bobwhite S

RAILS AND CRANES
* Yellow Rail N/S
  Black Rail (S)
* King Rail S
* Virginia Rail N/S
* Sora N/S
  Purple Gallinule (N)/(S)
* Common Moorhen (N)/S
* American Coot N/S
* Sandhill Crane N/S
  Whooping Crane (S)

SHOREBIRDS
  Black-bellied Plover N/S
* American Golden-Plover N/S
  Mongolian Plover (S)
  Snowy Plover (S)
  Wilson's Plover (S)
* Semipalmated Plover N/S
* Piping Plover N/(S)
* Killdeer N/S
  American Oystercatcher (S)
  Black-necked Stilt (N)/(S)
* American Avocet (N)/(S)
* Greater Yellowlegs N/S
* Lesser Yellowlegs N/S
  Spotted Redshank (S)
* Solitary Sandpiper N/S
  Willet (N)/S
  Wandering Tattler (S)
* Spotted Sandpiper N/S
* Upland Sandpiper N/S
  Eskimo Curlew (N)/(S)
* Whimbrel N/S
  Slender-billed Curlew (S)
  Long-billed Curlew (S)
  Black-tailed Godwit (S)
* Hudsonian Godwit N/S
* Marbled Godwit N/S
  Ruddy Turnstone N/S
  Red Knot N/S
  Sanderling N/S
* Semipalmated Sandpiper N/S
  Western Sandpiper (N)/S

  Little Stint (N)/(S)
* Least Sandpiper N/S
  White-rumped Sandpiper N/S
  Baird's Sandpiper N/S
* Pectoral Sandpiper N/S
  Sharp-tailed Sandpiper (S)
  Purple Sandpiper N/S
* Dunlin N/S
  Curlew Sandpiper (N)/(S)
* Stilt Sandpiper N/S
  Buff-breasted Sandpiper N/S
  Ruff (N)/S
* Short-billed Dowitcher N/S
  Long-billed Dowitcher N/S
* Common Snipe N/S
* American Woodcock N/S
* Wilson's Phalarope N/S
* Red-necked Phalarope N/S
  Red Phalarope N/S

**JAEGERS, GULLS,
TERNS & SKIMMERS**
  Pomarine Jaeger (N)/S
* Parasitic Jaeger N/S
  Long-tailed Jaeger N/(S)
  Laughing Gull (N)/S
  Franklin's Gull N/S
* Little Gull N/S
  Black-headed Gull (N)/S
* Bonaparte's Gull N/S
  Mew Gull (S)
* Ring-billed Gull N/S
* California Gull (N)/(S)
* Herring Gull N/S
  Thayer's Gull N/S
  Iceland Gull N/S
  Lesser Black-backed Gull (N)/S
  Slaty-backed Gull (S)
  Glaucous Gull N/S
* Great Black-backed Gull N/S
  Black-legged Kittiwake (N)/S
  Ross's Gull (N)/(S)
  Sabine's Gull N/S
  Ivory Gull (N)/(S)
* Caspian Tern N/S
  Royal Tern (S)
  Sandwich Tern (S)
* Common Tern N/S
* Arctic Tern N/(S)
* Forster's Tern N/S
  Least Tern (S)
  Sooty Tern (S)
  White-winged Tern (S)
* Black Tern N/S
  Black Skimmer (N)/(S)

ALCIDS
  Dovekie (S)
  Thick-billed Murre (S)
  Razorbill (S)
* Black Guillemot N/(S)
  Marbled Murrelet (S)
  Ancient Murrelet (S)
  Atlantic Puffin (N)/(S)

PIGEONS & DOVES
* Rock Dove N/S
  Band-tailed Pigeon (N)/(S)
  White-winged Dove (N)/(S)
* Mourning Dove N/S
* Passenger Pigeon (Extinct)

Inca Dove (N)

Common Ground-Dove (N)

CUCKOOS & ANIS

* Black-billed Cuckoo N/S

* Yellow-billed Cuckoo N/S

Groove-billed Ani (N)/(S)

OWLS

* Barn Owl (N)/(S)

* Eastern Screech-Owl (N)/(S)

* Great Horned Owl N/S

Snowy Owl N/S

* Northern Hawk Owl N/S

Burrowing Owl (N)/(S)

* Barred Owl N/S

* Great Gray Owl N/S

* Long-eared Owl N/S

* Short-eared Owl N/S

* Boreal Owl N/S

* Northern Saw-whet Owl N/S

NIGHTJARS

Lesser Nighthawk (S)

* Common Nighthawk N/S

Common Poorwill (N)

* Chuck-will's-widow (S)

* Whip-poor-will N/S

SWIFTS & HUMMINGBIRDS

* Chimney Swift N/S

Green Violet-ear (N)

Broad-billed Hummingbird (S)

* Ruby-throated Hummingbird N/S

Black-chinned Hummingbird (S)

Rufous Hummingbird (N)/(S)

KINGFISHERS

* Belted Kingfisher N/S

WOODPECKERS

Lewis's Woodpecker (N)/(S)

* Red-headed Woodpecker N/S

* Red-bellied Woodpecker (N)/S

* Yellow-bellied Sapsucker N/S

* Downy Woodpecker N/S

* Hairy Woodpecker N/S

* Three-toed Woodpecker N/S

* Black-backed Woodpecker N/S

* Northern Flicker N/S

* Pileated Woodpecker N/S

TYRANT FLYCATCHERS

* Olive-sided Flycatcher N/S

Western Wood-Pewee (N)

* Eastern Wood-Pewee N/S

* Yellow-bellied Flycatcher N/S

* Acadian Flycatcher S

* Alder Flycatcher N/S

* Willow Flycatcher (N)/S

* Least Flycatcher N/S

Dusky Flycatcher (N)

Gray Flycatcher (S)

* Eastern Phoebe N/S

Say's Phoebe (N)/(S)

Vermilion Flycatcher (S)

Ash-throated Flycatcher (S)

* Great Crested Flycatcher N/S

Sulphur-bellied Flycatcher (S)

Variegated Flycatcher (S)

Cassin's Kingbird (S)

* Western Kingbird (N)/(S)

* Eastern Kingbird N/S

Gray Kingbird (S)

Scissor-tailed Flycatcher (N)/(S)

Fork-tailed Flycatcher (N)/(S)

LARKS, MARTINS & SWALLOWS

* Horned Lark N/S

* Purple Martin N/S

* Tree Swallow N/S

Violet-green Swallow (N)

* Northern Rough-winged Swallow N/S

* Bank Swallow N/S

* Cliff Swallow N/S

Cave Swallow (S)

* Barn Swallow N/S

JAYS, MAGPIES & CROWS

* Gray Jay N/S

* Blue Jay N/S

Clark's Nutcracker (N)

* Black-billed Magpie N/(S)

Eurasian Jackdaw (S)

* American Crow N/S

Fish Crow (S)

* Common Raven N/S

TITMICE, NUTHATCHES & CREEPERS

* Black-capped Chickadee N/S

Carolina Chickadee (S)

* Boreal Chickadee N/S

* Tufted Titmouse S

* Red-breasted Nuthatch N/S

* White-breasted Nuthatch N/S

* Brown Creeper N/S

WRENS

Rock Wren (N)/(S)

* Carolina Wren (N)/S

* Bewick's Wren (S)

* House Wren N/S

* Winter Wren N/S

* Sedge Wren N/S

* Marsh Wren N/S

KINGLETS, GNATCATCHERS, THRUSHES & MIMIDS

* Golden-crowned Kinglet N/S

* Ruby-crowned Kinglet N/S

* Blue-gray Gnatcatcher (N)/S

Siberian Rubythroat (S)

Northern Wheatear (N)/(S)

* Eastern Bluebird N/S

Mountain Bluebird (N)/(S)

Townsend's Solitaire (N)/(S)

* Veery N/S

* Gray-cheeked Thrush N/S

Bicknell's Thrush (S)

* Swainson's Thrush N/S

* Hermit Thrush N/S

* Wood Thrush N/S

Eurasian Blackbird (S)

Fieldfare (S)

* American Robin N/S

Varied Thrush (N)/S

* Gray Catbird N/S

* Northern Mockingbird N/S

Sage Thrasher (N)/(S)

* Brown Thrasher N/S

PIPITS, WAXWINGS, SHRIKES & STARLINGS

* American Pipit N/S

Sprague's Pipit (N)

* Bohemian Waxwing N/S

* Cedar Waxwing N/S

Phainopepla (S)

* Northern Shrike N/S
* Loggerhead Shrike (N)/S
* European Starling N/S

VIREOS
* White-eyed Vireo (N)/S
  Bell's Vireo (S)
  Black-capped Vireo (S)
* Solitary Vireo N/S
* Yellow-throated Vireo N/S
* Warbling Vireo N/S
* Philadelphia Vireo N/S
* Red-eyed Vireo N/S

WOOD WARBLERS
* Blue-winged Warbler (N)/S
* Golden-winged Warbler N/S
* Tennessee Warbler N/S
* Orange-crowned Warbler N/S
* Nashville Warbler N/S
  Virginia's Warbler (S)
* Northern Parula N/S
* Yellow Warbler N/S
* Chestnut-sided Warbler N/S
* Magnolia Warbler N/S
* Cape May Warbler N/S
* Black-throated Blue Warbler N/S
* Yellow-rumped Warbler N/S
  Black-throated Gray Warbler (S)
  Townsend's Warbler (S)
  Hermit Warbler (S)
* Black-throated Green Warbler N/S
* Blackburnian Warbler N/S
  Yellow-throated Warbler (N)/S
* Pine Warbler N/S
* Kirtland's Warbler (N)/(S)
* Prairie Warbler (N)/S
* Palm Warbler N/S
* Bay-breasted Warbler N/S
* Blackpoll Warbler N/S
* Cerulean Warbler S
* Black-and-white Warbler N/S
* American Redstart N/S
* Prothonotary Warbler (N)/S
  Worm-eating Warbler S
  Swainson's Warbler (S)
* Ovenbird N/S
* Northern Waterthrush N/S
* Louisiana Waterthrush S
  Kentucky Warbler S
* Connecticut Warbler N/S
* Mourning Warbler N/S
  MacGillivray's Warbler (S)
* Common Yellowthroat N/S
* Hooded Warbler (N)/S
* Wilson's Warbler N/S
* Canada Warbler N/S
  Painted Redstart (S)
* Yellow-breasted Chat (N)/S

TANAGERS
  Summer Tanager (N)/S
* Scarlet Tanager N/S
  Western Tanager (N)/(S)

GROSBEAKS, BUNTINGS & SPARROWS
* Northern Cardinal (N)/S
* Rose-breasted Grosbeak N/S
  Black-headed Grosbeak (N)/(S)
  Blue Grosbeak (N)/(S)
  Lazuli Bunting (N)/(S)
* Indigo Bunting N/S

  Varied Bunting (S)
  Painted Bunting (N)/(S)
* Dickcissel (N)/S
  Green-tailed Towhee (S)
* Eastern Towhee (N)/S
  Spotted Towhee (N)/(S)
  Bachman's Sparrow (S)
  Cassin's Sparrow (N)/(S)
* American Tree Sparrow N/S
* Chipping Sparrow N/S
* Clay-colored Sparrow N/S
* Field Sparrow (N)/S
* Vesper Sparrow N/S
* Lark Sparrow (N)/S
  Black-throated Sparrow (N)
  Lark Bunting (N)/(S)
* Savannah Sparrow N/S
* Grasshopper Sparrow (N)/S
* Henslow's Sparrow (S)
* Le Conte's Sparrow N/S
* Nelson's Sharp-tailed Sparrow N/S
* Fox Sparrow N/S
* Song Sparrow N/S
* Lincoln's Sparrow N/S
* Swamp Sparrow N/S
* White-throated Sparrow N/S
  Golden-crowned Sparrow (N)/(S)
* White-crowned Sparrow N/S
* Harris's Sparrow N/(S)
* Dark-eyed Junco N/S
* Lapland Longspur N/S
* Smith's Longspur N/(S)
  Chestnut-collared Longspur (N)/(S)
* Snow Bunting N/S

MEADOWLARKS, BLACKBIRDS & ORIOLES
* Bobolink N/S
* Red-winged Blackbird N/S
* Eastern Meadowlark N/S
* Western Meadowlark N/S
* Yellow-headed Blackbird N/S
* Rusty Blackbird N/S
* Brewer's Blackbird N/S
  Great-tailed Grackle (N)/(S)
* Common Grackle N/S
* Brown-headed Cowbird N/S
* Orchard Oriole (N)/S
  Hooded Oriole (S)
* Baltimore Oriole N/S
  Bullock's Oriole (N)/(S)
  Scott's Oriole (N)

FINCHES
  Brambling (N)/(S)
  Gray-crowned Rosy-Finch (N)
* Pine Grosbeak N/S
* Purple Finch N/S
  Cassin's Finch (S)
* House Finch N/S
* Red Crossbill N/S
* White-winged Crossbill N/S
* Common Redpoll N/S
  Hoary Redpoll N/S
* Pine Siskin N/S
  Lesser Goldfinch (S)
* American Goldfinch N/S
* Evening Grosbeak N/S

OLD WORLD SPARROWS
* House Sparrow N/S
  Eurasian Tree Sparrow (S)

Field Checklist of Reptiles and Amphibians

(1988)

This list comprises all of the herpetofauna (reptiles and amphibians) species and subspecies (57) which have been recorded in the province of Ontario as of March 1988, on the basis of material evidence.

The classification and nomenclature follow 'Introduction to Canadian Amphibians and Reptiles' (Francis R. Cook, 1984, National Museum of Canada).

LOCALITY				
TIME/DATE				
MONTH				
YEAR				
OBSERVER				

LEGEND
e — protected by regulations of the Endangered Species Act, R.S.O. 1980
p — protected by regulations of the Game and Fish Act, R.S.O. 1980
i — there is good evidence the species may not be native to Ontario
n — no verified records during the past forty (40) years

REPTILES (30)

Turtles (10)

☐☐☐ Common Snapping Turtle
Chelydra serpentina

☐☐☐ Stinkpot [p]
Sternotherus odoratus

☐☐☐ Midland Painted Turtle [p]
Chrysemys picta marginata

☐☐☐ Western Painted Turtle [p]
Chrysemys picta belli

☐☐☐ Map Turtle [p]
Graptemys geographica

☐☐☐ Blanding's Turtle [p]
Emydoidea blandingi

☐☐☐ Wood Turtle [p]
Clemmys insculpta

☐☐☐ Spotted Turtle [p]
Clemmys guttata

☐☐☐ Eastern Box Turtle [i]
Terrapene carolina

☐☐☐ Spiny Softshell [p]
Trionyx spiniferus

Lizards (1)

☐☐☐ Five-lined Skink
Eumeces fasciatus

Snakes (19)

☐☐☐ Eastern Garter Snake
Thamnophis sirtalis sirtalis

☐☐☐ Red-sided Garter Snake
Thamnophis sartalis parietalis

☐☐☐ Northern Ribbon Snake
Thamnophis sauritus septentrionalis

☐☐☐ Butler's Garter Snake
Thamnophis butleri

☐☐☐ Northern Water Snake [p]
Nerodia sipedon sipedon

☐☐☐ Lake Erie Water Snake [ep]
Nerodia sipedon insularum

☐☐☐ Queen Snake [p]
Regina septemvittata

☐☐☐ Redbelly Snake
Storeria occipitomaculata

☐☐☐ Northern Brown Snake
Storeria dekayi dekayi

☐☐☐ Midland Brown Snake
Storeria dekayi wrightorum

☐☐☐ Eastern Smooth Green Snake
Opheodrys vernalis vernalis

☐☐☐ Northern Ringneck Snake
Diadophis punctatus edwardsi

☐☐☐ Eastern Hognose Snake [p]
Heterodon platyrhinos

☐☐☐ Black Rat Snake [p]
Elaphe obsoleta obsoleta

☐☐☐ Eastern Fox Snake [p]
Elaphe vulpina gloydi

☐☐☐ Eastern Milk Snake
Lampropeltis triangulum triangulum

☐☐☐ Blue Racer [ep]
Coluber constrictor foxi

☐☐☐ Eastern Massasauga
Sistrurus catenatus catenatus

☐☐☐ Timber Rattlesnake [epn]
Crotalus horridus

AMPHIBIANS (27)

Salamanders (14)

☐☐☐ Mudpuppy
Necturus maculosus

☐☐☐ Red-spotted Newt
Notophthalmus viridescens viridescens

☐☐☐ Central Newt
Notophthalmus viridescens louisianensis

☐☐☐ Jefferson Salamander Complex
Blue-Spotted Salamander
Ambystoma laterale

☐☐☐ Jefferson Salamander
Ambystoma jeffersonianum

☐☐☐ Smallmouth Salamander
Ambystoma texanum

☐☐☐ Yellow-spotted Salamander
Ambystoma maculatum

☐☐☐ Eastern Tiger Salamander [n]
Ambystoma tigrinum tigrinum

☐☐☐ Dusky Salamander
Desmognathus fuscus

☐☐☐ Two-lined Salamander
Eurycea bislineata

☐☐☐ Spring Salamander [n]
Gyrinophilus porphyriticus

☐☐☐ Four-toed Salamander
Hemidactylium scutatum

☐☐☐ Eastern Redback Salamander
Plethodon cinereus

☐☐☐ Red Salamander [in]
Pseudotriton ruber

Frogs and Toads (13)

☐☐☐ American Toad
Bufo americanus

☐☐☐ Fowler's Toad
Bufo woodhousei fowleri

☐☐☐ Spring Peeper
Hyla crucifer

☐☐☐ Tetraploid Gray Treefrog
Hyla versicolor

☐☐☐ Midland Chorus Frog
Pseudacris triseriata triseriata

☐☐☐ Boreal Chorus Frog
Pseudacris triseriata maculata

☐☐☐ Blanchard's Cricket Frog
Acris crepitans blanchardi

☐☐☐ Wood Frog
Rana sylvatica

☐☐☐ Northern Leopard Frog
Rana pipiens

☐☐☐ Pickerel Frog
Rana palustris

☐☐☐ Green Frog
Rana clamitans melanota

☐☐☐ Mink Frog
Rana septentrionalis

☐☐☐ Bullfrog [p]
Rana catesbeiana

FEDERATION OF ONTARIO NATURALISTS

Field Checklist of Ontario Mammals

(1993)

This list comprises all 82 wild mammal species recorded in the province of Ontario as of January 1, 1993.

The classification and nomenclature follow the Atlas of the Mammals of Ontario species list.

LOCALITY			
TIME/DATE			
MONTH			
YEAR			
OBSERVER			

LEGEND

(+) — Indicates a Provincial Priority Species for which complete documentation is requested.

(i) — Indicates a mammal that has been introduced to Ontario.

MARSUPIALS (1)
Virginia Opossum
Didelphis virginiana

INSECTIVORES (10)
Black-backed Shrew
Sorex arcticus
Common Shrew
Sorex cinereus
Smoky Shrew
Sorex fumeus
Pygmy Shrew (+)
Sorex hoyi
Water Shrew
Sorex palustris
Northern Short-tailed Shrew
Blarina brevicauda
Least Shrew (+)
Cryptotis parva
Hairy-tailed Mole
Parascalops breweri
Eastern Mole (+)
Scalopus aquaticus
Star-nosed Mole
Condylura cristata

BATS (9)
Eastern Small-footed Bat (+)
Myotis leibii
Little Brown Bat
Myotis lucifugus
Northern Long-eared Bat (+)
Myotis septentrionalis
Silver-haired Bat (+)
Lasionycteris noctivagans
Eastern Pipistrelle (+)
Pipistrellus subflavus
Big Brown Bat
Eptesicus fuscus
Eastern Red Bat (+)
Lasiurus borealis

Hoary Bat (+)
Lasiurus cinereus
Evening Bat (+)
Nycticeius humeralis

RABBITS AND HARES (4)
Eastern Cottontail
Sylvilagus floridanus
Snowshoe Hare
Lepus americanus
European Hare (i)
Lepus europaeus
White-tailed Jackrabbit (+)
Lepus townsendii

RODENTS (25)
Squirrels (9)
Least Chipmunk
Tamias minimus
Eastern Chipmunk
Tamias striatus
Woodchuck
Mormota monax
Franklin's Ground Squirrel (+)
Spermophilus franklinii
Gray Squirrel
Sciurus carolinensis
Fox Squirrel (i)
Sciurus niger
Red Squirrel
Tamiasciurus hudsonicus
Northern Flying Squirrel
Glaucomys sabrinus
Southern Flying Squirrel (+)
Glaucomys volans

Beavers (1)
Beaver
Castor canadensis

New World Mice and Voles (10)
White-footed Mouse
Peromyscus leucopus
Deer Mouse
Peromyscus maniculatus
Southern Red-backed Vole
Clethrionomys gapperi
Heath Vole (+)
Phenacomys intermedius
Rock Vole (+)
Microtus chrotorrhinus
Meadow Vole
Microtus pennsylvanicus
Woodland Vole (+)
Pitymys pinetorum
Muskrat
Ondatra zibethicus
Northern Bog Lemming (+)
Synaptomys borealis
Southern Bog Lemming (+)
Synaptomys cooperi

Old World Rats and Mice (2)
Norway Rat (i)
Rattus norvegicus
House Mouse (i)
Mus musculus

Jumping Mice (2)
Meadow Jumping Mouse
Zapus hudsonius
Woodland Jumping Mouse
Napaeozapus insignis

Porcupines (1)
Porcupine
Erethizon dorsatum

WHALES (3)
Beluga (+)
Delphinapterus leucas
Narwhal (+)
Monodon monoceros

Minke Whale (+)
Balaenoptera acutorostrata

CARNIVORES (21)
Wolves and Foxes (5)
Coyote
Canis latrans
Gray Wolf
Canis lupus
Arctic Fox (+)
Alopex lagopus
Red Fox
Vulpes vulpes
Gray Fox (+)
Urocyon cinereoargenteus

Bears and Raccoons (3)
Black Bear
Ursus americanus
Polar Bear (+)
Ursus maritimus
Raccoon
Procyon lotor

Mustelids (10)
Marten
Martes americana
Fisher
Martes pennanti
Ermine
Mustela erminea
Long-tailed Weasel
Mustela frenata
Least Weasel (+)
Mustela nivalis
Mink
Mustela vison
Wolverine (+)
Gulo gulo
Badger (+)
Taxidea taxus
Striped Skunk
Mephitis mephitis
River Otter
Lontra canadensis

Cats (3)
Cougar (+)
Felis concolor
Canada Lynx
Lynx canadensis
Bobcat (+)
Lynx rufus

SEALS (4)
Walrus (+)
Odobenus rosmarus
Ringed Seal (+)
Phoca hispida
Harbor Seal (+)
Phoca vitulina
Bearded Seal (+)
Erignathus barbatus

DEER (4)
Wapiti (i+)
Cervus elaphus
White-tailed Deer
Odocoileus virginianus
Moose
Alces alces
Caribou (+)
Rangifer tarandus

BISON (1)
Bison (i+)
Bison bison

Recommended Reading

The following list is an updated version of the one appearing in *Up North*.

The Best of the Raven (*The Friends of Algonquin Park*), by *Dan Strickland, is a rich compilation of 150 insightful natural history essays from 30 years of Algonquin Park's popular newsletter*, The Raven.

Familiar Amphibians and Reptiles of Ontario (*Natural History/Natural Heritage*), by *Bob Johnson, provides good accounts of all the province's frogs, salamanders, turtles and snakes, along with illustrations and range maps.*

Forest Plants of Central Ontario (*Lone Pine*), by *Brenda Chambers, features brief accounts on almost 700 of the region's herbs, shrubs, trees, ferns, mosses and lichens, with both colour photos and illustrations.*

Introduction to Canadian Amphibians and Reptiles (*National Museum of Natural Sciences*), by *Francis Cook, is good, handy, illustrated guide to all of Canada's herpetofaunal creatures.*

Legacy (*McClelland & Stewart*), *edited by John Theberge, now available in paperback, is a thick, comprehensive compendium of the natural history of Ontario, written by the province's leading naturalists and featuring some of the best colour nature photography.*

The Mammals of Eastern Canada (*Oxford*), by *Randolph Peterson, though academic in tone, is one of the best texts on the wildlife found in Ontario.*

Nightwatch: An Equinox Guide to Viewing the Universe (*Camden House Publishing*), by *Terence Dickinson, is an excellent guide to observing the night sky, with everything from superb star maps to advice on how to take pictures of the heavens.*

The Observer's Handbook (*The Royal Astronomical Society of Canada*) *is an annual publication containing a huge amount of information about stars, planets, eclipses, sunrises and sunsets, meteor showers, and so on, most of which is accessible to the average reader.*

Peterson's Field Guide to the Birds of Eastern and Central North America (*Houghton Mifflin*), by *Roger Tory Peterson, is perhaps the best field guide for Ontario birds, complete with detailed colour illustrations, brief descriptions and range maps.*

Seasons (the magazine of the Federation of Ontario Naturalists) and Equinox, Canadian Geographic, Nature Canada, Cottage Life *and* Wildflower *magazines are all excellent sources of ongoing information on nature in Ontario.*

Shrubs of Ontario (Royal Ontario Museum), by *Herb Hammond, offers the most comprehensive look at much of the province's plant life, from bunchberry to hawthorn trees.*

Tales the Elders Told (Royal Ontario Museum), by *Basil Johnston, is one of a number of intriguing books on Ojibway legends and culture written by this author.*

Trees in Canada (Fitzhenry & Whiteside), by *John Farrar, is the updated version of the Canadian Forestry Service's definitive* Native Trees of Canada, *with colour photos of leaves, seeds, flowers, buds and bark for each species.*

Wild Mammals of Canada (McGraw-Hill Ryerson), by *Frederick Wooding, provides popular accounts on all of Ontario's common mammals.*

Resouce Guide

Boy Scouts Canada, 9 Jackes Ave., Toronto, Ont., M4T 1E2, (416) 923-2461

Bruce Trail Association, P.O. Box 857, Hamiton, Ont., L8N 3N9, (905) 529-6821

Canadian Parks and Wilderness Society, 401 Richmond St. West, Suite 380, Toronto, Ont., M5V 3A8, (416) 979-2720

Canadian Recreational Canoe Association, P.O. Box 398, 446 Maine St. West, Merrickville, Ont., K0G 1N6, (613) 269-2910

Earthroots, 401 Richmond St. West, Suite 410, Toronto, Ont., M5V 3A8, (416) 599-0152

Federation of Ontario Cottagers' Association, 215 Morrish Rd., Suite 101, Scarborough, Ont., M1C 1E9, (416) 284-2305

Federation of Ontario Naturalists, 355 Lesmill Rd., Donmills, Ont., M3B 2W8, (416) 444-8419

Friends of Algonquin, P.O. Box 248, Whitney, Ont., K0J 2M0, (613) 637-2828

Girl Guides of Canada, 50 Merton St., Toronto, Ont., M4S 1A3, (416) 487-5281

Ministry of Citizenship, Culture and Recreation, 77 Bloor St. West, 6th Floor, Toronto, Ont., M7A 2R9, (416) 325-6200

Ontario Heritage Foundation, 10 Adelaide St. East, Toronto, Ont., M5C 1J3, (416) 325-5000

Ontario Parks, 300 Water St., Box 7000, Peterborough, Ont., K9J 8M5, (705) 755-7275

The Royal Astronomical Society of Canada, 136 Dupont St., Toronto, Ont., M5R 1V2, (416) 924-7973

Wildlands League, 401 Richmond St. West, Suite 380, Toronto, Ont., M5V 3A8, (416) 971-9453

World Wildlife Fund (Canada), 90 Eglinton Ave. East, Suite 504, Toronto, Ont., M4P 2Z7, (416) 489-8800

Acknowledgements

We would like to sincerely thank the following people for their advice and help in writing this book:

Richard Aaron • Robert Anderson • Michael Berrill • Roy L. Bishop • Chris Blomme • Michael Cadman • Luca Cargnelli • John Cartwright • John Casselman • Ted Cheskey • Nancy Clark • Francis R. Cook • William J. Crins • Doug Currie • Helene Cyr • Kenneth Dance • Judith Eger • J. Donald Fernie • Don Filman • Alan J. Hanks • Fred Helleiner • Tom Herman • Chris Heydon • James Hodgins • David Johnson • Joe Johnson • Colin D. Jones • Ellie Kirzner • Jaime Kirzner-Roberts • Henry Kock • Carole Ann Lacroix • Lawrence Lamb • Dave Martin • W.D. McIlveen • Peter L. McLaren • Deborah Metsger • A.L.A. Middleton • Sharmila Mohammed • Kong Njo • Erica Nol • Norm North • Judi Orendorff • James D. Rising • Jocelyne St-Onge • Heather Sangster • Alex Schultz • Carolyn Seburn • Sandra Shaul • Nik Sheehan • Mark Stabb • Dan Strickland • Ian Thompson • Ron Tozer • V.R. Vickery • Wayne F. Weller • Jan Whitford

We would also like to acknowledge the following organizations, to which many of the above individuals are attached: Canadian Forestry Service, Canadian Museum of Nature, Canadian Wildlife Service, The Friends of Algonquin Park, Laurentian University, Ontario Ministry of Natural Resources, Royal Ontario Museum and the ROM Herbarium, Trent University, University of Guelph and the U of G Abroretum, University of Toronto and *Wildflower* magazine

Index

This is a master index for both this book and *Up North*. Page numbers in **bold** indicate illustrations. *UN* refers to entries in *Up North*.